THE
BLIND
STRATEGIST

THE
BLIND
STRATEGIST

JOHN BOYD
AND THE
AMERICAN
ART OF WAR

– STEPHEN ROBINSON –

EXISLE
PUBLISHING

First published 2021
This edition published 2023

Exisle Publishing Pty Ltd
PO Box 864, Chatswood, NSW 2057, Australia
226 High Street, Dunedin, 9016, New Zealand
www.exislepublishing.com

A CiP record for this book is available from the National Library of Australia.

ISBN 978-1-922539-86-1

Designed by Nick Turzynski, redinc. Book Design, www.redinc.co.nz
Typeset in Baskerville Regular 11/15
Printed in China

This book uses paper sourced under ISO 14001 guidelines from well-managed forests and
other controlled sources.

10 9 8 7 6 5 4 3 2 1

Dedicated to William E. DePuy, an American soldier

William E. DePuy in Vietnam
(Author's Collection)

Stephen Robinson is the author of *False Flags: Disguised German Raiders of World War II*, *Panzer Commander Hermann Balck: Germany's Master Tactician*, *The Blind Strategist: John Boyd and the American Art of War* and *Eight Hundred Heroes: China's Lost Battalion and the Fall of Shanghai*. He studied Asian history and politics at the University of Western Sydney, graduating with First Class Honors. He has worked at the Department of Veterans' Affairs researching British atomic weapons tests and as a policy officer in the Department of Defence. Stephen Robinson is an officer in the Australian Army Reserve and has served as an instructor at the Royal Military College. He also graduated from Australian Command and Staff College.

CONTENTS

INTRODUCTION

A PHILOSOPHICAL FIGHTER PILOT

The legend of Colonel John Boyd is well known inside Western militaries but his ideas on competitive advantage have also inspired politicians, business leaders and many others driven by a desire to win. It is the story of a maverick fighter pilot who rebelled against the 'bomber barons' running the United States Air Force during the Cold War and later challenged the entire Pentagon system, fighting corruption and nepotism as leader of the Defense Reform Movement. However, Boyd is best remembered as a warrior philosopher and his theories on conflict and the human mind revolutionized the art of war.

Boyd, according to his biographer Robert Coram, may be 'the most influential military thinker since Sun Tzu wrote *The Art of War* 2,400 years ago'.[1] General Paul Van Riper, a retired United States Marine Corps officer, similarly announced, 'I believe the world's greatest military theorists are Carl von Clausewitz, Sun Tzu, and John Boyd.'[2] The scholar Daniel Ford considered Boyd to be 'arguably the most important American military thinker since the late-19th-Century sea power theorist, Admiral Alfred Thayer Mahan'.[3] William S. Lind, an acolyte of Boyd, described him as 'the greatest military theorist America ever produced'.[4]

John Richard Boyd, born on 23 January 1927 in Erie, Pennsylvania, enlisted in the United States Army in 1944 and participated in the occupation of postwar Japan.[5] He later joined the Air Force in 1951 and served as a fighter pilot during the Korean War, flying twenty-nine missions as a wingman in F-86 Sabres. However, he never completed the thirty

John Boyd serving as a United States Air Force fighter pilot
(Contributor: Military Collection/Alamy Stock Photo)

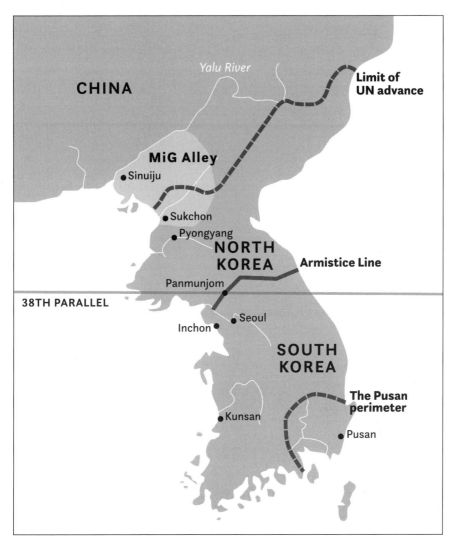

MiG Alley — the focus of the air war in Korea

missions required to become a flight leader but he did damage a MiG-15 in June 1953.[6] As a wingman, Boyd protected the lead plane which engaged the Chinese MiG-15s and rarely had the opportunity to open fire in combat.

After returning to America, Boyd taught tactics at the Fighter Weapons School at Nellis Air Force Base near Las Vegas in 1954. He challenged other pilots that he could outmaneuver any of them from a disadvantageous position within forty seconds. He never lost, and this feat earned him the nickname 'Forty Second Boyd'. During this time, he wrote the air-to-air combat manual *Aerial Attack Study*. The manual avoided the dogma of proscribing specific maneuvers in given situations and instead encouraged pilots to think for themselves by evaluating their options as they cycle through a sequence of moves and counter-moves.[7] *Aerial Attack Study* was integrated into the official Air Force manual on air-to-air tactics and became the international fighter pilot bible. By the end of the 1950s, many in the Air Force considered Boyd to be their finest fighter pilot.

In 1960, Boyd studied industrial engineering at Georgia Tech in Atlanta before being posted to Systems Command at Eglin Air Force Base in Florida two years later. At Eglin, with the help of the mathematician Thomas Christie, he formulated energy maneuverability theory. Boyd wanted to quantify fighter plane performance by comparing the ability of different airframes to alter altitude, speed and direction. Energy maneuverability could quantify how well aircraft can maneuver by analyzing how they change energy states in different conditions.[8] However, Boyd needed computer access to make the complex calculations but lacked authorization to use Air Force computers for this purpose. Undeterred, he created dummy accounts and stole the computer time, which he used to evaluate the flight performance data of all American and Soviet fighters.[9]

Boyd's covert research proved that Soviet MiG-17, MiG-19 and MiG-21 fighters all possessed greater maneuverability compared to American jets, a shocking revelation which shattered the myth of American Cold War air superiority.[10] The Air Force initially wanted to court martial Boyd for the stolen computer time but, after the realization of his achievement sunk in, it instead presented him with the Air Force Systems Command Scientific Achievement Award and the Air Force Research and Development Award for Aeronautical Engineering.

As energy maneuverability could improve aircraft design, the Air Force posted Boyd to the Pentagon to help the struggling F-X project, which aimed to develop the next generation air superiority fighter. In 1966, he arrived at the Pentagon and clashed with the senior 'bomber barons' who downgraded the importance of fighters. The F-86 Sabre was the last dedicated air superiority fighter as a trend toward more complex platforms designed for

A Soviet MiG-15 fighter
(Contributor: Malcolm Haines/Alamy Stock Photo)

American F-86 Sabre fighters during the Korean War
(Contributor: Alpha Stock/Alamy Stock Photo)

The destruction of a MiG-15 fighter taken from the gun camera of an F-86 Sabre during the Korean War
(Contributor: RBM Vintage Images/Alamy Stock Photo)

multi-role missions, such as dogfights and ground attack, had resulted in heavier, less maneuverable planes. During the Korean War, Sabres achieved a 10:1 kill ratio against MiG-15s, but in air combat over Vietnam, F-4 Phantoms experienced a ratio closer to a 1:1 against communist pilots. As Boyd knew, the existing American planes did not possess an edge over the latest Soviet designed air superiority fighters.[11]

Boyd believed the fighter envisaged by the F-X project was too heavy at 80,000 pounds with overly complex swing-wings. 'I've never designed an airplane before,' he declared, 'but I could fuck up and do better than this.'[12] In contrast, Boyd advocated a lighter 40,000 pound twin tailed plane with greater maneuverability. In this quest, he found allies among a group of officers who opposed the F-X project's multi-mission compromise plane. Boyd also found support from a handful of others in the Pentagon and industry and his 'Fighter Mafia' advocated a lightweight fighter based on energy maneuverability. He enhanced the design by eliminating the cumbersome swing-wing, resulting in a vastly improved prototype which was approved in 1968.

Boyd nevertheless believed the F-X design did not go far enough and began designing another lightweight fighter, without asking for permission from the Air Force hierarchy, which became the F-XX project. The 'bomber barons' planned to approve this fighter through the first two committees but would reject the concept at the final approval stage, which would give a pretense that the proposal had been genuinely considered. Boyd, alerted to the trap by an informer, used his network to pitch the F-XX directly to Deputy Secretary of Defense David Packard, who approved the project. After entering the generals' committee, Boyd announced, 'Gentlemen, this is not a decision briefing. Since the secretary of defense has already approved this program, today's briefing will be for information only.'[13] Boyd had outmaneuvered the stunned 'bomber barons'.

Boyd, a maverick by nature, followed none of the conventions of career Air Force officers, as his subordinate James Burton recalled:

> I thought Boyd was crazy. He did nothing right, according to what I had been taught since entering the Academy. His uniform was a mess; he never got to work on time; he ignored work deadlines; he even ignored the work itself. When the generals told him to do something, he would do something else. He was uncontrollable. He openly criticized numerous generals as either corrupt or incompetent, some as both.[14]

In the Pentagon, Boyd became known as 'The Mad Major', 'The Ghetto Colonel', 'Genghis John' and 'That Fucking Boyd'.[15] Nevertheless, the F-X program resulted in the F-15 Eagle and the F-XX project produced the F-16 Falcon — the first fighters designed using energy maneuverability — and they became the backbone of American airpower.

Boyd looked beyond fighter aircraft by championing the next generation ground attack plane. During the 1970s, the Air Force tasked Pierre Sprey, a member of the 'Fighter Mafia' who assisted Boyd on the F-X project, with designing its first dedicated ground attack aircraft, and he wanted historical

Colonel John Boyd
(Author's Collection)

lessons to influence the design. Sprey, Boyd and the design team interviewed German World War II veterans in CIA safe houses in Maryland to learn combat lessons, such as how pilots can best locate, approach and destroy ground targets.[16] The team interviewed Adolf Galland, a *Luftwaffe* fighter ace, and Hans-Ulrich Rudel, who flew 2,500 ground attack missions in Stuka dive bombers and is credited with destroying 519 tanks. The team learned that ground attack planes had to fly low toward their targets and be capable of absorbing considerable damage from anti-aircraft weapons, and their efforts resulted in the A-10 Warthog which demonstrated its worth as a tank killer during the Gulf War.

In 1975, the Vietnam War ended in defeat and the American military entered the darkest phase of its history. In that year, Boyd retired from the Air Force and became a civilian consultant for the Secretary of Defense with an office in the Pentagon from where he led the Defense Reform Movement, a network which spoke out against the corrupt relationship between military officials and industry. As the Pentagon often purchased poorly tested military hardware at inflated prices, the reform movement had a cause, as James Burton explained:

> . . . unbridled ambition and rampant careerism in the officer corps of all services, the incestuous revolving door between the defense industry and Pentagon officials, the almost daily revelation of horror stories about $600 toilet seats and $400 hammers, a steady stream of weapons systems either inadequately tested or purchased regardless of poor test results, and a regular diet of senior military and civilian officials lying to the public and Congress to cover up embarrassments were only a few of the symptoms of a corrupt business that cried out for reform.[17]

The 'Reformers' believed the American military was addicted to high-tech expensive weapons, resulting in small numbers of highly complex platforms with unreliable readiness due to a greater likelihood of systems failure, which would ultimately be less effective than a greater number of simpler systems.[18] In one noteworthy scandal, the 'Reformers' exposed that the Air Force had not properly funded maintenance so mechanics had been using their own pay to buy electronic spare parts at Radio Shack just to keep their aircraft flying. In another example, James Burton criticized the Bradley Fighting Vehicle project:

> They'd fired 400 rounds in a test — and not a single round was fired at a tank. They just detonated a warhead in a steel block, measured how big the hole was, then derived combat results from their computer models. I said to myself, 'These guys are crazy. What if their computer models are wrong?' So I said it's time to get some real data.[19]

Burton arranged a live-fire test program which fired rounds at vehicles loaded with weapons, fuel, ammunition and test dummies to realistically simulate combat.[20] The 'Reformers' forced the Pentagon to undertake proper testing which improved the design of the Bradley and Abrams tanks; this endeavor saved lives during the Gulf War.[21]

James Fallows, editor of *The Atlantic Monthly*, published an article, 'The Muscle-Bound Superpower', on 2 October 1979, propelling Boyd's crusade onto the national stage, and other journalists began covering the reform movement. Fallows again championed the reform agenda in his influential bestseller *National Defense* (1981) and later in articles for *The Washington Post*.

Boyd also formed alliances with politicians, including influential Republicans Dick Cheney and Newt Gingrich. He gained another powerful ally, Democrat Senator Gary Hart, who helped establish the Congressional Military Reform Caucus, which included Republicans and Democrats. Hart and Gingrich, an unlikely duo, wrote a series of articles on defense policy as part of the reform movement. In 1981, Hart, assisted by his legislative aide William S. Lind, wrote an opinion piece, 'The Case For Military Reform', in *The Wall Street Journal*. Hart later authored *America Can Win: The Case for Military Reform* (1984), again with Lind's help, which advocated inexpensive, simple and reliable weapon systems in tune with Boyd's demands. Hart later reflected:

> Through my staff assistant William Lind, I discovered a retired air force colonel named John Boyd and a handful of reformers, including Chuck Spinney and others. They let me sit in on some of their regular meetings, and I discovered an entirely new approach to thinking about the military.[22]

By 1985, the Congressional Military Reform Caucus had over 100 members and eventually included over one quarter of Congress.

During the early 1970s, Boyd developed an idea that would become his greatest contribution to military philosophy after becoming intrigued with the fly-offs between the two F-XX prototypes.[23] Before the test flights, he predicted that the YF-17 would perform better but the pilots agreed the YF-16 was superior. He realized the YF-16 discharged and regained energy quicker than the YF-17, which enabled it to perform faster transient maneuvers, giving the pilots superior responsiveness and tempo.[24] Boyd, through his insights concerning the test flights, developed his Observation–Orientation–Decide–Act (O–O–D–A) loop theory that later explained why F-86 Sabre pilots had inflicted a 10:1 kill ratio over Chinese MiG-15s in the skies over Korea — a curious statistic as the Soviet designed planes had superior acceleration, turning and climbing performance. However, the American fighters had a bubble cockpit, giving pilots excellent all-round visibility and hydraulic flight controls which enabled faster transitions between different maneuvers. Therefore, American pilots had superior situational awareness and could more easily translate their decisions into actions and, as dogfights required pilots to make a succession of decisions and actions, they established 'decision cycle' superiority over Chinese pilots.[25]

Franklin Spinney, an Air Force officer and Boyd acolyte, explained the O–O–D–A loop:

> He thought that any conflict could be viewed as a duel wherein each adversary observes (O) his opponent's actions, orients (O) himself to the unfolding situation, decides (D) on the most appropriate response or countermove, then acts (A). The competitor who moves through this OODA-loop cycle the fastest gains an inestimable advantage by disrupting his enemy's ability to respond effectively.[26]

Boyd, in addition to analyzing the implications of the test flights, also studied military history searching for a grand narrative to guide military success.

After eighteen months of research, Boyd prepared a briefing titled *Patterns of Conflict*, first delivered in 1977. In an early 1978 presentation, he explained the O-O-D-A loop in relation to the faster transient maneuvers related to the test flights and the Korean War.[27] He had been heavily influenced by Sun Tzu, Genghis Khan and the British military theorists J.F.C. (John) Fuller and Basil Henry Liddell Hart, as well as by the German stormtroopers of World War I and the *Blitzkrieg* of World War II. *Patterns of Conflict* became a living, never-ending project as Boyd constantly updated and expanded its content, later renaming it *A Discourse on Winning and Losing*. It began as a one-hour lecture and became a thirteen-hour marathon, which he delivered over 1,500 times during the next twenty years, reaching influential audiences in

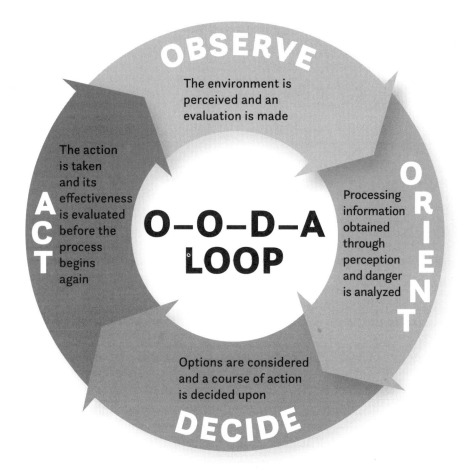

OBSERVE
The environment is perceived and an evaluation is made

O
R
I
E
N
T

Processing information obtained through perception and danger is analyzed

A
C
T

The action is taken and its effectiveness is evaluated before the process begins again

O–O–D–A LOOP

DECIDE
Options are considered and a course of action is decided upon

John Boyd's O–O–D–A Loop

the Pentagon and Washington who were seeking a new way of waging war after years of wasted attrition in Vietnam.

Patterns of Conflict explained Boyd's concept of maneuver warfare — the apparent Holy Grail of military theory — a means of rapidly defeating opponents by paralyzing their minds and ability to effectively react, mentally checkmating them with minimal violence. The key to understanding Boyd's philosophy is the realization that warfare is an art fought in the human mind. 'Terrain doesn't fight wars,' he said. 'Machines don't fight war. People fight wars. It's in the minds of men that war must be fought.'[28] Maneuver warfare rejected the Pentagon's Vietnam-era obsession with technology and managerialism — personified by Secretary of Defense Robert McNamara — which had created a risk-averse culture without a warrior ethos, as James Burton explained:

> Boyd embarrassed the nation's military leaders by showing that there were no real military theorists practicing their craft in this country. They had been replaced by scientists and technologists who thought in terms of bandwidth, gigahertz and computer memory.[29]

Robert Coram shared this scathing assessment:

> Military leaders of the 1970s were more familiar with business theory than with military theory. They read management books and talked at length of how things were done at the Harvard Business School. But some had never heard of Sun Tzu and could not spell 'von Clausewitz.' . . . Many Civil War buffs knew more about military tactics than did the average senior officer in the mid-70s.[30]

Boyd's journalist contacts championed maneuver warfare in the press. For example, James Fallows reported in *The Atlantic Monthly* after attending a *Patterns of Conflict* briefing in 1979:

> Deep within the Pentagon, on an inner hall of a lower floor, the retired colonel came to the end of his 'brief.' . . . 'I've been talking about war, waging it and winning it,' he said. 'People don't discuss that subject very often in this building.' His associate chimed in, 'It's really the Department of Technology, not the Department of Defense.'[31]

Boyd's ideas on maneuver warfare influenced General Donn Starry, who incorporated them into United States Army doctrine through the AirLand Battle concept in 1982. The Marine Corps Commandant General Alfred Gray, impressed with *Patterns of Conflict*, authorized the new manual *Warfighting*, which made maneuver warfare Marine doctrine in 1989. Boyd fundamentally changed the Corps and, as Grant Hammond from the Air War College explained, for 'five years, a retired Air Force Colonel taught every Marine officer that went through the Basic Course at Quantico, Virginia, about maneuver warfare'.[32] The Marine Corps later dedicated a section of their library at Quantico to hold Boyd's unpublished papers and notes.

The United States Navy and Air Force adopted the O–O–D–A loop as a standard decision-making tool. Maneuver warfare concepts are evident in Naval Doctrine Publication 1 *Naval Warfare* (1994) and Air Force Doctrine Document 1 *Air Force Basic Doctrine (*1997). Boyd's ideas are present in *Joint Vision 2010* (1996), authorized by the Joint Chiefs of Staff, which advocated gaining 'OODA-loop dominance'.[33] Boyd's ideas also are evident in the *Concept for Future Joint Operations* (1997) and in many other Department of Defense publications.

Dick Cheney, after becoming Secretary of Defense in 1989, sought Boyd's counsel during the planning of the Gulf War. Through this connection, Boyd is often considered the architect of the coalition's incredibly swift victory. For example, Secretary of Defense Robert Gates declared that Boyd developed 'the principles of maneuver warfare' which Cheney credited 'for the lightning victory in the first Gulf War'.[34] After the 9/11 terrorist attacks, Secretary of State Colin Powell used Boyd's language when articulating that America's response would get inside the enemy 'decision cycle'.[35]

The O–O–D–A loop and maneuver warfare initially gained national attention following articles in *The Washington Post* and other newspapers in 1981.[36] As Boyd believed his theories could be applied to competitive business strategies, he encouraged others to adapt his concepts in the private sector. George Stalk, who worked for the Boston Consulting Group in Japan, realized that time can be a source of competitive advantage, as companies which make faster decisions normally triumph over their competition. Stalk noticed similarities between his observations of the Japanese business world and Boyd's ideas, which he explored in *Competing Against Time* (1990): 'A time-compressed company does the same thing as a pilot in an OODA Loop . . . it's still the competitor who acts on information faster who is in the best position to win.'[37]

Chester Richards, an acolyte of Boyd from the Pentagon, later wrote *Certain to Win: The Strategy of John Boyd, Applied to Business* (2004). Richards noted that many military leaders who became familiar with Boyd's ideas 'later left the military and went into business where they began to use the concept of competing using time as their primary weapon'.[38] Numerous similar books appeared which further established Boyd's ideas in the commercial world, such as Santamaria, Martino and Clemon's *The Marine Corps Way: Using Maneuver Warfare to Lead a Winning Organization* (2003). Boyd's ideas have also been discussed in Forbes and the *Harvard Business Review*, and they are taught in business schools and by private sector consultants.

Boyd's ideas on strategy have been applied in politics. Newt Gingrich and Dick Cheney, both members of the Congressional Military Reform Caucus, applied the O–O–D–A loop to their political struggles. Gingrich even attributed Boyd's theories to the Republican takeover of Congress and stated:

> The key to success in politics as in war is the ability to stay on offense. . .
> Learning to stay on offense requires a strategic vision that enables you to
> constantly orient to the future, an operational system that allows you to
> be inside your opponent's decision cycle (see Boyd's work on OODA-loops
> for an explanation).[39]

Outside America, Boyd's ideas have been just as influential. Maneuver warfare is military doctrine in Britain, Canada, Australia and New Zealand as well as in numerous other Western countries. He has changed the world and, as Grant Hammond declared, from 'a Danish business school to military academies and war colleges from Australia to Norway, John Boyd is a familiar name'.[40] Frans Osinga, a Dutch Air Force officer, noted: 'Over the past two decades the image of the OODA loop has become an icon and has spread like a meme beyond military organizations, infecting business consultants, psychiatrists, pedagogues, and sports instructors.'[41]

At seventy years of age, Boyd died of prostate cancer on 9 March 1997, a slow and painful death. General Charles Krulak, Commandant of the Marine Corps, wrote a eulogy:

> How does one begin to pay homage to a warrior like John Boyd? He was
> a towering intellect who made unsurpassed contributions to the American
> art of war. . . From John Boyd we learned about competitive decision
> making on the battlefield — compressing time, using time as an ally. . .
> I was in awe of him, not just for the potential of his future contributions

but for what he stood for as an officer, a citizen and as a man. . . I, and his Corps of Marines, will miss our counselor terribly.[42]

Cheney, as Vice President, when asked about Boyd, reflected, 'We could use him again now. I wish he was around now. I'd love to turn him loose on our current defense establishment and see what he could come up with.'[43]

Boyd generated intense loyalty among his acolytes. 'To those who believed in him and his causes,' Grant Hammond remembered, 'he was more than a hero, he was a virtual saint and they would have followed him anywhere and taken on any foe, regardless of the odds'.[44] Boyd's legacy is seemingly assured as the scholar Michael Evans concluded: 'Today, in the second decade of the twenty-first century, those who opposed and impeded Boyd's career are forgotten men, while Boyd's influence permeates advanced military doctrine throughout the West.'[45]

Boyd, however, made a fatal mistake with the potential to undo his legacy. After formulating his views on air combat over Korea, he convinced himself that he had unlocked a universal truth. Therefore, he approached history with a preconceived view and sought confirmation of his theory, ignoring critical evidence which did not suit his quest. Far from discovering the Holy Grail of military theory, Boyd invented a mythological system of thought which the traumatized American military recovering from Vietnam mistook for reality.

A TEMPLE BUILT ON SAND

There is no denying the brilliance of John Boyd's mind and his legacy in relation to air-to-air combat, energy maneuverability and his battle against Pentagon corruption; however, the achievements of his Defense Reform Movement are overstated. Although Boyd influenced the design of the F-15 Eagle, he wanted an even smaller aircraft without radar and denounced the plane as too large and complex. The F-16 Falcon was also heavier and more technologically complex than Boyd envisaged. He wanted a smaller, short-ranged, single-engine, 25,000 pound fighter armed with a cannon and heat-seeking missiles without radar and advanced avionics.[46] However, the Air Force, based on recent combat experience over North Vietnam, required a long-range all-weather aircraft with advanced air-to-air missiles,

F-16 Falcon and F-15 Eagle aircraft during the Gulf War
(Contributor: Pictorial Press Ltd/Alamy Stock Photo)

radar, electronic countermeasures and the ability to perform ground attack missions. Boyd denounced the final design because it was not the 'pure' air superiority fighter he advocated, and as Robert Coram explained, his 'anger at what the Air Force did to the F-16 never abated. He had lost the last great battle of his Air Force career.'[47]

Boyd ultimately valued energy maneuverability over combat experience. When briefing his energy charts to Top Gun instructors, he claimed that F-4 Phantoms could not win dogfights against more maneuverable MiG-17s. The instructors, including two pilots who had shot down MiG-17s over North Vietnam, rejected Boyd's analysis and Commander Ron McKeown warned, 'never trust anyone who would rather kick your ass with a slide rule than with a jet'.[48]

Under Boyd's leadership, the Defense Reform Movement advocated cancelling the high-tech F-15 Eagles, F-16 Falcons and Abrams tanks in favor of outdated F-5 Tigers and Patton tanks.[49] The 'Reformers' believed that air superiority would be gained by pilots operating only in clear weather using their own eyes without the benefit of long-range missiles and radar — unnecessary burdens which compromise maneuverability. 'The Reform vision,' as John Correll from *Air Force Magazine* concluded, 'was perfectly suited to an imaginary war in which aerobatic fighters dueled in clear skies on sunny days. That war would never exist.'[50]

The Gulf War effectively ended the 'Reformers' crusade as the conflict demonstrated the effectiveness of the expensive and complex weapons they opposed, eroding their credibility. The F-15 Eagle's advanced radar, so despised by Boyd, has allowed its pilots to maneuver to advantageous positions prior to opening fire and the aircraft has been credited with 104 'kills' to date without suffering any aerial combat losses.[51] The F-16 Falcon has tallied 72 'kills' without any air-to-air losses.[52] The majority of these 'kills' were inflicted with missiles beyond visual range, clearly demonstrating that the age of Korean War dogfights has long since receded into the past.[53]

The O–O–D–A loop is a useful decision-making tool but is a far cry from being the universal key to victory, and maneuver warfare is essentially based upon fraudulent concepts. As Boyd had no direct experience of land warfare, he had little choice but to trust the insights of others when searching for confirmation of his theory. He trusted historical accounts of World War II which professional historians later exposed as dishonest fabrications and, as a result, maneuver warfare rests upon a foundation of deceit. Boyd at first innocently injected misinformation into his theory, unaware of the dishonesty of others, but after major anomalies eventually appeared, he failed to re-evaluate his grand narrative. He ignored damning evidence in complete contrast to his own intellectual standards.

Maneuver warfare originated from the ideas of the British military thinkers J.F.C. Fuller and Liddell Hart who, horrified by the slaughter in the trenches during World War I, sought new methods of waging war based on paralyzing the mind of enemy commanders as an alternative to blood-soaked attrition. Fuller and Liddell Hart both claimed that their concepts inspired the German *Blitzkrieg*. Boyd discovered their ideas while searching for his grand theory and expanded upon them when developing maneuver warfare. However, he only superficially studied the history of warfare and his analysis is reliant upon false dichotomies and faulty logic. Furthermore, his understanding of *Blitzkrieg* derived from fabricated history. Boyd and his key acolyte William S. Lind praised the *Wehrmacht* as the epitome of military virtue and depicted German generals as masters of maneuver warfare, but they had unknowingly fallen for a misinformation campaign conceived in 1945.

During the early days of the Cold War, the American military sought insights into the Red Army and asked *Wehrmacht* veterans to write accounts of their Eastern Front operations. However, this enterprise gave former German officers an opportunity to write myth-making propaganda and, instead of providing the Americans with genuine advice, these veterans salvaged their reputations by falsely claiming that their defeat originated from Hitler's interfering orders, which undermined their military genius. They also dishonestly insisted that the *Wehrmacht* had nothing to do with the Third Reich's criminal atrocities. These self-serving myths also reached wider audiences through popular memoirs such as Heinz Guderian's *Panzer Leader*, Erich von Manstein's *Lost Victories* and Friedrich von Mellenthin's *Panzer Battles*, which all contain a difficult to decipher mix of truth and deception. The myths of the *Wehrmacht*'s unparalleled military excellence and clean hands became largely accepted as fact in the English-speaking world, but the former German generals who conjured these fantasies were assisted by a collaborator.

World War II destroyed Liddell Hart's reputation, as his pre-war predictions turned out to be completely incorrect, but after the war he regained his former standing by fabricating historical evidence in an effort to persuade the world that his ideas had inspired *Blitzkrieg*. He achieved this aim by developing a co-dependent relationship with former *Wehrmacht* generals who used him to endorse their myths while they legitimized his fraudulent history, resulting in a distorted view of World War II gaining general acceptance. Boyd, unaware of this context, uncritically accepted the accounts of German veterans and Liddell Hart as truth, giving him an understanding of *Blitzkrieg* completely at odds with genuine history, and maneuver warfare is fatally tainted by this misinformation.

Boyd and Lind did not realize their ideas derived from dishonest individuals and, by confusing history and fantasy, they sowed dangerous myths in American military minds. However, they did become aware that something was not quite right with their theory after the *Wehrmacht* veterans Hermann Balck and Friedrich von Mellenthin became American military consultants during the late 1970s and early 1980s. During discussions at conferences and other events, Balck and Mellenthin rejected the central ideas of maneuver warfare and insisted that the *Wehrmacht* never fought according to its concepts. However, Boyd and Lind ignored this devastating testimony and inaccurately depicted Balck and Mellenthin as masters of maneuver warfare.

The misinformation inherent within maneuver warfare corrupted the art of war in the Western world, especially operational-level thinking. This became apparent during the 1980s when Boyd's acolytes applied its concepts to develop a potentially disastrous plan to defend Western Europe from a feared Soviet invasion. Nevertheless, maneuver warfare remained orthodoxy in large part because of a widespread misconception that Boyd's ideas resulted in America's victory during the Gulf War, but in reality General Norman Schwarzkopf followed an entirely different warfighting philosophy. Maneuver warfare did, however, contribute to disastrous decisions made in Iraq in 2003 when General Tommy Franks, a true believer in Boyd, formulated what historian Thomas Ricks referred to as 'perhaps the worst war plan in American history'.[54]

Boyd never genuinely studied history in the disciplined manner of a professional historian but instead relied upon dubious secondary sources, lacking the ability to analyze events in their proper historical context. He had a preconceived notion of proving the universal applicability of the O–O–D–A loop and his confirmation bias is clear in his own words. When reading a book on the French defeat in 1940, he noted that they became 'uncertain, confused, disordered — almost like I had said it, I felt like I had written the goddamn passage'.[55] Boyd is essentially a blind strategist, in the dark and cut off from the light of genuine historical inquiry, forever trapped in the feedback loop of his closed system. To understand why his flawed conception of war became so widely accepted, it is first necessary to understand the trauma the American military experienced after the Vietnam War.

CHAPTER ONE
EMERGENCE OF MANEUVER WARFARE

ACTIVE DEFENSE

During the final years of the Vietnam War, the American military unraveled as discipline broke down and forty-five officers and NCOs were killed by their own men in 'fragging' incidents between 1969 and 1971.[1] The institutional decline extended beyond the warzone as Donn Starry, who commanded the 11th Armored Cavalry Regiment in Vietnam and spearheaded the invasion of Cambodia in 1970, recalled:

> Forces that deployed to theaters other than Vietnam suffered mightily from personnel turbulence, the drug culture, multitudinous disciplinary infractions (the military jails were full to overcrowded), and depletion of the experienced NCO corps, all reflected in a serious lack of confidence in leadership at virtually every level.[2]

When final defeat came in 1975, the military suffered a traumatic shock as 58,318 Americans had died in a conflict ending with humiliating images of helicopters evacuating the embassy in Saigon. In the aftermath of Vietnam, the downward spiral continued as Roger Spiller from the Army's Combat Studies Institute explained:

> The indiscipline first appeared in Southeast Asia and was translated after the war to the European formations, manifesting itself in numerous racial incidents, drug and gang-related violence among soldiers. Some officers walked their night tours in the company areas with rounds chambered in their side-arms.[3]

At this time, the Army struggled with declining defense budgets and the challenge of transitioning to an all-volunteer force, creating the need for recruitment and retention at a time of extremely low morale and when public confidence in the military had collapsed and service lacked the social prestige it once had.

General William E. DePuy emerged out of this abyss and rebuilt the United States Army. He had served as a junior officer in World War II, fighting in the 90th Infantry Division in Normandy.[4] The soldiers, mostly poorly trained draftees, endured massive casualties while fighting under abysmal leadership. Several officers were relieved of command, leaving DePuy with a burning belief in the importance of training and competent leadership: 'I fought in Normandy with three battalion commanders who should have been relieved in peacetime. One was a coward, one was a small-time gangster from Chicago . . . and the other was a drunk.' He added, 'In the six weeks in Normandy prior to the breakout, the 90th Division lost 100 percent of its soldiers and 150 percent of its officers. . . That's indelibly marked on my mind.'[5] DePuy remembered the division as 'a killing machine — of our own troops!'[6]

Later in Vietnam, DePuy commanded the 1st Infantry Division and focused on search-and-destroy operations, gaining a notorious reputation for sacking incompetent officers, resulting in the Army Chief questioning this practice as he recalled: 'I either would have to be removed or I would continue to remove officers who I thought didn't show much sign of learning their trade and, at the same time, were getting a lot of people killed. You can't get a soldier back once he's killed.'[7]

In 1973, DePuy became commander of Training and Doctrine Command (TRADOC), which had been recently created to centralize training and doctrine, but he viewed his role as 'nothing less than to totally rethink the way the Army trained its forces and fought its wars'.[8]

William E. DePuy
(Author's Collection)

After America withdrew combat forces from Vietnam, the Army refocused on its traditional Cold War role of defending Western Europe against a possible Soviet invasion. Red Army forces in Central Europe had significantly modernized, resulting in more and better equipped soldiers being stationed along the borders of North Atlantic Treaty Organization (NATO) countries. In 1976, NATO had 6,655 tanks and 800,000 soldiers while the Warsaw Pact fielded 15,450 tanks and 925,000 soldiers.[9] The Red Army also had qualitative superiority as their BMP-1 infantry fighting vehicles, T-64 and T-72 tanks, and Mi-24 Hind attack helicopters outclassed obsolete American equipment such as Sheridan armored vehicles and Patton tanks. However, DePuy's response to NATO's defense challenge originated from the Middle East.

DePuy viewed the Arab–Israeli Yom Kippur War of 1973 as an opportunity to gain battle-tested insights into combat between modern

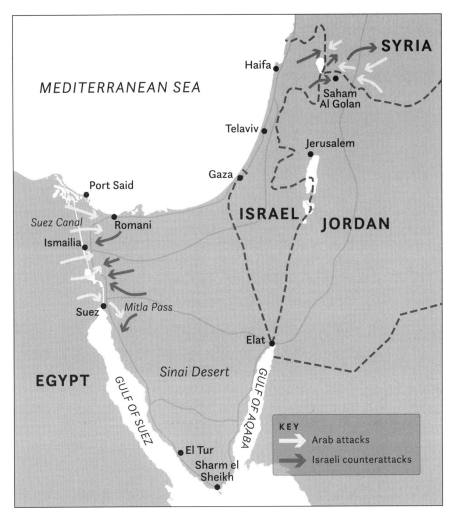

The Yom Kippur War, October 1973

American and Soviet weapons. TRADOC accordingly compared the performance of American weapons against Soviet arms, interpreting Yom Kippur as a micro-version of a possible US–Soviet war in Europe. This conflict witnessed the most intense armored battles since World War II and modern technology enabled tanks to engage targets at 4,000 meters and infantry effectively operated precision-guided anti-tank missiles. During World War II, a medium tank firing at a stationary target 1,500 meters away

An Israeli soldier holds a Soviet-made 'Sagger' anti-tank missile captured during the Yom Kippur War
(Contributor: Keystone Press/ Alamy Stock Photo)

A destroyed tank from the Yom Kippur War
(Contributor: Universal Images Group North America LLC/DeAgostini/Alamy Stock Photo)

would likely fire over twenty rounds before scoring a hit while a main battle tank would now in probability only need a single round.[10]

During Yom Kippur, over 400 Israeli tanks and 100 aircraft were destroyed while Arab forces lost 2,000 tanks and 400 aircraft.[11] Israeli and Arab forces both suffered 50 percent material losses in less than two weeks of fighting, and their tank and artillery losses combined exceeded American equipment levels in Europe.

To DePuy, Yom Kippur demonstrated the sheer destructiveness of modern battlefields due to technology which heralded a 'new lethality' or, as he put it, 'what we see we can hit; what we hit we can kill'.[12] However, he also observed the importance of training and leadership in the ultimate Israeli victory, as computer simulations predicted that the Israelis should have lost every battle.[13] DePuy remarked that 'training and leadership weighed more heavily than weapons systems capabilities on the actual battlefield'.[14] He concluded that contemporary conventional wars would be short but intense limited conflicts as 'modern weapons are so lethal that the outcome of the next war will be largely settled in weeks with the forces and weapons on hand at the outset'.[15]

DePuy decided to reform the Army based on his observations of Yom Kippur by rewriting Field Manual (FM) 100-5 *Operations*, initiating a 'program to reorient and restructure the whole body of Army doctrine from top to bottom'.[16] Doctrine shapes military culture, values and behavior, and DePuy perceived it as the 'unifying concept' which coordinates operations, training, education and leadership by articulating 'How to Fight'.[17]

FM 100-5 *Operations* is the Army's capstone doctrine at the top of the hierarchy and provides authoritative context and guidance for all subordinate doctrine manuals. This manual defines the Army's warfighting philosophy, as Roger Spiller explained: 'change 100-5 and one changes, ultimately, the way in which the Army fights'.[18] DePuy articulated his grand ambition on 10 October 1974:

We have now participated in enough discussions, listened to enough briefings and seen enough demonstrations to have the best consensus on how to fight that has probably ever existed in the school system of the

United States Army. It is now time to institutionalize and perpetuate this consensus through doctrinal publications.[19]

DePuy handpicked trusted loyalists to draft the new manual and General Donn Starry, who after Vietnam commanded V Corps in West Germany and was now commandant of the Armor School, became his principal collaborator. Starry shared DePuy's interpretation of Yom Kippur and the 'new lethality' as battlefields would be 'dense with large numbers of weapons systems whose lethality at extended ranges would surpass previous experience'.[20]

Starry genuinely believed in DePuy's doctrine reforms but warned about the need to gain consensus by involving the rest of the Army in open debate; however, DePuy had little interest in exposing his ideas to criticism.[21] He only tolerated minimal consultation with the rest of the Army and wrote much of the new manual himself with the help of his small team, dubbed the 'boat house gang' as it met in a building which had once been a yacht club. DePuy did, however, seek advice from General Bruce Clarke, who commanded an outnumbered force from the 7th Armored Division which opposed the panzer onslaught at St. Vith during the Battle of the Bulge. DePuy perceived this battle as an historical parallel to NATO's current position.

DePuy's efforts resulted in Active Defense, a new warfighting philosophy expressed in FM 100-5 *Operations* (1976), which planned to defeat a Warsaw Pact invasion of Western Europe close to the West German border. Given the 'new lethality' of modern weapons, the conflict would likely end before America could mobilize; therefore, troops already in Germany must defeat the invasion.[22] The outnumbered NATO troops would adopt an elastic defense and use firepower to destroy the initial Soviet assault.[23] NATO forces would initially conduct a series of defensive engagements from prepared positions and, after the Warsaw Pact's main effort was identified, they would concentrate mass force to counter the main blow. Active Defense viewed operations being tightly controlled by generals with limited independent action being tolerated down the chain of command, as DePuy insisted on 'the need for commanders to maintain near absolute control over subordinate units on the battlefield'.[24]

Active Defense centered on NATO defeating Warsaw Pact forces during the 'first battle' because the 'new lethality' would result in domestic and international pressure, forcing politicians on both sides to end the conflict before a 'second battle' could be fought.[25]

Active Defense, as DePuy announced, took 'the Army out of the rice paddies of Vietnam and places it on the Western European battlefield'.[26] He confidently told his staff that its 'impact will be a thousand fold. It will be more significant than anyone imagines' and 'will show up for decades'.[27] However, Active Defense drew immediate criticism from a new generation of American reformers, believers in a radically different warfighting philosophy.

THE REVOLT

DePuy discouraged criticism during the drafting of FM 100-5 *Operations* (1976) but he could not control the debate which followed its publication, and intense criticism soon came from a most unexpected individual, William S. Lind, a civilian defense analyst and legislative aide for Senator Robert Taft, Jr. Lind had graduated from Princeton with a Master's degree in German history and had an active fascination with the country's military past.

On 11 February 1976, Lind met DePuy and the 'Boathouse Gang' to listen to a presentation explaining Active Defense. Lind, unimpressed with the new doctrine, left the briefing determined to write an article critical of the new concept. DePuy, equally unimpressed with Lind, recalled:

> I had no intention of dealing with Lind anymore because I thought he was kind of a lightweight. . . I don't think I read him entirely correctly. I think he has more to offer than I perceived at that time. But I didn't particularly like the guy and I didn't intend to spend any more time with him, period.[28]

Starry similarly concluded, 'No one seems to know what he [Lind] is trying to prove. He is one of those instant field marshals. . . I guess the best thing to do is ignore Mr. Lind.'[29]

In May 1976, Lind submitted an article, 'Some Doctrinal Questions for the United States Army' but DePuy blocked its publication in TRADOC controlled journals, declaring, 'I have no intention of getting involved in a series of non-productive, point-by-point, exchanges with Mr. Lind.'[30] Lind instead shared the article with his political and military contacts, resulting in staff from the Army journal *Military Review* — based at the Command and General Staff College at Fort Leavenworth outside DePuy's control — offering publication. After DePuy learned this, he threatened the *Military Review* staff that he would demolish their building 'brick by brick' if they published Lind's article, causing them to withdraw their offer.

Lind, however, would not be silenced. The October 1976 issue of *Armed Forces Journal International* included four articles on Active Defense, including Lind's 'Banned at Fort Monroe, or the Article the Army Doesn't Want You to Read', accusing DePuy and TRADOC of censorship.

Military Review eventually published 'Doctrinal Questions for the United States Army' in March 1977, in which Lind challenged DePuy's win the first battle assumption:

> Can we assume that winning the first battle means that there will not be a second battle? If there is a second battle, will the concentration of our efforts on winning the first battle help us to win the second, or could it hinder us?[31]

Lind argued that Soviet doctrine assumed its first echelon would suffer heavy losses, but their follow-on echelons would fight subsequent battles. He also criticized Active Defense for being reliant upon technology which supposedly favors the defender but the 'connection between the "new lethality" and the superiority of the defense is assumed' and 'incomplete'.[32] Furthermore, Lind critiqued Active Defense for emphasizing 'firepower' at the expense of 'maneuver', which played to Soviet strengths, and condemned its forward defensive orientation as attritional and doomed to failure given the Warsaw Pact's numerical superiority.

Lind's critique triggered a revolt within the United States Army and over the next four years *Military Review* published around eighty articles criticizing Active Defense as DePuy lost control of the narrative.[33] This clash of ideas, as Israeli military theorist Shimon Naveh concluded, constituted 'the longest, most intoxicating and creative professional debate which ever occurred in the history of American military thought'.[34]

The rebels accused the Army of wrongly placing its faith in technology-based 'attrition warfare' designed to wear down the enemy by directly attacking strengths, rather than using cunning to indirectly exploit weaknesses. They viewed senior officers as trapped in a Vietnam-era attritional mindset and, as such, had learned nothing from their recent defeat.[35] The rebels, as General Huba Wass de Czege explained, perceived 'Army officers as hidebound bureaucrats cultivating managerial skills over leadership' with no interest in military art due to their 'tendency to treat military challenges as if they were simple engineering problems'.[36] The historian Thomas Ricks similarly concluded: 'DePuy's manual was very much a product of the late Cold War. It emphasized training, which prepares soldiers for the known, far more than education, which prepares them to deal with the unknown.'[37] In opposition to Active Defense, the rebels advocated an alternative warfighting philosophy — maneuver warfare — a concept first articulated by John Boyd.

THE O-O-D-A LOOP

Boyd's 1976 paper *Destruction and Creation* theorized that the human mind forms mental concepts, which help decide actions, in constantly changing environments. When new events supersede old ones, obsolete ideas must be destroyed and replaced with new concepts if decisions in tune with reality are to be made. The failure to adapt can be fatal, as any action taken not in harmony with reality can have disastrous consequences.

Destruction and Creation contains themes that echo Boyd's Observation–Orientation–Decision–Action loop theory which explained air combat over Korea. Although Chinese MiG-15s had superior speed, turning, climbing and acceleration performance compared with American F-86 Sabres, Boyd realized the Sabres had bubble cockpits providing superior observation and their hydraulic flight controls enabled pilots to more rapidly transition between different maneuvers. These factors gave American pilots an edge over the seemingly superior MiGs because they had superior situational awareness and transitioned through their 'decision cycles' quicker than Chinese pilots.

According to Boyd, individuals and groups transition through four stages of decision-making during conflict. During observation, the external environment is perceived through the senses as events unfold and an evaluation is made of one's place in the environment when scanning for

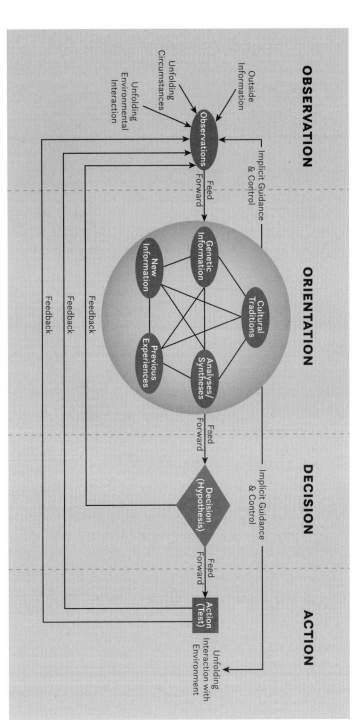

John Boyd's Final O–O–D–A Loop

threats. Orientation involves processing the information obtained through sensory perception, danger is analyzed and an assessment of reality is made.[38] During the decision stage, options are considered and a course of action is decided upon which is believed to offer the best chance of survival. Finally, the action is taken and its effectiveness is evaluated before the process begins again.

During conflict two minds going through O–O–D–A loops confront each other and a series of cycles continues until a victor, who is able to transition through the loops quicker, emerges. The victor has a more accurate sense of reality and thereby seizes the initiative. The loser, unable to keep up with the pace set by the victor, becomes paralyzed by confusion as his decisions and actions no longer correspond with reality as he completes cycles based on obsolete perceptions, resulting in poor decisions which, as historian Martin van Creveld explained, 'is comparable to that of a chess player who is allowed to make only one move for every two made by his opponent'.[39] The victor with quicker tempo will disorient the loser and operate inside his 'decision cycle' to generate mental collapse. As Boyd explained, the victor will create in their opponent's mind 'a world of uncertainty, doubt, mistrust, confusion, disorder, fear, panic, chaos'.[40] Boyd updated and refined the O-O-D-A loop over time into a vastly more complex idea involving multiple feedback loops towards the end of his life, and he only depicted the concept in a drawing in 1995.[41]

PROPHETS FROM THE TRENCHES

When Boyd studied military history looking for a grand theory, he was heavily influenced by two British military thinkers. As titanic armies clashed on the Western Front during World War I, J.F.C. Fuller, a British Royal Tank Corps officer, pioneered armored tactics and advocated using tanks as a massed mobile force to end the terrible carnage of trench warfare. Although tanks had been invented as a means of breaking into trenches, Fuller perceived them as the reincarnation of heavy cavalry with great potential to wreak havoc behind enemy lines. In 1918, he formulated 'Plan 1919', which would use tanks in a rapid surprise attack to overrun German headquarters to paralyze frontline units, allowing a follow-on force of tanks and lorry-based

The military theorist J.F.C. Fuller
(Author's Collection)

infantry to make deep advances while bombers targeted roads and supply depots to further paralyze the Germans.

Fuller perceived the German Army as a single organic being whose 'body', protected by the armor of trenches, had been ineffectively pounded with costly frontal assaults. He offered a less costly alternative by advocating a precision strike directly at the German 'brain':

> The brains of an army are its Staff — Army, Corps and Divisional Headquarters. Could they suddenly be removed from an extensive sector of the German front, the collapse of the personnel they control will be little more than a matter of hours.[42]

Fuller, convinced that an army deprived of leadership would quickly collapse, shaped 'Plan 1919' accordingly, but the war ended in 1918 and his concept remained hypothetical.

After the war, Fuller became the British Army's leading advocate of mechanization, prophesying that future conflicts would be decided by tanks operating across vast distances, resembling the movement of fleets at sea, outmaneuvering enemies and securing victory with minimal casualties. As a political reactionary, he detested the mass armies raised during the French Revolution and World War I, viewing them as degenerate while stressing that wars are best fought by small professional mechanized forces.

Fuller in *The Foundations of the Science of War* (1926) codified his 'organic' views on paralyzing enemy command (brain) and supply networks (stomach).[43] He above all wanted to avoid the World War I fixation on destroying enemy armies through attritional struggles.[44] Fuller's ideas became extremely influential, although his reputation suffered after he joined Oswald Mosley's British Union of Fascists and because his far-right ideals became increasingly intertwined within his military writing.[45] Furthermore, a younger colleague eclipsed him and took the spotlight.

Basil Henry Liddell Hart studied history at Cambridge before obtaining a commission in 1914 as a second lieutenant in the King's Own Yorkshire Light Infantry. After arriving on the Western Front the following year, he fought at Ypres. In 1916, Liddell Hart survived the first day of the Somme:

> After running the gauntlet of enemy snipers and other fire. . . we reached a slightly sunken road half a mile beyond the enemy's front trench, and there found what survived of the battalion. Only two officers were left, and one of them was wounded. . . The neighbouring battalion had no officers left, and I took charge of it temporarily until some fresh ones arrived.[46]

As the slaughter of the Somme continued, Liddell Hart was exposed to phosgene gas and he consequently served in a training battalion for the rest of the war. In this role, he developed unorthodox methods of training soldiers, motivated by a desire to prevent futile frontal attacks and later drafted training pamphlets in the Army Educational Corps. After the war, he helped write the new infantry training manual.

Liddell Hart's World War I experiences haunted him and preventing similar horrendous losses in future conflict became his overriding obsession because 'if war came again there should be no repetition of the Somme and Passchendaele'.[47] This mission became the central focus of his life.[48]

On 3 November 1920, Liddell Hart gave a lecture at the Royal United

The military theorist
Basil Henry Liddell
Hart in 1940
(Contributor: Pictorial Press
Ltd/Alamy Stock Photo)

Services Institute on his 'man-in-the-dark' and 'expanding torrent' theories. He explained that the modern battlefield is similar to two men fighting hand to hand in the dark and, unable to see, they stumble forward with raised arms searching for the other, an act of reconnaissance and self-protection.[49] Once contact is made, both men will try to hold and immobilize the other, and when the opponent becomes fixed a punch can be delivered 'from an unexpected direction in an unguarded spot, delivering out of the dark a decisive knock-out blow'.[50] The 'man-in-the-dark' theory is a metaphor explaining how to find and fix the enemy before maneuvering to exploit a vulnerability.

In the second part of the lecture, Liddell Hart explained his 'expanding torrent' concept, which envisaged striking 'the enemy's weakest spots instead of dashing one's head against his strongest points'.[51] 'We have learnt by bitter experience,' he explained, 'that it is sheer waste of force, when we come against an enemy position, to press our attack equally at all points.'[52] The 'expanding torrent' instead advocated probing for weak points across a broad front before breaching the line once 'soft spots' are identified, which reflects the natural flow of water.

The 'man-in-the-dark' and 'expanding torrent' concepts are complementary. The 'man-in-the-dark' concerns overcoming strong points that cannot be avoided while the 'expanding torrent' explains how to collapse the enemy by avoiding strong points and infiltrating into rear areas.

Captain Liddell Hart left the army in 1924 due to poor health and briefly earned a living as a sports journalist before becoming a military writer for the *Morning Post*. He later became the military correspondent for the *Daily Telegraph* and a military editor of *Encyclopedia Britannica*. By the mid-1920s, he gained an international reputation as a military thinker and became the most famous military journalist in Britain in the next decade.[53]

Liddell Hart moved beyond infantry tactics by embracing the armored warfare views of Fuller. During the early 1920s, he advocated the mass use of tanks to break through enemy defenses and praised 'Plan 1919' for heralding 'the dawn of scientific military thought' and for seeking 'the paralysis of the enemy's command and not the bodies of the actual soldiers'.[54] In 1924, Liddell Hart published a paper on his 'New Model Army' concept, which advocated applying the 'expanding torrent' to tank warfare, as mechanized forces could more easily exploit weak points to create breakthroughs by using superior speed to drive deep behind enemy lines.

Like Fuller, Liddell Hart viewed frontal assaults against trenches as insanity, but in explaining why such tragedies occurred, his ideas became distinct. He believed trench warfare resulted from the Prussian military theorist Carl von Clausewitz's concept of 'absolute war', found in his massively influential book *On War* (1832).[55] Liddell Hart believed that this idea advocated total war and maximum violence, which had been practiced by Napoleon, although Clausewitz 'analysed, codified, and deified the Napoleonic method'.[56] This 'Napoleonic Fallacy' is an unquestioning faith that 'victory can only be gained by defeating in battle the armed forces of the enemy'.[57] This delusion deceived the World War I generation into believing victory could only be obtained through the complete destruction of enemy armies, resulting in vast numbers of soldiers launching frontal attacks against trenches.

Liddell Hart explained how to overcome the 'Napoleonic Fallacy' in *Paris: Or the Future of War* (1925):

> The aim of a nation in war is, therefore, to subdue the enemy's will to resist, with the least possible human and economic loss to itself. . . [and] the *destruction* of the enemy's armed forces is but a means — and not necessarily an inevitable or infallible one — to the attainment of our goal.[58]

Therefore, the true aim of military planning is 'to discover and exploit the Achilles' heel of the enemy nation; to strike not against its strongest bulwark but against its most vulnerable spot'.[59] In modern nations these are usually capitals, industries, resources, communications and ports. Liddell Hart explained that attacking such vulnerabilities has traditionally been difficult because advancing armies marching at walking pace have only rarely been able to reach a vital center 'without first disposing of the enemy's main army'.[60] Therefore, a delusion arose that enemy armies had to be destroyed, but future conflict would be different because tanks could maneuver around enemy armies:

> Once appreciate [sic] that tanks are not an extra arm or a mere aid to infantry but the modern form of heavy cavalry and their true military use is obvious — to be concentrated and used in as large masses as possible for a decisive blow against the Achilles' heel of enemy army, the communication and command centre which form its nerve system.[61]

In *Paris*, Liddell Hart also predicted that strategic bombers would attack vital points as the use of aircraft 'enables us to *jump over* the army which shields the enemy government, industry, and people, and *so strike direct and immediately at the seat of the opposing will and policy*'.[62] He predicted that a nation with a strategic bomber force at war with a major land power would triumph 'within a few hours, or at most days' by paralyzing the enemy country.[63] Although this would necessitate bombing civilians, such actions are morally justifiable using utilitarian logic because less death would ultimately result from such actions, compared with direct attacks against enemy armies.

Liddell Hart ended *Paris* with a vision that the 'land "punch" of the future will be delivered by fleets of tanks' and 'air vehicles' advancing 'by rapid bounds into the enemy country to strike at its vitals'.[64] He continued:

> Speed, on land as in the air, will dominate the next war, transforming the battlefields of the future from squalid trench labyrinths into arenas where surprise and manoeuvre will reign again, resorted to life and emerging from the mausoleums of mud built by Clausewitz and his successors.[65]

In 1927, Liddell Hart began articulating the 'indirect approach': a means of winning wars without costly fighting by paralyzing the enemy through the use of subtlety, deception and avoiding strengths. The 'indirect approach' built upon ideas expressed in *Paris*, as tanks should strive 'to get by an indirect approach on the enemy's rear, knowing that once astride his line of communications and retreat he would either be paralysed or unhinged'.[66] This idea became fully expressed in *Strategy* (1929), which claimed that all successful commanders in history used the 'indirect approach' to dislocate their opponents by attacking where least expected to strike a fatal blow, as 'decisive results in war have only been reached when the approach has been indirect. In strategy, the longest way round is often the shortest way home.' [67]

The 'indirect approach' stressed the psychological aspect of war, viewing it as a contest between opposing minds, as 'in almost all the decisive campaigns the dislocation of the enemy's psychological and physical balance has been the vital prelude to a successful attempt at his overthrow'.[68] The 'indirect approach' avoids the 'Napoleonic Fallacy' of seeking decisive battles by instead seeking 'a strategic situation so advantageous that, if it does not of itself produce the decision, continuation by battle is sure to achieve this'.[69] Therefore, the 'indirect approach' would avoid excessive bloodshed by defeating the enemy through dislocation rather than destruction.

According to Liddell Hart, German stormtroopers in 1918 used the 'indirect approach' to break the trench deadlock by applying 'infiltration tactics', which involved probing and penetrating weak points in a manner resembling the 'expanding torrent'. The stormtroopers avoided direct attacks on strong points and infiltrated into rear areas to attack vital nodes, indirectly bringing about the collapse of the front. However, the Germans later unwisely abandoned 'infiltration tactics' by attacking strength and their forces failed to penetrate 'far enough to sever a vital artery'.[70]

Liddell Hart believed that if opposing sides rationally apply the 'indirect approach', war would become virtually bloodless as the 'perfection of strategy' is to 'produce a decision without any serious fighting'.[71] Future battles would be fought without horrendous casualties as victory would be won by the side gaining positional advantage, because once outmaneuvered a rational commander would surrender.

Fuller and Liddell Hart formulated their theories in the shadow of the trenches and their concepts remained largely theoretical until the outbreak of World War II. After the fall of France in 1940, they both argued that the British Army's conservative leadership had ignored their prophetic writings, in particular their views on armored warfare, and accordingly went to war stubbornly clinging to obsolete ideas. The Germans, in contrast, fully embraced their theories and used them to great effect in the early years of the war. Fuller accordingly declared that 'Plan 1919' was 'first put to the test in 1939, and became known as *Blitzkrieg*'.[72] He gave Liddell Hart co-credit for inventing *Blitzkrieg* as it 'was based on what Captain B.H. Liddell Hart calls "the indirect approach"'.[73] Liddell Hart similarly defined *Blitzkrieg* as 'the "expanding torrent", adapted to the new [panzer] arm'.[74]

The paralysis theories of Fuller and Liddell Hart and their association with *Blitzkrieg* eerily echo what Boyd independently concluded after studying the air war over Korea. When Boyd began looking for parallels between fighter pilots gaining 'decision cycle' superiority to mentally paralyze their opponents, he found kindred spirits in Fuller and Liddell Hart. They explained to him how the Germans defeated France in 1940 with rapid panzer attacks from unexpected directions, which set a pace too fast for French commanders to deal with, and their ideas became the foundation of maneuver warfare.

PATTERNS OF CONFLICT

Boyd, after retiring from the Air Force in 1975, searched for links between his O–O–D–A loop and other forms of conflict, looking for a grand theory to guide military success.[75] After spending eighteen months studying

A depiction of the Chinese military theorist Sun Tzu
(Contributor: Universal Art Archive/ Alamy Stock Photo)

history, he delivered his *Patterns of Conflict* briefing, the first expression of maneuver warfare.

Boyd admired Sun Tzu, who is believed to have written *The Art of War* around 550 BC, and praised the Chinese philosopher for advocating the virtues of avoiding protracted war and probing the enemy 'to unmask his strengths, weaknesses, patterns of movement and intentions' as well as shaping the 'enemy's perception of the world to manipulate his plans and actions'.[76] Boyd praised Sun Tzu's concept of *cheng* (ordinary force) and *ch'i* (extraordinary force); the *cheng* uses direct moves to fix the opponent while the *ch'i* applies indirect moves to strike a decisive blow, unexpectedly hurling strength against weaknesses, as Boyd explained in a more relatable way: 'Patton said, hold them by the nose and kick them in the ass. . . You get them to concentrate one way and you kick the shit out of them in a different direction.'[77]

Cheng and *ch'i* drew Boyd closer to Liddell Hart as they resemble the 'man-in-the-dark' theory of fixing the enemy before delivering a knockout blow. Sun Tzu also brought Boyd closer to Liddell Hart, as the Chinese philosopher observed: 'the army's disposition of force is like water. Water's configuration avoids heights and races downward. The army's disposition of force avoids the substantial and strikes the vacuous.'[78] Sun Tzu's metaphor echoed the 'expanding torrent' as Liddell Hart noticed: 'when I read Sun Tzu's two-thousand-year-old book on *The Art of War*, I found that he had used a close simile'.[79] This concept became central to Boyd who noted that Sun Tzu 'speaks many times of the idea that an army should behave like water going down hill. That you seek the crevices, the gaps and the voids' in order to 'find a path of least resistance.'[80]

In *Patterns of Conflict*, Boyd took a particular interest in the Greeks and Romans. He noted how the Theban commander Epaminondas during the Battle of Leuctra (371 BC) concentrated his numerically inferior force at a decisive point to defeat the Spartans. He attributed the Carthaginian general Hannibal's victory over the larger Roman Army at Cannae (216 BC) to the use of a double envelopment. Boyd noted that Leuctra and Cannae had been won by 'an unequal or uneven distribution of forces across a front as basis to concentrate forces for the main attack at the decisive point' that created 'local superiority and decisive leverage to collapse adversary resistance'.[81]

Furthermore, Boyd praised Genghis Khan and the Mongols who, despite being outnumbered, maneuvered 'in widely scattered arrays without being defeated separately or in detail' by using 'baited retreats, hard-hitting tactical thrusts, and swirling envelopments to uncover and exploit adversary vulnerabilities and weaknesses'.[82] He was also drawn to the psychological aspect of Mongol tactics, their 'clever and calculated use of propaganda and terror to play upon [an] adversary's doubts, fears, and superstitions in order to undermine his resolve and destroy his will to resist'.[83] Boyd concluded that the 'Mongols operated inside adversary observation–orientation–decision–action loops' and, despite being outnumbered, 'created impressions of terrifying strength — by seeming to come out of nowhere yet be everywhere'.[84]

In analyzing ancient battles, Boyd noticed a key difference between Western and Eastern commanders:

The Western commanders tended to apply these ideas within the context or within the frame of a battle. . . If you look at the Eastern commanders, particularly Genghis Khan, they played in full conformity with the ideas of Sun-Tzu. They tried to literally unravel their adversary prior to the battle or even to deny the opportunity of a battle.[85]

Boyd concluded that the Western obsession with winning battles epitomized the Napoleonic Wars and its principal theorist Clausewitz. He argued that Napoleon, as a younger general, used maneuver to threaten enemy communications and confuse them with feints, before attacking and destroying them after concentrating on their flank or rear.[86] However, Emperor Napoleon later fought grinding battles of attrition, without his earlier creativity, 'pitting strength against strength', which resulted in 'very high casualties on both sides'.[87]

Boyd shared Liddell Hart's criticism of Napoleon and Clausewitz's fixation on winning 'decisive battles' and seeking the complete destruction of enemy armies, rather than securing less costly victories by paralyzing opponents. He believed Clausewitz's central flaw was his obsession with overcoming the fog of war, rather than trying to increase uncertainty and confusion in the opponent's mind as Sun Tzu urged:

> Sun-Tzu was trying to magnify his adversary's friction and uncertainty or confusion and disorder, whereas Clausewitz generally thought in terms of trying to overcome it from a commander's perspective. In modern vernacular, Sun-Tzu was trying to drive his adversary bananas; Clausewitz was trying to keep himself from being driven bananas.[88]

According to Boyd, Clausewitz's obsession with reducing chaos and uncertainty, rather than projecting these fears into the enemy commander's mind, resulted in a failure to consider mentally paralyzing adversaries and 'operations end in a "bloodbath" — via the well-regulated stereotyped tactics and unimaginative battles of attrition suggested by Clausewitz'.[89] Boyd instead advocated avoiding battle and creating confusion and panic through deception and surprise to shape enemy perceptions to unravel their cohesion.[90] He also criticized the highly centralized command and control systems of Napoleonic-era armies with their rigid and predictable formations which 'minimized the possibility of exploiting ambiguity, deception, and mobility to generate surprise for a decisive edge'.[91]

In analyzing World War I, Boyd saw the legacy of Napoleon just as Liddell Hart had done. On the Western Front mass armies confronted each other across static trenches sustained by enormous rail-based logistics, in which flanking or enveloping the enemy became impossible, resulting in large-scale frontal attacks by massed infantry with enormous artillery bombardments.

To avoid the mass slaughter of industrial warfare, Boyd embraced Fuller and Liddell Hart's 'organic' view of the enemy, seeing it as a 'body' controlled by a 'brain' that can be paralyzed by severing its nerve centers. He embraced Liddell Hart's view of German stormtroopers using 'infiltration tactics' to overcome the trenches in 1918, involving small squads which 'flow into any gaps or weaknesses they can find in order to drive deep into [the] adversary rear'.[92] This resembled the 'expanding torrent' as the stormtroopers followed 'paths of least resistance to gain the opportunity for breakthrough and envelopment'.[93] They ultimately failed because the Germans violated their own logic by using reserves to reinforce attacks against hardened resistance. The stormtroopers also suffered from exhaustion, overextended supply lines and poor communications, but mechanization would later solve these problems.

To Boyd, the German *Blitzkrieg* of World War II combined stormtrooper 'infiltration tactics' with panzer warfare which he attributed to Fuller and the German general Heinz Guderian.[94] *Blitzkrieg* enabled the Germans with inferior numbers and equipment to defeat the French Army in 1940 because their panzers infiltrated the 'adversary front to find paths of least resistance'.[95] Boyd explained that German spearheads, striking deep into rear areas, created paralysis by shaping French perceptions, filling their minds with anxiety, fear and chaos. While the French attempted to fight Napoleonic-style centralized battles, *Blitzkrieg* relied upon de-centralized command and high levels of junior initiative, a feat made possible by *Auftragstaktik* (mission tactics) and *Schwerpunkt* (main effort).

Boyd believed the Germans overcame rigid Napoleonic top-down command through *Auftragstaktik*, a principle with deep Prussian roots, in which junior leaders are expected to exploit favorable situations on their own initiative, without waiting for orders, by acting in accordance with their higher commander's intent:

The German concept of mission can be thought of as a contract, hence an agreement, between superior and subordinate. The subordinate agrees to make his actions serve his superior's intent in terms of what is to be accomplished, while the superior agrees to give his subordinate wide freedom to exercise his imagination and initiative in terms of how intent is to be realized.[96]

Auftragstaktik did not produce anarchy because German commanders, despite decentralized leadership, maintained harmony through the *Schwerpunkt*:

Schwerpunkt represents a unifying concept that provides a way to rapidly shape focus and direction of effort as well as harmonize support activities with combat operations, thereby permit a true decentralization of tactical command within centralized strategic guidance — without losing cohesion of overall effort.[97]

In other words, a commander designates a *Schwerpunkt* or a 'main effort' and although subordinates use initiative to determine how to execute their missions in accordance with *Auftragstaktik*, they are also aware of the *Schwerpunkt* and, therefore, plan their missions in harmony with the overall plan. After reconnaissance teams detect weak points, the commander assigns the *Schwerpunkt* to direct the advance through the path of least resistance. The panzers accordingly bypass strong points and achieve rapid breakthroughs and, after reconnaissance identifies fresh weak points, the commander accordingly shifts the *Schwerpunkt* to ensure the path of least resistance is continuously followed.

Boyd believed that *Schwerpunkt* and *Auftragstaktik* gave the *Wehrmacht* an immense advantage by allowing them to compress time:

The secret of the German command and control system lies in what's unstated or not communicated to one another — to exploit lower-level initiative yet realize higher-level intent, thereby diminish friction and reduce time, hence gain both quickness and security.[98]

German junior leaders adapted to unfolding events and made quick decisions to rapidly exploit opportunities without waiting for orders, within the context of a unified plan, faster than the centralized French who patiently waited for orders which when finally arriving were no longer relevant in the changed situation, and their actions accordingly did not reflect reality. The French ultimately became overwhelmed and paralyzed by their inability to adapt to lightning panzer operations and rapidly changing situations — just like Chinese MiG-15 pilots during the Korean War — as Boyd explained:

> We see this idea of faster tempo or faster rhythm in terms of the Germans versus a slower tempo in rhythm by the French and the British. . . the Germans are going through these loops at a much faster pace, much quicker pace than the allies. The allies were trying to adapt. They kept getting this negative feedback. Pretty soon doubt and uncertainty began to emerge and confusion, disorder, panic and chaos developed.[99]

As such, Boyd found an example of an army transitioning through O–O–D–A loops decisively faster than its opponent and his theory moved beyond the cockpit into the realm of land warfare.

In *Patterns of Conflict*, Boyd articulated three distinct styles of warfare: attrition, maneuver and moral. In attrition warfare the destructive force of firepower is emphasized and success is determined by kill-ratio calculations. Its overall goal is the destruction of enemy armies, epitomized by Emperor Napoleon and the Allies during both world wars.[100] In attrition warfare 'firepower, as a destructive force, is king' and 'mobility is used to bring firepower to bear or to evade enemy fire'.[101] Boyd added, 'attrition warfare is easy. Christ, you just go out there and just slug off artillery and machine gun rounds and all that bullshit. You don't even have to think. Just pound away.'[102]

Maneuver warfare, in contrast, emphasizes ambiguity, deception, creativity and mobility to generate surprise and shock. According to Boyd, this will 'magnify friction, shatter cohesion, produce paralysis, and bring about his collapse' by overloading the enemy's 'immediate ability to respond or adapt.'[103] Maneuver warfare also reflected the 'organic' views of Fuller and Liddell Hart, as Boyd explained:

> I am talking about clipping the blood vessels of the organism or the

tendons or the nerves. Collapse them into jelly. If you do that, you just roll up the isolated resistance. What is the intent? Is it to kill? No. Here is the intent — to shatter cohesion, produce paralysis, and bring about adversary collapse by generating confusion, disorder, panic, and chaos.[104]

According to Boyd, maneuver warfare was practiced by Genghis Khan, Stonewall Jackson, Ulysses Grant, George Patton, Douglas MacArthur and *Wehrmacht* generals, notably Erich von Manstein, Heinz Guderian, Hermann Balck and Erwin Rommel.

Moral warfare, as Boyd explained, creates victory through the 'triumph of courage, confidence, and esprit (de corps) over fear, anxiety, and alienation when confronted by menace, uncertainty, and mistrust'.[105] The victors believe in the cause they are fighting for which legitimizes their struggle and amplifies morale while undermining enemy resolve and attracting the undecided toward their cause. For example, Pearl Harbor in a military sense was a Japanese victory but a strategic failure on the moral level of war as it united a divided America, as Boyd noted:

> The Japanese unified us. Before that happened, we had 'America First' units, we had the German-American Bund. . . I was a young kid at that time and I remember that. And as soon as they did that, the whole country unified. Goddamn it, if they're going to play that kind of game, we're going to kick them in the ass and win this thing.[106]

Through *Patterns of Conflict*, maneuver warfare became the philosophy of the rebels opposing Active Defense, which they associated with uncreative attrition and fixation on the physical destruction of the enemy. Boyd, always inquisitive, consistently modified and expanded *Patterns of Conflict* until 1986 before renaming it *A Discourse on Winning and Losing*, which brought together the different streams of his thinking.[107] The brief eventually included three sub-briefings on core ideas which Boyd on occasion delivered as standalone presentations: *An Organic Design for Command and Control* (1987), *The Strategic Game of ? and ?* (1987) and *The Conceptual Spiral* (1992).

An Organic Design for Command and Control concerns the role of people and communication technology in relation to tactics and strategy. As perfect knowledge is unobtainable and designs rarely unfold according to plan, Boyd asked how commanders are supposed to adapt to unexpected events in real time. He argued that communication is more than just advanced technology but also the bonds of trust and understanding the commander's intent and one's own purpose in the overall plan. From this realization, the most important flow of information is not from the top down the chain of command but bottom up feedback from subordinates which commanders can process to successfully adapt to changing situations.

The Strategic Game of ? and ? is a detailed explanation and overview of O–O–D–A loop process using the logic of destruction and creation. The central concept is a thought experiment involving the image of a skier, a motorboat, a bicycle and a toy tractor. All these images or concepts can be broken down into parts through a destructive process which results in skis, a motorboat engine, bicycle handlebars and rubber treads from the tractor. These parts can then be reassembled into something new through a creative process resulting in a new image or concept — a snowmobile. Through this snowmobile allegory, Boyd explained the process of synthesis and how to survive and win in a complex world through adaptation.

The Conceptual Spiral revisits the logic of destruction and creation and considers how individuals interact and cope with unfolding reality and successfully adapt to events as well as the relationship between science, engineering and technology. Boyd argued that these disciplines require self-correction and learning mechanisms to properly thrive and create innovation as progress continuously results in new uncertainties which must be accepted and overcome.

True to the philosophy of *Destruction and Creation*, Boyd hated the idea that his ideas might become dogma, so he avoided firmly defining them in writing which would immediately render them obsolete.[108] Therefore, he preferred to constantly modify his briefings and encourage audience feedback and no two presentations were ever identical. However, by refusing to write firm views, Boyd allowed his followers to define his ideas and even his closest acolytes disagree on the deeper aspects of the O–O–D–A loop.[109] William S. Lind, after listening to Boyd deliver *Patterns of Conflict*, became an acolyte and more than anybody else defined maneuver warfare to the wider world.

LIND AND THE OTHER THEORISTS

Lind explained maneuver warfare through numerous articles in military journals before systematically articulating his thoughts in *Maneuver Warfare Handbook* (1985). He translated Boyd's complex theories into easy to read passages, influencing a large audience of military minded individuals. For example, he considered that maneuver warfare is the opposite of attrition and 'can be thought of as military judo. It is a way of fighting smart, of out-thinking an opponent you may not be able to overpower with brute strength.'[110] Lind similarly articulated *Auftragstaktik* in a relatable way to soldiers: 'A mission-type order tells the subordinate commander what his superior wants to have accomplished. That is the mission. It leaves how to accomplish it largely up to the subordinate.'[111] *Auftragstaktik* does not result in the commander losing control as his intent is understood through the *Schwerpunkt*:

> It is where the commander believes he can achieve a decision, and it translates into a unit, as in 'Schwerpunkt is 2nd battalion'. When a unit is designated the focus of effort, all other units work to support it. . . Its neighbors each ask themselves, 'What can I do to support the Schwerpunkt?'[112]

As Lind explained, the key concepts of maneuver warfare are complementary. The superior tempo advocated by the O–O–D–A loop is achieved through *Auftragstaktik* because 'mission orders' allows lower-level initiative which facilitates faster tempo as commanders on the spot can complete their 'decision cycles' rapidly without the need to liaise with superiors.[113] The weakness of 'mission orders' is the potential for subordinates to act in isolation, but this is avoided through the 'main effort' when a commander designates a *Schwerpunkt*, as all other units focus their actions on supporting it. Furthermore, the 'main effort' will be most effective when directed against enemy 'gaps' or weak points which are best found through de-centralized 'recon pull' in which the direction of the 'advance is determined by the results of reconnaissance' and 'shifts in response to what the recon finds'.[114]

Brigadier Richard Simpkin, a retired British Royal Armoured Corps officer, wrote *Race to the Swift* (1985) which condemned the 'addicts of attrition', epitomized by the British and French during World War I, who 'simply seeks to achieve a shift of relative strengths in his favour by imposing on the enemy a higher casualty rate, or more broadly "attrition rate", than he himself suffers'.[115] To Simpkin, the British Army has been consistently addicted to attrition throughout its history and, in contrast, he praised the 'masters of maneuver' who draw their 'power mainly from opportunism — the calculated risk, and the exploitation both of chance circumstances and (to borrow a tennis term) of "forced and unforced errors" by the opposition'.[116]

Simpkin made a unique contribution by focusing on small-force maneuver, which can be practiced by nimble forces using light armored vehicles and helicopters capable of effortlessly moving through the land domain in a similar manner to warships at sea. This small force focus made maneuver warfare more relevant to smaller Western militaries such as the British, Canadian, Australian and New Zealand armies, in contrast to the tank heavy armored fist of the American superpower.

Lieutenant Colonel Robert Leonhard, a United States Army officer, wrote *The Art of Maneuver* (1991), which defined maneuver warfare in a similar way to Boyd and Lind:

> Maneuver warfare is, to put it simply, a kick in the groin, a poke in the eye, a stab in the back. It is quick, violent for a moment, and unfair. It is decisive, even preemptive, at the expense of protocol and posturing. Maneuver warfare puts a premium on being sneaky rather than courageous, and it is not at all glorious, because it typically flees from the enemy's strength.[117]

Leonhard condemned attrition 'in which the friendly force attempts to defeat an enemy through the destruction of the enemy's mass'.[118] Instead, he argues that maneuver warfare can defeat enemies through less costly preemption, dislocation and disruption.

Colonel Richard Hooker, a United States Army officer, edited *Maneuver Warfare: An Anthology* (1993), a collection of twenty-one essays written mostly by well-known contributors to military journals including Lind and Leonhard. The book summarized and analyzed maneuver warfare concepts which had been advocated in the journals since the late 1970s. Hooker had earlier defined the theory 'as a clash of wills, with victory going to the side that destroys the opponent's will to resist'.[119]

Although different maneuver warfare theorists disagree on details, they all share common core characteristics, as Francis Park explained:

> While the definitions of maneuver warfare have evolved over time, all of them reflected a method of combat that focused on the moral domain of warfare — defeating an adversary primarily through psychological collapse. Such an approach contrasted with a mechanistic use of firepower to destroy an enemy, a method consistent with the physical domain of warfare. Much of the practice of maneuver warfare implies a decentralized approach that trades synchronization and certainty for speed and initiative, accepting chaos and uncertainty as a matter of course.[120]

By the time *The Art of Maneuver* and *Maneuver Warfare: An Anthology* appeared, Boyd's ideas had already transitioned from a rebel philosophy to endorsed doctrine within the United States Army and Marine Corps.

CHAPTER TWO
THE MANEUVER WARFARE REVOLUTION

THE AIRLAND BATTLE

The rebels in the United States Army opposed to General William DePuy's Active Defense — codified in FM 100-5 Operations (1976) — expressed their dissent in *Military Review* articles. William S. Lind sustained this rebellion, relentlessly targeting senior leadership, while John Boyd, in retirement, openly attacked Active Defense: 'This is a disgrace! Even if you win the damn war, you're going to mow down thousands of your own soldiers!'[1] Boyd fueled the revolution through his *Patterns of Conflict* briefing which, in addition to spreading his philosophy, relentlessly denounced Active Defense as 'a piece of shit'.[2] The rebels won the hearts and minds of numerous junior officers and eventually senior officers with the power to change the system.

In 1981, General Jack Merritt, Commandant of Command and General Staff College, considered *Patterns of Conflict* 'a real tour de force' and considered Boyd 'really one of the most innovative and original guys I've ever had anything to do with'.[3] Lieutenant Colonel Huba Wass de Czege, an instructor at Staff College, impressed with *Patterns of Conflict*, arranged for Boyd and Lind to regularly lecture the students and they used this opportunity to continue their crusade against Active Defense by inciting the students against the doctrine.

General Donn Starry, a DePuy loyalist, ironically elevated Boyd's ideas into

Donn Starry
(Contributor: PJF Military
Collection/Alamy Stock
Photo)

doctrine. After DePuy retired in 1977, Starry took command of TRADOC and General Edward Meyer, the Army Chief of Staff, directed him to revise FM 100-5 *Operations* (1976).[4] The intensity of the rebellion against Active Defense convinced Starry of the need for doctrinal change, but in coming to this conclusion he found himself in an awkward position as he had strongly defended Active Defense but over time realized that some of the rebel ideas had merit.[5] He concluded that Active Defense was flawed as it did not address the possibility of, after defeating the initial Soviet onslaught in the 'first battle', fighting a 'second battle' against follow-on Warsaw Pact echelons.

Starry, having witnessed the backlash against Active Defense, wanted a more consultative approach to satisfy the rebels by allowing them to influence the new doctrine. He placed De Czege in charge of the writing team and invited the critics to contribute. Unlike DePuy, he did not rely upon a cabal of trusted subordinates and reached out to doctrine writers at Staff College. Starry also tasked Brigadier Donald Morelli to engage the rebels in genuine discussions about how to improve doctrine:

> We didn't agree with everything all of these people or many of the people in the Army said. But we certainly took into account all their thoughts. And I remember spending one whole day out at Leavenworth with Bill Lind and the authors, sitting around a table, going over this draft, page by page.[6]

Starry and De Czege met with Boyd and this consultative approach seemingly appeased the rebels by bringing them inside the doctrine development process.

The new manual, FM 100-5 *Operations* (1982), replaced Active Defense with the AirLand Battle concept, which retained DePuy's emphasis on the 'new lethality' of modern high-tech battlefields but introduced maneuver warfare concepts such as Boyd's O–O–D–A loop.[7] The manual also embraced *Auftragstaktik* and *Schwerpunkt* by introducing 'mission orders' and the 'main effort' into doctrine, completely overturning the Army's traditional centralized command philosophy. The AirLand Battle envisaged all soldiers understanding how their tasks contributed to the overall plan and small units would no longer be micro-managed by generals but would instead be trusted with autonomy.

The central idea of the AirLand Battle is seizing the initiative, as Starry explained:

> . . . the outcome of the battle at the tactical and operational levels will be decided by factors other than numbers, and other than who attacks and who defends. . . In the end, the side that somehow, at some time, somewhere during the battle seizes the initiative and holds it to the end is the side that wins.[8]

The AirLand Battle emphasized four core concepts: initiative, depth, agility and synchronization. The Army would initially be on the defensive as it faced the Soviet onslaught and soldiers would aggressively employ elastic defense involving combinations of strong-point defense, delaying actions and counterattacks. However, at the earliest possible moment, the Army would seize the initiative and go onto the offensive. Agility would help the Army do so as soldiers would be thinking and acting faster than their more centralized Eastern Bloc enemies. Depth would meanwhile be exploited by long-range air, missile and artillery strikes to interdict and disrupt the follow-on Soviet echelons before they reached the front line. Higher command would also shape operations by synchronizing combat functions such as firepower, electronic warfare, engineering, air defense, signals and logistics.

The AirLand Battle ended the rebellion in the United States Army as the consultative process injected core maneuver warfare concepts into doctrine. James Burton, a Boyd acolyte, triumphantly boasted, 'the Army threw out most of the dinosaurs' philosophy and embraced the philosophy espoused by Boyd'.[9] Four years later, the Army refined the AirLand Battle in FM 100-5 *Operations* (1986) to clarify the relationship between offensive and defensive operations and to expand operational-level content, but it retained Boyd's influence.

FM 100-5 *Operations* (1993) replaced the AirLand Battle after the Cold War when the new strategic environment necessitated greater emphasis on a wider range of military contingencies, such as peacekeeping and humanitarian intervention, but the new manual retained maneuver warfare ideals. During the War on Terror, FM 3-0 *Operations* (2008) preached Full Spectrum Operations with updated content on counterinsurgency and nation building but maneuver warfare remained. However, the Army never exclusively embraced maneuver warfare as Starry's consensus building attempted to reconcile Boyd's ideas with Active Defense.

The AirLand Battle is a hybrid concept which blends 'maneuver warfare' with its polar opposite 'destruction', as the new manual made crystal clear: 'The object of all operations is to destroy the opposing force.'[10] Therefore, the aspects of the AirLand Battle which embraced maneuver warfare were subordinated to this higher principle: 'Destruction of the opposing force is achieved by throwing the enemy off balance with powerful initial blows from unexpected directions and then following up rapidly to prevent his recovery.'[11] Therefore, achieving 'decision cycle' superiority is just a means to annihilate the enemy.[12]

The AirLand Battle's embrace of synchronization — the coordination of subordinate actions in physical space with precise timing — is inconsistent with the maneuver warfare ideal of *Auftragstaktik* as it is a form of centralized control. In 1982, when De Czege told Boyd at a West Point symposium that the new manual would stress initiative, agility, depth and synchronization, Boyd exploded, 'You synchronize watches not people. . . This idea of synchronization will ruin the Army.'[13] He explained his aversion to synchronization:

> How can the Army advocate initiative at the lower levels, agility of fast moving armored forces, and then insist upon everyone remaining synchronized? Synchronized forces can only advance at the pace of the slowest unit. Everyone has to stay in formation and advance together. This is wrong and flies in the face of the other three notions.[14]

Boyd, believing that synchronization ruined the new doctrine, denounced the AirLand Battle as based on an attritional 'high diddle diddle, straight up the middle' mindset and, like Active Defense, was another 'piece of shit'.[15] Destruction and synchronization remained in doctrine to the displeasure of the rebels, and James Burton lamented, 'the Army never did get things quite right'.[16] Robert Leonhard in *The Art of Maneuver* argued that the AirLand Battle constituted 'a move toward maneuver theory' but it 'succumbed to the irresistible pull of American warfighting traditions back toward attrition theory'.[17] However, the Marine Corps fully embraced 'pure' maneuver warfare.

WARFIGHTING

The Marine Corps adopted maneuver warfare in large part due to Lieutenant Colonel Michael Wyly, a key Boyd acolyte. Wyly served in Vietnam as a psychological warfare officer in 1965 before returning in 1968 to command D Company, 1st Battalion, 5th Marine Regiment based at An Hoa. D Company had suffered high casualties and the soldiers, with low morale, referred to themselves as the 'Dying Delta'; however, Wyly's leadership transformed the unit into an effective and lethal force. Nevertheless, he became disillusioned with the way the war was being fought. On one occasion Wyly witnessed a group of Marines advancing in a single line while the enemy simply waited until they passed before attacking them from behind.[18]

Wyly's disillusionment grew after returning home. As a student at the Amphibious Warfare School in Quantico, he found the lessons on World War II style beach attacks anachronistic:

> I had a lot of misgivings about our tactics. They were more casualty-producing than they needed to be. I said, 'Let's do some study. Let's have the courage to criticize our own efforts and move forward.' My career became sort of a crusade from then.[19]

After serving as a tactics instructor at Basic School, Wyly returned to Quantico as an instructor in 1979 and General Bernard Trainor, Director of Education, ordered him to develop a new tactics course.[20] As the existing lessons dated back to the 1930s, Wyly searched for something new and during a battalion exercise at Quantico he met Lind. 'I've read some of your stuff,' Wyly declared, 'you and I are obviously opposed to the same thing.' He then asked, 'What do you think we're for?'[21] Lind introduced Wyly to maneuver warfare and gave him Boyd's phone number.

In 1980, Wyly invited Boyd to Quantico to present *Patterns of Conflict* to his students and many of them found his ideas intriguing and stayed after class to further discuss maneuver warfare. Boyd became a feature at Quantico, giving lectures and participating in classes, and Wyly printed copies of his briefings, known as the 'Green Book', for the students.[22] Wyly incorporated maneuver warfare concepts into his tactics lessons and helped Lind edit *Maneuver Warfare Handbook*, which contained his lectures in an appendix. He also made the handbook compulsory reading for his students.[23]

The students in Wyly's class of 1981 played a more prominent role in advocating maneuver warfare. Lind gave them tactics lessons and one student, Captain William Woods, convinced him to lead a maneuver warfare study group.[24] The group, which called themselves the 'Young Turks', remained active for three years and attracted other like-minded Marines such as Captain Gary Wilson.[25]

Woods and Wilson wrote numerous articles advocating maneuver warfare in the *Marine Corps Gazette*, making Boyd's concepts accessible to fellow Marines.[26] Furthermore, Boyd and Lind helped their Marine colleagues bypass their chain of command. 'As civilians,' Wyly explained, 'they could bring pressures where we could not, finding ourselves at every turn "outranked".'[27] However, the relationship worked both ways as Wyly gave Boyd and Lind credible endorsement from a decorated land combat veteran.[28]

Before Wyly's encounter with Boyd, Marines had been advocating maneuver warfare in the *Marine Corps Gazette*, much like their Army colleagues had in *Military Review*. Captain Steven Miller wrote the first articles about the new concept in the journal in 1979 and this process intensified as the influence of Wyly and his students grew. The new ideas gained increasing credibility but not exclusive domination — a Marine Corps report sent to the House Armed Services Committee in 1983 noted that the 'Corps does not subscribe to any exclusive formula or recipe for warfare', although 'the concepts of maneuver warfare are evident throughout the Marine Corps'.[29]

Before graduating from Quantico, the study group students planned to promote their ideas in their future postings. Wilson and Woods later founded a study group at Camp Lejeune, North Carolina after being posted to the 2nd Marine Division.[30] They invited General Alfred Gray, their division commander, to a gathering and over dinner explained to him their desire to educate fellow officers and produce a divisional handbook for exercises. General Gray had served as an infantryman in Korea and, after being promoted to sergeant, became an officer in 1952. Gray later fought in Vietnam in 1965, 1967 and 1969 before commanding the 33rd Marine Amphibious Unit during the evacuation of South Vietnam in 1975.

At the dinner, Gray, already familiar with maneuver warfare having sat through *Patterns of Conflict* several times, said, 'This is no longer an informal study group. This is now the 2nd Marine Division's maneuver warfare board. The first thing you guys have to do is get John Boyd down here.'[31] Boyd soon delivered his briefing to the division, which became a maneuver warfare laboratory.

The Maneuver Warfare Board translated Boyd's concepts into tactics which could be tested during exercises. The board also published maneuver warfare reading lists, newsletters and training guides.[32] Lind often visited the division to observe training and discuss maneuver warfare with the officers. Gray developed the division's Battle Book, which outlined how to apply maneuver warfare principles, and travelled to Quantico to talk to the students about his reforms.[33] Former Quantico students also established a maneuver warfare study group at Camp Pendleton, California in the 1st Marine Division and other similar seminars appeared at other Corps institutions.

Despite maneuver warfare gaining traction with numerous Marines, General Paul Xavier Kelley, Commandant of the Corps, disapproved of the philosophy. Lind's attempts to incite the 'Young Turks' to rebel against the senior leadership alienated Kelley and other high-ranking officers, as Trainor recalled:

> Bill Lind was the source of friction. He publicly criticized Marine leadership and ascribed to it a calcified commitment to attrition warfare where it did not exist to the degree he claimed. . . The Marine Corps had a well-deserved reputation for innovative thinking and took umbrage at Bill Lind's charges.[34]

Kelley banned Lind from Quantico, so Lind could no longer lecture the students, as the rebellion lost steam. The maneuver warfare insurgency within the Marine Corps stagnated as it lacked a patron while Kelley remained Commandant, but this situation radically changed.

After Gray became Commandant in 1987, he decided to make maneuver warfare the Marine Corps' official philosophy and wanted a capstone doctrine similar to the Army's FM 100-5 *Operations* to guide all subordinate manuals. The Doctrine Division tasked Captain John Schmitt, a former platoon commander from the 2nd Division and member of its Maneuver Warfare Board, with drafting the new manual. He had previously helped draft Operational Handbook 6-1 *Ground Combat Operations*, adding elements of maneuver warfare, but the result was uneven as his passages did not align with the rest of the document.[35] After Wyly read the handbook, he praised Schmitt's isolated passages and demanded an official maneuver warfare manual: 'None of these new manuals would have a separate section entitled "maneuver warfare". Nothing could be less appropriate. All our doctrine will be maneuver warfare.'[36]

Alfred M. Gray in 1995
(Contributor: PJF Military
Collection/Alamy Stock Photo)

Gray never gave Schmitt specific instructions or guidance on how to write the manual. Schmitt consulted with Boyd, Lind and Wyly while bypassing the Marine Corps Doctrine Center.[37] In particular, Boyd advised Schmitt:

> Do not write it as a formula. Write it as a way to teach officers to think, to think in new ways about war. War is ever changing and men are ever fallible. Rigid rules simply won't work. Teach men to think. And keep the goddamn thing simple so generals can understand it.[38]

Gray only reviewed the document once during the drafting process and after Schmitt presented him with the final draft, he signed it without making any changes.[39] Fleet Marine Force Manual (FMFM) 1 *Warfighting* (1989) officially made maneuver warfare Marine doctrine and, unlike the AirLand Battle concept, there would be no diluting with opposing ideas. Boyd's influence in *Warfighting* is unmistakable:

> If the aim of maneuver warfare is to shatter the cohesion of the enemy system, the immediate object toward that end is to create a situation in which the enemy cannot function. By our actions, we seek to pose menacing dilemmas in which events happen unexpectedly and more quickly than the enemy can keep up with them. The enemy must be made to see the situation not only as deteriorating, but deteriorating at an ever-increasing rate. The ultimate goal is panic and paralysis, an enemy who has lost the ability to resist.[40]

Maneuver warfare also dominated its subordinate manuals, FMFM 1-1 *Campaigning* (1990) and FMFM 1-3 *Tactics* (1991). The rebels had triumphed as Lind proudly declared, 'The U.S. Marine Corps finally adopted maneuver warfare as doctrine in the late 1980s and I wrote most of their new tactics manuals.'[41] Marine Corps Doctrinal Publication 1 *Warfighting* (1996), developed later by Commandant Charles Krulak, replaced the original manual but maneuver warfare remained the official creed. This is unsurprising as Krulak directed Schmitt to revise the manual and Boyd again assisted. More recent Marine doctrines, such as *Expeditionary Force 21* (2014) and *Marine Corps Operating Concept* (2016), retained Boyd's philosophy.

Maneuver warfare is, as Anthony Piscitelli contended in *The Marine Corps Way of War* (2017), 'a day-in and day-out fact of life in the Marine Corps'.[42] Lieutenant Nathaniel Fick, whose exploits during the American invasion of Iraq in 2003 were made famous by the book and television series *Generation Kill*, explained how maneuver warfare is the Marine creed:

> The Marine Corps' hallmark is maneuver warfare, slipping around the enemy's hard surfaces and into his open gaps. Never attack into the teeth of the guns. We learned that indecision is a decision, that inaction has a cost all its own. Good commanders act and create opportunities. Great commanders ruthlessly exploit those opportunities and throw the enemy into disarray. The

focus on commanders recognized that war is a human enterprise. Even in the twenty-first century, wars are fought by people, not machines. Commanders must command from where they can influence the action. Marine officers, we were told, lead from the front. They thrive on chaos.[43]

The 1980s ended with the Marine Corps fully embracing Boyd's philosophy while the Army incorporated elements of maneuver warfare into doctrine but not exclusively. At the heart of this difference was Commandant Gray's true believer embrace of the theory while Starry viewed it as an idea with merit that should coexist with other concepts:

A lot of books have been written about maneuver warfare. . . That isn't what AirLand Battle is all about at all. AirLand Battle is about taking the initiative. If that means attacking and maneuvering, okay. But that's only one way to take the initiative.[44]

Starry ultimately had an ambivalent attitude toward Boyd's ideas: 'All the conversation about maneuver warfare. . . is kind of interesting but non-relevant. You can seize the initiative by maneuvering. You can also seize it by doing nothing.'[45] One reason for this contrast is an Army belief that attrition is not necessarily such a bad thing after all.

THE MYTHOLOGY OF ATTRITION

De Czege, when drafting the AirLand Battle, believed that maneuver warfare contained a specific flaw. Although genuinely impressed with *Patterns of Conflict*, he believed Boyd had created a false dichotomy between firepower and maneuver, concluding that a more balanced approach incorporating elements of both was required.[46]

Maneuver warfare is often seen as the epitome of all military virtue while its polar opposite — attrition warfare — is relentlessly demonized. For example, Lind declared, 'Firepower-attrition is warfare on the model of Verdun in World War I, a mutual casualty inflicting and absorbing contest where the goal is a favorable exchange rate.'[47] The mere mention of attrition normally conjures images of futile trench warfare, notably the Somme, and the meaningless 'body counts' of Vietnam. However, many military thinkers reject the maneuver versus attrition framework as a simplistic false dichotomy, as De Czege did. For example, the scholar Richard Betts said:

> William Lind presented attrition and maneuver as 'two complete, opposing and incompatible systems' and defined maneuver synonymously with initiative, speed, creativity, and virtually whatever military behavior is sensible in a given situation.[48]

However, attrition, as Carter Malkasian explained, is the 'gradual and piecemeal process of destroying an enemy's military capability' and 'has been a reasonably effective method of applying force, often preferable to many other operational strategies'.[49] For example, the Roman commander Quintus Fabius Maximus practiced a classic example of attrition. After Hannibal defeated the Roman Army at Cannae, he sensibly advocated his 'Fabian strategy' to pillage and harass Carthaginian supply lines which over time forced Hannibal to withdraw from Italy.

The use of attrition during World War I is misunderstood. In 1915, General Henry Rawlinson, commander of the British Fourth Army, believing attrition to be the key to defeating the Germans, advocated a 'bite and hold' strategy to quickly capture ground and to rapidly make it defendable. He believed this would force the Germans to counterattack and would inflict a favorable exchange rate of 2:1 over the enemy. Over time this would achieve a string of local victories and step by step the strength of the German Army would diminish. Rawlinson advocated this approach before the Somme, but Field Marshal Douglas Haig instead planned a breakthrough operation, hoping to create a massive gap in the German lines which cavalry would exploit to restart mobile warfare. The mass casualties sustained on the first day of the offensive resulted from a failed breakthrough operation which was retrospectively labeled 'attrition'.[50]

In 1917, Rawlinson tested his 'bite and hold' tactics during the Third Battle of Ypres, but the 'bites' were too large to hold and a favorable casualty ratio was not obtained. Rawlinson later used the tactics successfully at the Battle of Amiens on 8 August 1918. The British advanced 8 miles and captured over 400 guns and 20,000 prisoners while suffering 4,000 casualties. This

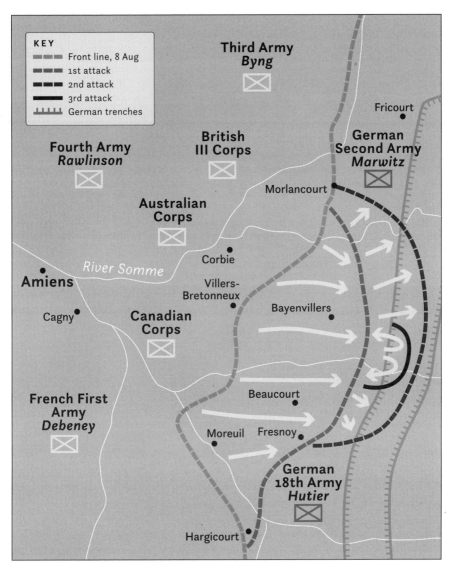

The Battle of Amiens, 8–11 August 1918

successful battle of attrition set the conditions for the continued wearing down of the German Army during the 'One Hundred Days' offensive, ultimately resulting in the Armistice.

Contrary to maneuver warfare assertions, attrition can reduce casualties. During the Korean War, General Matthew Ridgway, commander of United

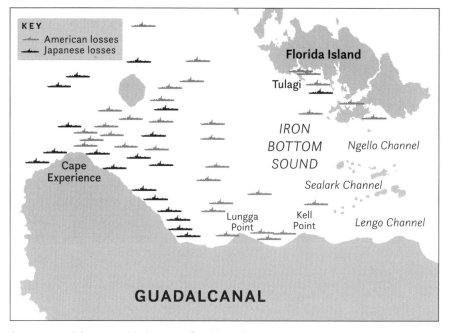

American and Japanese ship losses at Guadalcanal

Nations forces, used attrition to overcome Chinese numerical advantage by holding key terrain to weaken communist attacks before retreating to new defensive lines and conducting limited attacks under favorable circumstances. These tactics reduced American casualties and over time convinced the Chinese to sign an armistice favorable to the United Nations.[51]

Attrition is often a precondition to enable maneuver operations. After the 1st Marine Division landed at Guadalcanal on 7 August 1942, the Imperial Japanese Navy dispatched a large portion of its fleet to the island in an attempt to recapture Henderson Airfield, the key objective of the campaign. During the subsequent naval battles of attrition fought near the island, the Americans and Japanese both lost twenty-four capital ships. Battles of attrition were also fought on land and in the air and the eventual American victory severely weakened Japanese power in the Southwest Pacific. Guadalcanal set the conditions for operational maneuver and General Douglas MacArthur successfully executed Operation Cartwheel in 1943. During this offensive his forces perfected 'leapfrogging' tactics to seize

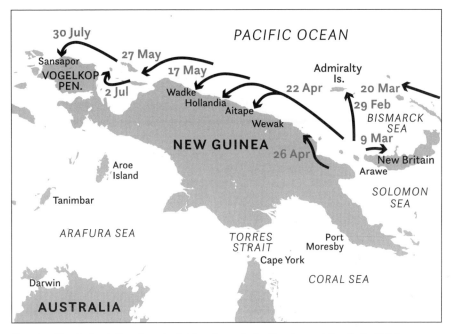

Douglas MacArthur's 'leapfrogging' drive through the South-west Pacific in 1944

the northern coast of New Guinea and established air bases in Bougainville, isolating the 100,000 Japanese defenders in Rabaul. This classic maneuver operation had only been made possible by the earlier attrition experienced at Guadalcanal.

The simplistic maneuver versus attrition framework is a false dichotomy as De Czege correctly identified. At times attrition is a preferable method and on other occasions it must precede maneuver. Therefore, a pragmatic complementary approach is required as William Owen, a British military theorist, argued:

> The whole edifice of Manoeuvre Warfare rests on the idea that there are two competing forms of warfare, manoeuvre and attrition, one of which is skilled and the other which is clumsy. This construct is false; it makes no sense to favour one form over the other. To do so is to limit available options by slavish adherence to ways over ends.[52]

The ultimate irony of the maneuver warfare rejection of attrition with its 'kill-ratio' and 'body-count' logic is that Boyd originally conceived the philosophy in response to the remarkable 10:1 kill ratio of F-86 Sabres versus MiG-15s in Korea. Therefore, maneuver warfare derived from an attritionist mindset, but the theory's false dichotomy is only one aspect of its flawed logic.

CLASSICAL MANEUVER

The idea of 'classical maneuver' pre-dates 'maneuver warfare theory' and is a tactical movement intended to gain positional advantage during battles and campaigns. In contrast, Boyd's philosophy aims to get inside the enemy 'decision cycle' to generate paralysis and collapse. These concepts are not mutually exclusive as a maneuver warfare practitioner can apply classical maneuver; however, classical maneuver does not necessarily involve maneuver warfare, as Lind made clear: 'A key to understanding maneuver war is to realize that not all movement is maneuver.'[53] For example, an army with a highly centralized command system can move through physical space to gain positional advantage, but this would not be an example of maneuver warfare. The term 'maneuver warfare' is inherently confusing and is not the best way of describing Boyd's ideas, as General Alfred Gray stated: 'You have to understand Maneuver Warfare is really a thought process. . . it is probably not even a good name but that's what we gave it.'[54]

Lind defined the essence of maneuver warfare as 'being consistently faster through however many OODA Loops it takes until the enemy loses his cohesion'.[55] Therefore, to practice maneuver warfare a force must get inside the enemy 'decision cycle' by using 'mission orders', designating a 'main effort' and exploiting 'gaps' in order to generate paralysis or disruption.[56] A frontal attack against an enemy trench, the antithesis of classical maneuver, can be maneuver warfare if certain conditions are met, as Lind explained:

> In the 1950s, the Israelis developed effective tactics against Arab fortified positions. They attacked frontally, got into the trench-works, and engaged the enemy in hand-to-hand combat. This may not sound like maneuver warfare, but it was. The Israelis had identified a specific weakness of their

opponent. The Arabs' lack of social cohesion outside the family made it very difficult for the Arab soldier to show initiative.[57]

However, despite articulating a clear distinction between classical maneuver and maneuver warfare, the theorists use examples of classical maneuver as evidence of their concepts working in practice, even though doing so betrays their own logic.

Lind claimed that maneuver warfare is a universal truth which 'probably dates from the first time a caveman surprised an enemy from behind instead of meeting him club-to-club'.[58] In this way, Boyd did not invent a theory but merely articulated a hidden truth, as Colonel Richard Hooker argued: 'Maneuver warfare is not new, although the work of modern students and practitioners has helped to crystallize and codify maneuver warfare as a coherent body of thought'.[59] Lind claimed that Boyd's ideas are historical because everything that maneuver warfare calls for 'has been done, in combat, by armies — successful armies. Focus of effort, surfaces and gaps, and mission-type orders are concepts with long combat histories.'[60]

Lind cited the ancient battles of Leuctra and Cannae — which Boyd had focused on in *Patterns of Conflict* — as specific examples of maneuver warfare working in history:

> The first clear case [of maneuver warfare] in recorded history was the battle of Leuctra in 371 B.C. The Thebans won that battle, thanks to a surprise strike against the right flank of the rigid Spartan phalanx. Hannibal's defeat of the Romans at Cannae in 216 B.C., one of the most decisive tactical victories of all time, was an example of maneuver warfare.[61]

At Leuctra, the Theban commander Epaminondas defeated the Spartans by attacking their right flank, rendering their left flank irrelevant. It was an example of classical maneuver, but no evidence links the battle with the key maneuver warfare concepts of 'mission orders', 'main effort' and 'surfaces and gaps'. In *Patterns of Conflict*, Boyd praised Epaminondas for 'having first discovered and employed an unequal or uneven distribution of forces across a front as a basis to concentrate forces for the main attack at the decisive point'.[62]

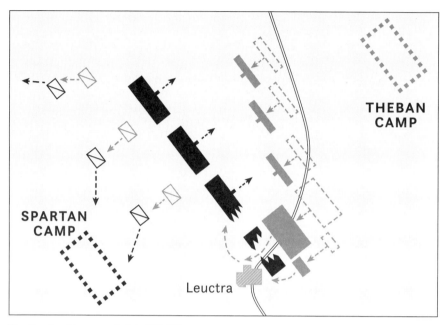

The Battle of Leuctra, 6 July 371 BC

A depiction of Epaminondas during the Battle of Leuctra
(Contributor: D.E. Luan/Alamy Stock Photo)

A statue of the
Carthaginian commander
Hannibal Barca
(Contributor: Science History
Images/Alamy Stock Photo)

However, Boyd never linked Leuctra with the virtues of maneuver warfare and gave no evidence that Epaminondas got inside the Spartan 'decision cycle'. At best, Leuctra represents a brilliant example of classical maneuver.

At Cannae, during the Second Punic War, the Carthaginian general Hannibal destroyed a numerically superior Roman army under the command of Terentius Varro by executing a double envelopment combined with a cavalry attack against its rear. Boyd became fascinated with Hannibal's triumph as the Carthaginians won a completely one-sided victory using clever tactics and believed that Hannibal had defeated Varro before the battle by operating inside the Roman O–O–D–A loop, which paralyzed their legions. Lind similarly praised Hannibal's victory at Cannae as the Carthaginian got inside the Roman 'Boyd Cycle'.[63] However, Boyd and Lind provided no

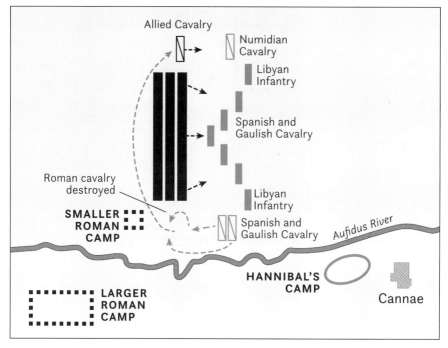

The Battle of Cannae — the Roman attack, 2 August 216 BC

evidence that Hannibal established 'decision cycle' superiority and there is little to link the Carthaginian victory with maneuver warfare.

Cannae was a battle of annihilation which saw approximately 50,000 Romans killed and, as historian Gregory Daly concluded, 'it is likely that no European army has ever suffered as heavily in a single day's fighting as the Roman forces did on that day in 216 BC'.[64] Hannibal did not disrupt or paralyze the Roman Army; he destroyed it in complete contrast to the philosophical essence of maneuver warfare and Boyd himself labeled Cannae a 'battle of annihilation' which automatically excludes it from being an example of his philosophy, as he believed destruction to be an integral aspect of attrition.[65]

Varro at Cannae attacked the weak Carthaginian center; however, Hannibal drew the Romans into a trap by using his center as bait to trick Varro into advancing. After the Carthaginian center retreated, Hannibal's Libyan infantry attacked the Roman flanks and his cavalry attacked their rear. Hannibal surrounded and annihilated the Roman Army, an outcome made possible through strict centralized control which would not have been

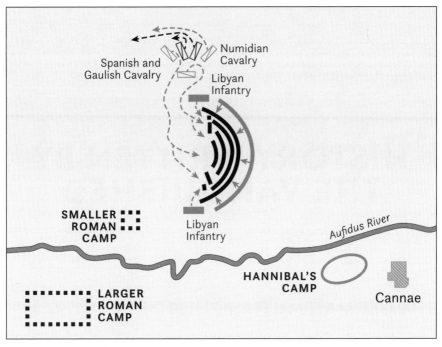

The Battle of Cannae — the Carthaginian attack, 2 August 216 BC

possible if he had applied the maneuver warfare principles of 'mission tactics' and 'main effort'. Hannibal did not allow junior leaders to exercise initiative and only delegated tasks to a handful of trusted commanders.[66] During the battle, he personally directed the fighting in the center and likely signaled the flank and cavalry commanders with horns when the time was right for their attack.[67] Hannibal's triumph represented an example of 'synchronization', a concept maneuver warfare theorists reject as it undermines initiative.

Hannibal's actions at Cannae are not examples of maneuver warfare.[68] The Romans actually fought more in accordance with the theory as Varro attempted to exploit a 'gap' — the weak Carthaginian center — while avoiding the 'surfaces' of Hannibal's flanks. Varro followed the principle of 'recon pull' but in doing so marched his army into a trap. Boyd and Lind attempted to provide maneuver warfare with a basis in history by linking their ideas to Leuctra and Cannae but only cited examples of classical maneuver.[69] In addition to approaching history with faulty logic, they relied upon historical sources tainted by fraud.

CHAPTER THREE
HISTORY WRITTEN BY THE VANQUISHED

THE GERMAN MILITARY HISTORY PROGRAM

On 20 July 1943, the United States Army established the Historical Branch to document its operations for historical purposes, which later expanded into the Historical Division.[1] The division produced work of immense value and contributed toward the publication of *The United States Army in World War II*, a vast history of the conflict. The division, in conducting this enterprise, realized that German insights would aid their efforts because it needed enemy viewpoints to properly understand events. Therefore, after the war, officers interrogated prominent German prisoners hoping to obtain historically valuable information and they persuaded some prisoners to write their own accounts.

In 1946, the Historical Division established the German Military History Program to make better use of willing prisoners and over 700 Germans worked for the program, writing manuscripts on *Wehrmacht* operations. After most prisoners were released in 1947, around 400 participants continued their work as paid civilians.

The emerging Cold War changed the program's focus as the Army faced the real prospect of war with the Soviet Union, and its leadership felt that guidance from former *Wehrmacht* officers would be invaluable as they had immeasurable experience fighting the Red Army.[2] The Americans had originally sought German reflections to help clarify the context of their operations but the Cold War massively increased demand for manuscripts on the Eastern Front. The Germans accordingly wrote manuscripts on how to fight the Red Army, effectively making themselves military advisers.[3] General Dwight D. Eisenhower, the Army Chief of Staff, realized the importance of this work and supported the program's continuation and the Germans had written over 2,500 manuscripts by 1954.

In July 1948, the Historical Division established a 'control group' within the program to translate American requests into German and assign the most qualified writers for each task.[4] The Americans believed General Franz Halder, former Chief of the General Staff, would be an ideal candidate to lead this group given his strong anti-Nazi credentials, as he had links with the pre-war German resistance through Generals Hans Oster and Ludwig Beck.[5] During the Munich Crisis in 1938, Halder, Oster and Beck planned a coup against Hitler which would have been triggered if war eventuated, but

Franz Halder in 1939
(Contributor: Sueddeutsche Zeitung Photo/ Alamy Stock Photo)

Franz Halder (right) briefing Hitler at the headquarters of the High Command of the Army on 7 August 1941
(Contributor: Sueddeutsche Zeitung Photo/Alamy Stock Photo)

the peaceful resolution of the crisis ended this prospect. After the failed plot against Hitler's life in July 1944, the Gestapo arrested Halder, who remained in concentration camps for the rest of the war. To American eyes, Halder appeared to be a trustworthy representative of the Kaiser-era General Staff, but his personality and motives were far more complex.

Halder's support of the German resistance in 1938 stemmed from a fear that Hitler's foreign policy ambitions would lead Germany toward catastrophe, but this dissipated after the fall of France in 1940 and he severed links with Oster and Beck before affirming loyalty to Hitler.[6] Halder then devoted himself to faithfully translating Hitler's will into military plans and only when the war turned decisively against Germany did his loyalty to Hitler again change.[7] Therefore, his opposition stemmed from strategic considerations, not moral principles.[8]

After 1945, a myth became popular in postwar Germany that Hitler had been a great military leader betrayed by incompetent generals, making

Halder and his colleagues primarily responsible for the defeat.[9] Former civilian members of the German resistance blamed the military conspirators for their failure to remove Hitler from power as they had constantly switched sides, making Halder an inglorious opportunist who cashed in on Hitler's early victories only to disgracefully desert him when defeat approached.[10] Halder struck back against these views in *Hitler as Warlord* (1949), arguing that Germany lost the war because of Hitler's amateurish interference in military operations, which made it impossible for professionals like him to fight a successful war.

Halder in his postwar years devoted himself to resurrecting the *Wehrmacht*'s reputation by constructing a false narrative of its unparalleled military excellence and divorcing it from Hitler's crimes.[11] The German Military History Program accidently gave Halder a powerful means of broadcasting this disinformation, but he nevertheless had genuine shared interests in working with the Americans. Halder held strong anti-communist views and believed America would be a future ally with a resurgent Germany against the Soviet Union. Therefore, he convinced other former German officers to work with the Americans as a means of continuing 'the battle against Bolshevism'.[12] Nevertheless, Halder's primary motive remained rehabilitating the *Wehrmacht*'s image. He accordingly explained to his colleagues that their work would be a means of fighting 'defamation' as they would have the chance to 'correct' postwar criticism of the *Wehrmacht* by highlighting Hitler's 'interference'.[13] Most German participants in the program shared this goal. For example, Field Marshal Georg von Küchler told his colleagues that their work would highlight 'German deeds, seen from the German standpoint' which 'will constitute a memorial to our troops'.[14]

Halder used his 'control group' to handpick former *Wehrmacht* officers who shared his worldview.[15] He maintained tight editorial control over manuscript development by closely supervising his writers and wrote the most politically sensitive work himself.[16] Halder's manuscripts contain irreconcilable contradictions, as he wanted to give the Americans sound military advice in case World War III broke out, but he could not permit genuine self-criticism of the *Wehrmacht*'s professional conduct, making wholly genuine advice impossible to give.

The Americans realized that Halder was producing misinformation as Army intelligence secretly recorded his conversations, noting that 'he is extremely frank on what he thinks should be suppressed or distorted'.[17] Halder ultimately left the Americans a dangerous legacy of interwoven fact and fiction.

MEMOIRS AND HISTORIES

Halder and his manuscript writers were not the only former *Wehrmacht* officers producing misinformation in the postwar years. Many former German generals wrote memoirs containing a mix of truth and mythology, notably Heinz Guderian's *Panzer Leader* (1952) and Erich von Manstein's *Lost Victories* (1958). Guderian commanded the 19th Panzer Corps in France in 1940 and later the Second Panzer Army in Russia. After the war, he participated in the German Military History Program. Manstein theorized the 'sickle cut' plan used by the *Wehrmacht* to outflank the Maginot Line during the invasion of France and later served on the Eastern Front, conquering the Crimea in 1942, and is best known for his 'backhand blow' counter-stroke which recaptured Kharkov in the Ukraine in March 1943.

Guderian and Manstein's narrative slightly differed from Halder's manuscripts as their elevation up the ranks owed much to Hitler's direct patronage. Therefore, their memoirs are less critical of Hitler and are scathing of the High Command, an attitude Halder did not tolerate within his 'control group'. For example, Guderian in *Panzer Leader* praised Hitler's 'remarkable powers of memory' and 'willpower' but condemned his leadership:

> I had repeated angry altercations with him, because over and over again he would sabotage the taking of necessary military measures for the sake of the obscure political game that he was playing. He would also attempt to interfere in matters that purely concerned the Army, always with unfortunate results.[18]

Manstein likewise did not completely condemn Hitler's leadership as 'one should certainly not dismiss him with such clichés as "the lance-corporal of World War I"'.[19] Nevertheless, he concluded that Hitler became

Heinz Guderian in 1941
(Contributor: Sueddeutsche Zeitung Photo/Alamy Stock Photo)

Erich von Manstein
(Contributor: Sueddeutsche Zeitung Photo/Alamy Stock Photo)

'increasingly accustomed to interfering in the running of the army groups, armies and lower formations by issuing special orders which were not his concern at all'.[20]

Friedrich von Mellenthin's *Panzer Battles* (1956) also became highly influential. Mellenthin served as an operations and intelligence officer, notably working in Rommel's *Afrika Korps*, before becoming chief of staff of the 48th Panzer Corps on the Eastern Front. After the war, he wrote five manuscripts under Halder's direction.

Guderian, Manstein and Mellenthin all blamed the German defeat on Hitler's interference, which undermined the professional military conduct of operations.[21] Their accounts, like any book, contain biases but beyond subjectivity is a deeper issue of deliberate deceit as historian Geoffrey Megargee explained:

Hermann Balck (front left) and Friedrich von Mellenthin (front right)
on the Eastern Front
(Author's Collection)

> . . . the generals had much to hide, especially in connection with their
> politics and the crimes that their forces had committed, and so they
> conspired to deceive their audiences on some points. Thus, for reasons
> both innocent and insidious, their accounts constitute a mix of truth, half-
> truth, omission, and outright lies that has been difficult to untangle.[22]

Hermann Balck's little read memoir *Order in Chaos*, first published in English
in 2015, stands out as an attempt to give a more honest account of the
war. Balck commanded the 1st Motorized Infantry Regiment in France and
created the decisive breakout at Sedan after his troops crossed the Meuse
River, which allowed Guderian's panzers to race to the English Channel.
After taking command of the 11th Panzer Division, Balck established
himself as one of the finest armored warfare commanders in history during
the Chir River battles in the Stalingrad campaign. He avoided the spotlight
after the war, refusing to work for Halder, and remained obscure until the

late 1970s when he became a consultant to the American military alongside his former chief of staff Mellenthin.[23]

Balck refused to solely blame Hitler for Germany's defeat and, unlike the famous accounts written by his colleagues, he acknowledged the *Wehrmacht*'s shortcomings. *Order in Chaos* is not influential but provides invaluable counterpoints to the deceptive memoirs of other German generals, and to understand the scale of their dishonesty it is necessary to investigate their myths in more detail.

MYTHS OF HITLER'S LEADERSHIP

Hitler did not trust General Staff officers because on numerous occasions their advice turned out to be incorrect. For example, senior generals cautioned him against the reoccupation of the Rhineland in 1936 and annexation of the Sudetenland in 1938, due to fears of Anglo-French reactions, but on both occasions the Allies failed to intervene.[24] The General Staff subsequently warned against invading Poland while leaving only ten divisions defending the Western Front as the French Army would immediately invade Germany, but Hitler correctly concluded that the French would remain passive.[25]

After the Polish campaign, Halder had no faith that Germany would triumph over France, predicting that panzer spearheads, while successful in Poland, would not be effective in Belgium and northern France given the less open terrain and more effective enemy defenses.[26] Halder also conceived an unimaginative plan to invade France, a repeat of the Schlieffen Plan attempted in 1914, in which the main German attack would concentrate on the right wing and enter France via northern Belgium in a circular maneuver.[27] Manstein criticized Halder's plan for being predictable and instead proposed a feint into the Netherlands and Belgium to lure the Allied armies north, before launching the main attack through the Ardennes toward the French coast to cut off the Allied armies advancing into the Low Countries. Halder rejected Manstein's 'sickle cut' as too risky, labeling it 'senseless'.[28] Hitler approved the plan, which resulted in the fall of France, but Halder in *Hitler as Warlord* dishonestly claimed that Hitler had formulated his plan while giving himself credit for Manstein's 'sickle cut':

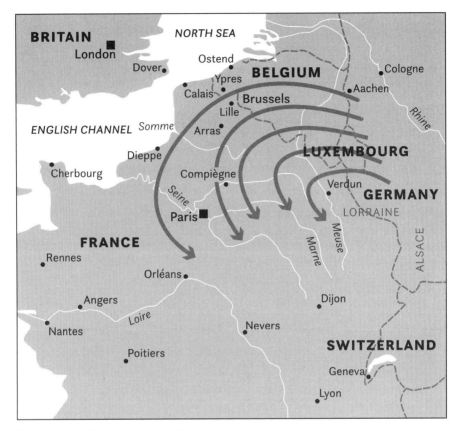

The Schlieffen Plan attempted in 1914

The bitter dispute which ensued was settled by a firm order from Hitler to make preparations for an early German attack with its principle thrust through the Belgian provinces of Limburg and Brabant. It was an unimaginative replica of the Schlieffen plan, the weaknesses of which had been shown by the First World War. The Army High Command opposed this plan and arranged to shift the centre of operations into the Ardennes.[29]

Numerous postwar German accounts blame Hitler's decision to halt the panzers near Dunkirk in May 1940 as a fatal blunder that lost Germany the opportunity of capturing the British Expeditionary Force (BEF). After the war, Field Marshal Gerd von Rundstedt, Commander of Army Group A, insisted that he could have captured the BEF if his hands had not been tied

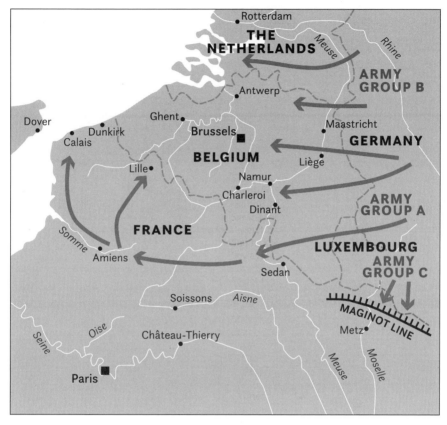

Manstein's 'Sickle Cut' plan to invade France in 1940

by Hitler. 'If I had my way the English would not have got off so lightly at Dunkirk,' he argued. 'But my hands were tied by direct orders from Hitler himself.'[30] Halder backed Rundstedt's account in *Hitler as Warlord*, as Hitler 'actually withdrew the German tanks already standing behind the British front, and thus opened the way for the British Army's retreat to Dunkirk'.[31] Guderian in *Panzer Leader* similarly declared that the opportunity to capture the BEF 'was wasted owing to Hitler's nervousness'.[32]

The reality of the Dunkirk halt order is somewhat different. Rundstedt himself, believing that his panzers had advanced too far from the infantry and were vulnerable, ordered the halt and Hitler a few hours later confirmed his decision.[33] Given the weight of evidence, historian Kenneth Macksey concluded that 'Rundstedt lied. . . when stating that the order came from

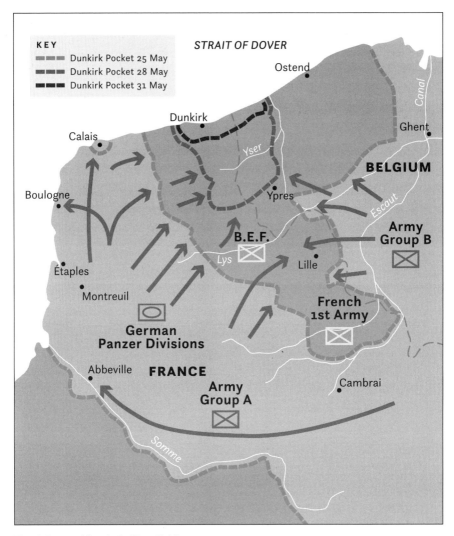

KEY
STRAIT OF DOVER
▰▰▰ Dunkirk Pocket 25 May
▰▰▰ Dunkirk Pocket 28 May
▰▰▰ Dunkirk Pocket 31 May

The defense of Dunkirk, May 1940

Hitler. In fact, as the War Diary of Army Group A shows, it was he who gave the order.'[34] On 28 May, Guderian advised against reducing the Dunkirk pocket with panzers, fearing heavy losses, advocating instead the use of infantry and artillery to complete the assault, making his later account in *Panzer Leader* dishonest.[35]

The postwar German accounts claim the General Staff opposed Hitler's decision to invade the Soviet Union. For example, Halder in *Hitler as Warlord* claimed to have opposed this decision, but he actually prepared the first invasion plan — Operation Otto — on his own initiative before Hitler announced his desire to invade Russia. As Halder welcomed and anticipated the invasion, his postwar claim is clearly untrue.[36] Halder also claimed to have warned Hitler about the military potential of the Red Army, but the German dictator 'brushed aside arguments stressing the incalculable strength of Russian manpower'.[37] Hitler underestimated the Red Army, but Halder shared Hitler's optimism and senior *Wehrmacht* leaders believed that Stalin's purges had 'beheaded' the Red Army, making it a 'colossus with feet of clay'.[38] For example, General Günther Blumentritt noted on 18 April 1941, 'there will be fourteen days of heavy fighting. Hopefully, by then we shall have made it.'[39]

After Operation Barbarossa, the German invasion of the Soviet Union, began on 22 June 1941, the *Wehrmacht's* optimism continued and Halder noted in his diary on 3 July 1941: 'It is thus probably no overstatement to say that the Russian Campaign has been won in the space of two weeks.'[40] Halder only realized the scale of his misjudgment on 11 August 1941:

> The whole situation makes it increasingly plain that we have underestimated the Russian Colossus. . . At the outset of the war we reckoned with about 200 enemy Divisions. Now we have already counted 360. These Divisions indeed are not armed and equipped according to our standards, and their tactical leadership is often poor. But there they are, and if we smash a dozen of them, the Russians simply put up another dozen.[41]

In September 1941, as the Russian winter approached, Hitler had to decide whether to halt the campaign to make a strong winter defensive line or to attempt an offensive to capture Moscow. Rundstedt argued against an offensive in favor of making proper winter preparations, but Halder and Guderian favored pressing on to Moscow.[42] Guderian falsely claimed after the war that Hitler alone had been responsible for this mistake:

> Hitler believed that he could still reach Moscow before the arrival of cold weather, although the season was already very advanced, and he

succeeded in convincing his counselors of the Wehrmacht and of the Army High Command.[43]

In fact, Guderian had strongly advised Hitler to capture Moscow despite the onset of winter.[44] Halder similarly advocated continuing the offensive toward Moscow despite his postwar claims.[45]

Halder in *Hitler as Warlord* blamed Hitler for the *Wehrmacht*'s failure to prepare for the Russian winter:

> When the army Commander-in-Chief asked for immediate preparations to be made for the provisions of special winter clothing, he received a curt refusal [from Hitler] with the remark that by the beginning of winter the fighting would long since have been over.[46]

However, in reality sufficient winter clothing existed in depots but could not reach the front because of insufficient transport, as the priority given to the Moscow offensive resulted in trains bringing up fuel and ammunition instead of winter supplies.[47] The General Staff failed to prioritize winter operations until it was too late and the *Wehrmacht* in Russia found itself overextended and, at this critical time, the Red Army launched a devastating winter counter-offensive.

The Soviet counterattack in December 1941 resulted in Hitler's famous 'no retreat' order which, accordingly to postwar mythology, resulted in unnecessary casualties as Halder declared:

> A proposal for a planned withdrawal over a few days' march to a line more suitable for defence was contested by Hitler with fanatical fury and he ordered the Army to 'fight to the last man' where it stood — even where its positions were tactically impossible to hold. . . In consequence there were heavy losses in men and material which could, without the slightest doubt, have been avoided.[48]

Guderian in *Panzer Leader* similarly accused Hitler of refusing to allow him to retreat to a better defensive line, 'But this was exactly what Hitler refused to allow.'[49]

Hitler's 'no retreat' order actually saved the *Wehrmacht* during the Russian winter. The Germans held the line and, given the absence of winter equipment, large scale withdrawals were not realistic. 'Considering the conditions of the Russian winter,' as Balck explained in *Order in Chaos*, 'any withdrawal on our part would result in a catastrophe of Napoleonic dimensions'.[50] He also recalled his part in this decision:

> I pleaded with Hitler not to withdraw under any circumstances. Operations were completely impossible in the snow that was two meters deep, and in the -58 degree Fahrenheit weather river crossings and the building of positions were impossible anywhere. . . The demand to hold under such conditions might sound brutal, but in reality it was the greatest clemency.[51]

General Fritz Bayerlein also agreed with Hitler's decision:

> All higher commanders requested of the OKW [*Wehrmacht* High Command] that their lines be withdrawn to 'winter positions' which actually did not exist. Hitler stood up against this with all the demoniacal willpower which seized him in such moments.[52]

Numerous myths persist concerning Hitler's leadership during the *Wehrmacht*'s disastrous Stalingrad campaign. The German summer offensive of 1942 aimed to seize the oilfields of the Caucasus but capturing Stalingrad on the Volga River later became an objective, and Halder blamed Hitler for this dispersal of effort:

> Stalingrad was to be a stepping stone along the approach road toward the Caucasus. In the Fuehrer's mind, however, the desire to conquer the city on the Volga by house-to-house fighting gradually became a fixation. . . The diversion of more and more forces toward Stalingrad was made to the detriment of the principal drive into the Caucasus, and eventually both efforts were to bog down for lack of strength.[53]

Mellenthin in *Panzer Battles* similarly claimed, 'Hitler committed the oldest and simplest mistake in warfare — neglect of the principle of concentration.

The diversion of effort between the Caucasus and Stalingrad ruined our whole campaign.'[54]

Hitler made his fatal decision to simultaneously attack the Caucasus and Stalingrad on the false assumption that Red Army reserves were running out. Hitler's judgment was incorrect but Halder shared this delusion contrary to his postwar claims. On 15 July 1942, Hitler declared, 'The Russian is finished!' Halder responded, 'I must say, it is beginning to look uncommonly like it.'[55] Halder, in a manuscript written for the United States Army not intended for public reading, acknowledged his error:

> On 9 September the Eastern Intelligence Division submitted an estimate according to which the Russians seemed to have no sizeable reserves along the entire front. . . Halder accepted this estimate and concluded that the Russians lacked strategic reserves.[56]

The Red Army offensive in November 1942 surrounded the Sixth Army in Stalingrad, which later surrendered in February 1943. Hitler is condemned in postwar accounts for not permitting the Sixth Army to break out by ordering its commander, General Friedrich Paulus, to await rescue from the hastily assembled Army Group Don commanded by Manstein. Halder in *Hitler as Warlord* condemned Hitler's order: 'There remained therefore only one possible military decision — to give up Stalingrad immediately and to order the Sixth Army to fight its way through to the west.'[57] Manstein in *Lost Victories* similarly claimed that the Sixth Army's 'destruction at Stalingrad is obviously to be found in Hitler's refusal — doubtless mainly for reasons of prestige — to give up the city voluntarily'.[58]

Hitler's refusal to withdraw the Sixth Army from Stalingrad is often criticized as the beginning of his descent into irrational orders to hold all ground against military logic. As Hitler's 'no retreat' order had saved the *Wehrmacht* during the previous Russian winter, he apparently believed that his 'iron will' would again produce the same result, as Manstein argued:

> When, therefore, a fresh crisis arose in autumn 1942 after the German offensive had become bogged down outside Stalingrad and in the Caucasus, Hitler again thought the arcanum of success lay in clinging at all

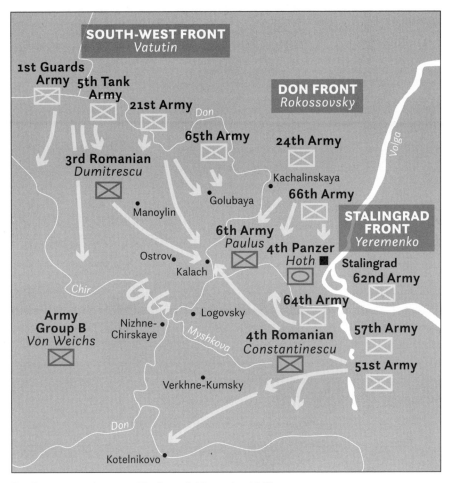

The Soviet encirclement of Stalingrad, November 1942

costs to what he already possessed. Henceforth he could never be brought to renounce this notion.[59]

However, Hitler had sound reasons for not allowing Paulus to retreat. The Sixth Army's stand at Stalingrad secured the Rostov corridor, which enabled the much larger Army Group A to retreat from the Caucasus.[60] Therefore, in contradiction to postwar mythology, Hitler had authorized an enormous withdrawal, an act which sacrificed the Sixth Army to save the far larger Army Group A.

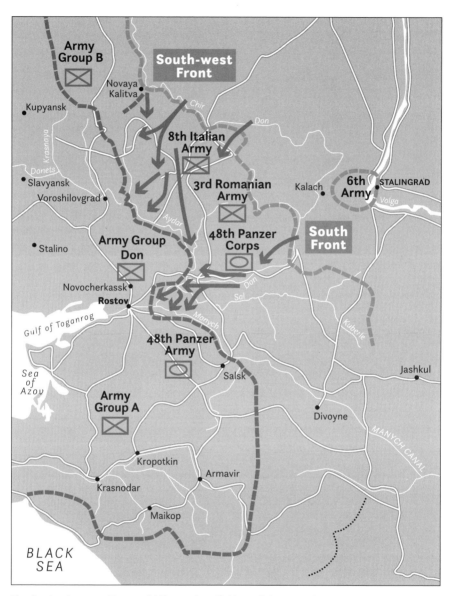

The Soviet threat to Rostov, 16 December 1942 to 19 January 1943

Manstein in *Lost Victories* criticized Hitler's refusal to allow the Sixth Army to withdraw while simultaneously acknowledging the wisdom of this decision as the 'enemy had obviously committed his main forces primarily in the ring enclosing Sixth Army'.[61] Without the Sixth Army tying down these forces, 'the fate of the whole southern wing of the German forces in the east would have been sealed — including Army Group A'.[62] Manstein clearly understood the bigger picture but refused to credit Hitler with making the hard decision to sacrifice the Sixth Army to save Army Group A. Mellenthin also tried to have it both ways. He predictably condemned Hitler's order to Paulus and 'the senseless sacrifice of 250,000 men of the Sixth Army'.[63] However, he also acknowledged that their sacrifice was anything but senseless:

> The Russians already had about 90 large formations around Stalingrad, and had they been suddenly released by the surrender of the Sixth Army, a catastrophe of the greatest proportions would have over taken the German forces on the Eastern Front. By the refusal to surrender, the Sixth Army's heroic stand during the final phase of the Stalingrad disaster still made military sense.[64]

Balck acknowledged the logic of Hitler's decision as 'German forces at Stalingrad had tied down the majority of the Russians, blocked their supply lines, and thus established the conditions to establish the new front line necessary to withdraw our armies from the Caucasus'.[65] He never inconsistently argued that Paulus should have somehow retreated from Stalingrad while simultaneously defending the city to tie down the siege forces.

MYTH OF CLEAN HANDS

In November 1945, during the Nuremberg War Crimes Trials, several former generals, including Halder and Manstein, wrote a memorandum denying the General Staff had committed war crimes.[66] Halder's manuscripts similarly make no reference to *Wehrmacht* war crimes and *Russian Combat Methods in World War II* even claimed that the army faced disadvantage due to its high regard for human life: 'the Germans had to contend with a great number of difficulties which simply did not exist for the Russian high command. . . the low valuation placed on human life freed the Soviet high command from moral inhibitions'.[67]

In reality the *Wehrmacht*'s leadership long held views not vastly different from Hitler's racial fantasies and shared his vision of a war of conquest in the east.[68] Since the beginning of the twentieth century, German generals believed in a Slavic threat to Western Europe, which became more acute following the Russian Revolution.[69] During the mid-1920s, the German Army planned to create a German Empire in the east, an aim shared by Halder.[70]

Before the German invasion of Poland, Reinhard Heydrich, head of the *SS* security service *Sicherheitsdienst* (SD), planned *Einsatzgruppen* death squad operations to murder the Polish intelligentsia and Jewish communities. General Eduard Wagner, the *Wehrmacht*'s quartermaster general, met with Heydrich to integrate the *Einsatzgruppen* into the army's logistics system.[71] Halder fully understood Hitler's plans for Poland and noted in his diary: 'Polish intelligentsia must be prevented from establishing itself as a non-governing class. Low standard of living must be conserved. Cheap slaves. All undesirable elements must be thrown out of German territory.'[72]

Shortly after the German invasion of Poland on 9 September 1939, soldiers from the 15th Motorized Infantry Regiment, acting upon the orders of Colonel Walter Wessel, murdered 300 recently surrendered Polish soldiers near Ciepielów.[73] The massacre, a *Wehrmacht* war crime, did not involve the *Einsatzgruppen* and was not an isolated incident as army soldiers committed over fifty similar atrocities during the invasion of Poland.[74] While some army officers protested against *Einsatzgruppen* operations, the *Wehrmacht* as an institution did nothing to prevent massacres and army soldiers murdered between 16,000 and 27,000 Poles during the campaign.[75]

Hitler envisaged the invasion of Russia as a war of extermination against Bolsheviks, Jews and Slavs in order to acquire living space. On 30 March 1941, shortly before the invasion, he summoned senior military leaders including Halder to the Reich Chancellery to explain that commissars and the intelligentsia would be liquidated, requiring German soldiers to 'forget the concept of comradeship between soldiers'.[76] As Barbarossa would be an ideological struggle between two worldviews represented by two opposing races, the *Wehrmacht* needed to be ideologically committed to the destruction of 'Jewish Bolshevism'.[77]

Halder claimed in his affidavit at Nuremburg that, after hearing Hitler's plans, 'listeners on the part of the army were of course outraged by this speech'.[78] However, he expressed no outrage in his diary when summarizing Hitler's words: 'The intelligentsia put in by Stalin must be exterminated. . . In

Polish prisoners of war at Ciepielów
(Contributor: UtCon Collection/Alamy Stock Photo)

Wehrmacht soldiers marching Polish prisoners to their fate at Ciepielów
(Contributor: UtCon Collection/Alamy Stock Photo)

The aftermath of the Ciepielów massacre: a *Wehrmacht* war crime
(Contributor: World History Archive/Alamy Stock Photo)

Great Russia force must be used in its most brutal form.'[79] General Hermann Hoth, commander of the Third Panzer Group, also present during Hitler's speech, later echoed Hitler's language in orders to his troops:

> We clearly recognise that our mission is to save European culture from the encroachment of Asiatic barbarism. . . Any trace of active or passive resistance, or of any machinations by Jewish-Bolshevik agitators, is to be crushed immediately and mercilessly. . . They constitute the same Jewish subhumanity that has already caused great harm to our fatherland through hostility to our people and culture.[80]

Before Barbarossa, Halder laid the foundations of the barbarous conflict in two criminal orders drafted by his staff: the 'Commissar Order', which called for the immediate execution of all Soviet political officers, and the 'Jurisdictional Decree', which suspended military justice, allowing German soldiers to commit atrocities with immunity.[81] When Halder first read a draft of the Commissar Order, he declared, soldiers 'must do their share in the ideological struggle of the eastern campaign'.[82]

Halder and the Army High Command oversaw the negotiations between General Wagner and Heydrich concerning army support for *Einsatzgruppen* operations as they had done before the invasion of Poland.[83] After the invasion, the *Wehrmacht* carried out its assigned role as *SS Brigadefuehrer* Ernst Rode testified at Nuremberg:

[The military commanders] approved of these [*Einsatzgruppen*] missions and operational methods because, apparently, they never opposed them. The fact that prisoners, such as Jews, agents, and commissars, who were handed over to the SD, underwent the same cruel death as victims of so-called purifications, is a proof that the executions had their approval.[84]

The memoirs of former German generals deny any involvement in these crimes. For example, Guderian in *Panzer Leader* claimed:

I forbade its [the Jurisdictional Decree] forwarding to the divisions and ordered that it be returned to Berlin. This order. . . was consequently never carried out in my Panzer Group. . . The equally notorious, so-called 'Commissar Order' never even reached my Panzer Group. No doubt Army Group Centre had already decided not to forward it. Therefore the 'Commissar Order' was never carried out by my troops either.[85]

However, the war diaries of units within Guderian's Second Panzer Army indicate the Commissar Order was indeed implemented and his headquarters recorded the execution of 183 commissars in October 1941.[86] This is unsurprising as Guderian viewed Barbarossa as a noble mission to save Western civilization from the 'Asiatic Bolshevik-Jewish menace'.[87]

After the war, Guderian claimed, 'I never had anything to do with the

A mass execution of Jews by *Einsatzgruppen D* near the Ukrainian town of Vinnytsya in 1942. *Wehrmacht* soldiers are watching in the background.

(Contributor: Everett Collection Inc/Alamy Stock Photo)

SD and its *Einsatzkommandos* (Operational commandos) and am therefore not able to give any firsthand information concerning them.'[88] However, he actively supported *Einsatzgruppen* operations under the guise of fighting 'partisans'.[89] During Barbarossa, *Wehrmacht* involvement in massacres was often referred to in reports as 'pacification' against 'partisans'.[90] General Hans Röttinger, Chief of Staff of Fourth Army, confirmed the nature of these operations at Nuremburg as 'the harshest conduct of the anti-partisan war can only have been intended to make possible a ruthless liquidation of Jews and other undesirable elements'.[91] Ernst Rode testified at Nuremburg that he collaborated with Guderian during 'partisan warfare' and added that 'since police troops for the most part could not be spared from the Reich Commissariats, the direction of this warfare lay practically always in the hands of the army'.[92]

Manstein in *Lost Victories* claimed not to have implemented the Commissar Order:

An order like the *Kommissarbefehl* was utterly unsoldierly. To have carried it out would have threatened not only the honour of our fighting troops but also their morale. Consequently I had no alternative but to inform my superiors that the Commissar Order would not be implemented by anyone under my command.[93]

Manstein did implement the Commissar Order and his soldiers executed captured commissars.[94] This is unsurprising as he viewed Barbarossa in ideological terms, a fact evident in his orders on 20 November 1941:

Jewry constitutes the middleman between the enemy in the rear and the remainder of the Red armed forces which are still fighting and the Red leadership. . . The Jewish-Bolshevist system must be exterminated once and for all. Never again must it encroach upon our European living-space.[95]

Manstein claimed ignorance of *Einsatzgruppen* operations in the Crimea during his war crimes trial, but as Eleventh Army commander he received reports on their activities. Furthermore, his soldiers provided the *Einsatzgruppen* with logistics support and cordoned off areas during operations.[96] After Otto

Ohlendorf, the *Einsatzgruppen* commander in the Crimea, murdered 11,000 Jews near Simferopol, Manstein ordered him to distribute watches taken from the dead to his soldiers.[97] The *Einsatzgruppen* murdered the 90,000 strong Jewish population of the Crimea while Manstein had responsibility over the area.

The *Wehrmacht* committed war crimes independent of the *SS*. During 1941, the army captured 3.3 million Red Army prisoners and approximately two million of them died in captivity due to inadequate preparations and deliberate starvation.[98] On 13 November 1941, General Wagner, the officer responsible for Russian prisoners, remarked:

> Those non-working prisoners of war in the prison camps are to starve. Working prisoners of war can in individual cases be fed from army provisions. But unfortunately this cannot be ordered on a general basis, given the overall food situation.[99]

Many *Wehrmacht* war criminals never faced justice due to the *realpolitik* of the Cold War. In 1950, as the United States Army in Germany grew from an occupation force to a field army designed to defend Western Europe from a feared Red Army invasion, NATO decided that it needed a German contribution.[100] However, creating a West German Army necessitated changes to American–German relations as the formerly occupied country would become an important ally.[101] The Americans could not achieve German re-armament without the support of former *Wehrmacht* officers, but their cooperation would come at a price.

On 9 October 1950, five former German officers, all veterans of the German Military History Program, met at the Cloister Himmerod, near the town of Wittlich, and drafted the 'Himmerod Memorandum'. This document advised the West German Chancellor Konrad Adenauer that a precondition of a West German Army included the release of *Wehrmacht* war criminals and the government would have to announce that German soldiers had fought honorably.[102] Adenauer agreed and pressured the American Government to release war criminals in custody.[103] The Cold War helped legitimize the myth of the *Wehrmacht*'s clean hands as the abandonment of trials and release of war criminals created an impression of innocence.

Halder stood as a defendant in a German court facing charges of aiding the Nazi war of conquest. He denied any knowledge of *SS* crimes and claimed to have been outside the regime's key decision-making processes. In October 1948, the court found him guiltless, but afterward the prosecutor discovered his diaries which proved the dishonesty of his testimony. The Bavarian Government sought a second trial, but American authorities refused to hand Halder over, as his work for the German Military History Program made him indispensable. In 1950, the Bavarian Government gave up and Halder never answered for his crimes.

Guderian never faced justice because during the trials no substantial documentary or eyewitness evidence directly linked him to war crimes and the prosecution focused on easier cases.[104] He also gained the good graces of the prosecutors due to his willingness to inform on his colleagues, and he died a free man in 1954.[105]

In 1949, a British military court found Manstein guilty of nine war crimes including the failure to prevent murder, shooting prisoners and carrying out the Commissar Order. The court sentenced Manstein to eighteen years in prison, a decision Mellenthin noted was 'a sad reflection of the times'.[106] However, in 1950 his sentence was reduced to twelve years, and three years later he walked free following high-level talks between Churchill and Adenauer.

INFLUENCE OF MYTHOLOGY

In 1949, John Morgan, a retired British general working as a legal adviser at Nuremberg, accused Halder of conducting a dishonest misinformation campaign: 'There is an illuminating German document in the American archives at Nuremberg which puts the existence of the concerted policy of dual exculpation beyond doubt. It was written in November, 1945, by General Halder.'[107] This 'dual exculpation', as Morgan explained, consisted of a deceptive portrayal of the *Wehrmacht* as an essentially undefeated army, whose battlefield failures solely resulted from Hitler's 'interference', and a false claim that the *Wehrmacht* played no role in the Third Reich's criminal enterprises.[108] Unfortunately, Morgan's warning failed to stop these myths from becoming largely accepted as truth in the English-speaking world.

The Halder manuscripts and the postwar memoirs distorted scholarship as historian James Wood concluded:

> The resulting body of work therefore came to be characterized by the absence of war crimes (with the exception of those committed by the Red Army), an unquestioning admiration of the professional skill of the German soldier, and an explanation of the loss of the war that is almost invariably linked to Allied material strength and/or the interference of a certain Austrian corporal.[109]

Halder's manuscript writers had a strong advantage over other accounts of the war as the Americans had given them access to archival sources unavailable to most historians, giving their narratives considerable authority.[110] The manuscripts strongly shaped perceptions of the Eastern Front as Western historians initially had few other sources to use.[111]

When archival sources eventually became available to all historians, the sheer size of the material took decades to evaluate; therefore, it took time for historians to effectively challenge postwar myths. Historians have more recently rewritten history and within academic circles these myths have been demolished.[112] However, such historians write for professional readers and not the general public, so the *Wehrmacht* myths live on in popular culture as the memoirs, and popular works based on them, continue to influence the wider public. *Lost Victories*, *Panzer Leader* and *Panzer Battles* continue to be popular among readers of military history.

The German Military History Program ended in 1961 and President Kennedy awarded Halder the United States Meritorious Civilian Service Award for 'a lasting contribution to the tactical and strategic thinking of the United States Armed Forces'.[113] Halder died in 1972, having successfully restored the *Wehrmacht*'s reputation.

THE PRUSSIAN RENAISSANCE

Postwar German misinformation deceived many American military officers.[114] For example, Lieutenant Colonel J.L. Frothingham reviewed *Panzer Leader* in the *Marine Corps Gazette* in 1953: 'Guderian and his *Panzer*

Leader of World War II is just as essential to the student of mobility as is the study of Sherman and Forrest in our own Civil War.'[115] S.L.A. (Samuel) Marshall, in a 1958 *Marine Corps Gazette* review of *Lost Victories*, praised Manstein's integrity as 'to be honest about years of great personal defeat can hardly come easy'.[116] Marshall believed Manstein was a professional soldier far removed from Third Reich politics: 'He was neither a Hitler admirer nor an anti-Hitler plotter. In his mind there was no tormenting struggle about the course to be run. He held to the "line of military duty" and his defense of that position is profoundly logical.'[117]

Colonel R. Tompkins, in a 1956 *Marine Corps Gazette* review of Mellenthin's *Panzer Battles*, concluded that if Hitler had 'let his generals fight their war, rather than forcing impossible orders on them, the results might well have been in Germany's favor' before declaring, 'I would like to recommend to your early attention a first-class book entitled *Panzer Battles*. . . I'm delighted to have it in my library.'[118]

Although many American officers admired the *Wehrmacht*, this had limited utility as the German experience of World War II lacked relevance during the limited war in Korea and unconventional conflicts in Southeast Asia. However, after experiencing defeat in Vietnam, the American military lost its confidence and found inspiration in the *Wehrmacht* as historians Ronald Smelser and Edward Davies explained:

> Why did the U.S. Army seem to lack cohesion? Why did discipline seem to collapse? Why were American soldiers in disproportionate numbers overindulging in drugs and alcohol, deserting, and fragging their officers? As the Americans struggled to come to grips with these questions, they rediscovered the Wehrmacht.[119]

The triumphant United States Army originally approached the *Wehrmacht*'s legacy after World War II seeking insights on the Eastern Front. However, humbled by Vietnam, they began searching for something to emulate and the *Wehrmacht* became the model. Major Bruce Gudmundsson, a Marine officer, recalled this time:

> A generation of readers of military history had grown up with postwar

accounts of the German Army in World War II that, while they decried the ends that army served, lauded the skill with which its members fought. In the minds of many observers of military affairs, both in and out of uniform, the German became a paragon of military virtue whose institutions and tactics were worthy of close study, if not outright imitation.[120]

Colonel Trevor Dupuy, an American World War II veteran, wrote the highly influential *A Genius for War* (1977), which became critical in establishing this mindset. Dupuy declared, 'the Germans, uniquely, discovered the secret of *institutionalizing* military excellence'.[121] He argued that after Napoleon imposed the humiliating Tilsit Treaty on Prussia in 1807, General Scharnhorst, with the help of reformers including Gneisenau and Clausewitz, laid 'the foundations of the military excellence that characterized Prussian and German armies for more than a century'.[122] However, Dupuy unknowingly accepted postwar mythology when explaining why German military excellence failed to win World War II, conveniently blaming the defeat solely on Hitler. For example, Hitler was entirely to blame for the German disaster at Stalingrad: 'because of Hitler's obstinacy, Germany suffered its most decisive military defeat since November 1918'.[123] Dupuy also incorrectly believed Halder was 'strongly anti-Nazi' and 'a totally apolitical soldier'.[124]

The historian Martin van Creveld wrote *Fighting Power* (1982), another influential work which mirrored Dupuy's observations. According to Van Creveld, the *Wehrmacht*'s defeat in no way diminished its excellence: 'Confronted with impossible political and economic odds, a qualitatively superior force may go down to defeat through no fault of its own.'[125] He also praised the *Wehrmacht*'s heroic defeat in contrast to American behavior in Vietnam:

> [The *Wehrmacht*] was outnumbered three, five, even seven to one. Yet it did not run. It did not disintegrate. It did not frag its officers. Instead, it doggedly fought on. . . [and] its units, even when down to 20 percent of their original size, continued to exist and to resist — an unrivalled achievement for any army.[126]

Dupuy and Van Creveld's high opinion of the *Wehrmacht* derived from numerous references to Halder's manuscripts. Furthermore, Dupuy heavily relied upon *Panzer Leader*, *Lost Victories* and *Panzer Battles* in forming his conclusions.

Postwar German mythology and works derived from it had profound influence on the United States Army. General William DePuy, the architect of Active Defense, accepted Halder's myths, believing the German High Command had been 'crippled' by 'the personal interference of Hitler who appointed and relieved its chiefs on the basis of their compliance with his wishes and the degree to which they shared his delusions'. DePuy concluded, 'the German Army fought a bitter battle with Adolf Hitler, as well as the massive forces of the Russians. Hitler wished to hold every inch of ground. The German generals desperately wanted to fight a maneuvering defense.'[127] General Donn Starry, architect of the AirLand Battle, similarly expressed his admiration of the German General Staff with its 'intellectual prowess and staff brilliance'.[128]

As the American military emulated the *Wehrmacht*, its officers did not distinguish genuine lessons of German military history from the distorted postwar accounts written by unreliable former generals. Therefore, their admiration of the *Wehrmacht* often mistook illusion for reality and in this context the maneuver warfare theorists embraced German military mythology with evangelical fire.

ABSORPTION OF MYTH INTO MANEUVER WARFARE

Halder's manuscripts and postwar German memoirs contain useful historical information alongside myth and, as such, can be used as source material but only after careful analysis with a full understanding of the context of their creation as extreme caution is required to separate history from fantasy.[129] However, the maneuver warfare theorists did not apply such care and their ideas are accordingly grounded in myth.

After John Boyd retired from the Air Force, he studied military history hoping to find a grand narrative and his efforts resulted in *Patterns of Conflict*, the first expression of maneuver warfare. During this formative time, to understand *Blitzkrieg*, he read *Panzer Leader* and *Lost Victories*.[130] Boyd's

understanding of German military history during World War II was largely
formed from unreliable information and his source list for *Patterns of Conflict*
unsurprisingly included *Panzer Leader, Lost Victories, Panzer Battles* and Halder's
manuscripts. Boyd took his sources very seriously and made reading all the
listed books a prerequisite for entering his inner circle.[131] However, he was
unaware of postwar German agendas and accordingly praised *Lost Victories*
without any understanding of historical context:

> I think that is a masterpiece and I think there are some very important
> lessons in there. For some reason it is not articulated or is not brought
> out and I think if you do not read this book you are not going to really
> have a deep understanding of how the modern German general staff
> worked or actually how that Blitzkrieg unfolded and the thinking that
> went behind it.[132]

William S. Lind's *Maneuver Warfare Handbook* included an annotated
bibliography in which he, like Boyd, expressed deep admiration for *Panzer
Leader*: 'The discussion of the French campaign is especially useful, with its
stress on the need for quick decisions, bold actions, an understanding of
the operational art and, above all, speed.'[133] He was skeptical of one aspect
of *Panzer Leader* as 'Guderian somewhat overstates the resistance he met in
developing the Panzer divisions' but displayed no further critical thinking.[134]
Lind also praised *Lost Victories* without qualification:

> Manstein was probably the best operational and strategic thinker in
> the *Wehrmacht*, and this book, his memoirs, is an important tool for
> understanding those arts. The section where he leads the reader through
> his thought process as he developed the plan for the invasion of France in
> 1940 is especially valuable.[135]

Furthermore, Lind considered *Panzer Battles* 'an excellent account of
German armored warfare in World War II'.[136] He accepted postwar German
mythology while remaining unaware of the historical problems inherent
within his sources.

Michael Wyly, who helped introduce maneuver warfare to the Marine

Corps, recalled discovering Halder's work for the German Military History Program with no understanding of his dark motives:

> While studying at the National Archives one day, I came across a thick, dusty document by Gen Franz Halder. . . As a professional who had studied warfare all his life yet seen the finest soldiers he had served with go down in defeat, he endeavored to extract the things that they had done right, to leave a legacy to the Americans.[137]

Wyly praised Halder who 'convinced the defeated German generals to be cooperative with their American captors. In Halder's view, it would be left to Americans to carry the baton as the Soviet Union's main military opponent.'[138] He also uncritically praised *Lost Victories*: 'Unlike many soldiers who write their memoirs, Manstein makes no attempt to glorify his own record.'[139] Wyly made chapters of *Lost Victories* and *Panzer Battles* compulsory reading for his Marine students at Quantico.[140] The Amphibious Warfare School later created a professional reading list which included the Halder manuscript *Small Unit Action During the German Campaign in Russia*, *Panzer Leader*, *Panzer Battles* and *Lost Victories*.[141]

The theorists, when faced with the uncomfortable question of why the Germans lost the war, found solace in myth. For example, Boyd blamed their defeat on Hitler: 'if you go back to Poland in 1939, we find that Hitler really did not get down to the operational or tactical level. He gave them pretty much what he wanted to do and they carried it out according to the way they thought best.' But during the French campaign, 'Hitler started undermining the structure. As a result we find that the so-called decentralized control became more and more centralized.' In Russia, Boyd continued, 'Hitler interfered more and more with that so-called freedom of the lower level commander. We see hardening of the arteries of the blitz system.'[142]

Lind, consistent with Boyd's logic, blamed the German defeat solely on Hitler:

> . . . what happened at Kursk, and on the Eastern Front generally after 1941 on the German side, was not the defeat of the maneuver doctrine but, rather, its abandonment by those whom it had best served. On Hitler's

orders, the desires of the general staff to continue a maneuver war, where holding of territory is not of prime importance, were overridden.[143]

Wyly similarly blamed Hitler for Manstein's defeats as the German commander 'detested Hitler's meddling' and 'had Hitler not tampered with Clausewitz's ideas and Manstein's genius, even despite the awesome odds against her, Germany would have won'.[144] The maneuver warfare theorists are victims of misinformation, but they also trusted another deceiver, Liddell Hart, who had his own reasons to fabricate history.

CHAPTER FOUR

THE FATHER OF
BLITZKRIEG

THE MISUSE OF HISTORY

Liddell Hart wrote in order to champion his own theories at the expense of genuine historical inquiry. For example, in *Sherman: Soldier, Realist, American* (1929) his purpose was to convince readers that General William Tecumseh Sherman's Atlanta campaign during the American Civil War embodied the 'indirect approach' as historian Albert Castel concluded:

> Should Sherman, as he often did, outflank an impregnable enemy position instead of attacking it frontally, futilely, and fatally, he did not merely exercise, as a newspaper correspondent accompanying his army put it, 'common sense', he displayed 'strategic artistry' by way of the 'indirect approach'.[1]

Liddell Hart depicted Sherman's division of forces into separate columns as an example of the 'indirect approach' because it disguised his intentions, as the Confederates did not know from which direction the main blow would come. However, in reality, Sherman's army of over 100,000 men through necessity alone had to march in different columns just like all large armies of that era; therefore, there was nothing special about Sherman's maneuvers.[2] Liddell Hart also depicted Sherman's March across Georgia as an indirect attack on the Confederacy's morale, hastening the end of the war, but failed to mention other disasters the South experienced during this time, such as the Union advance through the Shenandoah Valley, Robert E. Lee's defeat at Fort Fisher and the fall of Wilmington.[3] By 1865, the Confederacy no longer possessed enough military strength to resist the North, a result of the preceding years of grinding attrition; therefore, morale by this time had ceased being a deciding factor.[4] The ultimate purpose of *Sherman* is not biography but to convince the reader to believe in the 'indirect approach'.

In *Great Captains Unveiled* (1927), Liddell Hart praised Genghis Khan and Mongol warfare for its 'amazingly rapid sequence of successes'.[5] He explained how in 1220, Genghis Khan created a diversion by splitting his army in three forces when invading the Karismian Empire. Two Mongol armies fixed the Shah's attention and drew in his reserves before the third army 'like a thunder-clap' appeared in the rear, causing the downfall of the empire.[6] Liddell Hart also attributed the Mongol victory to their superior tactics:

> The Mongol tactics were to avoid closing with the adversary until he was weakened and disorganised by fire. . . Thus they proved that mobility is the king-pin of tactics, as of strategy; that lightly armed troops can beat more heavily armed ones if their mobility is sufficiently superior.[7]

Liddell Hart then used this example to comment on contemporary military debates:

> Mobility was the weakest point in the World War. The armies of Europe were relatively as immobile as those of the Shah of Karismia and medieval Christendom. . . The development of mechanical firepower has negatived the hitting power of cavalry against a properly equipped enemy. But on land the armoured caterpillar car or light tank appears the natural heir of the Mongol horseman, for the 'caterpillars' are essentially mechanical cavalry.[8]

Liddell Hart actually distorted Mongol warfare in an attempt to champion his own concepts and, as historian Patrick Porter explained, 'The Mongols at his hands became an ideal-type of warrior that reflected his ambitions for

The rise of the Mongol Empire

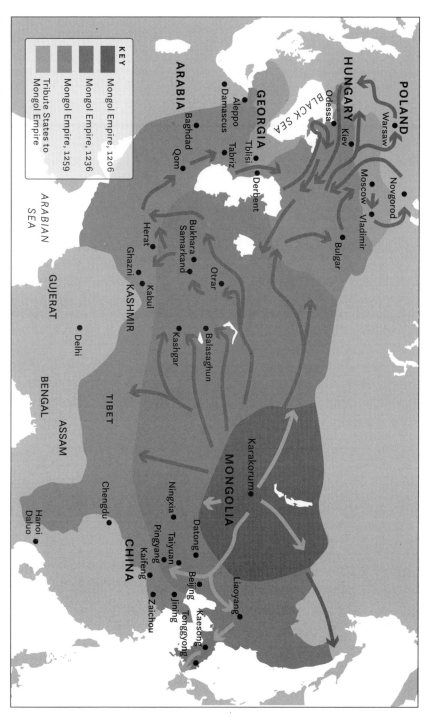

tanks and aircraft.'[9] Liddell Hart neglected to mention that Mongol operations focused on the destruction of their enemies, the antithesis of the 'indirect approach', as Patrick Porter concluded:

> Precisely because they often were numerically limited, Mongol campaigns also had a logic of annihilation. . . To prevent defeated or fleeing enemy armies regrouping at their rear and menacing their long supply lines, the Mongols frequently hunted them down and wiped them out to a man.[10]

As detailed historical understanding of Mongol warfare was largely unknown in the 1920s, Liddell Hart simply projected his own theories onto a largely blank canvas with few being able to challenge his narrative.[11]

Liddell Hart's *Strategy* continued his propagandistic approach to history by presenting the 'indirect approach' as having a firm basis in historical fact; however, analyzing his methodology causes his credibility to collapse as William Owen, a British military theorist, argued:

> [Liddell Hart] did not want historical fact, argument or complexity to get in the way of promoting what he saw as his good idea. He, therefore, set about ransacking the historical and operational record for selected examples to prove his point.[12]

Liddell Hart relied upon superficial historical research and shallow sources as Robert Graves, author of *I Claudius*, declared to him in 1943: 'My criticism of your history is that you have (in the past) tended to accept school textbook accounts of generals or religious disputes or campaigns which you have not yourself studied in intimate detail.'[13] Liddell Hart essentially wrote propaganda and, as Albert Castel explained, 'his purpose throughout his career being not to understand the past but to shape the future'.[14] Liddell Hart's credibility did eventually erode but not before he modified his most famous idea.

THE BRITISH WAY IN WARFARE

In 1931, Liddell Hart recalibrated his thinking on the 'indirect approach' when devising a new concept — the 'British Way in Warfare'. He argued that Britain should avoid massive continental commitments in favor of using the Royal Navy to blockade enemies while the British Army could, under favorable circumstances, provide limited support to allies on the continent. The army should be a small mechanized force capable of conducting selective strikes, in contrast to the mass conscript army of World War I. Furthermore, Britain should initially only send a small expeditionary force to the continent while maintaining a strategic reserve for later use against the greatest threat.[15]

Rather than directly engaging continental armies, Britain should indirectly attack opponents with strategic bombing and by providing financial support to allies. Liddell Hart argued this would constitute a return to a traditional 'Rule Britannia' strategy based on maritime power and economic influence.[16] In this scheme, resurgent German power would be deterred by fear of blockade, strategic bombing and the French Army's Maginot Line, as German leadership would acknowledge the impossibility of victory and rationally seek a negotiated settlement to any crisis.[17]

The 'British Way in Warfare' constituted a grand strategy expression of the 'indirect approach'. Liddell Hart believed it would limit British involvement and avoid continental Napoleonic warfare.[18] However, this vision contradicted the original 'indirect approach' as the mass bloodshed of direct battles between continental armies would still occur; however, Britain alone would avoid the slaughter.[19] Therefore, the 'indirect approach' transformed from a universally applicable method into a cynical British strategy which relied upon the French stopping a German invasion with blood sacrifice. As such, George Orwell condemned the strategy as 'not likely to be successful unless you are willing to betray your allies whenever it pays you to do so'.[20] In opposing large-scale continental commitments, Liddell Hart rejected any basis to build a large mechanized army as he had advocated during the 1920s.

Liddell Hart also altered his earlier views on future conflict by advocating the superiority of defensive war.[21] During the 1930s, he became increasingly convinced that defenders possessed decisive advantages over attackers, as 'the dominant lesson from the experience of land warfare, for more than a generation past, has been the superiority of the defense over attack'.[22] For example, in *When Britain Goes to War* (1935), he stated:

I think that the motorization of armies is more likely to strengthen the defensive than to revive the power of the offensive; that it may hasten a renewed stalemate rather than restore the open warfare for which every keen soldier ardently longs.[23]

In *Europe in Arms* (1937), Liddell Hart further argued that defenders would triumph over armored attacks by destroying bridges and using rivers as natural barriers, unless taken by surprise or if their own forces lack mechanization.[24]

The Spanish Civil War seemingly confirmed this vision as rough terrain and poor roads limited mobility and tanks fell prey to anti-tank guns.[25] Liddell Hart observed that offensive operations with tanks were disappointments, again arguing that armored mobility better favors defenders. The war in Spain further convinced him that massed armored offensives were not viable as defenders could just as rapidly launch counterattacks.[26]

In 1937, Liddell Hart, under the patronage of Neville Chamberlain, became an unofficial adviser to the War Minister Leslie Hore-Belisha, and his ideas became policy as the Chamberlain Government intended to restrict British involvement in any future continental war.[27] Liddell Hart convinced Hore-Belisha to purge the Army Council, removing 'old guard' generals, and to reform the officer promotion system by reducing the length of appointments and promoting 2,500 officers, significantly reducing the average age of officers.[28]

Hore-Belisha and Chamberlain, impressed with the 'British Way in Warfare', abandoned the policy of continental commitment. Chamberlain, in a letter to Liddell Hart in March 1937, accordingly stated: 'I found your articles in *The Times* on the role of the Army extremely useful and suggestive. I am quite sure we shall never again send to the Continent an Army on the scale of that which we put into the field in the Great War.'[29] When budget pressures compelled funding cuts, Hore-Belisha oversaw decreased army expenditure by reducing heavy equipment and tanks, justified by the secure knowledge that Britain would avoid large-scale continental deployments. However, as Hitler's aggressive foreign policy propelled Europe closer to war, Liddell Hart opposed Chamberlain's appeasement policy, while still opposing large-scale support for France, and in May 1938 Hore-Belisha rejected some of Liddell Hart's ideas, resulting in the termination of their partnership. In the following year, the Chamberlain Government doubled the size of the Territorial Army and introduced conscription, arousing the hostility of Liddell Hart, who still opposed mass armies.[30]

Liddell Hart's influence slowed the modernization and expansion of the British Army, particularly in terms of mechanization, and it was critically short of tanks and artillery when World War II commenced. In May 1940, Britain fielded only ten divisions on the Western Front compared with ninety-three French divisions. As this conflict would be a total war of a completely different nature to Liddell Hart's pre-war predictions, events soon shattered his illusions.

A REPUTATION LOST

After the outbreak of World War II, Liddell Hart advocated a negotiated peace with Hitler. Given the superiority of defensive war, the Allies should wait for, and defeat, a German attack on France, after which negotiations would follow as all sides would see the irrationality of offensive actions, as he advocated on 8 September 1939:

> To pursue a military offensive against Germany would be the most unwise strategy and policy from every point of view. . . A declaration that we are renouncing military attack as a means of combating aggression would be a far sighted move, strengthening our moral position. . . It would throw on the Germans the responsibility of taking the offensive, with all its disadvantages.[31]

Liddell Hart ironically did not advocate defeating Germany through the 'indirect approach' and made no effort to identify an Achilles heel which could be exploited along a 'line of least resistance' to paralyze the German war machine.[32] He opposed the Norwegian campaign, which aimed to stop German iron-ore imports from Sweden, a classic expression of the 'indirect approach', by arguing against 'getting strategically frozen in trying to get a flanking grip on some remote part of the enemy's territory'.[33] When the Allies intervened in Norway, their application of the 'indirect approach'

Basil Henry Liddell Hart in his London home in 1940
(Contributor: Pictorial Press Ltd/Alamy Stock Photo)

completely failed, resulting in German control of the country for the rest of the war.

As panzers broke through the Allied lines in May 1940, Liddell Hart, given his belief in the superiority of defensive war, dismissed Germany's chances of success:

The German break-through. . . does not compare with the serious
strategic effect of the three great bulges which the Germans made in the
Allied front in 1918, still less with the desperately ominous situation of the
Allied armies on the eve of the Battle of the Marne in 1914.[34]

Liddell Hart remained supremely confident that the offensive would quickly
run out of steam and vindicate his predictions.

The *Wehrmacht*'s crushing victory during the French campaign destroyed
Liddell Hart's reputation and many public figures blamed him for the
fall of France. *Time* magazine specifically blamed him for the failure of
Allied strategy.[35] Although Liddell Hart did not deserve sole blame for the
catastrophe, he was responsible for the Chamberlain Government's policy of
avoiding continental commitments, which fatally undermined British troop
strength in France.[36] The German victory demonstrated the emptiness of
his faith in defensive war, shattering his standing in the eyes of the world.[37]

Liddell Hart in *Paris* championed strategic bombing and his views on
airpower had changed little during the 1930s. However, he changed his mind
in *The Defence of Britain* (1939) as the bombing of Spanish and Chinese cities
inflicted devastation on civilians 'out of proportion to the results achieved
against any kind of military objective'.[38] Once war commenced, he publicly
opposed strategic bombing on moral grounds.

The Allied strategic bombing campaign against the Achilles heel of
German industry, far from quickly ending the war, resulted in a battle of
attrition in the skies over Europe.[39] Strategic bombing failed to create the
sudden collapse predicted by Liddell Hart in *Paris* because civilian populations
and industry adapted. For example, during the 1943 raids against Hamburg,
the RAF devastated the city, killing 48,000 people, but five months later
industry operated at 80 percent of its former capacity.[40] Strategic bombing
contributed to Allied victory through sheer destructiveness but created the
bloodshed that Liddell Hart — until the end of the 1930s — believed would
be avoided.[41]

Liddell Hart publicly condemned the naval blockade of Germany,
again distancing himself from the 'indirect approach', as it would starve
German civilians and the populations of occupied countries, making the
British worse than Hitler as the blockade constituted 'a greater crime

against humanity and civilisation than anything that even a tyrannical dictator has contemplated'.[42]

The Allies suffered a series of disasters during the war when attempting to implement the 'indirect approach'. Instead of the strategic paralysis promised by Liddell Hart, these efforts often ended in defeat or blood-soaked slogging matches. The indirect Anglo-American attack on Germany through Italy in 1943 — the soft underbelly of Europe — resulted in a slow and protracted campaign with limited strategic gains and never broke out of the Italian peninsula.[43] The Italian campaign was an ineffective sideshow which diverted disproportionate Allied forces away from the decisive Western Front, undermining Allied operations in France and the Low Countries in 1944.[44] The 'indirect approach' resulted in periphery operations that absorbed large numbers of Allied soldiers, which the Germans contained with minimal troop numbers.[45]

The 'indirect approach' also failed at the tactical level. Before the war Liddell Hart advocated dispersing armored units in several directions to find weak points in accordance with his 'expanding torrent' concept: 'One must advance on a wide front in order to be able to envelop the enemy and find and penetrate through gaps in his front. For that purpose it is best to advance on as many roads and with as many spearheads as possible.'[46] In *Europe in Arms*, Liddell Hart condemned the concentration of force:

> . . . there have been some instances in recent exercises of a tendency towards movement on wider fronts, but it has not gone far enough for its promise to mature. The greatest hindrance is the dogma of 'concentration', imperfectly understood.[47]

The British Army in North Africa unsuccessfully applied the 'expanding torrent' by dispersing its armor to divergent objectives, but the German *Afrika Korps*, in contrast, concentrated force at the decisive point, resulting in numerous British defeats.[48] Friedrich von Mellenthin confirmed this when commenting on North Africa: 'The British failure was due purely and simply to the inability of their command to concentrate and co-ordinate the armoured and motorized Brigades.'[49]

The chasm between Liddell Hart's pre-war prophesies and actual World

War II combat shattered his reputation with justification and a reviewer of *The Current of War* (1941) concluded: 'its main prophecies have been shown by recent events to have been false: its leading principles have been decisively discredited. . . As a guide to the future Captain Liddell Hart has ceased to count.'[50] After the war, Liddell Hart endured a Siberian-like exile but later resurrected his public standing.

NEW ASSOCIATES

Liddell Hart had a burning desire to regain his reputation and, through good fortune, an opportunity presented itself after discovering that the British Army held many senior German prisoners at Drysdale Hall near his Lake District home. After interviewing the prisoners, their conversations became the basis of *The German Generals Talk* (1948). Through this book and other postwar writing, Liddell Hart helped rehabilitate the *Wehrmacht*'s reputation in the English-speaking world by giving German veterans a platform to spread misinformation which he endorsed as historically accurate. For example, he legitimized the myth of Hitler's Dunkirk halt order:

> 'At that moment', Rundstedt told me, 'a sudden telephone call came from Colonel von Grieffenberg at O.K.H. [Army High Command], saying that Kleist's forces were to halt on the line of the canal. It was the Führer's direct order — and contrary to General Halder's view. I questioned it in a message of protest, but received a curt telegram in reply, saying: "The armoured divisions are to remain at medium artillery range from Dunkirk".'[51]

Liddell Hart also endorsed the myth of the General Staff opposing the invasion of Russia:

> Blumentritt told me that the Commander-in-Chief, Brauchitsch, and the Chief of the General Staff, Halder, as well as Rundstedt, were opposed to the attempt to invade Russia. All three realized the difficulties presented by the nature of the country from their experiences in the 1914-18 war — above all, the difficulties of movement, reinforcement, and supply.[52]

In *The German Generals Talk*, Liddell Hart made sweeping conclusions that no credible historian would have made as he had no evidence beyond the word of *Wehrmacht* veterans. German generals accordingly quoted his statements on their military performance as evidence of objective conclusions. For example, Field Marshal Albert Kesselring declared, 'I am only stating a truism when I say that our performance in the war was something of an achievement, as Liddell Hart confirms.'[53] Franz Halder also used his statements to gain credibility as they seemingly came from an objective observer.[54]

Liddell Hart also legitimized the myth of the *Wehrmacht*'s clean hands by becoming an apologist for war criminals:

Many [German generals] would have looked in their natural place at any conference of bank managers or civil engineers. They were essentially technicians, intent on their professional job, and with little idea of things outside it. It is easy to see how Hitler hoodwinked and handled them, and found them good instruments up to a point.[55]

Liddell Hart made their supposed ignorance a virtue:

The German generals of this war were the best-finished product of their profession — anywhere. They could have been better if their outlook had been wider and their understanding deeper. But if they had become philosophers they would have ceased to be soldiers.[56]

Liddell Hart understood the *Wehrmacht*'s guilt because he supported war criminals facing justice by publicly opposing their trials and assisting their defense teams. As he followed the trials closely, it is inconceivable that he did not become aware of the mountains of incriminating evidence against the defendants. Nevertheless, Liddell Hart depicted defendants, such as Erich von Manstein and Gerd von Rundstedt, as elderly ill men, fighting charges based on unconvincing evidence.[57] After courts handed down guilty verdicts, he then campaigned for acquittal. For example, Liddell Hart wrote a letter to *The Times* declaring that Manstein had been found guilty only of two minor charges.[58] However, in actuality, the court found Manstein guilty of nine charges including shooting prisoners, implementing the commissar order and allowing subordinates to shoot civilians – facts Liddell Hart must have known.[59] The historian Alex Danchev accordingly concluded:

> These crimes — war crimes — were perpetrated by the overwhelming majority of Liddell Hart's most favoured generals, always knowingly and often willingly. Afterwards they tried to cover them up. In other words these pampered patriots did their best to evade both responsibility and truth — which is to say that they lied, and continued to lie, until death.[60]

Liddell Hart faced criticism for being too close to former German officers and accepting their claims at face value, but this was initially attributed to naivety. For example, Robert O'Neil, a colleague, stressed that he possessed 'a certain innocence' resulting in 'a willingness to believe the best of people and to discount what others had said against them'. Therefore, he had a 'tendency to believe the words of German generals' which 'possibly led to some distortion in his thinking about events on the Eastern Front during World War II'.[61] Another colleague, his biographer Brian Bond, ruled out any sinister motive in his dealing with former *Wehrmacht* officers as 'he was too big a man deliberately to "use" the German generals — or anybody else — to further his career'.[62] However, Liddell Hart did ally himself with German veterans to obtain the means of resurrecting his shattered public image.

THE FABRICATION OF EVIDENCE

Liddell Hart distorted history by soliciting manipulative statements from *Wehrmacht* veterans, which he used to 'prove' that they had been profoundly influenced by his ideas before the war. Above all, he wanted to convince the world that his ideas inspired *Blitzkrieg*. Liddell Hart, as historian Azar Gat explained, used 'his connections with the German generals for extracting, inviting, and planting accolades, which he later inflated beyond their original context, modified, inserted in key publications'.[63] For example, in *The German Generals Talk*, Liddell Hart wrote:

I was fortunate in getting a long account of the rise of the 'Panzers' from General von Thoma, the most famous of the original German tank leaders next to Guderian. . . [who said] 'The German tank officers closely followed the British ideas on armoured warfare, particularly your own; also General Fuller's.'[64]

Liddell Hart similarly claimed that Field Marshal Walther von Reichenau had 'shown an enthusiastic interest in the new theory of tank strategy' and 'personally translated several of my books, describing them as "setting new rules" for warfare'.[65]

Wehrmacht veterans had a motive to inflate Liddell Hart's importance because he publicly championed their causes; therefore, they tended to tell him what he wanted to hear.[66] Former German generals accordingly made flattering comments, such as Blumentritt in 1949:

Liddell Hart and Fuller were for us young officers after 1920 'the modern military authors.' Particularly in the *Reichswehr* they were carefully studied and all their articles read. In those days we were lieutenants and captains aged 38 to 35 and took delight in the modern spirit of these writers.[67]

These comments 'proved' that Liddell Hart had influenced German generals, but he needed a stronger statement to decisively link his theories with *Blitzkrieg*; therefore, he fabricated evidence, as historian John Mearsheimer exposed in his book *Liddell Hart and the Weight of History* (1988):

He needed evidence that showed his prewar writings had influenced the German plan to defeat the Allies in the West, but in *The German Generals Talk* Liddell Hart does not point to a single instance of a German general claiming such an influence. Liddell Hart had to manufacture the evidence. This is a serious charge, I know, but the evidence warrants it.[68]

In 1948, Liddell Hart became acquainted with Heinz Guderian and inquired if he had considered writing his memoirs. Guderian was living in near poverty, but Liddell Hart helped him find British and American publishers and helped edit *Panzer Leader*.[69] He also wrote the foreword to the English language version. This presented Guderian as a genius who defeated France with his panzer force which 'measured by any standard, have hardly been matched in the records of warfare'.[70] Writing the foreword gave him the opportunity to take credit for Guderian's triumph by linking it with his ideas, but to complete the illusion of credibility, he needed a definitive statement from Guderian to corroborate this claim; however, the former panzer general had written nothing to this effect. In the original German version, Guderian merely stated that Liddell Hart had been a source of inspiration alongside other theorists:

> It was principally the books and articles of the Englishmen, Fuller, Liddell Hart and Martel, that excited my interest and gave me food for thought. These far-sighted soldiers were even then trying to make of the tank something more than just an infantry support weapon. They envisaged it in relationship to the growing motorisation of our age, and thus they became the pioneers of a new type of warfare on the largest scale.[71]

As Liddell Hart needed a statement emphasizing his unique importance, he wrote to Guderian requesting an additional paragraph for the English edition:

> . . . because of our special association, and the wish that I should write the foreword to your book, people may wonder why there is no separate reference to what my writings taught. You might care to insert a remark that I emphasized the use of armoured forces for long-range operations against the opposing army's communications, and also proposed a type of armoured division combining panzer and panzer-infantry units — and that these points particularly impressed you.[72]

Guderian, indebted to Liddell Hart who had arranged publication, obliged and the English version contains an additional paragraph:

> Further, it was Liddell Hart who emphasised the use of armoured forces for long-range strokes, operations against the opposing army's communications, and also proposed a type of armoured division combining

panzer and panzer-infantry units. Deeply impressed by these ideas I tried to develop them in a sense practicable for our own army. So I owe many suggestions of our further development to Captain Liddell Hart.[73]

Liddell Hart did not keep a copy of this letter in his well-maintained files, presumably because he did not wish the outside world to know how he had manipulated Guderian.[74] He defined *Blitzkrieg* to suit his own needs and forced Guderian to endorse his definition, but the panzer general also did well out of the arrangement as Liddell Hart endorsed his myths.[75]

Guderian in *Panzer Leader* claimed to have been the principal creator of panzer divisions, overcoming strong opposition from a reactionary high command personified by General Ludwig Beck.[76] However, after Beck became Chief of the General Staff in 1933, he oversaw the creation of the first panzer divisions two years later, making Guderian's claim to have fought a long struggle a fantasy.[77] Beck did not oppose the development of panzers; he simply sought holistic mechanization across the whole army.[78] Guderian also ignored the contribution of other panzer pioneers such as Ernst Volckheim who commanded a tank in World War I and wrote *German Tanks in the World War* (1923) and *Tanks in Modern Warfare* (1924).[79] Volckheim, in fact, personally educated Guderian, but he only got one fleeting reference in *Panzer Leader*.[80] Furthermore, Guderian did not acknowledge his former commander Oswald Lutz, who wrote numerous articles on tanks in the journal *Militär-Wochenblatt (Military Weekly)* and oversaw early exercises involving dummy tanks.[81]

Guderian, through *Panzer Leader*, convinced the English-speaking world of his unique pioneering importance, but in reality the formation of panzer divisions had been a team effort.[82] Liddell Hart unsurprisingly legitimized Guderian's myth by endorsing the historical accuracy of his memoir: 'This book is the fullest, most factual, and most revealing personal account of the war from the German side that has yet emerged.'[83] Liddell Hart and Guderian ultimately needed each other to spread their mutually supportive myths.[84]

Despite Liddell Hart's postwar propaganda, Guderian had actually rejected the 'expanding torrent' during the French campaign in 1940 through his *Schwerpunktprinzip* (concentration principle), which he expressed as *Klotzen, nicht kleckern!* (Hit with the fist, don't feel with the fingers!)[85]

Guderian accordingly concentrated his 19th Panzer Corps, containing 60,000 soldiers and 22,000 vehicles, at Sedan into a thrust 6 miles wide — a move completely contrary to Liddell Hart's advice to disperse armor using multiple thrusts to uncover weak points.

Although Field Marshal Erwin Rommel, commander of the famed *Afrika Korps*, died in 1944, after the war he became a retrospective 'pupil' of Liddell Hart. Rommel had written many papers on his military experiences and after the war his family, wanting them edited and published, approached Liddell Hart. After accepting the job of editing Rommel's papers, he used this opportunity to emphasize his supposed influence on the Desert Fox. He obtained from General Fritz Bayerlein, Rommel's former chief of staff in North Africa, a statement that during the war Rommel had twice blamed British defeats on their failure to apply the armored warfare theories of J.F.C. Fuller and Liddell Hart.[86] Manfred Rommel similarly told Liddell Hart:

My father had a great admiration for you and I remember that he read one or more of your books when he was appointed commander of the 7th Armoured Division in France. In North Africa he studied the articles you wrote during the war.[87]

Bayerlein and Manfred likely gave their statements with a certain 'understanding' as John Mearsheimer explained:

They recognized Liddell Hart could do much to advance their efforts to present a highly favourable picture of Rommel to the English-speaking world. At the same time, however, they understood they would have to say something about Liddell Hart's positive influence on the field marshal. . . . In effect, a de facto bargain was struck: Liddell Hart would describe Rommel as a brilliant general with a few faults; Bayerlin and the Rommels would tell Liddell Hart that the field marshal had been his dutiful student.[88]

Liddell Hart used his foreword to *The Rommel Papers* (1953) and subsequent editorial comments to demonstrate his influence as the Desert Fox allegedly understood 'the value of indirect rather than direct reply to the enemy's moves'.[89] For example, Liddell Hart linked Rommel with his theories when commenting on his avoidance of the mined main road to Cherbourg: 'That calculation of the advantages of the indirect approach, as the line of least expectation, showed his insight and foresight.'[90] In actuality, avoiding a mined road is simply a sensible decision. In another dubious example, Rommel's casual use of the words 'directly rather than indirectly' provided a pretext for Liddell Hart to declare his 'shrewd grasp of the psychological basis of the "strategy of indirect approach"'.[91] He also twisted Bayerlein's words into a supposed direct quote from Rommel which conveniently no longer mentioned Fuller: 'The British would have been able to prevent the greatest part of their defeats if they had paid attention to the modern theories expounded by Liddell Hart before the war.'[92] Of course, Rommel had never uttered these words, but there was nothing the dead field marshal could do to correct the record.

There is no genuine evidence that Rommel had been highly influenced by Liddell Hart.[93] Rommel condemned Liddell Hart's views on dispersing armor in line with the 'expanding torrent', blaming this practice on early British defeats in North Africa:

> The result of these tactics of dispersal was that the British formations were either badly battered or destroyed one after the other and disappeared from the theatre while the battle was still in progress. The British Command did not once, during the whole of this battle, succeed in conducting operations with a concentration of its forces at the decisive point.[94]

Mellenthin confirmed that Rommel did not apply the 'indirect approach' in North Africa: 'At no time did I hear Rommel express any interest in the supply dumps of Eighth Army. We knew of their location from captured documents, but Rommel's aim was not to attack the British supplies, but to destroy their field army.'[95] A true 'pupil' of Liddell Hart would have avoided the British Army, as seeking the destruction of the enemy is a 'Napoleonic Fallacy', and instead attacked the Achilles heel of its supply system.

Liddell Hart wrote the foreword to Manstein's *Lost Victories*, providing him with yet another opportunity to write mythology. He praised Manstein, who possessed 'a superb sense of operational possibilities' and 'military

Erich von Manstein during his war crimes trial in 1949
(Author's Collection)

genius'.[96] Liddell Hart unsurprisingly praised Manstein's 'sickle cut' plan to attack France through the Ardennes in 1940 as an example of the 'indirect approach': 'The new plan, for making the decisive thrust through the hilly and wooded Ardennes — the line of least expectation — has come to be called the "Manstein Plan".'[97]

Liddell Hart even attempted to take credit for Manstein's 'sickle cut'. In *The Decisive Wars of History* (1929) he wrote, 'this idea of the Ardennes [being impassable] must have arisen from a lack of knowledge of the district, for it is well-roaded, and most of it is rolling rather than mountainous country'.[98] After the war, he claimed that Manstein based his plan on these words, but he needed a statement from him. Liddell Hart had eased the hardship Manstein endured in a prisoner-of-war camp, transported his family to the French occupied zone of Germany, publicly defended him during his trial, fought for his acquittal, secured a place for his son at Cambridge and helped find a publisher for *Lost Victories*. Nevertheless, an apparently ungrateful Manstein refused to provide a supportive statement.[99] Undeterred, Liddell Hart fabricated one by claiming in his *Memoirs* (1965) that Manstein had privately admitted this 'truth':

> Manstein, who devised the new German plan for an armoured thrust through the Ardennes, told Mr. R.T. Paget, K.C. (who conducted his defence in a 1949 war-trial), that the idea of such a thrust developed in his mind on recalling what I had written before the war about its possibilities and practicability.[100]

However, there is no evidence that Manstein ever read *The Decisive Wars of History* and, as numerous German officers had fought in the Ardennes during World War I, there were many other sources of information Manstein could have referred to when formulating his plan.[101] Despite Manstein's lack of cooperation, Liddell Hart used former German generals to legitimize his myths and used their statements to define *Blitzkrieg* in the English-speaking world.

BLITZKRIEG DEFINED

Liddell Hart lost his reputation because his pre-war predictions became the basis of failed Allied strategy and tactics. Nevertheless, after the war, he used dubious statements from *Wehrmacht* veterans to construct a fable which attributed initial German success to his ideas.[102] Guderian's testimony became vital to his enterprise and, as Alex Danchev explained, 'Guderian's good opinion was Liddell Hart's most treasured possession. If the past master of *Blitzkrieg* was a self-confessed pupil, then the paternity of the idea was securely his.'[103] Liddell Hart wasted little time in using these endorsements:

> The notion that my teachings were 'proved wrong' in 1940 has become comic in view of the fact that Guderian, who made the decisive breakthrough, called himself my 'disciple' and 'pupil' — while Manstein, who conceived the plan of the tank stroke through the Ardennes, has

stated that the idea came to him from an article of mine in which I had pointed out the possibilities of an armoured move in the Ardennes.[104]

Of course, Guderian's comment had been made in dubious circumstances and Manstein never made such a claim. Furthermore, Liddell Hart contended:

Germany's greatest generals — Rommel, Guderian, Manstein — have said that they won their victories early in the war by applying my ideas — and that *our* defeats could have been prevented if our leaders had applied them. It should thus be plain that I could have saved the West in 1940, if officialdom had let me help.[105]

In fabricating this mythology, Liddell Hart defined *Blitzkrieg* as an expression of his early views on armored warfare combined with the 'expanding torrent' and 'indirect approach', as he explained in new editions of *Strategy*:

The tactics of the German forces corresponded to their strategy avoiding head-on assaults, seeking to find 'soft spots' through which they could infiltrate along the line of least resistance. . . While the Allied commanders thought in terms of battle, the new German commanders sought to eliminate it by producing the strategic paralysis of their opponents.[106]

Liddell Hart, in *Memoirs*, similarly defined *Blitzkrieg* as 'little more than a natural adaptation of the "expanding torrent" method for application by forces which had mechanized mobility'.[107]

The word *Blitzkrieg* normally conjures images of the mass use of panzers with tactical air support — personified by Stuka dive bombers — employed to confuse the enemy with rapid surprise blows to achieve breakthroughs and encirclement at a lightning pace. Liddell Hart could plausibly define *Blitzkrieg* because it has no objective meaning and, as Israeli military theorist Shimon Naveh concluded, it is 'a typical historical myth' in which 'reality and fantasy are interwoven'.[108]

In the early days of the war, *Blitzkrieg* gained widespread currency after British newspapers used the word to describe an alleged revolutionary German mechanized warfare doctrine.[109] British commentators witnessing rapid German triumphs over Poland, Denmark and Norway convinced themselves that Germany had unleashed a new method of waging war. On 25 September 1939, *Time* magazine announced: 'This was no war of occupation, but a war of quick penetration and obliteration — *Blitzkrieg*, lightning war.'[110] This statement popularized the word *Blitzkrieg* in the Western press, which was used to convey a sense of rapid and destructive German operations.[111] However, the *Wehrmacht* never had a *Blitzkrieg* doctrine and, as Azar Gat concluded, it 'was not the name of any official or at first even unofficial German doctrine allegedly crystallized during the interwar period'.[112]

Before the outbreak of war, the word *Blitzkrieg* was virtually non-existent in German military writing, but it did occasionally appear in articles without any of the various interpretations commonly associated with it. In 1935, the *Deutsche Wehr* (German Defense) journal used the term to describe a rapid war to force a decision against an adversary with resource superiority, and the *Militär-Wochenblatt* in 1938 spoke of 'lightning war' involving a surprise attack at the strategic level being implemented at the operational level by tanks, planes and paratroopers.[113] On 24 May 1939, General Georg Thomas, Chief of the War Economy and Armaments Office, declared in a speech: 'I personally do not believe that a conflict between the Axis Powers and the states of the West will be a question of blitzkrieg — in other words a question of days and weeks.'[114] These references implied a rapid war at the strategic level with little or no concept of how this would be fought at the tactical and operational levels; therefore, they have no relationship with Anglo-Saxon notions of *Blitzkrieg*. Furthermore, these obscure references in no way shaped — let alone revolutionized — German military thinking or practice.

After the *Wehrmacht* invaded France and the Low Countries in May 1940, the mirage of *Blitzkrieg* appeared as Allied soldiers conditioned by the press convinced themselves they were facing 'lightning war'. However, the *Wehrmacht* experienced just as much surprise over the speed of their victory as the Allies, a clear indication that no *Blitzkrieg* idea existed. General Johann Adolf Graf von Kielmansegg, who fought in France with the 1st Panzer Division, dismissed 'some kind of *Blitzkrieg* concept, whatever it was', claiming instead that German success resulted from improvisation.[115]

Nevertheless, the Germans exploited the Allied fear of *Blitzkrieg* through propaganda, as Samuel Cook made clear:

> The mythical images of Blitzkrieg still permeate popular history, much as they did with contemporary observers in 1940. And that is just as Joseph Goebbels intended it. Laced with images of tanks rolling through France, Goebbels' films created the popular image of a numerically and technologically superior German army cruising effortlessly through France.[116]

The *Wehrmacht* never officially defined *Blitzkrieg* and it remained largely a propaganda term. Hitler himself dismissed the concept on 8 November 1941, announcing, 'I never used the word *Blitzkrieg* because it is a very stupid word.'[117] Liddell Hart's definition of *Blitzkrieg* did not have to compete with a genuine German concept and exploited an Anglo-Saxon misconception that the word represented a revolutionary doctrine.

Liddell Hart's claim that the British military establishment ignored his prophetic visions is fiction. Far from being an overlooked prophet, he was an adviser to War Minister Leslie Hore-Belisha who made his ideas policy.[118] He also argued for the supremacy of defensive warfare during the 1930s and failed to predict the success of the German offensive in May 1940, making his claim to have invented *Blitzkrieg* absurd. Nevertheless, Liddell Hart convinced the English-speaking world of his fantasy version of World War II.

THE ACCEPTANCE OF MYTHOLOGY

Liddell Hart's collaboration with German generals gave him the illusion of credibility and his myths largely became accepted; as Brian Bond confirmed, 'Liddell Hart is universally recognised as the prophet of mechanized warfare or *Blitzkrieg*.'[119] John Mearsheimer similarly concluded that he is 'widely seen as a prophet whose prescient advice had been tragically ignored'.[120] Liddell Hart was knighted in 1966 and he became the most famous military writer in the world before his death in 1970. The postwar editions of *Strategy* sold significantly more copies than the earlier versions, becoming one of the most influential military books of the twentieth century.[121]

Liddell Hart's myth-making fundamentally damaged historical inquiry and military thinking by obscuring how the Germans actually conducted operations.[122] For example, he stated in the *Marine Corps Gazette*:

> In 1940 the West was overrun, and the course of history changed by the German armored forces applying a new blitzkrieg technique of swiftly maneuvering concentration, exploited by deep strategic penetration. Guderian, the creator and leader of these 'Panzer troops', has generously stated in his memoirs that their organization and technique were inspired by my theories and writings of the 1920s.[123]

Unfortunately, many military officers were deceived by fraudulent history. For example, Lieutenant Colonel Brooke Nihart reviewed *Strategy* in the *Marine Corps Gazette* in 1954:

> Liddell Hart has been much maligned for his alleged defensive doctrine prior to World War II. This doctrine is further alleged to have been responsible for the French Maginot Line complex which is considered to have resulted in their defeat in 1940. Nothing could be further from the truth.[124]

Nihart concluded, 'the French were defeated by a German application of the indirect approach'.[125] He also explained that the evidence for this assertion came from testimonials by Guderian and Rommel before adding that *Strategy* should 'become a classic in military literature', highly recommending it to 'those who aspire to a knowledge of the art of war'.[126] *Wehrmacht* officers were actually unaware of the 'indirect approach' as Bayerlein confirmed in 1950: 'The strategy of the indirect approach was still unknown to us at that time [before the war].'[127]

Lieutenant John Walden praised Liddell Hart's integrity in *Military Review* in 1954, as in 'all of his writings are seen the objectiveness of the historian combined with the thirst for knowledge and truth of the philosopher and scientist'.[128] Unfortunately, Walden accepted the myth that the 'expanding torrent' method 'was used with great success by the German armies'.[129]

When Robert Walters interviewed Liddell Hart in the *Marine Corps Gazette*, he asked:

The Germans since the war have been quite eloquent in their praise of
you. Gen Guderian, who originated the idea of the 'blitzkrieg', claims that
he got most of his ideas from your pre-war writings. Could you give us an
insight into the 'blitzkrieg'?[130]

Liddell Hart replied: 'It's a high-speed indirect approach to the enemy's rear.
That is what Guderian epitomized in his shorter definition of the *blitzkrieg*
method as "mobility, velocity, indirect approach".'[131]

The acceptance of Liddell Hart's myths continued in the 1980s and
General John Woodmansee wrote in *Military Review*: 'The German success of
1940 would confirm both Fuller's views and Liddell Hart's observations.'[132]
Major Jerry Morelock similarly claimed that Liddell Hart 'has been called
"the creator of the theory of the conduct of mechanized war" by the *blitzkrieg*'s
most famous executioner, panzer leader Heinz Guderian'.[133] Liddell Hart's
myths also became foundational ideas within maneuver warfare.

LIDDELL HART AND MANEUVER WARFARE

Maneuver warfare derived many of its core concepts from Liddell Hart, as
R.J. Brown declared in the *Marine Corps Gazette*, 'The first and most important
concept in maneuver warfare was the proper use of Liddell Hart's concept of the
"indirect approach".'[134] J.R. Benson similarly stated in the *Marine Corps Gazette*:

Do we owe our concepts of maneuver war to Hart? Yes, to an extent. The
first working model of maneuver war was the *blitzkrieg*, with Guderian its
chief disciple. Guderian states that Hart and his predecessors excited his
interest in what came to be the *blitzkrieg*.[135]

In *Strategy*, Liddell Hart described the 'indirect approach' in terms
unmistakably similar to John Boyd's *Patterns of Conflict*. For example, he
advocated psychological means to defeat the mind of the enemy commander:

In the psychological sphere, dislocation is the result of the impression
on the commander's mind of the physical effects which we have listed.
The impression is strongly accentuated if his realization of his being at a

disadvantage is *sudden*, and if he feels that he is unable to counter the enemy's move. *Psychological dislocation fundamentally springs from this sense of being trapped.*[136]

This is very similar to Boyd's ideal of getting inside an opponent's 'decision cycle' or O–O–D–A loop. Liddell Hart also stated:

. . . the pace of panzer warfare paralyzed the French Staff, whose minds were still moving at 1918 tempo. The orders they issued might have been effective, except that they were repeatedly 24 hours late for the situation they were intended to meet.[137]

This comment clearly echoes Boyd's ideas, which is unsurprising as his source list for *Patterns of Conflict* included Liddell Hart's *A Science of Infantry Tactics Simplified*, *The Future of Infantry*, *The Ghost of Napoleon*, *The German Generals Talk*, *Strategy* and *History of the Second World War*. Boyd, despite the conceptual closeness of his ideas and the 'indirect approach', disagreed with Liddell Hart's focus on generating psychological collapse through dislocation in favour of disorientation, which he believed to be a far more effective mechanism to trigger mental collapse. In order to distinguish his own theories, Boyd would exaggerate and overemphasize this point of difference. For example, during one *Patterns of Conflict* presentation, Boyd ungratefully referred to *Strategy* as 'garbage' and he called Liddell Hart the 'chiropractor of war' given his emphasis on dislocation.[138] On another occasion, Boyd even discouraged the audience from reading *Strategy* despite the book's critical influence upon him.[139]

Despite such unacharacteristic rhetoric, Boyd understood *Wehrmacht* operations and postwar German accounts through the prism of Liddell Hart's writing, as the scholar Grant Hammond from the Air War College explained:

. . . Boyd began to read military history in the Pentagon library. He began to learn about using aircraft to kill tanks and so read Von Mellenthin, Von Manstein, Hans Rudel and books about WWII. Then he went back to study the 1930s, the theories of Liddell-Hart, Guderian, and how German ideas had developed about blitzkrieg and infiltration tactics in WWI.[140]

Basil Henry Liddell Hart
during World War I
(Author's Collection)

Boyd accepted Liddell Hart's myth that *Blitzkrieg* was a German application of the 'expanding torrent' and 'indirect approach'. For example, in *Patterns of Conflict* he identified *Blitzkrieg* with avoiding destruction and generating paralysis.[141] He further linked *Blitzkrieg* with the 'indirect approach' as armored forces 'advance rapidly from least expected regions and infiltrate adversary front to find paths of least resistance'.[142] Boyd used the language of Liddell Hart's 'expanding torrent' when describing stormtrooper 'infiltration tactics' as they 'flow into any gaps or weaknesses they can find in order to drive deep into adversary rear'.[143]

William S. Lind in *Maneuver Warfare Handbook* praised Liddell Hart's *Strategy* and acknowledged how it inspired Boyd:

> This book contains the heart of Liddell Hart's thinking, his strategy of the indirect approach. The basic principal he espouses applies to tactics and operations as well, which makes this volume valuable to officers of all ranks. It is interesting to compare Liddell Hart's theory, which focuses on

place, with John Boyd's, where time is the critical element.[144]

Lind claimed that the fall of France vindicated Liddell Hart as it 'demonstrated that a maneuver doctrine, particularly when combined with its natural partner, an indirect approach, constitutes a form of jujitsu'.[145]

Robert Leonhard in *Art of Maneuver* similarly praised Liddell Hart's contribution to the development of maneuver warfare:

> The indirect approach involves subtlety, deception, and the avoidance of enemy strength. As we read his accounts, it is instructive to explore in each campaign the specific purpose of the indirect approach, because Liddell Hart's insights can then be integrated into a modern theory of maneuver.[146]

Furthermore, Richard Simpkin in *Race to the Swift* paid tribute to Liddell Hart: 'Manoeuvre theory is about amplifying the force which a small mass is capable of exerting; it is synonymous with the indirect approach.'[147]

Despite Liddell Hart's tireless advocacy of the 'indirect approach', he did not genuinely believe in the concept. As his fraudulent history was not solely motivated to regain his lost reputation, he had a higher motive for deceiving his readers. Traumatized by the Somme, Liddell Hart believed bloodshed in future conflict could be reduced if combatants applied the virtue of limitation as outlined in *Strategy*. Therefore, the 'indirect approach' is a noble lie intended to serve the greater good by diminishing the level of violence experienced during combat, which would be achieved if both sides apply its logic.

Liddell Hart covertly agreed with Allied strategy in 1914 which prioritized operations on the Western Front — a direct application of force — but he never admitted this publicly because doing so would have destroyed the credibility of the 'indirect approach', as he privately noted: 'Is it too unkind to suggest that to do so would have ruined a memorable metaphor?'[148] His noble lie failed to moderate conflict and his myths grew beyond his control by merging with the deceit of *Wehrmacht* generals to form the intellectual foundation of maneuver warfare. As the theorists are victims of fraud, it is unsurprising that their understanding of *Wehrmacht* operations does not align with genuine historical evidence.

CHAPTER FIVE
WEHRMACHT OPERATIONS: MYTH AND REALITY

THE CANNAE IDEAL

John Boyd depicted *Wehrmacht* generals as masters of maneuver warfare who 'were able to repeatedly operate inside their adversary's observation-orientation-decision-action loops'.[1] William S. Lind similarly asserted:

> . . . in the West in this century, Germany was the only country to *institutionalize* maneuver warfare. That is, only the Germans endeavored to make every element of their military — their education system, officer selection, officer promotion, the way their army made its choices and decisions, etc. — supportive of maneuver warfare.[2]

Robert Leonhard in *Art of Maneuver* agreed as 'Lind expertly describes the fundamentals of maneuver warfare and provides a worthy extrapolation of WWII German theory'.[3]

The theorists, however, formed their views of German operations based on superficial and unreliable accounts of World War II.[4] The *Wehrmacht*, contrary to mythology, never sought to paralyze their enemies — the essence of maneuver warfare — as historian Daniel Hughes concluded:

There is a disturbing and quite erroneous view that a German doctrine of blitzkrieg called for maneuver and deep penetration to paralyze the enemy's command and control system. . . This is sheer invention, both in theory and in practice. The German army's armored forces, contrary to unexamined expectations and assumptions, did not attempt to disrupt the enemy's command apparatus as their primary or even secondary objectives. Nor was paralysis of the enemy their ultimate goal.[5]

General Daniel Bolger similarly concluded, 'whatever the Germans did to their unlucky neighbors, it was not maneuver warfare, a concept unrecognizable in German doctrine'.[6] In fact, the *Wehrmacht* adhered to a warfighting philosophy with deep Prussian roots which was the polar opposite of maneuver warfare.

German strategy reflected its unfavorable geography in central Europe, bordering hostile states which collectively possess population and resource superiority. As such, the Prussian military tradition always sought to avoid long wars, seeking instead rapid and decisive victories.[7] In the eighteenth century, Frederick the Great envisaged swift campaigns achieving victory before opponents mobilized their superior numbers:

Our wars must be short and lively, because it is not good for us to drag the thing out, because a long, drawn-out war inevitably will cause our admirable discipline to fall apart and would depopulate the land and exhaust our resources.[8]

During the nineteenth century, Helmuth von Moltke the Elder sought rapid victories and German military thinkers envisaged a *Niederwerfungsstrategie* — strategy of annihilation — to swiftly seek a decisive battle to destroy the enemy's army. In this way, the Germans hoped to rapidly destroy one opponent before engaging other adversaries.

After Alfred von Schlieffen became Chief of the General Staff in 1891, he faced the dilemma of planning a two-front war against France and Russia. He decided that a defensive war against both great powers would be unwinnable; therefore, Germany's best hope would be to rapidly defeat France before Russia fully mobilized.[9] To avoid the fortified French border,

Germany in 1914

Schlieffen planned a flanking maneuver through Belgium to attack the French Army in the rear — his famous Schlieffen Plan.

Schlieffen later experienced a revelation in retirement when reading an account of Cannae by Hans Delbrück and became obsessed with Hannibal's destruction of the larger Roman army — the 'perfect battle of annihilation'.[10] Schlieffen convinced himself that all great commanders, either consciously or unconsciously, emulated Hannibal's triumph and Cannae became a mystical ideal.[11] In *Cannae* (1909), he argued that a double envelopment combined with an attack on the rear, seeking the complete destruction of the enemy, was the universal key to victory.[12] 'The battle of extermination,' Schlieffen

Alfred von Schlieffen
in 1895
(Contributor: Granger
Historical Picture Archive/Alamy
Stock Photo)

noted, 'may be fought today according to the same plan as elaborated by Hannibal in long forgotten times.'[13]

The Cannae ideal resembled the Prussian tradition of *Kesselschlacht* (cauldron battles), which sought to encircle and destroy enemy forces from all sides.[14] Schlieffen used Cannae as a yardstick to evaluate other battles and praised Sedan during the Franco-Prussian War as an encirclement battle 'on three, eventually four sides' which completely destroyed the French Army.[15] Sedan had been a Cannae-like victory but, as it lacked the equivalent of the cavalry attack on the enemy rear, Schlieffen noted that it did not completely fulfill the ideal. He also argued that any battle which failed to destroy the enemy army could at best only be considered an 'ordinary victory'.

The Schlieffen Plan of 1905, before his Cannae revelation, envisaged the

A depiction of the Battle of Cannae during the Second Punic War, 2 August 216 BC
(Contributor: FALKENSTEINFOTO/Alamy Stock Photo)

right wing of the German Army moving through Belgium and the Netherlands in a giant wheel which would sweep around Paris before enveloping the French Armies while the left wing defended the Franco-German border. This resembled Frederick the Great's victory of Leuthen in 1757 more than Cannae as it was a single envelopment designed to force the enemy against a barrier.[16]

Schlieffen's successor Helmuth von Moltke the Younger, a convert to the Cannae ideal, modified the plan in the image of the 'perfect battle'. The strengthened left wing could now potentially attack through the French forts to form the second pincer of a double envelopment.[17] Moltke, concerned about the distance the right wing would have to march to reach Paris, reduced this distance by deciding not to envelop Paris from the west. When Moltke executed the revised plan in 1914, the German Army approached Paris but reached the limit of its supply lines and could no longer advance. However, the failure of the plan did not diminish Schlieffen's legacy in Germany as the failure was blamed on Moltke's modifications.[18]

In the 1925 edition of *Cannae*, the editor Freytag-Loringhoven warned that the ideal needed reassessment given the destructive power of modern weapons which made cavalry operations impossible and prevented the decisive attack on the rear.[19] The 'perfect battle' seemed unobtainable because without mobile cavalry, the enemy rear could not be threatened. As such, Karl Justrow, a German Army officer, critiqued the Schlieffen Plan as unable to fulfill the Cannae ideal due to the obsolescence of cavalry and the slow speed of marching infantry, declaring 'The age of Cannae is over.'[20]

The German Army after World War I, seeking a means of avoiding trench warfare, continued to seek inspiration in Schlieffen's legacy. Officers considered the encirclement battle of Tannenberg in 1914 a modern Cannae and their map exercises stressed operational encirclement as the epitome of military art.[21] Hans von Seeckt, the commander-in-chief, embraced Schlieffen-like ideals, believing that Germany needed to avoid getting drawn into long conflicts of attrition against larger enemies.[22] He also stressed that a small professional army could use superior mobility to outflank, encircle and destroy slower mass armies, as the German Army had achieved on the Eastern Front during World War I.[23] Seeckt predicted, 'I see . . . the future of warfare residing in the use of high-quality and mobile, hence smaller, armies, whose effectiveness is considerably enhanced by the air force.'[24]

In 1926, Major Friedrich von Rabenau argued that while the Schlieffen Plan failed because men and horses became exhausted, a motorized army could maintain the momentum required to successfully attack the enemy rear.[25] German military thinkers realized that panzers concentrated in independent units could be the new cavalry within the Cannae ideal. Heinz Guderian embraced this concept and argued that panzers could be the decisive weapon in future Cannae-style battles of annihilation.[26]

The *Wehrmacht*'s embrace of the Cannae ideal rejected the 'indirect approach' and maneuver warfare because it envisaged the complete destruction of enemy armies.[27] Therefore, German operations never followed the concepts of J.F.C. Fuller, Liddell Hart and Boyd, who all stressed the avoidance of destruction and advocated paralyzing opponents.[28] General Hermann Hoth confirmed this fact:

> Outflanking the enemy is decisive. It leads to his encirclement and destruction. The greater the number of units employed, the further the lunge of the envelopment manoeuvre. More enemy forces will then fall prey to annihilation.[29]

The invasion of Poland, September 1939

Hermann Balck in *Order in Chao*s echoed this sentiment:

> Complete victory over a superior enemy was the problem. Frederick the
> Great solved it at Leuthen; Clausewitz underscored it in theory; Schlieffen
> made it the focus of his studies of the Battle of Cannae; and Seeckt
> planted these tenets deeply with us.[30]

The German invasion of Poland involved two powerful enveloping wings
designed to destroy the Polish Army, a plan derived from the Cannae ideal
as Friedrich von Mellenthin confirmed: 'This conception of a weak center
with two powerful attacking wings was traditional in German strategy, and
found its roots in Count von Schlieffen's classic study of Hannibal's victory
at Cannae.'[31]

The 'sickle cut' plan devised by Erich von Manstein to invade France
through the Ardennes with the main panzer force in Army Group A
attacking the Allied armies in the rear, forcing them against the Channel

coast and Army Group B, resembled Cannae logic.[32] After Dunkirk, the Germans viewed the second phase of the campaign, which sought the encirclement and annihilation of the remaining French forces, in the spirit of Cannae, as Franz Halder noted in his diary on 10 June 1940, 'A "Battle of Cannae" is in the making.'[33] Friedrich von Rabenau, now a *Wehrmacht* general, analyzed the French campaign and concluded, 'The basic trend in the war of movement simultaneously contained the basic old Schlieffen truth, the idea of Cannae, involving envelopment and annihilation by means of encirclement.'[34]

The *Wehrmacht* continued its Cannae obsession during Operation Barbarossa as the Germans viewed operations in Russia as a series of Cannae-like battles of annihilation, involving great encirclement battles to surround and destroy Soviet armies.[35] For example, Guderian's orders to the Second Panzer Group on 8 June 1941 emphasized the destruction of the Red Army and made no reference to 'indirect' attacks on headquarters or 'critical nodes' to generate paralysis.[36] Hoth also stressed the Cannae logic of Barbarossa:

> Since the campaigns of Frederick the Great it had become an axiom of warfare to make the objective not a geographical point but the enemy army itself, the destruction of which in a decisive battle all operations must be directed towards. . . The operational orders [of Barbarossa] took this into account.[37]

General Günther Blumentritt accordingly referred to the encirclement battle near Vyazma and Bryansk as 'a modern Cannae' but 'on a greater scale'.[38] Rommel in North Africa similarly focused on destruction, dreaming of Cannae. On 8 April 1941, he noted, 'Our main force is on its way up after a 220-mile march over the sand and rock of the desert. . . It's going to be a "Cannae", modern style.'[39]

The *Wehrmacht* fought World War II with doctrinal concepts inherited from Frederick the Great, Moltke and most importantly Schlieffen, maintaining a near-religious belief in fighting battles of annihilation. However, the maneuver warfare theorists failed to understand this as they were blinded by a false vision of *Blitzkrieg*.

LIDDELL HART'S ACTUAL INFLUENCE

The inaccurate maneuver warfare belief that the *Wehrmacht* sought to avoid battle and paralyze opponents originated from Liddell Hart's fraudulent definition of *Blitzkrieg*. However, as the Germans accepted limited aspects of his thinking, it is necessary to consider his actual impact. Liddell Hart did have some influence in Germany after World War I and, as historian Azar Gat concluded, 'the fact that he was fraudulent does not necessarily mean that he was wholly incorrect'.[40] John Mearsheimer overstated his case when claiming that Liddell Hart had almost no influence in Germany, but he did not have access to primary sources which recorded German enthusiasm for his early ideas on armored warfare. As such, Azar Gat concluded that Liddell Hart did have a decisive influence on the development of the panzer arm.[41]

By the late 1920s, Fuller and Liddell Hart had become extremely popular within German military circles. The journal *Militär-Wochenblatt* summarized Liddell Hart's 'New Model Army' mechanized concept and his book *Paris* in the mid-1920s, and frequently repeated his observations on armored warfare made in the *Daily Telegraph*.[42] Colonel Geyer von Schweppenburg, the German military attaché in Britain, reported on British maneuvers in 1935: 'Liddell Hart highly praises the fact that in these exercises the tanks were assigned a strategic mission. In his view it is against the nature of the armoured arm to be solely employed as a tactical assistant of infantry.'[43]

Liddell Hart influenced the development of panzer divisions as the Germans noted his belief that tanks should be organized in independent units and assigned operational missions — rather than dispersed throughout the army as infantry support weapons. However, the *Wehrmacht* rejected the other aspects of his theories. Liddell Hart believed in applying his 'expanding torrent' concept to armored warfare, as tanks should be dispersed across a wide front seeking 'soft spots' to infiltrate into rear areas.[44] He also considered the purpose of armored operations was to attack 'nerve centers' in order to generate paralysis, as stated in *When Britain Goes to War*:

The aim of such moves, if wisely directed, will not be to strike the enemy troops in the back. . . but to cut the communications on which they depend. The object will be to dislocate their organization by destroying headquarters and signal centres; to cut off supplies by destroying railways and road transport; even, if possible, to reach and attack the sources of supply.[45]

However, panzer generals in contrast concentrated their force at the decisive point with the aim of destroying enemy armies by attacking their flanks and rear in accordance with the Cannae ideal.[46] Therefore, the *Wehrmacht* rejected the 'expanding torrent' and the paralysis theory found in the 'indirect approach'.

Guderian firmly believed in concentrating armor, rejecting Liddell Hart's principle of dispersing tanks along a broad front to search for weak points as 'we have derived from the last war the three requisites for the success of a tank attack: suitable terrain, surprise, and the concentration of all available forces at the decisive point — in other words attacking *en masse*'.[47] This is the basis of Guderian's concentration principle, which is the opposite of the wide front dispersal philosophy expressed in the 'expanding torrent'.

Liddell Hart perceived annihilation operations as originating from the 'Napoleonic Fallacy' of seeking the complete destruction of enemy armies. For example, in *Paris* he rejected the Cannae ideal by criticizing the Schlieffen Plan's focus on destroying French armies, rather than striking at the 'critical node' of Paris:

> History may well decide that had the German Higher command been less obsessed with the dream of a Cannae manoeuvre, and struck at Paris first instead of attempting to surround the French armies, 'Deutschland uber alles' might now be an accomplished fact.[48]

If Guderian had truly been a 'pupil' of Liddell Hart, after his breakthrough at Sedan in May 1940, he would have headed directly toward 'nerve centers' to paralyze the French Army. Instead, his panzers headed for the channel coast to surround and destroy the main Allied armies.[49] During Barbarossa, Guderian again focused on destroying enemy armies and made no attempt to strike at Achilles heels.[50] Furthermore, after the war Guderian reaffirmed his belief in destruction in relation to the German offensive in southern Russia in 1942:

. . . Hitler was driving for objectives of economic and ideological significance without first ensuring that the enemy's military strength was broken. The capture of the Caspian oilfields, the cutting of the Volga as a maritime artery, and the neutralisation of the industrial centre of Stalingrad, such were the motives that led him to undertake operations which, from a military point of view, were nonsensical.[51]

Therefore, Guderian perceived the destruction of enemy armies as a prerequisite to securing 'vital nodes', which rejected the 'indirect approach' and maneuver warfare. Furthermore, as Liddell Hart spent his postwar years writing mythology in favor of conducting genuine historical inquiry, he failed to understand the principal reason for Germany's initial victories.

TRUPPENFÜHRUNG AND COMBINED ARMS

After World War I, Seeckt oversaw a study of the conflict, resulting in the 1923 manual *Führung und Gefecht der Verbundenen Waffen (Leadership and Battle with Combined Arms)*, which envisaged infantry, artillery, armor, cavalry and aircraft all working together in mutually supporting roles — a vision of combined arms warfare.[52] In 1933, the Generals Ludwig Beck, Werner von Fritsch and Otto von Stülpnagel wrote the manual *Truppenführung (Unit Command)*, which built upon Seeckt's legacy, further emphasizing combined arms cooperation by advocating mobile operations involving tanks and other supporting elements working closely together as combined arms teams.[53] The *Truppenführung* stressed that no single arm, not even panzers, can achieve tactical success independently as only the harmonious cooperation of all arms can achieve victory.

After the fall of France, the *Wehrmacht* further enhanced its combined arms methods due to Balck who realized the shortcomings of the panzers. The Germans had organized panzers in rigid groups which lacked flexibility and diminished combined arms cooperation. After Balck and his men from the 1st Motorized Infantry Regiment crossed the Meuse River on 13 May 1940, Guderian held the panzer regiments back to preserve them for the operational breakthrough, effectively keeping his infantry and panzer units separate. As a result, the first panzer did not cross the Meuse until the next day, leaving Balck without armored support. Consequently, his men endured savage combat, assaulting French bunkers at close quarters with pistols, grenades and hand-to-hand fighting.

Balck realized that the French counterattack at Chémery on 14 May was almost successful and his men would not have been able to stop the French tanks on their own and only the arrival of the 1st Panzer Brigade in the nick of time saved his regiment. Balck concluded that Guderian's separation of infantry and panzers in distinct echelons was a mistake: 'The idea of separate assignments for tanks and infantry was a sin against the essence of tactics.'[54] The assault across the Meuse exposed the weakness of German armored doctrine as Mellenthin explained:

> At that time it was customary to draw a sharp distinction between rifle units and armored units. This theory proved unsound. Had Colonel Balck had tanks under his command during the Meuse crossing, things would have been much easier. It would have been possible to ferry single tanks across the river, and there would have been no need to send the troops forward without any tank support on the night 13/14 May.[55]

Balck accordingly advocated that infantry and tanks needed to work closer together and proposed mixing infantry, armor and other supporting arms into more flexible *kampfgruppen* (battlegroups). After the fall of France, the *Wehrmacht* accepted Balck's flexible combined arms *kampfgruppen* concept.[56] Mellenthin stressed that the '*Kampfgruppen* embodied a principle as old as war itself — the concentration of all arms at the same time in the same area.'[57] The *Wehrmacht* subsequently developed flexible *kampfgruppen* in which task orientated combined arms teams would be created to conduct specific missions.

Before the war, Liddell Hart failed to understand the value of combined arms cooperation but after the conflict claimed that the balanced force structure of panzer divisions originated from his ideas.[58] For example, he stated in *Memoirs*:

> . . . in a 1922 proposal for a New Model Army I had put forward the 'mixed' idea in a less radical form, suggesting that tanks, infantry in

armoured vehicles, and artillery should be combined in combat groups of brigade size. When published two years later in the *Army Quarterly* it made little impression in British quarters, but caught the attention of fresh-minded soldiers in the German Army.[59]

Before the war, Liddell Hart did envisage 'land marines' in *Paris*:

These quick-moving and quick-hitting [tank] forces will advance by rapid bounds into the enemy country to strike at its vitals, establishing behind them, as they progress, a chain of fortified bases, garrisoned by heavy artillery and land marines — *late* infantry. A proportion of land marines might also be carried in this tank fleet to be used as 'landing parties' to clear fortifications and hill defences under cover of the fire from the tank fleet.[60]

After the war, Liddell Hart claimed that his 'land marines' were the basis of German mechanized infantry which accompanied the panzers.[61] However, in *Paris* he only viewed 'land marines' as a 'shore party' designed to garrison captured territory which *might* be used to clear strong points in support of tanks. As such, 'land marines' are not an essential component of the tank fleet which is virtually autonomous and lacking combined arms flexibility.[62]

German panzer divisions did not resemble Liddell Hart's advice which envisaged a small infantry force assigned to a tank army while panzer divisions fully integrated tanks with infantry, artillery and other supporting elements.[63] As such, mechanized infantry in panzer divisions were never restricted to secondary tasks and formed an essential element of integrated combined arms teams.[64]

During the North African campaign, the British Army adopted Liddell Hart's tank-centric views with disastrous consequences, as their armor charged German lines without support, falling victim to German 88-mm anti-tank guns with heavy losses.[65] Colonel Bonner Fellers, a US Army observer in North Africa, reported this fact to Washington in 1942: 'the British Army has twice failed to defeat the Axis in Libya. . . Its tactical conceptions were constantly faulty; it neglected completely the use of combined arms.'[66] Mellenthin made the same observation: 'British experts did indeed appreciate that tanks had a great part to play in the wars of the future. . . but they did not stress sufficiently the need for cooperation of all arms within the armored division.'[67] In contrast to British practices, Mellenthin praised the flexibility of the *Afrika Korps*' combined arms formations:

> To my mind, our victories depended on three factors — the superior quality of our antitank guns, our systematic practice of the principle of *Co-operation of Arms*, and — last but not least — our tactical methods. . . In short, a German panzer division was a highly flexible formation of all arms, which always relied on artillery in attack or defense.[68]

After the fall of France, Hitler decided that Germany's ten panzer divisions were insufficient for the invasion of Russia and expanded the force to twenty-one divisions, although this halved the number of tanks in each division. The new panzer divisions nevertheless contained a better balance of armor and other arms, and the inclusion of heavier Panzer III and IV models, which progressively replaced the lighter Panzer II tanks, compensated for the reduction in overall tank numbers.[69] Most of the new divisions had enough armored personnel carriers to carry a rifle company which could support the panzers in forests and villages by assaulting enemy infantry and anti-tank guns.[70]

The reformed panzer divisions were better able to eliminate pockets of resistance and protect their flanks due to the increased levels of infantry, and smaller tank numbers reduced bottlenecks on the roads and logistics requirements.[71] However, after Guderian became inspector-general of armored troops in 1943, he pleaded with Hitler to reduce the number of panzer divisions to allow each unit to possess 400 tanks, quoting a recently published Liddell Hart article on the subject.[72] After the war Liddell Hart, still failing to appreciate combined arms cooperation, condemned the improved panzer divisions in *The German Generals Talk*:

> Thoma argued that the net effect would be disadvantageous on balance, since it meant doubling the number of staffs and auxiliary troops without any effective increase in the armoured punch. 'But I could not persuade Hitler — he was obsessed with the advantage of having an increased number of divisions. Numbers always inflamed his imagination.'[73]

However, German field commanders, guided by combat experience, favored the reformed panzer divisions as the older model hindered combined arms operations.[74]

Guderian failed to appreciate the right balance between armor and supporting arms due to his tank-centric obsession. For example, he opposed the mechanization of cavalry units, believing in a completely autonomous panzer arm.[75] He also challenged Beck's idea to provide motorized transport to pull anti-tank and field guns in infantry units, demanding such resource allocation strictly for panzer units, but this increased mobility and provided the infantry with great advantage during the war.[76]

Guderian opposed one of Germany's great armored innovations by arguing against tanks without rotating gun turrets. In 1935, Manstein recommended manufacturing turretless assault guns to support infantry, but Guderian argued against the idea as he opposed allocating any armor to infantry support roles.[77] Nevertheless, *Sturmgeschütz* assault guns and turretless tank destroyers, such as *Jagdpanzers*, proved their worth in combat.[78] Although the absence of rotating turrets made them less tactically flexible, they could be mass-produced in vast numbers and, as historian Jon Mosier explained, they 'became the backbone of German mechanized forces, even though men like Guderian remained bitterly opposed to them throughout the war'.[79]

As Liddell Hart and Guderian failed to understand that German tactical excellence originated from combined arms cooperation and balanced force structures, their competence as military thinkers can be questioned along with the adoration of their ideas within maneuver warfare. The theorists similarly misunderstood what they believed was the *Wehrmacht*'s greatest asset — its command philosophy.

AUFTRAGSTAKTIK AND FORWARD COMMAND

The maneuver warfare theorists praised the *Wehrmacht*'s embrace of *Auftragstaktik*. Boyd in *Patterns of Conflict* claimed that Balck personified 'mission tactics' and declared that his example taught 'Wide freedom for subordinates to exercise imagination and initiative — yet harmonize within intent of superior commanders.'[80] Simpkin in *Race to the Swift* similarly stated 'manoeuvre theory can only be exploited to the full by the practice of directive control (*Auftragstaktik*) in the full German meaning of that term'.[81] The *Wehrmacht* encouraged junior leaders to use initiative and exploit fleeting opportunities as Mellenthin confirmed:

> Our panzer corps and divisions not only had the advantage of excellent training and communications, but the commanders at every level appreciated that panzer troops must be commanded from the front. Thus they were able to take immediate advantage of the rapid changes and opportunities which armored warfare brings.[82]

The *Truppenführung* manual likewise noted: 'The command of an army and its subordinate units requires leaders capable of judgment, with clear vision and foresight, and the ability to make independent and decisive decisions and carry them out unwaveringly.'[83] Nevertheless, *Auftragstaktik* in reality differed greatly from how the theorists imagined the *Wehrmacht* functioned because 'mission tactics' was balanced by 'forward command'.

Lind in *Maneuver Warfare Handbook* presented forward command as coexisting alongside *Auftragstaktik* as German commanders monitored their subordinates but only intervened 'to exploit opportunities or shift the *Schwerpunkt*'.[84] However, *Wehrmacht* forward commanders frequently micro-managed their subordinates, making *Auftragstaktik* as understood by the theorists impossible. For example, Guderian in *Panzer Leader* recalled an incident during the Polish campaign when he took charge after his subordinates failed to cross the Brahe (Brda) River under their own initiative:

> I walked angrily away and tried to decide what measures I should take to improve this unhappy state of affairs. A young Lieutenant Felix came over to where I was standing. . . 'Herr General,' he said, 'I've just come from the Brahe. . . The bridge is crossable. The advance has only stopped because there's no one to lead it. You must go there yourself, sir.'[85]

Balck in *Order in Chaos* similarly recalled taking charge at the village of Bouvellemont during the French campaign after his subordinates failed to act:

I called the officers together and they told me that after a good night's sleep we would press on the next day. I cut them off. 'Gentlemen, we will attack, or we will lose the victory.' It was a situation where no matter what you ordered, the soldiers were not going to move. So I turned around and said, 'If you're not going, then I'll just take the village myself', and I started in the direction of Bouvellemont across the open field, fifty meters, one hundred meters. Then it all broke loose. Troops and officers, who just a few seconds ago could not move anymore, started to pass me.[86]

As a general principle Balck preferred *Auftragstaktik*: 'As much as possible, I tried not to tell my people what to do. As long as I saw that a man was sound, I let him do things his way, even if I would have done them differently.'[87] However, he also knew that *Auftragstaktik* did not always work and that forward command needed to be imposed from time to time as less-talented subordinates could not be trusted with too much independence. 'It depended entirely on the subordinate,' Balck explained. 'If he was a stupid fellow, you had to go into much detail explaining the situation to him; if he was an intelligent officer, a word was sufficient for him.'[88]

Rommel similarly believed in forward command because subordinates cannot always be trusted to use initiative:

It is a mistake to assume that every unit officer will make all that there is to be made out of his situation; most of them soon succumb to a certain inertia. Then it is simply reported that for some reason or another this or that cannot be done — reasons are always easy enough to think up. People of this kind must be made to feel the authority of the commander and be shaken out of their apathy. The commander must be the prime mover of the battle and the troops must always have to reckon with his appearance in personal control.[89]

The widespread use of radio made it possible for German forward commanders to immediately alter their subordinate's actions when required. During World War I, high-ranking commanders had used telegraphs and telephones to control their units, but static lines could never keep up with advancing units, which diminished command authority. Guderian, who

Erwin Rommel in North Africa in 1941 — the epitome of a German forward commander
(Contributor: World History Archive/Alamy Stock Photo)

served as a signals officer during World War I, realized that radios could synchronize the actions of fast-moving panzers and accordingly advocated that every tank should have one.[90] He also envisaged special command vehicles following the panzers with powerful long-range radios, allowing forward commanders to race from one decisive point to the next to synchronize operations.[91]

Guderian's marriage of the tank and radio was a critical German innovation which, as Balck explained, freed the leadership 'from the telephone line, and the German general was once again leading personally from the front'.[92] Balck realized that equipping all panzers with radios 'allowed both small and large tank units to be commanded and maneuvered with a swiftness and flexibility that no other army was able to match'.[93] Balck praised Guderian's contribution which gave 'the panzer division a signal organization that allowed the division commander to command from any point within the division'.[94] As maneuver warfare rejects 'synchronization' and the micro-managing tendencies of 'forward command' made possible through radio, the *Wehrmacht* did not follow its principles.

In maneuver warfare 'mission tactics' permits subordinates to disobey

Heinz Guderian in an armored command vehicle in 1941
(Contributor: Chronicle/Alamy Stock Photo)

orders provided that the commander's intent is achieved, as outdated orders in a new situation may be detrimental to the success of the commander's plan, as Lind explained:

> Your actions must always fit in with what your commander is trying to accomplish — with his intent and the mission. If he also suggests some means, you cannot disregard his suggestions, but if you find that the situation changes or is different from what your commander envisaged, you put the ends above the means and do what you think is appropriate.[95]

However, Guderian frequently ignored his commander's intent, instead seeking personal glory. For example, on 9 July 1941 he advanced toward the Dniepr River without orders from his superior Günther von Kluge, an action which undermined the actions of all other units within the command.[96] Guderian later initiated a river crossing over the Desna, in contradiction to Kluge's intent, which resulted in heavy German losses before the unwanted bridgehead was evacuated.[97] Guderian failed to act in accordance with the commander's intent, as Israeli military theorist Shimon Naveh concluded: 'Between 8 August 1941 and mid-September, Guderian as commandant of Panzer Army 2 perpetrated four independent acts of insubordination against the high command's operational orders.'[98] Guderian further alienated Kluge during the Battle of Moscow by retreating from Chern without permission and lying about his actions.[99] Given the dysfunctional relationship between Guderian and Kluge, Balck noted:

> Guderian had assured Kluge that he would hold a certain line, even though the troops of his 4th Panzer Division were already falling back from that position. Kluge cited two other similar instances in Guderian's previous conduct of the operation when he supposedly had not played with open cards.[100]

The reality of *Auftragstaktik* in the *Wehrmacht* differed greatly from the assumptions of maneuver warfare, but the theorists blame the dysfunction on Hitler. For example, Michael Wyly, who helped introduce maneuver warfare to the Marine Corps, blamed Hitler for destroying trust:

Why did the Germans lose World War II? After 1942, after Stalingrad, Hitler relieved talented generals, actually taking personal command, himself, of a field army group. In other words, trust broke down, and this was felt through the chain of command so that finally the smooth, well-oiled machine stopped working.[101]

However, in reality the dysfunctional lack of trust in the *Wehrmacht* had little to do with Hitler as army officers frequently feuded. Balck recalled one occasion: 'Guderian told me that Kluge once challenged him to a duel, but Hitler had prohibited it.'[102] In another example, Rommel during the North African campaign clashed with Halder and the General Staff, completely lacking faith in his superiors:

The African campaign and the new aspects of warfare which it brought were never understood by men like General Halder. They [the General Staff] stuck to their established methods and precedents, even though these often showed themselves to be outdated and hence false. . . many officers of the academic type, steeped in their ancient theories, failed to understand us and so took us for adventurers, amateurs and the like.[103]

Halder likewise had no faith in Rommel:

Personal relations are complicated by Gen. Rommel's character and his inordinate ambition. . . Rommel's character defects make him extremely hard to get along with, but no one cares to come out in open opposition, because of his brutality and the backing he has on top level.[104]

The theorists' idealized vision of *Auftragstaktik* is at odds with historical accounts as they misunderstand genuine *Wehrmacht* operations and the French campaign best illustrates their flawed logic.

THE FALL OF FRANCE

Maneuver warfare theory explains the French defeat in 1940 as having a psychological origin, as Lind argued: 'The Germans presented the French with a succession of new and unexpected situations at a pace too rapid for the French observation-decision-action cycle. The nerve of the French high command broke under the strain.'[105] Lind presented the French campaign as a contest between two opposing ideals: 'The clash in 1940 between the German Army, with its maneuver doctrine, and the French Army, with a firepower doctrine, was resolved decisively in favor of the former.'[106]

The French defeat in reality primarily resulted from General Maurice Gamelin's strategic decision to move the best Allied units into Belgium and the Netherlands to defend the Dyle River on the assumption that the Germans would repeat the Schlieffen Plan.[107] He originally planned to send ten French and five British divisions to the Dyle line but in March 1940, concerned with defending the Netherlands, increased this force to thirty divisions, including his best mechanized units. These would race into the Low Countries to establish formidable defensive zones to stop the Germans before they reached French soil. This revision changed the role of the French Seventh Army from being a central reserve deployed near Reims to being the spearhead of the advance to Breda.[108] As such, Gamelin committed his mobile strategic reserve, which had previously been poised to counter any German attack from Belgium to Switzerland, before the start of the campaign.[109]

Manstein's 'sickle cut' plan intended to lure the Allied armies into Belgium with a feint before launching the main attack through the Ardennes to cut off and destroy them. On 10 May 1940, Germany invaded the Low Countries and the best Allied troops advanced into the trap of Belgium.[110] A small German glider force famously captured the Belgium fortress of Eben Emael and paratroopers in the Netherlands attempted to capture key bridges ahead of Army Group B, actions which convinced the Allies that Army Group B constituted the main attack.[111] German radio news deliberately highlighted the deeds of Army Group B, with little mention of Army Group A which was quietly advancing through the Ardennes toward the Meuse River.[112] On 13 May, French intelligence continued to believe the main German attack was advancing through Belgium further north.[113] After Army Group A crossed the Meuse, Guderian ordered two panzer divisions to advance from Sedan toward the English Channel, which closed the trap.[114]

The French high command began to realize the true situation and, contrary to legend, did not become overwhelmed by paralysis. On 15 May,

Gamelin reported to the French war minister Edouard Daladier that panzers had broken through the lines and were near Rethel and Laon. Daladier responded, 'Then you must counterattack at once, like 1918!' but Gamelin announced, 'With what? I don't have the reserves.'[115] The next day Churchill met Daladier and Gamelin, who showed the British prime minister a map of the Sedan bulge. Churchill asked about the strategic reserve and Gamelin replied, 'None.'[116] The French commander's mind had not been shocked into paralysis, he had simply committed his reserves to the wrong sector, which denied him the ability to make contingency plans. As this decision had been made prior to the start of the campaign, the most critical decision was not made in the context of a rapid sequence of time critical O–O–D–A loops during the heat of combat. In contrast it had been made in complete isolation to German 'decision cycles', making Boyd's central prism irrelevant when analyzing the fall of France.

By the time the French high command realized the main attack was advancing through Sedan, it was too late to redeploy their finest mechanized troops out of the trap. When Guderian's panzers reached the coast they surrounded around 1.7 million Allied troops.[117] General Maxime Weygand recalled the scale of this disaster: 'Three-quarters, if not four-fifths, of our most modern equipment was captured. Our units in the north were the best armed. They were our spear-head. The best of the French army was captured.'[118] After Dunkirk the balance of power decisively shifted in Germany's favor as Mellenthin noted: 'the French Army had sacrificed most of its armored and motorized formations, and was left with barely sixty divisions to hold the long front from the Swiss Frontier to the English Channel'.[119]

The maneuver warfare theorists claim that superior German tempo had prevented the French from implementing their 'methodical battle' plans. However, the French did implement their plan by racing into Belgium, which turned out to be an unwise move. Historian Robert Doughty correctly concluded that the French 'mistake was preparing inflexibly and stubbornly to charge into Belgium and the Netherlands' while not adequately preparing 'for the possibility of a rapid enemy move through the Ardennes'.[120] The Germans formulated a high-risk yet unpredictable plan which accurately anticipated how the French would act. Maneuver warfare concepts had little to do with the fall of France as German success primarily resulted from a daring German plan which exploited French mistakes.

The *Wehrmacht* displayed tactical excellence during the French campaign which resulted from its command philosophy — which balanced *Auftragstaktik* with forward command — and combined arms cooperation, not maneuver warfare. This cooperation included the integration of tactical airpower with ground operations and enabling close air support provided by Stuka dive bombers, a key advantage.[121] On 13 May, the *Luftwaffe* conducted its largest bombing mission of the campaign at Sedan, enabling the German breakthrough at this decisive point.[122]

The *Wehrmacht* had another critical advantage over the French not mentioned by the theorists — actual combat experience. Around 20,000 German soldiers fought on the Nationalist side during the Spanish Civil War, giving participants experience and teaching soldiers how to best employ their excellent 88-mm guns.[123] The *Luftwaffe* in Spain improved its ground support operations, learning how to concentrate its support at decisive points. The devastating German air attacks against Republican fortifications at Bilbao in 1937 became a dress rehearsal for the *Luftwaffe*'s decisive mass bombing of Sedan.[124] Even the bloodless annexation of Austria in 1938 gave the *Wehrmacht* valuable logistics experience as advancing units encountered and overcame problems with route clearance, fuel and maintenance.[125] The *Wehrmacht* experienced combat on a large scale in Poland, gaining further experience denied to the Allies during the 'Phony War', as Mellenthin explained: 'the operations were of considerable value in "blooding" our troops and teaching them the difference between real war with live ammunition and peacetime maneuvers'.[126]

The maneuver warfare theorists misinterpreted the French campaign as they sought confirmation of their ideas, which prevented them from understanding the deeper causes of the Allied defeat. Furthermore, as the theorists' main source of credibility rests upon their insistence that the *Wehrmacht* practiced maneuver warfare, the inaccuracy of this claim fatally undermines their theory. Boyd and Lind would also have their mythology challenged when they became acquainted with Balck and Mellenthin.

CHAPTER SIX

RIDDLE OF THE STORMTROOPERS

INFILTRATION TACTICS

The maneuver warfare understanding of *Blitzkrieg* derived from Liddell Hart's association of World War I German stormtrooper 'infiltration tactics' with his 'expanding torrent' and 'indirect approach' concepts. In *The Future of Infantry* (1933), he defined 'infiltration tactics' in a manner reflecting his own theories:

> . . . the idea underlying these [German] tactics was that a widely dispersed chain of little groups should probe the enemy's front to discover its weak points, and then penetrate between the posts and machine-gun nests of the defence. While the leading groups pushed onwards through the enemy's position, the 'islets' of the defence, cut off from help, were outflanked and reduced by fresh troops from the reserve.[1]

After World War II, Liddell Hart linked 'infiltration tactics' with *Blitzkrieg* as 'fast tanks were the ideal agents of infiltration or "soft-spot" tactics — to push on along the line of least resistance while other troops dealt with the cut-off "islets" of the defence'.[2]

Liddell Hart's understanding of 'infiltration tactics' became an article of faith in maneuver warfare theory and John Boyd explained the concept in *Patterns of Conflict*:

> The idea was to try to get through the crevices, the gaps, the voids in
> the defense. In other words, seep in or infiltrate. Try not to hit the strong
> points, press on, and work their way through. . . The purpose was to go
> through paths of least resistance.[3]

Boyd speculated that stormtrooper tactics originated from the French officer
Captain André Laffargue who wrote a pamphlet on infiltration which the
Germans captured, or from General Oskar von Hutier who used 'infiltration
tactics' to capture Riga on the Eastern Front in 1917.[4]

Boyd explained that stormtrooper tactics, while initially successful during
the 1918 German offensives, eventually failed:

> Even though Ludendorff seemed to start out right, at least seen through
> Liddell Hart and others, later on he seemed to start burning his reserves
> against these regions of strong resistance. . . Those Sturmtruppen got very
> tired. . . They just could not keep pace with the assault to bring up the
> artillery, supplies, and so forth. They did not have logistics or the gasoline
> engine to support that kind of thing, plus the terrain was all torn up.[5]

Boyd, however, insisted that stormtrooper tactics formed the basis of
Blitzkrieg which 'really is a mechanized variant of the infiltration tactics
that the Germans applied during World War I'.[6] Boyd's fascination with
stormtrooper 'infiltration tactics' made an impression on his audience. For
example, the journalist James Fallows, after sitting through *Patterns of Conflict*
in 1979, reported: 'Boyd cites reports from World War I and the Battle of
the Bulge in World War II about the terror of Allied soldiers when German
infiltrators suddenly "loomed up out of nowhere" from the fog.'[7]

William S. Lind and Gregory Thiele also defined *Blitzkrieg* as a mechanized
version of stormtrooper tactics:

> On the offensive, the German 'storm-troop tactics' of 1918 flowed like
> water around enemy strong points, reaching deep into the enemy's rear
> area and also rolling his forward units up from the flanks and rear. These
> World War I infantry tactics, when used by armored and mechanized
> formations in World War II, became known as 'Blitzkrieg'.[8]

A German stormtrooper during World War I
(Author's Collection)

Lind linked 'infiltration tactics' with Liddell Hart as stormtroopers followed 'the lines of least resistance, drawing reserves after them to create the "expanding torrent" of which Liddell Hart writes'.[9] Robert Leonhard in *The Art of Maneuver* concurred:

> Combining the successful infiltration tactics with the rapidly developing technologies of the tank and combat aircraft, the Germans created the *blitzkrieg* — lightning war. Some have suggested that Guderian borrowed somewhat from Liddell Hart in his innovations. The concept of the 'expanding torrent', for example, is fundamental to *blitzkrieg* theory.[10]

Michael Wyly, who helped introduce maneuver warfare to the Marine Corps, similarly linked stormtrooper tactics with Liddell Hart: 'Von Hutier did not invent the tactic. However his name is still attached. Basil Liddell Hart, the British author, called it the expanding torrent system tactic.'[11]

The maneuver warfare understanding of *Blitzkrieg* stressed that German operations avoided battle and destruction in order to defeat enemies through paralysis. For example, Liddell Hart claimed that German commanders avoided battle when practicing *Blitzkrieg*:

> While the Allied commanders thought in terms of battle, the new German commanders sought to eliminate it by producing the strategic paralysis of their opponents, using their tanks, dive-bombers, and parachutists to spread confusion and dislocate communications.[12]

J.F.C. Fuller similarly believed the Germans had adopted his 'Plan 1919' and explained the secret of *Blitzkrieg* in a manner similar to Liddell Hart:

> It was to employ mobility as a psychological weapon: not to kill but to move; not to move to kill but to move to terrify, to bewilder, to perplex, to cause consternation, doubt and confusion in the rear of the enemy, which rumour would magnify until panic became monstrous. In short, its aim was to paralyse not only the enemy's command but also his government.[13]

Maneuver warfare incorporated Liddell Hart and Fuller's understanding of

German stormtroopers during World War I
(Author's Collection)

Blitzkrieg. Boyd in *Patterns of Conflict* argued that the 'basic idea' of *Blitzkrieg* 'was to cut the lines of communication, disrupt movement, paralyze the command and their support activities'.[14] He rejected 'destruction' as an essential element of 'attrition warfare' while praising 'paralysis' and 'disruption'.[15] Lind agreed that the essence of maneuver warfare 'is to break the spirit and will of the opposing high command by creating unexpected and unfavorable operational or strategic situations, not to kill enemy troops or destroy enemy equipment'.[16] He also said:

> The Germans also discovered as early as the Polish campaign that a maneuver doctrine reduces casualties. Because the object is not the physical destruction of the opponent's men and equipment but, rather, the destruction of his mental cohesion and will, a maneuver doctrine permits the offensive forces to avoid rather than seek tactical engagements.[17]

Leonhard accepted this logic as 'maneuver theory attempts to collapse or disrupt the enemy (rather than destroying his physical components) in order to bring about his defeat'.[18] Richard Simpkin in *Race to the Swift* similarly stated, 'The distinguishing feature of the *blitzkrieg* offensive is the avoidance of battle.'[19]

Nevertheless, *Wehrmacht* operations in reality never resembled Fuller and Liddell Hart's understanding of *Blitzkrieg*, as historian Robert Doughty concluded:

> When the Germans broke through the French defenses. . . their objective was not to 'make straight', as Fuller said, for divisional, corps, and army headquarters; instead, they headed west toward the English Channel [to attack the rear of the Allied armies in Belgium].[20]

The German attack through the Ardennes accordingly resembled a traditional German *Kesselschlacht* battle of encirclement and destruction.[21] Fuller actually admitted in 1943 that his 'belief that demoralization rather than destruction would become the aim of warfare was an overstatement'.[22] Boyd and Lind would also be forced to confront their assumptions when two *Wehrmacht* veterans visited America.

MELLENTHIN AND BALCK IN AMERICA

Boyd and Lind cannot be blamed for incorporating German misinformation and Liddell Hart's fabricated history into maneuver warfare during the 1970s because the difficult work of professional historians in separating fact and fiction had yet to make a noticeable impact in the English-speaking world. At that time, little information critical of postwar German accounts existed in America and Britain.[23] The key works available in English on the depth of Franz Halder, Heinz Guderian and Erich von Manstein's deceit appeared decades later in works such as Wolfram Wette's *The Wehrmacht: History, Myth, Reality* (2006) and Ronald Smelser and Edward Davies' *The Myth of the Eastern Front* (2008). Furthermore, John Mearsheimer only exposed Liddell Hart's fraud in *Liddell Hart and the Weight of History* in 1988. Nevertheless, Boyd and Lind were exposed to critical information which challenged their concepts.

After the United States experienced defeat in Vietnam, the Army refocused on its traditional Cold War role — defeating a possible Red Army invasion of Western Europe — but it faced a dilemma in determining how this could be achieved given the numerical superiority of Warsaw Pact forces compared with NATO. Many officers sought the solution to this problem by studying the *Wehrmacht*'s Eastern Front operations. The Army accordingly invited Friedrich von Mellenthin and Hermann Balck to America where they became military consultants. Battelle Columbus Laboratories interviewed Balck in 1979 and Mellenthin attended an armored warfare conference on 10 May 1979; they both participated in a conference and wargame on NATO tactics hosted by the BDM Corporation in May 1980.

When Boyd and Lind met Mellenthin at the armored warfare conference they naturally assumed he would confirm the fundamentals of maneuver warfare. Mellenthin made comments supportive of 'mission tactics':

I would say it was part of our training to learn to make independent decisions, because as we have seen in the North African campaign, the Commander of the Army was gone, there had to be made a decision, you can't wait until the Commander is back — then the battle is lost, therefore you have to make an independent decision even as a lower General Staff Officer.[24]

The spirit of confirmation continued after Lind asked, 'Was this a basic principle of the German command system always to try to make the decision at the lowest possible level so that it could be made as quickly as possible?'[25] Mellenthin replied, 'Yes, you are right, this was a principle in our operations to make the decision as low as possible.'[26] The tone changed when Lind asked Mellenthin another question:

General, in the counterattacks you discussed, you emphasized how the attempt was always made to hit the Russian penetration in the flank or in the rear. In your view, what was the decisive point in the counterattack? Was it the destruction that was inflicted on the enemy by firepower or was it the disorganization and disruption of his cohesion that was caused by appearing suddenly from an unexpected direction?[27]

Mellenthin's reply shattered Boyd and Lind's illusions:

The main point was to destroy the enemy. . . The only chance you have
with the Russian units is to attack them not from the front line but from
the rear or from the flank, therefore, our aim was to attack the enemy by
surprise and destroy him.[28]

As Mellenthin rejected the philosophical basis of maneuver warfare by
advocating destruction, Lind asked a clarifying question: 'Would you then
say that the destruction was in effect a *denouement* in the tactical action, but
that the actual decision, the point where he came apart, was where he was
surprised?'[29] Mellenthin re-confirmed that German operations sought the
physical destruction of the enemy: 'The actual decision was to get him by
surprise and destroy him.'[30] He then rejected disruption as its effects quickly
fade: 'There is no doubt that the Russians succeeded in reorganizing their
divisions and groups very quickly, and the only hope for us was not to disrupt
them, but to destroy them.'[31]

Boyd, stunned by Mellenthin's rejection of maneuver warfare, asked
his own clarifying question, 'General, on your comments relative to the
destruction of the forces, are you talking about every element or are you
talking about their organic whole?'[32] Mellenthin again confirmed his belief
in destruction, 'You see, always the aim of our tank corps was not to destroy
the single man, but to destroy the whole unit.'[33] In fact, Mellenthin had
earlier explained in *Panzer Battles* how the *Wehrmacht*, after Stalingrad, pinned
its hopes on destruction and attrition to bleed Red Army reserves:

. . . in this grim month of December 1943, the German soldiers in the
Ukraine felt a flicker of hope, for it was clear that the limits of Soviet
manpower were being reached; the Russians could not continue to
suffer these huge losses indefinitely and 'the bottom of the barrel' was
already visible. . . A cautious and circumspect policy combining strategic
withdrawals with tactical offensives — would have played havoc with the
Russian masses, while conserving our own manpower and material.[34]

Major G.S. Lauer confirmed Mellenthin's assertion as the 'Germans never avoided battle, on the contrary, they sought the destruction of the enemy at every opportunity.'[35] As such, he correctly concluded, 'the German army cannot be shown to possess the intent or experience in war which supports the contention that they practiced a maneuver style of warfare'.[36]

Balck rejected the maneuver warfare understanding of *Blitzkrieg* when interviewed in 1979. When asked, 'Could you tell us some of the aspects of German military tradition that created a particularly fertile ground for the ideas of *blitzkrieg* and *panzer* warfare?' Balck responded:

> Prussia was a small country surrounded by superior forces. Therefore, we had to be more skillful and more swift than our enemies. In addition to being more clever than our opponents, we Prussians also needed to be able to mobilize much more quickly than our enemies. These ideas were then further developed by Clausewitz and then by Schlieffen. Schlieffen wanted above all to bring home the lessons of the battle of Cannae.[37]

Balck associated *Blitzkrieg* with the Cannae ideal and made no mention of mechanized stormtrooper 'infiltration tactics' or 'expanding torrents'. When he later attended the NATO conference, Pierre Sprey raised the topic of 'infiltration tactics':

> In the U.S. we talk a lot about the infiltration technique of the First World War. By that they mean the breaking in with shocktroops to open the enemy position, and then to follow with the other forces. The question is, does the mentality of the shock troop leader have any influence on the tank troops (leader) or otherwise?[38]

Balck, a stormtrooper veteran who had served in a *Jäger* (hunter) infantry battalion during World War I, responded, 'The last part of the First World War, I was in attack units (Stosstruppen).'[39] Sprey then asked, 'Was not the so-called Alpen Corps predominately attack-oriented?'[40] Balck's reply stunned the American audience: '[It was] one of the best attack units, and I never noticed anything of this method of infiltration, we did not use it. We suppressed the enemy fire by strong artillery and then we deployed.'[41] As Balck defined stormtrooper tactics in terms of combined arms cooperation, not 'infiltration tactics', a shocked Sprey asked, 'What here in the States is called "Von Hutier tactics" is not known in Germany?'[42] Balck replied, 'I can only say that I went through practically everything, but that is something that I did not experience.'[43] As Balck had never heard of 'infiltration tactics', the report from the NATO event noted:

> British and American historians have long put forth the theory that General von Hutier's infiltration tactics using Stosstruppen (assault troops), first employed with great success against the Russians at Riga in World War I, were the lineal forebearers of the Blitz tactics of World War II. General Balck professed ignorance of this connection.[44]

The report continued:

> In a separate conversation later, Col. von Uslar-Gleiden, the German Army Attache in Washington, told this reporter that the 'Von Hutier' theory seemed to be confined to the British and Americans. He knew of no such ideas in German military doctrine or publications. Given the wide adherence to the theory outside Germany, this may be a fertile field for further research.[45]

Balck had never heard of 'infiltration tactics' or its supposed influence on *Blitzkrieg* as these ideas, alien to Germany, are fantasies conjured in Anglo-Saxon minds.

THE VIEW FROM OLIFA

After the British Army experienced, and recovered from, the shock of the 1918 German offensives, many officers naturally searched for an answer to explain the initial success of the stormtroopers. As many British defenders, during the chaos of battle, first spotted German troops in rear areas, they naturally assumed the enemy had 'infiltrated' through their lines.[46] Therefore, the fog of war had created a mirage of 'infiltration tactics' which was attributed to General Oskar von Hutier, who commanded the Eighteenth Army during the campaign. General Hubert Gough, the defending British commander, encouraged the notion that Hutier had invented some kind of completely novel tactic, which he supposedly used earlier at Riga.[47] By associating Hutier with an innovative tactical revolution, Gough misdirected attention away from his poor defensive plan, as historian Stephen Bull explained: 'Gough had an interest in building up the reputation and importance of von Hutier: for the more omnipotent the opponent appeared, the more excusably his own performance could be interpreted.'[48] Gough's misdirection explains the origin of so-called 'Hutier tactics', but English language history has also attributed 'infiltration tactics' to a Frenchman.

André Laffargue wrote the pamphlet *L'Etude sur L'Attaque (The Attack in Trench Warfare)* based on his experience at Neuville St Vaast in May 1915, and he is often credited with the invention of 'infiltration tactics'. Laffargue commanded a company during an attack which became pinned down by two machine guns for four hours until German reinforcements arrived. After the Germans bloodily repulsed subsequent attacks, Laffargue concluded that if he had initially destroyed the machine guns, a breakout could have been achieved before the reinforcements arrived.[49] Based on this insight, his pamphlet proposed a new technique for attacking trenches, in which small howitzers and 37-mm guns would be used by the attacking infantry to destroy machine guns and companies would advance rapidly without the need to keep aligned with neighboring units.[50]

In 1916, the Germans captured a copy of Laffargue's pamphlet which supposedly inspired them to develop 'infiltration tactics'.[51] For example, the British writer Captain G.C. Wynne in *If Germany Attacks* (1939) gave Laffargue a central role in the creation of stormtrooper tactics.[52] However, Laffargue's solution to trench warfare envisaged a mass assault across an entire sector of front with overwhelming firepower to break through the entire trench system.[53] As the attacking infantry would advance in lines to overcome all points of resistance, Laffargue never advocated the use of small squads to 'infiltrate' through enemy lines into rear areas by avoiding strong points and seeking gaps. Therefore, he never advocated 'infiltration tactics' as understood by Anglo-Saxon commentators.[54]

Liddell Hart, in *Foch: The Man of Orleans* (1931), attributed 'infiltration tactics' to Captain Hermann Geyer who had 'framed the infiltration tactics and written the textbooks on which the German army had been trained for its devastating punches in the spring'.[55] Liddell Hart's writing popularized the notion of 'infiltration tactics' in postwar Britain, but a colleague also inflamed the public imagination with this concept.

After the outbreak of World War I, John Buchan worked for the British War Propaganda Bureau and for *The Times* as a war correspondent in France. He soon shot to fame through his thriller *The Thirty-Nine Steps* (1915) before becoming an officer in the British Army's Intelligence Corps. Buchan later contributed to the twenty-four volume *Nelson's History of the War*, further propelling his fame.

In 1920, Buchan read a transcript of Liddell Hart's famous lecture on the 'expanding torrent', which inspired him to inquire into stormtrooper 'infiltration tactics', seeking to understand their origin and principles.[56] Buchan's later bestseller *A History of the Great War* (1922) included an account of German 'infiltration tactics' based on his reading of Liddell Hart's *Framework of a Science of Infantry Tactics* (1921).[57]

The myth of 'infiltration tactics' also penetrated the Anglo-Saxon mind through fiction. In Buchan's novel *Huntingtower* (1922) a character declares, 'I do not know to whom the Muse of History will give the credit of the tactics of 'infiltration', whether to Ludendorff or von Hutier or some other proud captain of Germany.'[58] Buchan's novel *The Courts of the Morning* (1929) further popularized 'infiltration tactics' and the 'indirect approach' in a story involving British and German World War I veterans assisting belligerents in the Republic of Olifa, a fictional South American country. The protagonist Sir Archibald Roylance insists that a motivated small force using human cunning can defeat the larger enemy through surprise and attacking their morale; and through these means he defeats the pro-German faction in the Olifa Civil War. Liddell Hart unsurprisingly endorsed the novel and recommended it to his readers.[59]

As the concept of 'infiltration tactics' developed in British minds as a means of dealing with the initial success of the German 1918 offensives, it is unsurprising that stormtrooper veteran Balck had never heard of the concept. The fantasy of stormtroopers infiltrating through the trenches resulted from confusion inherent in the fog of war and became codified in immediate postwar British histories and novels before becoming a central idea in maneuver warfare as the theorists failed to distinguish history, fantasy and fiction.

STORMTROOPER REALITY

World War I German stormtroopers originated from a variety of special attack units, in particular assault pioneers, which formed storm battalions and assault squads (*Stosstrupp*).[60] Captain Willy Rohr, a key stormtrooper innovator, took command of an experimental pioneer troop in August 1915, which he transformed into a stormtrooper unit named *Sturmbataillon Rohr* and his troops fought in small squads armed with grenades, machine guns, trench mortars, flamethrowers and light artillery. They would advance behind a creeping barrage using ground as cover when attacking French strong points.[61] Rohr established a one-week training course in December 1915 to teach his tactics to other units and wrote the manual *Instructions for the Employment of an Assault Battalion*, published in May 1916, which explained how small squads of attackers should assault enemy trenches using grenades, flamethrowers, trench mortars and infantry guns.[62] He stressed the importance of conducting detailed reconnaissance and taking the troops through full-scale rehearsals. Ludendorff, impressed with *Sturmbataillon Rohr*, ordered stormtrooper battalions to teach their methods to the entire army, resulting in a large-scale training program, and every field army had a storm battalion.[63]

The German Army formed numerous specialized stormtrooper units, often modeled on *Sturmbataillon Rohr*, designed to destroy strong points such as machine gun posts. The 2nd Pioneer Company attacked French trenches at Schratzmannle on the Western Front in October 1915, using flamethrowers, hand grenades and trench mortars to overcome points of resistance.[64] A stormtrooper detachment also successfully attacked French trenches at Hartmannsweilerkopf on 10 January 1916, using combined arms squad tactics.[65] Furthermore, assault troops led the first attack at Verdun using grenades to clear French defenses, and during the battle the Bavarian Life Guards Regiment specialized in rolling up trenches from the flanks and rear.[66] After the battle the Germans resumed a defensive posture on the Western Front but, nevertheless, small-scale attacks continued which enabled stormtroopers to further develop their tactics.[67]

As the stormtroopers originated from a pioneer tradition of fortress-busting, they never possessed a mentality to bypass strong points, and in contradiction to Liddell Hart's mythology and the imagination of maneuver warfare theorists, they were strong point destroyers. Lind and Thiele incorrectly depicted the stormtroopers as masters of 'light infantry' tactics:

> Light infantry offensive tactics usually use infiltration to avoid casualties. Infiltration allows light forces to surprise the enemy and engage him at short distances. In close, light infantry can exploit its small arms skills while denying the enemy effective employment of his superior firepower.[68]

Lind further identified the stormtroopers with light infantry: 'In August 1914, German infantry was all line infantry with the exception of a small number of Jaeger battalions. By the end of the war in 1918, German infantry is virtually all using a form of light infantry tactics.'[69] However, stormtroopers in 1918 used infantry guns and trench mortars to destroy strong points, which excludes their methods from being 'light infantry' tactics.[70]

German *Jägers* originally were indeed light infantry, embodying a tradition of small unit stealth skills learned in forests and mountains and, accordingly, they were normally recruited from hunters and forest-dwellers.[71] However, after 1914 the *Jägers* adapted their small unit tactics, retaining initiative and teamwork, to the challenge of trench warfare, learning pioneer methods and acquiring heavy weapons.[72] For example, Rohr had been a *Jäger* and he incorporated elements of their tradition, mixing it with pioneer skills, when overseeing the conversion of *Jägers* into stormtroopers.[73] Furthermore, Balck's *Jäger* platoon transitioned from light infantry tactics to pioneer methods and his men used grenades and wire-cutters after learning how to assault fortified positions.[74] The *Jägers* ceased being light infantry and Lind failed to understand this transition as stormtroopers did not use stealth to infiltrate through enemy positions — they instead used firepower to create gaps.[75] As such, Captain Jon Hoffman correctly concluded that stormtroopers 'were not light infantry' and 'the storm battalion itself contained support companies of heavy machineguns, trench mortars, flamethrowers, and even horse-drawn artillery!'[76]

Specialized assault troops did participate in the German offensive at Riga on the Eastern Front in 1917. The German High Command wanted to capture Riga and destroy the Russian Twelfth Army and three divisions belonging to Hutier's Eighth Army assaulted across the Dvina River on

1 September. Lieutenant Colonel Georg Bruchmüller planned the artillery support which envisaged a short but intense 'hurricane bombardment'. This involved a highly centralized fire plan involving different task organized artillery groups implementing detailed plans to suppress Russian infantry and artillery.[77] Bruchmüller's synchronized plan consisted of five phases which would begin with gas attacks followed by high explosive shells in a creeping barrage.[78]

The bombardment commenced at 0400h with gas attacks and two hours later artillery and trench mortars fired high explosive and shrapnel shells on the riverbank opposite the assaulting troops. At 0910h, assault companies armed with flamethrowers, machine guns and grenades crossed the river in boats while trench mortars continued to suppress the defending Russians. After reaching the opposite bank, the attackers launched green rockets to trigger the rolling barrage and, as the advance continued, the attackers used infantry guns to destroy Russian strong points.[79] The surviving Russian troops mostly surrendered or fled, and German engineers quickly constructed pontoon bridges, allowing reinforcements to exploit the gap and Riga soon fell.

The Riga offensive was a complex and meticulously planned operation involving high levels of synchronization, which maneuver warfare theorists normally associate with French methodological battles. In particular, the highly centralized artillery plan contradicted basic maneuver warfare principles as it allowed no room for 'mission tactics'. The offensive witnessed little innovative infantry tactics but its 'hurricane bombardment' method was later used on the Western Front in 1918.[80] Hutier and Bruchmüller did bring their experience to France but the so-called 'Hutier Tactics' of the Anglo-Saxon imagination were completely absent in the complex river crossing assault.

The German infantry, when training for the 1918 offensives, focused on squad-level tactics using combined arms cooperation to quickly destroy machine gun posts. Their training included rehearsals using exact replicas of enemy trenches, complete with barbed wire. In 1917, Ludendorff ordered the creation of a new manual to guide the upcoming offensives and directed all generals commanding armies to contribute ideas. The result, *Attack in Position Warfare*, was drafted by Captain Hermann Geyer with the assistance of Lieutenant Colonel Max Bauer, who had previously helped raise assault battalions.[81] The manual largely reflected Western Front experiences but it also incorporated the 'hurricane bombardment' method from Riga and lessons from the Italian front. *Attack in Position Warfare* called for the elimination of strong points by attacks from the flanks and rear, utilizing surprise and suppression through artillery and machine guns. After the war, Crown Prince Wilhelm, an Army Group Commander during the 1918 offensives, wrote a memoir, *My War Experiences* (1922), and when recalling the new manual, never mentioned 'infiltration tactics' and stressed combined arms cooperation:

> . . . companies, battalions and regiments were trained in the co-operation of infantry with machine-guns, trench-mortars, escort batteries, aircraft and tanks, the use of searchlight and visual signals, the employment of gas and smoke shell, etc.[82]

Contrary to the assertions of Liddell Hart, the new manual never envisaged stormtroopers 'infiltrating' through enemy lines into rear areas in a manner resembling his 'expanding torrent' and Captain Geyer did not invent 'infiltration tactics'.

Ludendorff's plan for the 1918 offensives envisaged a brief artillery barrage using high explosives and gas to suppress defenders followed by a creeping barrage to protect the assaulting infantry, controlled with flares to allow the infantry to determine the pace of the bombardment.[83] It would involve highly synchronized control, as had been the case at Riga, in total contradiction to maneuver warfare principles.

After the 'hurricane bombardment' stormtrooper reconnaissance patrols would move forward, looking for concealed routes to British strong points in order to guide the assault troops toward their objectives. The stormtroopers would then destroy the strong points to allow regular infantry to exploit the gaps.[84] If the first wave of stormtroopers encountered resistance beyond their ability to overcome, the second wave armed with heavy machine guns, trench mortars, infantry guns and flamethrowers would complete the destruction.[85] Stormtrooper tactics did not seek to bypass strong points as their reason for existence was to destroy them.[86] The stormtroopers did not infiltrate through no-man's land into rear areas but instead assaulted strong points from the approach which offered the best tactical advantage.

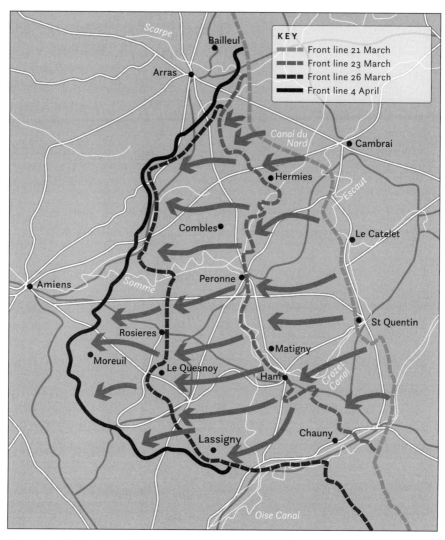

Operation Michael, March 1918

The first German offensive, Operation Michael, commenced on 21 March 1918. The stormtroopers in Hutier's 18th Army had considerable success as the 'hurricane bombardment' successfully suppressed the British machine guns and artillery and heavy fog concealed the attackers.[87] On the first day, the 18th Army broke through the British defensive zone and captured artillery as the British 5th Army retreated, while the 17th and 2nd

Armies failed to break through.[88] The attacking stormtroopers attempted to destroy strong points without any intention of 'infiltrating' into British rear areas, as Paul Kretschmer, a stormtrooper in the 28th Pioneer Battalion, confirmed: 'Then we reached the barbed wire, our objective. But there is nothing for us to do. The wire is completely destroyed.'[89]

On the second day, the British 13th Corps retreated to the Somme, creating a gap in the British 5th Army's line, which Hutier's 18th Army exploited.[90] By 23 March, the 2nd and 17th Armies attacked the British rear-zone and Ludendorff succeeded in creating a 50-mile gap in the British line, which convinced him it was possible to force the British Army toward the English Channel, so he ordered the 2nd and 17th Armies to advance north.[91] Although the Germans succeeded in restoring mobile operations, stormtrooper casualties increased as they no longer could conduct detailed reconnaissance or rehearsals prior to attacks.[92] Stormtroopers advancing into rear areas suffered high death rates as they were no longer protected by their own trenches.[93] Exhaustion, along with British counterattacks, slowed German progress and Ludendorff cancelled Michael on 5 April.[94]

The other German offensives of 1918 — Georgette, Blücher, Gneisenau and Marne — achieved less success and during these battles the British suffered 177,739 casualties, the French 77,000 and the Germans 250,000, making them just as attritional as other battles on the Western Front despite increased mobility.[95]

After the war, General Wilhelm Balck, Hermann Balck's father, wrote *Development of Tactics — World War* (1922), which never mentioned 'infiltration tactics' and unsurprisingly emphasized combined arms cooperation:

Success of the attack does not lie in the number of infantry units inserted, but in the manner of artillery preparation and the immediate utilization of the moral impression created by our fire effect and in the use of the auxiliary arms (machine guns, light minenwerfers [trench mortars], flame throwers and accompanying guns) that accompany the infantry.[96]

Wilhelm Balck explained that shock squads created gaps in enemy defenses by rolling up hostile trenches and overrunning machine guns and pillboxes.[97] Instead of avoiding strong points, he stressed that shock troops 'should be

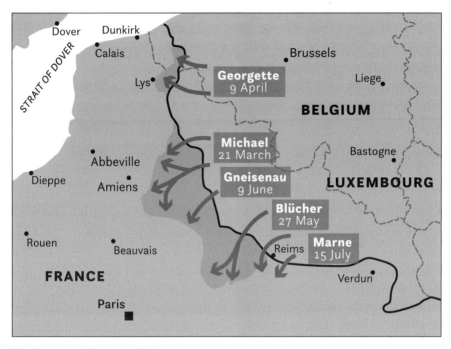

The German offensives of 1918

placed at points where the strongest hostile resistance is expected'.[98] In other words, stormtroopers did not follow the path of least resistance, in contradiction to the mythology of Liddell Hart and maneuver warfare.

Hermann Balck, like his father, attributed stormtrooper tactical success to combined arms cooperation. As a *Jäger* company commander in April 1918, he received orders to attack, not bypass, a strong point because 'Mount Kemmel lay threateningly on the right flank of the German attack, dominating for quite a long distance the flat lands to the north and south'.[99] On 25 April Balck's attack succeeded due to combined arms cooperation: 'At 0400 the gas attack began. . . At 0620 our trench mortars started to fire. . . At 0703 hours I could clearly observe our zone. As a single man the battalion rose and stormed forward.'[100]

Balck criticized stormtrooper tactics because they were actually forbidden from advancing into rear areas: 'we had exceeded the day's objective by one kilometer. That was strictly prohibited because we had advanced beyond the range of our own artillery.'[101] He explained that his unit failed to exploit the

A German *minenwerfer* team during World War I
(Author's Collection)

gap it created after capturing Mount Kemmel, which allowed the French 3rd Cavalry Division to close the gap:

> If we had taken advantage of the great tactical success we had gained, and had used it for a push northward toward Poperinge, we would have gotten into the rear of the Allied forces there. Pushed against the sea, they would have been totally destroyed.[102]

Haunted by this wasted opportunity, Balck wrote an article on Mount Kemmel in the *Militär-Wochenblatt* in 1935 and this memory later became a decisive factor during the French campaign in May 1940, after he captured the French bunkers defending Sedan:

> The enemy was gone and there was a huge gap in his lines. I thought back to Mount Kemmel, where we had achieved a similar great success, but no senior leadership had been at the point to follow through to a victory. It was my great good luck that I was allowed to lead at a point where I had

seen others in the First World War fail so critically. I walked off a distance, thought about it, and made a decision. We had to advance another ten kilometers into the enemy.[103]

In other words, Balck's success in France was inspired by the failure of stormtrooper tactics to think beyond strong point capture — a far cry from the myth of mechanized 'infiltration tactics'.

The non-existence of 'infiltration tactics' critically undermines the maneuver warfare principle of 'surfaces and gaps' as stormtrooper attacks never resembled Liddell Hart's 'expanding torrent'. As Balck had been a stormtrooper and his father had written an authoritative book on German tactics, his testimony cannot be ignored, but this is precisely what Boyd and Lind did.

BETRAYAL OF DESTRUCTION AND CREATION

John Boyd's paper *Destruction and Creation* (1976) outlines his intellectual methodology, which underpins the O–O–D–A loop and maneuver warfare, by explaining how the human mind forms mental concepts by synthesizing information. In this framework, any mental concept which does not reflect reality will inevitably contradict observed experience and a new, more accurate concept will replace it through a process of destruction and creation. Therefore, when faced with a situation that challenges a preconceived notion, the logic of destruction and creation necessitates re-evaluation as Boyd argued:

> . . . this does not necessarily mean we reject and throw away the entire structure. Instead, we should attempt to identify those ideas (particulars) and interactions that seem to hold together in a coherent pattern of activity as distinguished from those ideas that do not seem to fit in.[104]

Following this logic, Boyd continued, 'Over and over again, this cycle of Destruction and Creation is repeated until we demonstrate internal consistency and match-up with reality.'[105] However, this process is never-ending as mental concepts can never truly reflect reality; therefore, there is always room for improvement as 'a concept must be incomplete since we depend upon an ever-changing array of observations to shape or formulate it'.[106]

Destruction and Creation is the basis of the O–O–D–A loop because the winner in a 'decision cycle' contest will be able to form better mental concepts by more effectively applying the logic of destruction and creation to acquire a better sense of reality, while the actions of the loser will increasingly fail to reflect what is actually going on in a changing situation.

The principal lesson of *Destruction and Creation* is to embrace ideas that challenge preconceptions as they offer the opportunity to destroy mistaken concepts and replace them with a better understanding of reality:

> . . . we can expect unexplained and disturbing ambiguities, uncertainties, anomalies, or apparent inconsistencies to emerge more and more often. . . Fortunately, there is a way out. Remember, as previously shown, we can forge a new concept by applying the destructive deduction and creative induction mental operations.[107]

The avoidance of dogma is central to Boyd's philosophy and failure to apply the logic of destruction and creation results in a closed inward-looking system 'talking to itself'.[108]

Destruction and Creation had been inspired by three key scientific ideas. First, Kurt Gödel's principle that one cannot determine the true nature of a system from within itself as this is only possible from the vantage point of another system. Second, Werner Heisenberg's uncertainty principle which warned that observers change the nature of systems, which limits the extent of what can actually be known with precision. Third, the second law of thermodynamics which states all processes create entropy and individuals working within closed systems are subjected to increased internal confusion and disorder. Boyd explained that these three concepts form a single grand idea: 'Taken together, these three notions support the idea that any inward-oriented and continued effort to improve the match-up of concept with observed reality will only increase the degree of mismatch.'[109] In other words, the observer can never be sure their perceptions of reality are accurate and must constantly break down their observations and rebuild them in accordance with the logic of destruction and creation — otherwise they risk their survival as they will make decisions based on inaccurate perspectives.

Boyd had also been heavily influenced by Thomas Kuhn's *The Structure of Scientific Revolutions* (1962) which argued that 'normal science' operates within a paradigm until anomalies are detected, and when the paradigm cannot be modified to account for them, a crisis arises, triggering a scientific revolution and a new paradigm. For example, in the sixteenth century Copernicus realized that astronomical anomalies could not be explained within the Ptolemaic earth-centered paradigm, resulting in the Copernican revolution and the emergence of the new heliocentric sun-centered paradigm.[110] In this way, Boyd warned that any paradigm could be subjected to confusing anomalies as mismatches with reality are bound to occur.

Boyd is frequently depicted by his acolytes as maintaining high intellectual standards. For example, Franklin Spinney declared that he 'set a standard for integrity seldom equaled in this age of flexible ethics. He's going to be a tough act to follow.'[111] Spinney attributed Boyd's success to his uncompromising application of Destruction and Creation:

> . . . his uninhibited imagination was tightly coupled to a maniacal discipline to follow the truth wherever it might lead — even if it meant trashing his own creations. Boyd subjected each new synthetic analogy to rigorous analysis and testing, rolling it over and over in his mind, checking it obsessively for internal consistency as well as its matchup to reality.[112]

As such, Boyd never finished *Patterns of Conflict* as he always altered its content with improved insights.[113] He spent twenty years refining the briefing, later renamed *A Discourse on Winning and Losing*, as Grant Hammond from the Air War College explained: 'It was a discourse, a conversation, refined over and over again through nineteen different versions, and it was never quite right. It was always tentative.'[114] Apart from *Destruction and Creation*, Boyd never published written words because doing so fixes ideas and allows for the possibility of dogma.

In reality, Boyd never lived up to the standards expressed in *Destruction and Creation*, as his biographer Robert Coram revealed:

> [Boyd] expected those who disagreed [with him] to come around to his viewpoint — and quickly. If someone belittled his ideas, they were instantly

and forever dismissed from his life. They ceased to exist. He never spoke to them again.[115]

Boyd's inability to deal with conflicting information became all too apparent after he encountered Mellenthin and Balck.

Mellenthin's statements at the armored warfare conference on destroying the Red Army completely contradicted Boyd's understanding of how the *Wehrmacht* operated, which had deep implications as it exposed a fundamental flaw in maneuver warfare. He should have used Mellenthin's testimony as an opportunity to revise his assumptions and modify his theories in accordance with the logic of *Destruction and Creation*, as an anomaly emerged which the paradigm of maneuver warfare could not account for, but he instead ignored this evidence. Boyd's source list for *Patterns of Conflict* included the report from the armored warfare conference, which contained a transcript of Mellenthin's words, but Boyd's final briefing slides insisted that the *Wehrmacht* avoided attrition (destruction) in order to paralyze and collapse its opponents even though strong evidence suggested this was not the case.[116]

The transcripts of the Balck interviews also appeared in Boyd's source list, but in *Patterns of Conflict* he inaccurately referred to Balck as a practitioner of maneuver warfare by selectively quoting his comments on decentralized leadership while ignoring his association of *Blitzkrieg* with the destructive principles of the Cannae ideal.[117] Boyd included the report from the NATO conference in his source list so he certainly read Balck's testimony denying the existence of stormtrooper 'infiltration tactics'. The source list also included Wilhelm Balck's *Development of Tactics* so Boyd knew that German stormtroopers attacked 'at points where the strongest hostile resistance is expected'. However, the final version of the *Patterns of Conflict* slides claimed that German stormtroopers used 'infiltration tactics' and followed the path of least resistance despite authoritative and compelling evidence that these concepts were completely alien to German military history, which should have triggered the destruction of the maneuver warfare paradigm and the search for a new paradigm which better reflects reality.[118]

Boyd took his source list for *Patterns of Conflict* extremely seriously, as his acolyte James Burton explained: 'Those of us on the telephone net had to read most of them, some more than once.'[119] He added:

Boyd's favorite time for talking about the publications in this list, as well as his ideas and theories, was during the middle of the night. In order to delve into this brilliant mind, Boyd's friends had to be willing not only to read all of these books and articles but also require a limited amount of sleep.[120]

Therefore, it is inconceivable that Boyd casually read his sources and never noticed the critical anomalies.

Lind similarly failed to reconcile the contractions he encountered with his pre-conceptions. He commented on Mellenthin's testimony at the armored warfare conference in his *Maneuver Warfare Handbook*:

The discussion is valuable because it addresses a number of specific questions such as night combat, resupply, communications and reconnaissance. However, the value is greatly enhanced if the reader is well familiar with the basics of maneuver warfare beforehand; this should not be the first thing on your reading list.[121]

Lind implied that Mellenthin embraced maneuver warfare ideals but failed to mention that he repeatedly rejected the essence of the theory at the conference. Lind also commented on the Balck interviews in *Maneuver Warfare Handbook*:

The Balck interviews are particularly useful; General Balck was probably the finest tank tactician of World War II, and his insights on the nature of tank warfare against the Russians cannot be overvalued. . . They show how theory turns into practice — the hardest task maneuver warfare presents to Marines.[122]

Furthermore, Lind referred to Balck as 'one of the most successful practitioners of maneuver warfare'.[123] This is a strange comment as Balck used forward command when 'mission tactics' failed, synchronized operations in person and via radio, insisted that the *Wehrmacht* followed the destructive logic of Cannae and denied that stormtroopers used 'infiltration tactics'.

In another key statement, Lind referred to stormtrooper tactics as 'the basis of modern maneuver warfare tactics' and claimed that the stormtroopers represented 'maneuver warfare's full conceptual development'.[124] Lind's source for this bold comment is 'a dinner conversation with General Hermann Balck'.[125] However, there is no genuine evidence that Balck ever uttered such ideas which certainly contradict his earlier comments. Like Boyd, Lind failed to mention that Balck denied the existence of 'infiltration tactics' and refused to explore how this observation critically undermined maneuver warfare, even though he was certainly aware of Balck's testimony.

Boyd and Lind's refusal to update and modify their ideas after encountering inconvenient information, or even to acknowledge its existence, can bring their integrity into question as others have done regarding different issues. Lind had earlier been accused of dishonesty by Major F.G. Sanford in the *Marine Corps Gazette* after he refused to correct an error:

> In a June 1984 GAZETTE article Lind lashed out at AWS [Amphibious Warfare School] for administering a 1983 'final exam in tactics' that queried potential combat leaders on such inane issues as the type of stove to be used in the 10-man tent and the basic ski technique for down hill movement. Rebuttals in the September 1984 GAZETTE explained that there were no final tactical exams at AWS. Tactics evaluations were continuous and involved substantial subjective problem solving evolutions. Despite irrefutable evidence to the contrary, Lind repeated his educational denunciation one year later in his book.[126]

Marshall Michel, an Air Force officer, similarly accused Boyd of making dishonest claims:

> Boyd's self-aggrandizing characteristics are clear in his oral history. One example is his claim to have written a textbook on philosophy used at the Air Force Academy and a textbook in engineering used at the University of California, Berkeley. There is no evidence these books ever existed.[127]

As Boyd and Lind ignored damning evidence, maneuver warfare according to the logic of *Destruction and Creation* is a dogmatic system 'talking to itself'.

Nobody noticed this problematic issue because when the reports containing the critical testimony were published, they were difficult to obtain even for American officers.[128] Therefore, few people initially had the opportunity to scrutinize these sources, making their highly selective use of this material difficult to detect. Furthermore, casual readers would not understand the implications of the problematic testimony as a deep appreciation of maneuver warfare is required. Therefore, nobody joined the dots and challenged Boyd and Lind's dubious insistence that the *Wehrmacht*, and Balck in particular, practiced maneuver warfare.

Boyd's dialectic process of destruction and creation intended to break ideas or concepts into their component parts, reject what is useless or untrue, and use the new material to construct a better concept more in tune with reality — his 'snowmobile' allegory. However, Boyd in practice injected the fraud of others into his synthesis and failed to separate history from deceit because he refused to follow his own advice and embrace the anomalies.

Boyd's failure to apply the O–O–D–A loop process highlights the central flaw of his 'decision cycle' theory. Boyd assumed that competing cycles inherently bring a mind closer to reality through the logic of destruction and creation. Therefore, relative speed is the key as the faster thinker will gain 'decision cycle' superiority. However, it never occurred to him that accuracy is just as important as speed. There is little point completing cycles if dubious data is obtained and analyzed through deficient mental processes, as this will result in a greater disconnect from reality — as happened with Boyd's personal O–O–D–A loop when creating *Patterns of Conflict*. In fact, his mind was closer to reality in 1975 before he analyzed military history because he had not yet exposed his mind to vast amounts of misinformation. Therefore, a slower but more accurate O–O–D–A loop is preferable to fast and mentally lazy cycles.

Before Mellenthin and Balck visited America, Boyd and Lind had been victims of misinformation spread by former German officers and Liddell Hart, but after refusing to deal with problematic evidence by engaging in genuine historical inquiry, they remained in the fantasy world of their closed system, which is evident in their views on the operational level of war.

CHAPTER SEVEN
MANEUVER WARFARE AND OPERATIONAL ART

SOVIET OPERATIONAL ART

In the 1830s, the Napoleon-era theorist Antoine-Henri Jomini spoke of 'grand tactics' — a level between tactics and strategy. Tactics is the art of winning battles while strategy is the high-level employment of national resources to achieve state goals which involves diplomacy, economics and industrial planning. As political leaders at the strategic level define military objectives, soldiers at the tactical level attempt to translate tactical success into strategic victory. Jomini's 'grand tactics' is the intermediate level in which campaigns — sequences of battles — are planned which better determine how tactical actions can serve a strategic purpose.[1]

The Red Army moved beyond 'grand tactics' by first articulating the operational level of war in the aftermath of the Russian Civil War (1918–21). During this revolutionary time, Bolshevik military theorists felt liberated from the perceived conservatism of imperialist armies, encouraging creative thinking and an iconoclastic attitude to established concepts.[2] The Russian Civil War involved mobile armies fighting on multiple fronts across vast expanses of great depth and the Red Army conducted rapid strategic redeployments and deep cavalry raids in rear areas.[3] Given the massive scale of the conflict, the idea of winning the war through a single decisive battle had no meaning.[4]

The Russian Civil War, 1918–21

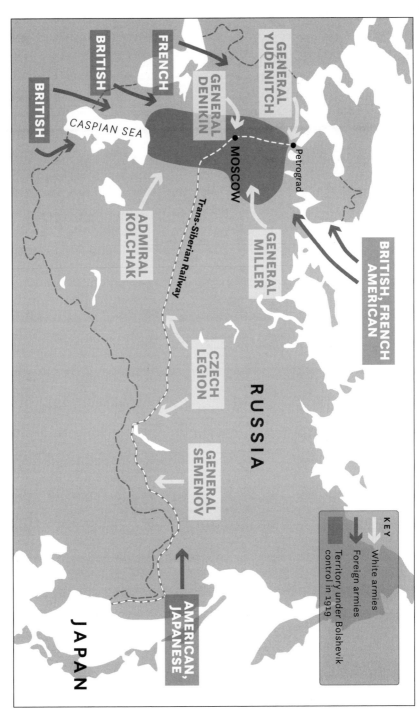

CASPIAN SEA

BRITISH

BRITISH

FRENCH

GENERAL
YUDENITCH

GENERAL
DENIKIN

MOSCOW

Petrograd

ADMIRAL
KOLCHAK

Trans-Siberian Railway

GENERAL
MILLER

BRITISH, FRENCH
AMERICAN

CZECH
LEGION

R U S S I A

GENERAL
SEMENOV

J A P A N

AMERICAN,
JAPANESE

KEY

White armies

Foreign armies

Territory under Bolshevik
control in 1919

After the war in 1926, Aleksandr Svechin, a leading Red Army theorist, spoke of the 'operational level' connecting tactics and strategy and 'operational art' which linked battles together in a series of operations: 'Tactics make the steps from which operational leaps are assembled; strategy points out the path.'[5] According to Svechin, operations are normally lengthy and involve numerous interrelated battles:

> Only in very infrequent cases can one rely on achieving the ultimate goal of combat operations in a single battle. Normally this path to the ultimate goal is broken down into a series of operations separated by more or less lengthy pauses.[6]

Therefore, operational art aims to conduct battles in a systematic manner through successive operations to ultimately achieve strategic victory.

Soviet operational art developed into 'deep battle' theory under Georgii Isserson, a Red Army officer, who argued that although sound tactics can propel a force through enemy defenses, such an act serves no purpose unless an operational breakthrough is achieved. In his view, the German 1918 offensives solved the riddle of the trenches but failed to capture a strategically important objective.[7] Isserson accordingly advocated using tanks to smash enemy defenses at the tactical level followed by 'deep battle' in which separate breakthrough echelons would exploit the initial tactical success and strike at the enemy's operational depth.[8] He also developed the idea of a 'shock army' to enable operational breakthroughs.[9]

The Red Army's field regulations of 1929 spoke of 'deep battle' involving tanks, artillery and aircraft organized in shock groups, which would break through the front line, allowing highly mobile armored forces to advance deep into the enemy rear. The mobile tank groups aimed to annihilate retreating troops and destroy enemy reserves.[10]

Mikhail Tukhachevsky, a Red Army officer who commanded the Western Front during the Russo–Polish War (1919–20), expanded the 'deep battle' concept by advocating 'deep operations' centered on massed tank and combined arms formations, striking deep into the rear to encircle and destroy enemy armies. Tukhachevsky shared Svechin's operational-level thinking:

The nature of modern weapons and modern battle is such that it is impossible to destroy the enemy's manpower by one blow in a one-day battle. Battle in modern operations stretches out into a series of battles not only along the front but also in depth until that time when either the enemy has been struck by a final annihilating blow or the offensive forces are exhausted.[11]

Tukhachevsky advocated a unified campaign plan to coordinate sequential battles and 'deep operations' became Red Army doctrine in 1936.

Robert Leonhard in *The Art of Maneuver* argued that maneuver warfare is comprised of German and Soviet schools and, as such, 'deep operations' is a Soviet variant of the theory. He claimed that Red Army maneuver warfare under Tukhachevsky's guidance 'evolved in the thirties' but 'died in the Purges' only to be 'reborn in the face of the German onslaught' and it subsequently co-opted many elements of *Blitzkrieg*.[12] Leonhard distinguished Red Army maneuver warfare through its command and control as 'mission-type orders (*Auftragstaktik*) was never feasible given the political nature of the Soviet military'.[13] Leonhard continued that Soviet commanders display 'imagination, flexibility, and dash' when planning but once an operation commences they become inflexible as 'there is great pressure upon the Soviet commanders to conform to the plan'.[14] Richard Simpkin also discussed Soviet maneuver warfare in *Race to the Swift* when commenting on 'deep operations': 'The Soviet model is the only one in existence at the moment, and at theoretical level it is better developed and documented than any other version of manoeuvre theory in history.'[15]

The Red Army, however, never practiced anything akin to maneuver warfare. Svechin's operational art embraced the heretical concept of 'attrition', automatically excluding his ideas from the theory.[16] Tukhachevsky's 'deep operations' sought the destruction of enemy armies and, as General David Zabecki concluded, he was 'the champion of the "annihilation" school of Soviet military thought'.[17] Red Army 'deep operations' envisaged massive firepower to enable operational breakthroughs with the goal of destroying enemy reserves. For example, the Red Army's *Instructions on Deep Battle* (1935) declared: 'Deep battle is battle with the massive use of new mobile and shock forces for the simultaneous attack of the enemy to the entire depth of his combat formation with the aim of fully encircling and destroying him.'[18] Tukhachevsky's belief in destruction prevents 'deep operations' from being Soviet maneuver warfare as it contradicts the essence of the theory. Furthermore, the theorists largely ignored the Red Army's sophisticated ideas on operational art, in preference to shallow *Wehrmacht* operational concepts, and the American military accordingly learned the wrong lessons from poor teachers.

WEHRMACHT OPERATIONAL ART

The United States Army 'discovered' the operational level during the 1970s. General Donn Starry believed that narrow tactical focus contributed to defeat in Vietnam and, therefore, an operational focus would better translate tactical success into strategic victory.[19] General William DePuy, to his credit, noted his operational shortcomings:

> You only see the things you've been doing well, not the big mistakes you've made. When I was commanding the 1st Division [in Vietnam], I was totally preoccupied with trying to find the 9th VC [Viet Cong] Division and the other main-force elements in my area. I was deficient at the next level up — the operational level.[20]

Starry first made the operational-level doctrine in FM 100-5 *Operations* (1982), and FM 100-5 *Operations* (1986) further developed operational thinking by defining operational art.

The 'discovery' of the operational level was concurrent with the Army's embrace of maneuver warfare concepts, which was not coincidental as John Boyd and William S. Lind championed operational thinking. Lind's critique of Active Defense centered on DePuy's assumption that if the Red Army invaded Western Europe, the first battle had to be won, which did not consider the possibility of a second battle. Lind in contrast stressed the importance of winning the overall campaign, potentially involving numerous battles.

To apply maneuver warfare at the operational level, Lind used the *Wehrmacht* as a model of operational excellence as 'the Germans were consistently superior to their opponents at the tactical and operational' levels.[21] Lind accordingly recommended Erich von Manstein's *Lost Victories* as a guide to operational thinking:

> Memoirs of accomplished practitioners of the operational art are also valuable. One of the best is Field Marshal Erich von Manstein's *Lost Victories*. You could do worse than taking the advice one Army general gave the officers of his division: 'Read this book once a year for 30 years.'[22]

The historian Martin van Creveld, a maneuver warfare convert, similarly concluded: 'by dint of a superb performance on the tactical and operational levels, the *Wehrmacht* achieved some triumphs so great, and so unexpected, that they have become almost legendary'.[23]

Lind and van Creveld uncritically accepted the postwar self-assessment of German veterans who depicted themselves as masters of operational art and conveniently explained away their defeat as resulting from Hitler's 'amateur' misuse of their genius. For example, Franz Halder argued in *Hitler as Warlord*:

> The man [Hitler], to whom the artistry of a modern General Staff map was a complete mystery, believed that he was living up to his role of a great military leader by interfering from his Headquarters, hundreds of miles behind the Eastern Front, in the movement of single Divisions, and by deciding tactical details which could only be judged aright by the commander on the spot.[24]

Manstein in *Lost Victories* similarly spoke of futile attempts to educate Hitler:

> On one side we had the conceptions of a dictator who believed in the power of his will not only to nail down his armies wherever they might be but even to hold the enemy at bay. . . On the other side stood the views of military leaders who by virtue of their education and training still firmly believed that warfare was an *art* in which clarity of appreciation and boldness of decision constituted the essential elements.[25]

Friedrich von Mellenthin in *German Generals of World War II* blamed Hitler for the *Wehrmacht*'s operational shortcomings as he 'had no eye for the necessary relationship between the setting of operational objectives and available forces'.[26]

Hermann Balck in *Order in Chaos*, in contrast, spoke well of Hitler's operational abilities but condemned his faith in willpower:

> Operationally, Hitler had a clear and one might even say an exceptional understanding. He combined this with a rare ability to influence men. He was incapable, however, of judging what could be accomplished with the available forces and when the correlation of forces was completely against him. He believed that he could bridge any gaps with his iron will.[27]

Balck blamed Hitler and Halder equally for failing to work together:

> The General Staff and Hitler had opposing views on the conduct of the war. Each brought to the table what the other lacked. They could have complemented each other so well. That they did not come together was part of the German tragedy.[28]

The *Wehrmacht* in reality performed poorly at the operational level. For example, Operation Barbarossa, the German invasion of Russia, demonstrated shallow operational planning as it envisaged three army groups simultaneously advancing toward three different objectives — Leningrad, Moscow and Kiev — which dissipated strength.[29] Therefore, Barbarossa, as Israeli military theorist Shimon Naveh concluded, 'was flawed and indicated deep operational ignorance'.[30]

Hitler was not solely responsible for this weakness as he did not articulate Barbarossa's operational vision, as this was the responsibility of Halder and the General Staff.[31] Manstein ironically condemned Hitler's strategic-level Barbarossa Directive for not providing sufficient operational guidance as 'this "formula" could never replace an operations plan'.[32] Therefore, Manstein bizarrely condemns Hitler for 'interfering' in operational matters while simultaneously complaining that he failed to provide sufficient operational detail — a ridiculous argument. Nevertheless, Hitler cannot be solely blamed

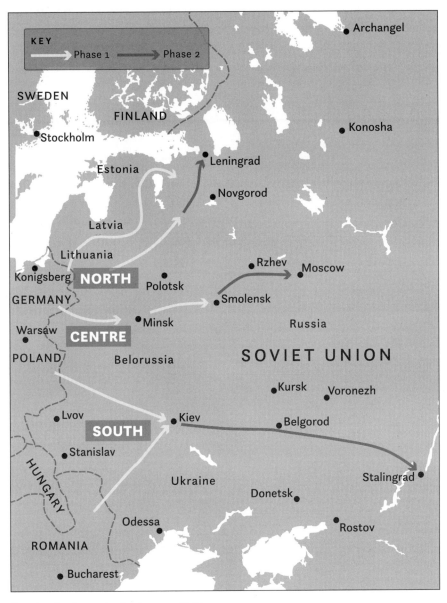

The plan for Operation Barbarossa, 1941

for Barbarossa's flaws and Heinz Guderian in *Panzer Leader* rightly criticized the General Staff's operational deficiencies:

> Three army groups, each of approximately the same strength, were to attack with diverging objectives; no single clear operational objective seemed to be envisaged. Looked at from a professional point of view this did not appear at all promising. I arranged for my Chief of Staff to convey my views to the OKH [Army High Command], where they produced absolutely no effect.[33]

Halder in *The German Campaign in Russia*, written for the US Army and not intended for public release, acknowledged his failure: 'Halder then summarized the instructions issued to the three army groups in the operation order. . . [Hitler] added that he had no basic objection to the Army's operation plan as presented by Halder.'[34]

The *Wehrmacht*'s deficient operational planning in part resulted from a poor intelligence system. The Germans erroneously believed the Soviets had 10,000 tanks when in fact they had over 20,000.[35] The General Staff also believed the Red Army could mobilize only 300 divisions but by December 1941 it had raised around 600 divisions.[36] Furthermore, the *Wehrmacht*'s operational planning methods failed to properly use intelligence, as historian Geoffrey Megargee explained:

> The role of intelligence was to determine what the Wehrmacht would face when it carried out the plan of campaign, rather than to shape that plan to best advantage: in other words, the planners drew up the plan first, then tried to figure out the enemy's situation and intentions.[37]

Megargee also explained that *Wehrmacht* logistics planning suffered from the same flaw as 'planners created the scheme of maneuver first, then called in the (more junior) supply officers and told them to make sure the supplies got through'.[38]

Once Barbarossa commenced, the *Wehrmacht*'s logistics system struggled to support units in the field as its supply and transportation systems deteriorated.[39] The vast distances of the Soviet Union had not been factored into logistics planning, as Halder later admitted: 'During the planning stage the vastness of the Russian theater had not been fully taken into consideration.'[40] This had severe consequences because German soldiers found themselves unprepared for the Russian winter toward the end of 1941.

Poor operational planning also plagued the *Wehrmacht* in North Africa. Rommel's initial orders instructed him to secure the southern flank of the Axis by propping up the Italian position in Libya, but he instead advanced toward Egypt and overextended his *Afrika Korps*.[41] Rommel's leadership style in the desert mirrored his command of the 7th Panzer Division in France — forward presence on the battlefield and tactical excellence. However, this style was not appropriate in North Africa — a strategic theatre of vast distances — and he became fixated on tactical issues at a narrow portion of the front and, in doing so, lost operational control.[42] Rommel fought and won several remarkable battles but failed as an operational commander, as Colonel James Robinson concluded:

> Rommel came to North Africa, fought countless battles over two years, shaped his legend, but achieved no enduring political goals. In all this, he never met the challenges of operational art and never blended time, space, means and purpose. Rommel fought battles, but never determined why. . . By any measure of success at the operational level of war, Rommel failed.[43]

Rommel hinted at his lack of operational focus in a letter to his wife on 8 April 1941, 'I've no idea whether the date is right. We've been attacking for days now in the endless desert and have lost all idea of space or time.'[44] Halder noted the Desert Fox's shortcomings in his diary:

> Rommel is not up to his operational task. All day long he rushes about between the widely scattered units and stages reconnaissance raids in which he fritters away his forces. No one has a clear picture of their disposition and striking power.[45]

Gerd von Rundstedt after the war criticized Rommel's operational ability: 'He was a brave man, and a very capable commander in small operations, but not really qualified for high command.'[46]

The *Wehrmacht* failed to master operational art largely because the concept went against the grain of Prussian military thinking. As the dilemma of German geography encouraged a search for rapid operations and avoiding two front wars, German military thinkers dreamed of rapidly defeating the most vulnerable enemy before swiftly redeploying forces to counter the next threat. This line of thought found full expression in Schlieffen's Cannae ideal, which sought the 'perfect battle' of annihilation to achieve rapid victory.

The Cannae obsession demonstrated poor operational thinking as it narrowly focused on winning one 'decisive battle' at the tactical level. The Germans also ignored the bigger operational picture of the Second Punic War — despite Hannibal's victory at Cannae the Romans won the war.[47] After Cannae, Hannibal lacked sufficient logistics to march on Rome and the means of conducting a successful siege; he had no plan to defeat the Romans who continued to resist despite suffering a comprehensive defeat.[48] Hannibal failed to translate his battlefield victory into a victorious war and, as historian Karl-Heinz Frieser explained, 'Cannae was only a passing operational success by Hannibal over Rome, the strategically superior sea power.'[49]

Schlieffen's Cannae ideal elevated a tactical formula to the operational level without considering the difficulties of executing the vision on a larger scale.[50] Balck acknowledged the Cannae delusion after the war in a rare instance of genuine *Wehrmacht* self-examination:

> After Cannae, Hannibal did not march on to Rome, which caused his cavalry commander Marhabal to exclaim, 'Vincere scis, Hannibal, victoria uti nescis. [You know how to gain a victory, Hannibal, but you do not know how to make use of it.]' Did Hannibal lack military leadership greatness, or did he correctly know the limits of his power? He probably was right because he was vulnerable in human resources and space. Both of these factors were on the side of Rome, as well as decisive maritime dominance. Germany also achieved legendary victories but in the end succumbed to the human factor, space, and maritime domination, all of which were clearly on the side of Russia. Unfortunately, we did not have the sense of proportion and reality, like the great Carthaginian.[51]

The *Wehrmacht* never excelled at operational art because its leaders convinced themselves they had to win rapidly or not at all. German commanders accordingly could not embrace the idea of fighting many battles across great depth linked into numerous campaigns without first admitting the unfeasibility of rapid knockout blows. Therefore, German operational thinking never made a clean break with tactics, as Bruce Condell and David Zabecki concluded:

> The idea of winning a war through a single decisive battle is a purely tactical notion. It is the very antithesis of operational art and the operational level of war, for which sequential operations and cumulative effects are the keys. . . . Thus, many historians have argued that what passed for operational art in the German Army was really little more than tactics on a very large scale.[52]

The *Wehrmacht* in Russia did not look beyond encirclement and annihilation battles and, as its forces moved deeper into Russia, they became overextended and exhausted without securing victory.[53] Even the disaster at Stalingrad did not alter the German mindset, as Shimon Naveh concluded: 'when the Russians deliberately offered the Germans the Kursk Bulge, the tactical urge for encirclement reappeared, and against all possible logical thinking led the Germans to commit operational suicide'.[54]

Although the German Army won spectacular tactical victories, its lack of operational perspective and strategic bankruptcy failed to translate its initial success into a victorious war. Despite a tradition of poor operational planning, the *Wehrmacht* is commonly viewed as the model of operational excellence and the Red Army, which invented operational art, is not seen this way. This misunderstanding is attributable in part to the actions of the Soviet State.

MISUNDERSTANDING THE RED ARMY

The Red Army lost its operational excellence before Barbarossa only to regain it through painful experience after the German invasion. During Stalin's great purge of the Red Army, Tukhachevsky was executed on 12 June 1937 and Svechin on 29 July 1938 while Isserson spent fourteen years in gulags. As the purges continued, Red Army soldiers fought in the Spanish Civil War and attempts to conduct mechanized offensives around Madrid failed.[55] After Dmitry Pavlov, who commanded a tank brigade in Spain, returned home in 1938, he argued that 'deep operations' had failed due to the superiority of defensive war caused by technological advances and terrain, and accordingly argued against massed tank formations in favor of using tanks as infantry support weapons.[56]

Tukhachevsky's murder and the Spanish Civil War signaled the end of 'deep operations'. Soviet authorities banned the Red Army from engaging in theoretical work on operational art and its key books.[57] The great purge destroyed the 'shock army' concept and Red Army tanks became infantry support vehicles.[58] Therefore, on the eve of Barbarossa the Red Army possessed 1,000 modern T-34 medium tanks and 500 KV-1 heavy tanks but they were not concentrated in armored units.[59] The great purge transformed the Red Army from a modern innovative force into a slow, inflexible mass army.[60]

The Germans had a low opinion of the Red Army before Barbarossa due to the purge and its poor performance in Finland during the Winter War (1939–40). After the German invasion, the Red Army's initial poor performance also resulted from inexperienced officers engaging German combat veterans.[61] The Soviet High Command abandoned its large pre-war units in favor of creating simpler units that less experienced officers could control, and this decision ended any possibility of resurrecting 'deep operations' as the newly mobilized units, out of necessity, were an interim force designed to stop the German advance.[62]

The Soviets could not initiate 'deep operations' until they recovered from the invasion, and after the *Wehrmacht* culminated in late 1942, the Soviets resurrected operational principles and force structures. The Red Army unleashed their new tank armies at Kursk in July 1943, creating an operational penetration of 75 miles into German lines in five days. After Kursk, Red Army operations began resembling Tukhachevsky's vision.[63]

Operation Bagration demonstrated Soviet operational excellence. The Red Army planned an offensive along a 450-mile front against the *Wehrmacht*'s Army Group Center, involving four army fronts, designed to encircle German forces near Minsk. The Soviet deception plan convinced the Germans that the coming offensive would be in the Ukraine through the use of dummy positions and fake signals, which diverted the 56th Panzer Corps south, leaving Army Group Center with only 11 percent of German armor on the Eastern Front.[64] On 23 June 1944, the offensive began and the Red Army surrounded Minsk, resulting in 350,000 German casualties, effectively destroying Army Group Center.

The Red Army recovered from the German invasion and became the greatest practitioner of operational art, as Shimon Naveh noted: 'The last two years of the war saw a succession of strategic-operational manoeuvres, which have no equal in scope, intensity and creativity in the history of modern war.'[65] Nevertheless, given the Red Army's initial incompetence, many *Wehrmacht* officers did not understand the resurrection of Soviet operational art, viewing Red Army victories as resulting from seemingly limitless manpower reserves. As such, German Eastern Front accounts normally portray themselves as having been defeated by a less skilled enemy, as historian David Glantz explained:

> We have gazed in awe at the exploits of those Germans who later wrote their personal apologies, and in doing so we have forgotten the larger truth: their nation lost the war — and lost it primarily in the east against what they portrayed as the 'artless' Soviets.[66]

Many former *Wehrmacht* officers did, however, acknowledge superior Red Army leadership at the strategic level. For example, the Halder manuscript *Russian Combat Methods in World War II* stated: 'The higher echelons of Russian command proved capable from the very beginning of the war and learned a great deal more during its course. They were flexible, full of initiative, and energetic.'[67] Nevertheless, the manuscript credits the *Wehrmacht* for 'teaching' operational art to the Soviets, who supposedly mimicked German techniques: 'The way operations were launched and carried out revealed the influence of German methods on the Soviet high command.'[68]

Manstein, failing to understand 'deep operations', similarly praised high-level Soviet leadership while insisting they copied the *Wehrmacht*:

> Although the enemy had possessed large numbers of tanks as early as

1941, he had not known then how to use them as individual members of a united whole. By now he had them properly organized in his tank and mechanized corps and had also taken over the German technique of penetration in depth.[69]

Liddell Hart in *The German Generals Talk* endorsed Rundstedt's claim that Marshal Zhukov's skill reflected German influence:

I asked Rundstedt which were the best of the Russian generals in his experience. He replied: 'None were any good in 1941. . . But in later years there is no doubt of the improvement in their generalship. Zhukov was very good. It is interesting to recall that he first studied strategy in Germany under General von Seeckt — this was about 1921–23.'[70]

The postwar German accounts fail to understand that the Red Army's operational excellence reflected its own concepts. Balck, however, acknowledged that the Red Army counter-offensive during the winter of 1942–43 'was well planned, well prepared, and brilliantly executed'.[71] He added, 'I also underestimated the Russians considerably.'[72] Balck recognized superior Soviet operational art in relation to Stalingrad without claiming German influence:

You had to hand it to the Russians. Their leadership at the strategic-operational level was excellent. They had managed together with the Anglo-Americans in North Africa to launch a major offensive in two decisive locations at the same time. Hats off to their clear vision, consistency, and organizational talent.[73]

Boyd in contrast dismissed Soviet operational art and embraced the myth of *Wehrmacht* operational excellence, believing the Germans taught the Red Army about speed and tempo: 'Where the hell did they [the Russians] get that? Because they got their head handed to them by the first part of the blitzkrieg, they didn't have it before World War II.'[74] Boyd, as Major Ian Brown concluded, insisted 'the Germans were superior at the operational and tactical level of winning battles; and the Russians' only real strength in war came from a large population that was used as cannon fodder'.[75]

Although the maneuver warfare theorists correctly champion the operational level, their understanding of operational art contains deep flaws due to their belief in *Wehrmacht* operational superiority. Therefore, their contribution to operational art would accordingly be just as flawed as their superficial understanding of German operations.

THE CENTER OF GRAVITY

In attempting to apply maneuver warfare at the operational level, the theorists made the same mistake as the *Wehrmacht* in seeking short cuts to secure rapid victories. The root cause of this failure was Boyd's reinterpretation of the Clausewitzian idea of 'center of gravity'. Clausewitz in *On War* used the term 'center of gravity' several times, most notably:

> . . . one must keep the dominant characteristics of both belligerents in mind. Out of these characteristics a certain center of gravity develops, the hub of all power and movement, on which everything depends. That is the point against which all our energies should be directed.[76]

What Clausewitz meant by 'center of gravity' is commonly believed to be the enemy's 'strength' or 'source of strength', and he also noted, 'A center of gravity is always found where the mass is concentrated most densely. It presents the most effective target for a blow.'[77]

Boyd viewed Clausewitz's 'center of gravity' as a siren's call encouraging commanders to deliberately attack strength with strength in order to destroy armies. He accordingly redefined the term under the influence of J.F.C. Fuller and Liddell Hart, who advocated avoiding battle and striking directly at vulnerable 'nerve centers' to paralyze the enemy:

> Clausewitz incorrectly stated: 'A center of gravity is always found where the mass is concentrated most densely' — then argued that this is the place where the blows must be aimed and where the decision should be reached. He failed to develop [the] idea of generating many non-cooperative centers of gravity by striking at those vulnerable, yet critical, tendons, connections, and activities that permit a larger system to exist.[78]

A portrait of Carl
von Clausewitz, by Karl
Wilhelm Wach
(Contributor: ART Collection/Alamy
Stock Photo)

In other words, Boyd believed an enemy force can be collapsed by attacking multiple 'critical vulnerabilities' to generate paralysis.

Lind made Boyd's 'center of gravity' concept the central pillar of maneuver warfare operational art: 'The operational art is the art of using tactical events — battles and refusals to give battle — to strike directly at an enemy's strategic center of gravity.'[79] Robert Leonhard in *Art of Maneuver* similarly defined 'center of gravity' as 'critical vulnerabilities' which should be attacked to paralyze the enemy army.[80] Therefore, he shared Boyd's vision of attacking 'nerve centers' to bring about systematic collapse:

> . . . maneuver theory defines the center of gravity as the enemy's critical vulnerability — that aspect of the enemy whose neutralization causes paralysis within the enemy force. After disruption occurs, the enemy is typically unwilling or unable to fight.[81]

After Vietnam, the US Army 'discovered' Clausewitz's 'center of gravity' concept, making it an essential element of its approach to operational art, but it understood the idea through Boyd's interpretation and accepted his belief that enemy strength can be undermined through indirect attacks against 'critical vulnerabilities'.[82] For example, Huba Wass de Czege, who drafted the AirLand Battle, said, 'Genius finds and uses the line of least expectation and least resistance to the enemy's center of gravity by way of an unguarded vulnerability.'[83] The same trend exists in the Marine Corps as *Warfighting*, heavily influenced by Boyd, declared that a 'critical vulnerability is a pathway to attacking a center of gravity'.[84]

Maneuver warfare operational art, by focusing on 'critical vulnerabilities', was the latest incarnation of Liddell Hart's eternally elusive quest to find an Achilles heel. In *Strategy*, he insisted that in all circumstances an 'indirect approach' can be found to rapidly defeat an enemy without excessive bloodshed. Boyd similarly taught that an enemy can always be defeated by striking at 'critical vulnerabilities' to produce a swift collapse with minimal fighting. Of course, selective examples in history can be found of rapid and unexpected victories but it is dangerous to assume that this will always be possible and even more reckless to focus operational-level planning exclusively on this assumption. The scholar Adam Elkus accordingly warned that for 'every lightning campaign like the 1940 German conquest of France, there are ten campaigns that swiftly degenerated into slugging matches'.[85]

The problem with the maneuver warfare understanding of 'center of gravity' is that in most cases targetable 'critical vulnerabilities' don't exist. Colonel Mark Cancian, a Marine officer, explained why this is the case:

> These concepts may be good in theory, but they rarely exist in the real world in a way useful for military planners. . . the problem is that centers of gravity and critical vulnerabilities just are not there. In addition, their pursuit often overpromises what a campaign can achieve and can distract from more limited, but achievable, objectives.[86]

To illustrate this point, Cancian considered the Battle of Tarawa in 1943: 'Japanese capabilities had to be destroyed piece by piece. There was no point so vulnerable that its destruction would produce the collapse of resistance

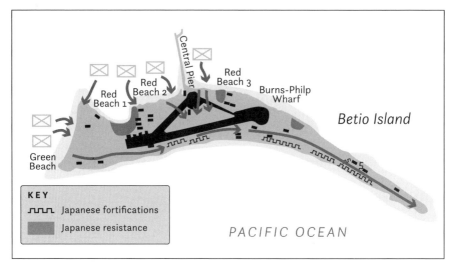

The Battle of Tarawa, November 1943

. . . there was nothing that could be termed a critical enemy vulnerability.'[87] Boyd even acknowledged that 'critical vulnerabilities' can rarely be targeted, which contradicted the heart of his teaching:

> If you go after something that's vulnerable, a critical vulnerability, he [the enemy] probably knows it is too. So therefore, he's going to put a lot of forces there. Now you've got strength going against strength. In other words, you've got Verdun. . . So it's sometimes better to exploit the weakness. As a result, you can get to the vulnerability.[88]

Boyd conceded that 'critical vulnerabilities' are likely to be well-protected and instead advocated locating and exploiting weakness in order to expose a 'critical vulnerability'. To achieve this he recommended probing the entire front through multiple thrusts in a manner resembling the 'expanding torrent' to locate weak points.[89] However, probing the entire front to locate weak points which *might* expose a 'critical vulnerability' is an appeal to hope because in most cases the enemy will defend pathways to 'critical vulnerabilities'. Therefore, Boyd's advice cannot be the general basis for operations because attacking weak points will likely be a road to nowhere.

Maneuver warfare operational art is largely an empty promise because its 'center of gravity' concept is useless unless targetable 'critical vulnerabilities' can be found. Furthermore, even when 'critical vulnerabilities' can be attacked, collapse does not necessarily result because enemies adapt, as Cancian explained:

> Army and Air Force doctrine regard networks as vulnerabilities — knock out one node and the whole network may collapse. The problem is that networks, by definition, have many paths leading to the same end. So it is with military activities. If a bridge at point A is destroyed, then the enemy will use the bridge at B, or the ford at C, or the ferry at D, or repair the bridge.[90]

The notion that enemies can always be rapidly defeated through the 'indirect approach' or maneuver warfare is delusional, as the scholar Eliot Cohen concluded, 'When two comparable military powers fight, much blood will flow. To think otherwise, as Hart and Lind do, is to indulge in fantasy, and dangerous fantasy.'[91] Major Craig Tucker, a Marine officer, made a similar point:

> In the entire history of warfare there is no credence to the illusion that an enemy's cohesion can always be shattered by rapid thought and action and that once shattered his remnants will always be defeated with relative ease. Those opportunities do present themselves but their occurrence is rare and determined not by the illusion of method perpetuated by Hart, Lind, and FMFM-1 [Warfighting] but by a confluence of circumstances that can be exploited but cannot be created.[92]

Maneuver warfare operational art encourages planners to search for an elusive defeat mechanism which rarely exists and, as Cancian warned, 'Where such vulnerabilities are not evident, they will manufacture them.'[93] Operational planning has been undermined by enormous amounts of wasted time spent arguing over what constitutes an enemy 'center of gravity' without any tangible advantage being gained through the long process.[94] In contrast to such useless processes, Cancian concluded that operational art does not need 'centers of gravity' and 'critical vulnerabilities' as campaigns should focus on gaining advantages through sequential actions:

> In the Falklands Campaign of 1982, the British struck many Argentine points. Their naval campaign quickly swept the Argentine Navy from the sea. Their air campaign held the Argentine Air Force at bay. Their ground campaign reduced the outlying Argentine outposts, pushed the Argentines into the capital, then cracked the main line of resistance, finally forcing surrender. It is hard to see this campaign as a strike at a center of gravity or at a critical vulnerability. What one does see is a classic joint campaign, each move of which sets up the subsequent move.[95]

Ironically what Clausewitz meant by 'center of gravity', according to Antulio Echevarria, from the United States Army War College, was something quite different from what Boyd interpreted due to imperfect translation, which created a 'false impression' that centers of gravity are sources of strength.[96] Clausewitz's term, as Echevarria explained, is better understood by thinking of the relationship between gravity and balance:

> In general, a center of gravity represents the point where the forces of gravity can be said to converge within an object, the spot at which the object's weight is balanced in all directions. Striking at or otherwise upsetting the center of gravity can cause the object to lose its balance, or equilibrium, and fall to the ground.[97]

Therefore, Echevarria defined 'center of gravity' as a 'focal point' which 'exerts a certain centripetal force that tends to hold an entire system or structure together'. He added, 'a blow at the center of gravity would throw an enemy off balance or even cause the entire system (or structure) to collapse'.[98] As such, the maneuver warfare theorists misunderstood a key term in German military thinking.

In Clausewitz's original German 'center of gravity' is *Schwerpunkt*, which is best translated as 'weight of effort' or 'focus of effort', but maneuver warfare defines this term as 'main effort'.[99] To Clausewitz, the *Schwerpunkt* is a strategic concept which can be the enemy's army, capital, alliance or public opinion.[100] Schlieffen redefined *Schwerpunkt* as an operational term to mean 'decisive point', a location where a local action can achieve a decisive victory.[101] The historian Karl-Heinz Frieser explained the genuine operational meaning of *Schwerpunkt*: 'The important thing each time was to convert the enemy's absolute strategic superiority into one's own relative operational superiority at the decisive point.'[102] Following this logic, the *Schwerpunkt* during the German invasion of France was the Ardennes because defeating the weak French forces in this sector could generate a wider defeat by cutting off the Allied armies in the Low Countries.[103]

The maneuver warfare theorists are in error when they define 'center of gravity' and 'main effort' as two different concepts because there is a difference between a unit *being* the main effort and a unit being *at* the decisive point. This confusion originated from Boyd who attempted to define *Schwerpunkt* in both ways when discussing the Ardennes:

> So the schwerpunkt wasn't set because the unit was set, because that sector would give them a weakness they could exploit. So the schwerpunkt was set in that sector, and once it's set there, the units then are part of that schwerpunkt. So don't just designate a unit. You want to look at the sector you're looking at. And you say, okay. This is the area I want to do it because they're weak here. And then those units become the schwerpunkt to go through there.[104]

To add to the confusion, Boyd also stated, 'I notice in some of the Marine documents, you say you designate a unit as being the schwerpunkt or focus of effort. You may do that. You may not.'[105] No wonder his acolytes struggled to consistently define *Schwerpunkt*! Lieutenant Colonel Mark Hamilton correctly observed: 'Ask three US officers to define the term *Schwerpunkt*. You will get three different answers. Or ask one maneuver warfare advocate to define *Schwerpunkt*. You will still get three answers.'[106]

Maneuver warfare undermined operational art by misunderstanding the 'center of gravity' concept, but the theorists further corrupted operational thinking, creating greater confusion, by retrospectively imposing their concepts on *Wehrmacht* operations.

THE KIEV CONTROVERSY

A notable historical issue generated by German postwar accounts is the Kiev controversy. During Barbarossa, Hitler detached Guderian's Second Panzer Army from Army Group Center and diverted it to the Ukraine to support Army Group South's efforts to annihilate Red Army forces near Kiev to secure the Ukraine's vast economic resources. On 19 September 1941, the *Wehrmacht* eliminated the Kiev Pocket, but Hitler's decision generated fierce controversy.

Halder strongly disagreed with Hitler's decision, believing that Guderian should have been allowed to advance toward Moscow since threatening the capital would have drawn out the Red Army's last reserves, creating an opportunity to destroy them.[107] Therefore, Hitler's decision to encircle Kiev was a 'crucial mistake' which lost Germany the 'opportunity of knocking the Russians out of the war' before the onset of winter.[108] Guderian in *Panzer Leader* made a similar claim:

Moscow was the great Russian road, rail and communications centre: it was the political solar plexus; it was an important industrial area; and its capture would not only have an enormous psychological effect on the Russian people but on the whole of the rest of the world as well . . . I tried to show [Hitler] how a victory in this decisive direction, and the consequent destruction of the enemy's main forces, would make the capture of the Ukrainian industrial area an easier undertaking.[109]

Manstein in *Lost Victories* strongly argued that Hitler's decision went against military logic as capturing Moscow 'would split the Russian defences in two and prevent the Soviet command from ever mounting a single, co-ordinated operation'.[110]

Despite the postwar criticism, Hitler's order to send Guderian's panzers into the Ukraine was a sound military decision because an advance on Moscow before the elimination of the Kiev Pocket would have been unwise as Army Group Center first needed to secure its southern flank. As historian Alan Clark argued, Hitler's decision was correct 'because military orthodoxy suggested the salients had to be eliminated to secure the flanks before further advances could be made'.[111] David Glantz agreed as the Kiev operation

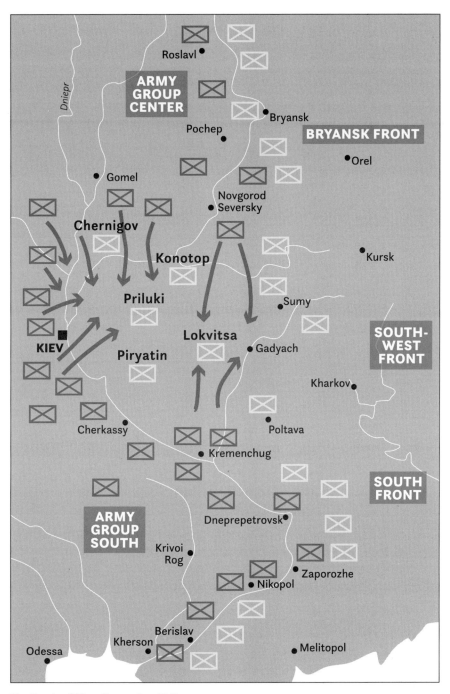

The Battle of Kiev, September 1941

'eliminated four armies and over 600,000 men that, had they not been destroyed, would have threatened Army Group Center's extended right flank as it advanced on Moscow'.[112]

Professor Russel Stolfi from the Naval Postgraduate School, and a Marine reserve officer, rekindled the Kiev controversy with a novel maneuver warfare argument in *Hitler's Panzers East* (1992). Stolfi understood the fall of France through the prism of Boyd's 'decision cycle' theory:

> The term *psychological equilibrium* conveys the idea that the French opposite the German *Schwerpunkt* army were thrown off balance psychologically by the unexpected pace of the Germans and the accompanying casualties and damage. The French command lost its capability to react to German moves, and French troops were overwhelmed.[113]

Following this logic, Stolfi argued that Germany almost lost the campaign because, after the *Wehrmacht* crossed the Meuse, Kleist ordered Guderian's panzers to halt, but he ignored this order and kept advancing.[114] Stolfi speculated that if Guderian had halted, the Germans would have ceased being inside the French 'decision cycle': 'The French had lost the war by the evening of 15 May 1940. Kleist by his single, discrete decision offered them the opportunity to rise from the operational death and pack forces around Germans held in the Meuse bridgehead.'[115] In other words, once the Germans got inside the French 'decision cycle', the French could do nothing to reverse their impending defeat, but a German blunder could have given them an opportunity to recover.

Stolfi applied this logic to Barbarossa by claiming the *Wehrmacht* quickly got inside the Red Army's 'decision cycle': 'In the first hours of the campaign, Soviet command and control broke down.'[116] Therefore, the Germans could not lose as long as they maintained this advantage as 'only a German mistake of the highest magnitude could thwart victory'.[117] Stolfi accordingly argued that the Red Army could do nothing to alter the situation because 'the Soviets had no control over their own destiny'.[118] However, Hitler's Kiev decision ended German 'decision cycle' superiority and allowed the Red Army to recover, but if Guderian's advance to Moscow had been allowed:

. . . the Red Army would have been destroyed and Soviet mobilization terminated by the German advance, leading to a revisionist view that the Germans would have defeated Soviet Russia by the end of October 1941. By the magnitude of the victory and its timing, the Germans would have won the war in Europe.[119]

To Stolfi, Moscow constituted a 'critical vulnerability' as its loss would have paralyzed the Soviet Union: 'Moscow was the communications and transportation plexus of European Russia and the core of an area accounting for more than 18 percent of the industrial production of the Soviet Union.'[120] Stolfi concluded that Barbarossa was 'a race on the part of the Germans into Soviet mobilization space. . . to paralyze the arming and organizing of the additional 4.1 million Soviet troops'.[121]

The postwar German accounts heavily influenced Stolfi's high opinion of the *Wehrmacht* and he uncritically praised Halder's professionalism, viewing him as someone 'whose competence can scarcely be doubted'.[122] He believed Barbarossa was a sound operational plan and rejected any notion that the *Wehrmacht* underestimated the Red Army while planning the invasion.[123] Stolfi freely admitted that his argument was based on one-sided sources: 'The greatest potential for bias in the results probably lies in my conscious decision to concentrate on German documentation to support conclusions about the summer of 1941.'[124]

Hitler's Panzers East contains numerous dubious sources which Stolfi uncritically uses, including Halder's *The German Campaign in Russia and Decisions Affecting the Campaign in Russia*, the Halder manuscripts *Combat in the East* and *Small Unit Actions during the German Campaign in Russia* as well as Guderian's *Panzer Leader*, Manstein's *Lost Victories* and Liddell Hart's *History of the Second World War*. Therefore, Stolfi simply repackaged postwar *Wehrmacht* mythology related to the Kiev controversy, which he interpreted through the prism of maneuver warfare dogma.[125]

Richard Hooker, editor of *Maneuver Warfare: An Anthology*, similarly argued that Hitler's Kiev decision 'robbed the *Wehrmacht* of a victory that would have changed the world for generations'.[126] Hooker's claim centered upon a maneuver warfare understanding of operational art as he also viewed Moscow as a critical vulnerability which represented 'the true center of gravity of the Soviet defense'.[127] He added that without the central railway hub at Moscow, the Red Army could not have shifted strategic reserves into European Russian fronts, making effective operations west of the Volga River impossible.[128] Hooker concluded, 'In correctly assessing the true Soviet center of gravity and how to destroy it, the German military and its leaders gave Hitler the key to victory'.[129]

Hooker's thesis, like *Hitler's Panzers East*, is built on postwar *Wehrmacht* myths and repeats much of the misinformation contained in the accounts of former German officers. For example, he declared, 'leading German commanders were astounded at Hitler's decision to invade Russia'.[130] However, in reality Halder drafted the first invasion plan, Operation Otto, before Hitler issued his Barbarossa Directive. Hooker's views are not surprising given his sources and his uncritical acceptance of their accounts. He unsurprisingly praised German operational-level planning:

> If it is true that Hitler's strategic fumbling, not German operational and tactical failures, saved Russia in 1941, then much of the history of the Second World War must be viewed in a new light. Had Germany succeeded in knocking Russia out of the war in a lightning two-month campaign, after overrunning the rest of the continent from the Arctic circle to the tip of Greece, the virtues of the German operational method could not have been denied.[131]

The Stolfi-Hooker thesis that a German capture of Moscow before winter would have won them the war is unconvincing. The Red Army had contingency plans to continue the war without Moscow and the Soviet railway system would still have connected the non-European theatres with the industrial base in the Urals. Allied lend lease would have supplemented Soviet industry in the Urals and compensated for the loss of Moscow's industry as Red Army soldiers fighting from the Urals would have been supplied with lend lease through Persia.[132] After the war, Halder conceded that Soviet resistance could have been sustained from the Urals:

> In the event that all territory west of the Volga was seized by the Germans, the Soviet armament potential would be greatly weakened without

necessarily collapsing. A complete economic breakdown of the Soviet system was not to be expected unless the industrial area of the Urals was occupied by the Germans.[133]

Furthermore, even if Moscow fell the Red Army could have brought great pressure to bear on Army Group Center's bulge as historian Dennis Showalter concluded:

> It is an overlooked paradox that the failure to reach Moscow may have averted a German catastrophe. . . Army Group Center would be forward-loaded at the far end of a long salient vulnerable to systematic counterattacks, containing a tenuous supply line exposed to constant harassment from a developing partisan movement.[134]

After writing *Panzer Leader*, Guderian, the central figure in the Kiev controversy, later doubted that Germany could have defeated Russia in 1941, in complete contradiction to the Stolfi-Hooker thesis: 'As a rule the outcome of military operations is hard to foresee, and this is particularly the case in Russia. No plan, however well conceived, can be relied upon to ensure the success of a "blitz war" in this country.'[135] Balck similarly changed his mind after the war:

> When we advanced on Moscow, the general opinion, including my own, was that if we take Moscow the war will be ended. Looking back in the light of my subsequent experience, it now seems clear that it simply would have been the beginning of a new war. The Russians would have switched from modern warfare to the most primitive and ancient means of warfare. After all, they had plenty of room to run all the way back into the vastness of Siberia, and they could have started a partisan war that would have cost us such large forces that our invasion would not have succeeded.[136]

Stolfi and Hooker superimposed maneuver warfare concepts, formulated in the 1970s and alien to *Wehrmacht* commanders, onto historical events in direct contradiction of the evidence. They argued that the capture of Moscow would have paralyzed the Soviet Union while in contrast German generals believed that *threatening* Moscow would have committed the bulk of the Red Army and its last reserves into a final Cannae-style battle of annihilation. The Germans wanted to force the Red Army into a situation where it could be defeated in the field and, as such, the true value of Moscow lay not in the flow on effects of its capture but in creating the conditions of a super Cannae.

As the primary purpose of maneuver warfare is to avoid battles of destruction by exploiting 'critical vulnerabilities', German plans for Moscow have little in common with the theory. For example, after the war Halder said: 'according to all available intelligence the bulk of the Russian forces were massed in front of Moscow. Their destruction and the seizure of the Russian capital were therefore the primary objectives for the German Army.'[137] Manstein in *Lost Victories* also prioritized the destruction of the Red Army over targeting 'critical vulnerabilities':

> By seizing these territories [the Donetz Basin and Caucasus oilfields] he [Hitler] hoped to cripple the Soviet war economy completely. O.K.H. [Army High Command], on the other hand, rightly contended that the conquest and retention of these undoubtedly important strategic areas depended on first defeating the Red Army. The main body of the latter, they argued, would be met on the road to *Moscow*.[138]

General Hermann Hoth agreed with this logic as Hitler's Kiev 'decision violated the principle that the destruction of the Russian field army must precede economic and political war aims'.[139]

These statements by key *Wehrmacht* generals reject maneuver warfare by insisting that 'critical vulnerabilities' should be secured only *after* fighting battles of destruction. Hitler's Kiev decision ironically conforms with maneuver warfare logic as he advocated avoiding the Red Army's expected concentration at Moscow (strength) and instead advocated a surprise attack against the exposed flank of the Red Army in Kiev (weakness) in order to seize the 'critical vulnerability' of the Ukraine's resources. Hitler's thinking clearly mirrored Liddell Hart and Boyd's ideas as he prioritized the capture of strategic resources over destroying enemy armies.[140] However, Stolfi and Hooker were too blinkered by *Wehrmacht* myths to see this truth.

The maneuver warfare theorists rightfully championed the concept of operational art but failed to apply sound operational thinking as their ideas originated from poor *Wehrmacht* operational logic and Liddell Hart's elusive Achilles heel, and these deep flaws would become all too apparent when maneuver warfare moved beyond the theoretical realm and was applied in the real world.

CHAPTER EIGHT
MANEUVER WARFARE AND THE DEFENSE OF NATO

THE VEXING PROBLEM

During the early days of the Cold War, the United States Army planned to defend West Germany through forward defense, hoping to buy time for NATO countries to mobilize their military potential. However, the Americans soon realized that its Seventh Army in Germany could never match the numerical superiority of the Warsaw Pact. Therefore, it sought a means of winning while fighting outnumbered by studying German Eastern Front experiences. Planners who read Franz Halder's manuscripts became convinced that Germany would have won the war if the *Wehrmacht* had not been undermined by Hitler's 'interference' and insane 'no retreat' orders.[1]

As NATO intended to defeat a Soviet invasion using static linear defense, American officers under Halder's influence perceived a parallel between their plan and Hitler's supposed inflexible orders. As linear defense, expressed in FM 100-5 *Operations* (1949), seemed doomed to repeat Hitler's blunder, American planners abandoned it in 1952 and asked Halder to help them develop a new plan by critiquing the existing manual. Halder agreed and explained his motive to other German veterans:

> I have undertaken this task, because I am of the opinion, that with a serious handling of this task, we will be in a position to make an

intellectual contribution to the defensive potential of the West, which no one else can do. I'll also not conceal the fact that the old German General Staff, which is still rejected in public, is at least valued behind the scenes as unparalleled experts.[2]

Halder's critique condemned linear defense and advocated mobile defense, which would allow the Soviets to make deep advances into West Germany but their forces would be cut off and destroyed by counterattacks conducted by highly mobile armored units.[3] The Americans accepted mobile defense as the answer to their dilemma and the Seventh Army in Germany accordingly planned to counter a Red Army invasion using fluid defense.[4]

As the US Army embraced mobile defense, the importance of Halder's manuscripts increased.[5] The Americans also began identifying with the *Wehrmacht* as they envisaged conducting operations similar to German Eastern Front experiences between 1943 and 1945, facing the offensive might of the Red Army.[6] As the Americans lacked experience fighting a long-term defensive campaign, the Halder manuscripts filled this void and shaped the new mobile defense doctrine.[7]

The Army's fascination with the *Wehrmacht* and mobile defense was a short-term affair. In 1954, one year after embracing mobile defense, the Army abandoned the concept in favor of 'Massive Retaliation' — deterrence backed up by tactical nuclear weapons.[8] Consequently, the importance of the Halder manuscripts sharply declined and they were declassified, a clear indication the Americans no longer viewed the *Wehrmacht*'s experience as relevant.[9] The Army lost further interest in the *Wehrmacht* as it focused on waging unconventional wars in Southeast Asia.

After the Vietnam War, the Army refocused on its traditional Cold War role of defending Western Europe against a feared Soviet invasion and it no longer viewed nuclear deterrence as a sole guarantor of security.[10] The Red Army had conducted a massive build-up of conventional strength near Western Europe and Warsaw Pact forces fielded more than twice the number of tanks compared with NATO forces. General Donn Starry, commander of V Corps in West Germany, accordingly noted:

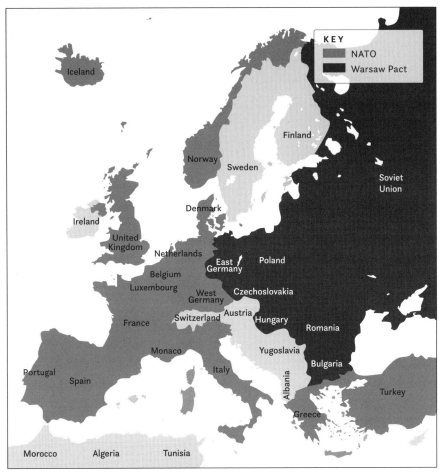

NATO and Warsaw Pact countries during the Cold War, 1975

Historically, we in the US have been wedded to the notion that, to win in battles and so in war, it was necessary simply to outnumber the other side. Therefore the growing conventional strength of Soviet and Soviet surrogate or client state ground forces, especially those arrayed against NATO Europe's Central Region, has been and is a most vexing problem.[11]

General William DePuy's Active Defense concept sought to defeat a Soviet invasion as close to the West German border as possible, which William S. Lind associated with static defense: 'As Guderian, amongst others with

Soviet tanks during a Warsaw Pact exercise in 1973
(Contributor: SPUTNIK/Alamy Stock Photo)

experience, warned, a forward, linear defense is the least advantageous posture when facing a Soviet-style attack.'[12] Lind concluded, 'the Army's approach produces a linear defense. Such a defense would have little or no chance of stopping an opposing thrust by mechanized forces.'[13] Robert Leonhard in *Art of Maneuver* associated Active Defense with Hitler's insanity: 'The forward defense of West Germany. . . begat an operational anomaly, reminiscent of Hitler's irrational "no retreat" orders to the *Wehrmacht*.'[14] As an alternative to Active Defense, Lind proposed maneuver as 'military authorities believe that Germany could have beaten the Soviet Union had the maneuver doctrine not been abandoned after 1941 on Hitler's orders in favor of a policy of holding ground'.[15] Therefore, his concept to defend Western Europe resurrected Halder's vision of mobile defense, but this vision rested upon mythology.

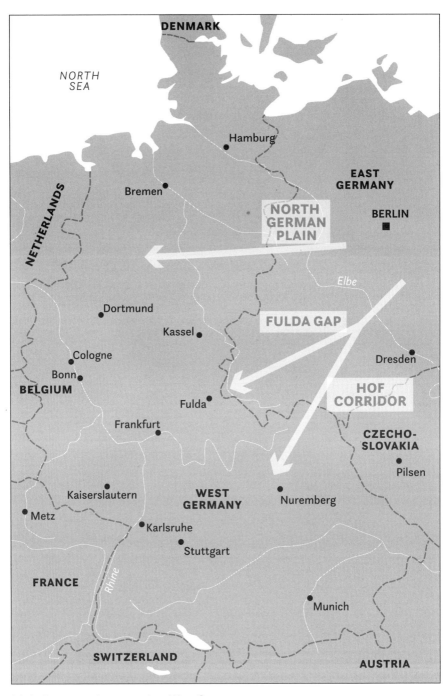

Likely Soviet invasion routes into West Germany

A Sheridan tank from the 11th Armored Cavalry guards the border between East and West Germany in 1979
(Contributor: Hum Images/Alamy Stock Photo)

THE 'SLAVIC' O-O-D-A LOOP

The postwar accounts by former *Wehrmacht* officers portrayed the Red Army as a peasant force comprised of Slavic-Mongol hordes, a myth that did not result from deception but rather ignorance.[16] As German officers held a racist worldview similar to National Socialism, they understood the Red Army through a fatally flawed prism.[17] The Halder manuscripts accordingly contain a mythical view of a primeval 'Slavic' Red Army.[18] For example, *Night Combat* warned about the danger of Russian soldiers due to their animal instincts:

> . . . the Russian soldier demonstrated that he was closer to nature than his west European counterpart. . . From early childhood he had been used to covering long distances across difficult terrain, orienting himself by conspicuous features on the ground, by the stars, and often simply by following his natural instincts. . . His natural cunning as well as his typically Slavic astuteness and cleverness stood him in good stead.[19]

Russian Combat Methods in World War II similarly declared, 'The characteristics of this semi-Asiatic, like those of his vast country, are strange and contradictory.'[20] The manuscript continued:

> The unpredictability of the mood of the Russian soldier and his pronounced herd instinct at times brought on sudden panic in individual units. As inexplicable as the fanatic resistance of some units, was the mystery of their mass flights, or sudden wholesale surrender. . . His emotions drive the Russian into the herd, which gives him strength and courage.[21]

As the Red Army had a 'herd mentality', its offensive actions consisted of nothing more than human wave attacks made possible by the cruel discipline of commissar overlords without any regard for tactical considerations:

> The Russian disdain for life — always present, but infinitely heightened by communism — favored this practice. A Russian attack which had been twice repulsed with unheard of losses would be repeated a third and a fourth time at the same place and in the same fashion.[22]

On the Fighting Qualities of the Russian Soldier went into greater detail about the Red Army's racial worth:

> . . . [in Russians] there can be traced a weak Germanic blood strain from the Gothic period and the Middle Ages. Of special importance, however, I consider the infusion of Mongol blood during the 300 years of Tartar domination, since it very definitely put its stamp on the Russian national character. . . The greatest patience and endurance of suffering, a certain inertness and submissiveness to life and fate, little initiative, and in many of them. . . an easily aroused inclination toward cruelty and harshness which may be considered as part of their Mongol heritage in view of the good-natured disposition of the people.[23]

The Halder manuscripts contain a low opinion of Red Army tactical leadership, as *Night Combat* concluded:

Russian junior officers were accustomed to act in accordance with rigid orders. Upon encountering unexpected resistance they were easily confused and, in the event of a surprise counterattack against the flank of their unit, often helpless.[24]

The same view of Slavic-Mongol hordes is found in the memoirs.[25] Erich von Manstein in *Lost Victories* noted that Red Army commissars possessed 'contempt for human life which had become a principle of this Asiatic Power!'[26] Friedrich von Mellenthin in *Panzer Battles* stated: 'No one belonging to the cultural circle of the West is ever likely to fathom the character and soul of these Asiatics, born and bred on the other side of the European frontiers.'[27] He continued: 'As part of a mob he is full of hatred and utterly cruel, but when alone he can be friendly and generous. These characteristics apply to the Asiatic Russian, the Mongol, the Turkoman, and the Uzbek, as well as to the Slavs west of the Urals.'[28] Despite facing such a 'primitive' enemy, Mellenthin explained the German defeat in terms of overwhelming Russian numbers:

Even in the critical years of 1944–45 our soldiers never had the feeling of being inferior to the Russians — but the weak German forces were like rocks in the ocean, surrounded by endless waves of men and tanks which surged around and finally submerged them.[29]

According to historian David Glantz, *Lost Victories* and *Panzer Battles* 'portray the Red Army as a faceless enemy, an armed host which possessed neither concrete form nor precise features'.[30] He noted, 'That psychological image of the Soviets portrayed in German works has persisted ever since.'[31] Lind fell for this myth based upon his uncritical reading of *Panzer Battles*: 'Mellenthin writes to give present-day soldiers and Marines a feel for the Soviets as opponents, not just to write history.'[32] Colonel Graham Vernon similarly praised the Halder manuscripts and the memoirs in *Military Review* for their assessment of Russian character:

National characteristics or traits tend to reflect the unique history, culture and ideology of a particular nationality. Methods of warfare are, in turn, a function of these national characteristics, and Russian methods of warfare are no exception.[33]

Vernon concluded that the Russian 'Slavic' mentality is their Achilles heel because 'the Soviets had difficulty coping with mobile warfare. It is here that their lack of initiative, herd instinct and vulnerability to surprise found their greatest exposure as Manstein demonstrated in the Kharkov battle.'[34]

Hermann Balck and Mellenthin, when visiting the United States as military consultants, provided advice on how to destroy Red Army tank formations, but their advice had a darker side. During the armored warfare conference in 1979, Mellenthin maintained his mythical view of Slavic-Mongol hordes:

> I am, of course, aware that the Slavs migrated into Russia from the West, and were originally a European people but the Mongol invasion of 1241, and the two centuries of domination which followed, gave an Asiatic twist to the Russian outlook and character, a development accentuated by the policy of the Tsars. There is no way of telling what the Russian will do next; he will tumble from one extreme to the other.[35]

Balck made similar statements at the NATO conference in 1980 when noting that Russians tend to 'fall back into primitive existence' after experiencing setbacks.[36] When asked if the Red Army might have improved its levels of initiative since the war, he responded, 'That won't change.'[37] Mellenthin added, 'Believe us, they are masses and we are individuals. That is the difference between the Russian soldier and the European soldier.'[38] The report on the NATO conference noted Mellenthin and Balck's invaluable 'understanding' of the Russian mentality:

> In World Wars I and II the Germans learned many valuable, if enormously costly, lessons about the Russians as a people with a distinctive cultural heritage, and as soldiers whose military traditions, proclivities and character in battle derive from these same cultural roots. Owing to their intrinsic nature, these same basic traits and broad patterns of behavior would likely find similar expression on any future battlefield.[39]

Mellenthin, Russel Stolfi and E. Sobik, a *Wehrmacht* veteran and *Bundeswehr* intelligence officer, later wrote *NATO Under Attack* (1984), a maneuver warfare solution to the 'vexing problem' of Soviet conventional superiority. They argued that the *Wehrmacht* should be used as a model to defeat the Red Army as 'German defeats on the eastern front were due not to Russian tactical superiority but rather to grave strategic errors by Hitler and Russia's ultimate superiority in manpower and material'.[40] Given this familiar narrative, *NATO Under Attack* unsurprisingly relied upon Halder manuscripts, *Panzer Leader*, *Lost Victories* and *Panzer Battles*. *NATO Under Attack* also depicted the Red Army as an unsophisticated Slavic-Mongol horde, recycling entire paragraphs from *Panzer Battles*:

> In 1943, and indeed throughout the war, the Russian soldier seemed to the Germans temperamentally unstable. They were swept up by a herd instinct, which ill prepared them to tolerate the sudden reversal from a triumphal advance to a precipitous retreat. . . Manstein demonstrated that Russian mass attacks must be met with maneuver rather than rigid defense to force fluid conditions of combat and exploit the Russians' often displayed temperamental instability.[41]

NATO Under Attack recommended exploiting the Russian 'Slavic' mentality by getting inside their 'decision cycle' using mobile defense because Red Army soldiers were incapable of dealing with unexpected situations due to their lack of initiative: 'Command reaction in the Soviet army, based largely on historical style. . . can be considered slow — deadly slow — and is a powerful numbers-cancelling weakness.'[42] Therefore, *NATO Under Attack* proposed exploiting an imagined vulnerability.

NATO Under Attack concluded that the defense of Western Europe should be modeled on Balck's battles at the Chir River.[43] In December 1942, during the Stalingrad campaign, the Soviet 5th Tank Army launched an offensive across the Chir River and the 1st Tank Corps occupied the collective farm Sovchos 79. On 8 December, Balck's 11th Panzer Division counterattacked into the Soviet rear, destroying 53 tanks, effectively annihilating the 1st Tank Corps. Balck later attacked a Red Army tank force near Nizhna Kalinovski on 19 December, destroying 65 tanks from the 5th Mechanized Corps.

Although Balck won outstanding tactical victories, Mellenthin failed to acknowledge that these battles occurred within a disastrous campaign, as David Glantz contended:

> Mellenthin's work, written without benefit of archival materials, tended to treat tactical cases without fully describing their operational context. . . In it he describes the brilliant operations of that panzer corps [at the Chir River] in fending off assaults by Soviet 5th Tank Army's units. . . Mellenthin only in passing describes the operational disaster that provided a context for these fleeting tactical successes.[44]

Mellenthin had little genuine understanding of the Red Army, as Glantz wrote:

> Mellenthin did not mention (probably because he did not know) that Soviet 1st Tank Corps had been in nearly continuous operation since 19 November and was under strength and worn down when it began its march across the Chir. Similar flaws appear elsewhere in Mellenthin's work, many of which result from a lack of knowledge of opposing Soviet forces or their strengths.[45]

The maneuver warfare theorists happily used Mellenthin's ignorant observations as they conveniently suited their preconceived notions. Michael Wyly, who helped introduce maneuver warfare to the Marine Corps, praised *NATO Under Attack*:

> According to the authors, the Soviets will find it difficult, if not impossible, to achieve the same skill, for creative thought in the Soviet Union is too constrained by a rigid political system to allow revolutionary change. It is this, the authors argue, that we must exploit.[46]

Wyly viewed the recycling of *Panzer Battles* in *NATO Under Attack* as a strength, not a flaw:

> In order to develop a characterization of the Soviet command style and

the Soviet Army, the book draws most heavily on Gen von Mellenthin's experience fighting against the Russians in World War II. Anyone who has read his classic, *Panzer Battles*, will find the characterization familiar, in fact, unchanged.[47]

Richard Simpkin in *Race to the Swift*, when considering the defense of Western Europe, presented the same false hope based on myth:

> . . . lasting weakness stems from Russian character and is compounded by the paranoia that seems to permeate the Marxist-Leninist system from top to bottom. The amount of noise the Soviet Army makes in public about flexibility, initiative and tempo shows how well aware its higher echelons are of weakness in these respects.[48]

The maneuver warfare defense plan depended upon exploiting a mythical Russian vulnerability and accordingly violated a fundamental principle of warfare by grossly underestimating the enemy, as is revealed through analyzing the Red Army's actual tactical performance.

RED ARMY TACTICS

The *Wehrmacht* on the Eastern Front used flexible combined arms techniques with high levels of initiative, demonstrating clear tactical excellence and superiority over the Red Army during the early years of the conflict. A combination of factors explains the Red Army's initial poor performance, notably Stalin's purges and the surprise of the German invasion; however, the Red Army's tactical performance significantly improved as the war continued.

The Red Army, despite the postwar complaints of German generals, did not have unlimited manpower reserves and if it did not improve its tactical performance, it would have run out of soldiers. Stalin, as historian John Mosier concluded, 'could not afford to sustain losses of more than 2:1 without eventually running out of cannon fodder'.[49] Red Army attacks in the later period of the war did not resemble hordes conducting human wave assaults. For example, the Red Army during Operation Bagration in 1944 successfully used combined arms tactics involving infantry attacks supported by specialist tank and combat engineer support.[50]

The maneuver warfare theorists used Eastern Front operations as examples of what a surprise Red Army invasion of NATO might look like, but in doing so they studied the wrong war. To the Soviets, the 'Great Patriotic War' on the Eastern Front was a conflict of necessity, not a war of choice, as they had been the victim of a surprise attack and it took the Red Army over two years to seize the initiative. The Soviet Union logically would only have invaded Western Europe if it believed surprise could be achieved; therefore, such a conflict would have been a war of choice more resembling their surprise invasion of Japanese-controlled Manchuria in 1945 — Operation August Storm.

During August Storm, the Red Army employed sophisticated combined arms tactics with tailored force structures designed to achieve specific missions.[51] The Red Army demonstrated tactical excellence in complete contrast to the myth of a 'herd mentality', as Glantz outlined:

> At every level in every sector, Soviet commanders in Manchuria took great risks, planned bold operations, and executed their plans with abandon. They demonstrated a flexibility exceeding that displayed in earlier operations, not only because of the particular demands in the theater of operations, but also because Soviet military leadership had matured.[52]

Furthermore, the Japanese defenders, like the maneuver warfare theorists, unwisely based their defense plan on German accounts of Red Army human waves and, as Glantz explained, 'fell victim to the false image of Soviet clumsiness projected by the early years of the war — a stereotype that reality had shattered by 1945'.[53] He continued: 'Most surprising to the Japanese was the Soviet commanders' new display of initiative at all levels. Non-existent in 1941 and 1942, that initiative was evident in 1945, and it surprised and confused the Japanese.'[54]

The maneuver warfare mobile defense plan rested upon false hope found in mythology. A Red Army invasion of Western Europe would not have resembled Mellenthin's Mongolian horde and would have echoed August Storm. Furthermore, the Red Army during the 1980s increased

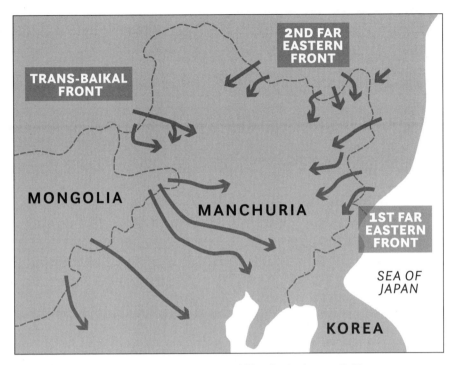

Operation August Storm: the Soviet invasion of Manchuria, August 1945

lower-level initiative as a more flexible approach was required to fight guerrillas in the mountains of Afghanistan.[55] General William DePuy criticized the myth of slow Russian tempo:

> Suffice it to say that they [the Soviets] seek to execute an operation at army level (a big U.S. corps) five to six hours after receipt of orders. Even if it takes them twice as long, say 12 hours, they would not be the slow, sluggish organization we happily describe to ourselves. If we intend to operate inside his decision cycle we have our work cut out for us.[56]

The historical Red Army which executed August Storm is not the same force found in the fantasy world of maneuver warfare, but the theorists also embraced another German myth.

MYTH OF STATIC DEFENSE

The US Army in the 1950s based its mobile defense strategy on the assumption that the *Wehrmacht* had been prevented from fighting in this manner, and therefore from winning the war, through Hitler's inflexible vision of a static war. The Americans believed they could prevail over the Red Army using mobile defense because, unlike their *Wehrmacht* mentors, they would not be handicapped by Hitler's 'interference'.[57] However, Halder's desire to rehabilitate the *Wehrmacht*'s reputation by blaming its defeat on Hitler outweighed the provision of genuine military advice. Therefore, the Americans failed to realize that his advice on mobile defense derived from fantasy.

After the war, former *Wehrmacht* generals complained about being constrained by Hitler's 'no retreat' orders which made it impossible for them to fight cleverly with mobile defense, as Halder argued in *Hitler as Warlord*:

> . . . the military advisers of Hitler in the Army High command all made desperate efforts to guide him along the only path which would avert the serious operational danger in the East, the only path which promised success — the path of flexible operational warfare.[58]

Halder's manuscripts cite numerous examples of Hitler's disastrous 'no retreat' orders. For example, *Improvisations During the Russian Campaign* stated:

> Being aware of the army's numerical inferiority and its loss of combat efficiency caused by heavy casualties, Hitler perhaps doubted its capability of conducting a flexible active defense and therefore ordered all army units to cling rigidly to prepared positions. But such tactics could never prevent an enemy break-through, let alone lead to victory.[59]

Operations of Encircled Forces similarly claimed:

> It was Hitler who originally pronounced: 'I must hold all pockets to the last in order to tie up superior enemy forces as long as possible'. This may be correct in exceptional cases, but can never be elevated to the level of a general principle.[60]

Military Improvisations During the Russian Campaign stated that Hitler's 1944 fortress orders meant that 'many towns suddenly became improvised fortresses and had to suffer encirclement and siege as if they were well-equipped strongholds'.[61]

Manstein in *Lost Victories* complained about Hitler's orders: 'Obstinate defence of every foot of ground gradually became the be all and end all of that leadership.'[62] He concluded: 'Only in mobile operations could the superiority of the German staffs and fighting troops have been turned to account and, perhaps, the forces of the Soviet Union ultimately brought to naught.'[63]

Heinz Guderian in *Panzer Leader* recalled protesting against Hitler's 'no retreat' order during the Russian winter:

> . . . this means taking up positional warfare in an unsuitable terrain, as happened on the Western Front during the First World War. In this case we shall have the same battles of material and the same enormous casualties as then without any hope of winning a decisive victory.[64]

Mellenthin in *Panzer Battles* similarly complained about the impossibility of reasoning with Hitler:

> Hitler rightly said that the Russians 'must lose their breath some time', but what he could not see was the best way to wear them down was to adopt an elastic strategy, and in no circumstances to permit the German armies to be caught in dangerous salients. But it was impossible to argue with the man.[65]

Liddell Hart endorsed these views in *The German Generals Talk* as the *Wehrmacht* veterans all 'felt that Russia's offensive power could have been worn down by elastic defence — If they had only been allowed to practice it.'[66] However, he had a vested interest in championing mobile defense.

After Dunkirk, Liddell Hart's reputation had been shattered because he had argued the superiority of defensive war and predicated the defeat on the German breakout through the Ardennes. However, after the war he claimed the Allied defeat resulted from a failure to apply the 'antidote' to *Blitzkrieg*:

As Guderian stated, in his war memoirs and elsewhere, that he owed his success largely to applying my ideas of tank strategy and tactics — describing himself as my 'disciple and pupil' — I have particularly good reason to gauge how this fatal thrust could have been checked. Having thought out the new method of attack in the nineteen-twenties, it did not require any great effort to discover the antidote well before 1940.[67]

By antidote Liddell Hart meant mobile defense and he claimed that writing *The Defence of Britain* constituted a last minute attempt to warn the Allies about the dangers of *Blitzkrieg*, which could only be countered through mobile defense: 'I devoted most of my effort to the problem of meeting a German offensive in the West, and emphasising the need to develop a new technique of defence capable of checking it.'[68] He continued:

The prime element in such an antidote must, I insisted, be the development of armoured divisions for mobile defence and swift counterstroke. Static defence, however strong, was not enough — in view of the inherent advantage that the attacker enjoys of selecting the spot for his thrust and being able to gain initial surprise.[69]

Liddell Hart made the same claim in a *Marine Corps Gazette* interview, 'I was never an advocate of the Maginot line, or of static defense, but always of mobile defense and counterstroke.'[70] However, before the war in *Europe in Arms*, he had actually advocated a combination of fixed and mobile defense:

By utilizing rivers, canals, and railways as barriers, by demolishing bridges and blocking defiles, the defender may go far to nullify the new menace. Moreover, mechanization itself enables the means of obstruction and demolition to be moved swiftly to any threatened spot.[71]

Therefore, Liddell Hart viewed defense as primarily establishing fixed positions along natural obstacles, supplemented by a mobile force designed to counter specific enemy moves. Furthermore, in *The Defence of Britain* he stressed that defense would be predominantly linear as the 'problem of Belgium turns on the course of the Meuse, and its solution largely depends on the maintenance of the obstacle to an invader that is offered by this great natural moat'.[72] Liddell Hart concluded that a successful German offensive was unlikely: 'If we credit the German Staff with a sense of realities, the possibility of a serious German offensive in the West becomes more than doubtful.'[73]

Nevertheless, Liddell Hart in *Memoirs* explained away the absence of a definitive statement on the superiority of mobile defense in *The Defence of Britain* by claiming that his printed words failed to reflect his true meaning due to impossible time pressure:

> Time was so short that it was not possible to do much more than produce a composition of what I had said in private memoranda and in articles during the past two years. . . But, in trying to foster interest in the possibilities of defence with a better technique, I did not rub in these essential qualifications as hard as I should have done — and might have done if there had been time to go over the proofs more carefully.[74]

This argument is unconvincing as Liddell Hart before the war clearly believed that any German offensive action had little chance of success and was therefore, not preoccupied with an 'antidote' to *Blitzkrieg*; therefore his retrospective claim of an impossible race against time to warn the Allies is sheer fantasy.

Despite the postwar claims of German generals and Liddell Hart, *Wehrmacht* operations on the Eastern Front included mobile defense. Manstein in *Lost Victories* spoke of ignoring Hitler's orders after Stalingrad as he 'acted contrary to Hitler's orders whenever it was absolutely necessary to do so. Success proved me right, and Hitler had to tolerate my disobedience'.[75] Manstein mentioned major retreats on numerous occasions; for example, in August 1943 'Kharkov was abandoned to obtain forces for the two threatened wings of Army Detachment Kempf and prevent its encirclement.'[76] He also noted Hitler's agreement to withdraw east of the Dnieper bend and the Nikopol bridgehead as well as his retrospective approval of the breakout from the Cherkassy pocket.[77] Furthermore, Manstein ignored Hitler's 1944 fortress orders:

> Since 'strongholds' without proper fortifications or adequate garrisons must inevitably fall to the enemy sooner or later without fulfilling their

intended purpose, the Army Group in every case but one contrived to get them abandoned before they were hopelessly surrounded.[78]

Guderian in *Panzer Leader* also cited examples of Hitler authorizing large-scale withdrawals. In reference to the Russian offensive against Army Group South in August 1944, he stated, 'Although Hitler immediately authorised the withdrawal of the Army Group's front, the troops attempted to hold out in places and to carry out a fighting retreat step by step.'[79] Mellenthin in *Panzer Battles* similarly wrote:

> A classic example of a retreat, smoothly and efficiently conducted, occurred in March 1943, when Hitler was persuaded to evacuate the dangerous salient of Vyaz'ma — Rzhev on the front of Army Group Centre. This operation was known by the code name of *Buffalo* and is worth describing in detail; indeed it may serve as a model for staff officers who want to learn the intricate art of withdrawal.[80]

Mellenthin further detailed mobile defense operations in the Ukraine, a method that Hitler supposedly forbade:

> On the whole, the defensive battles in the Western Ukraine were successful because there was no rigid defence line, but an elastic one, which was allowed to bend but not break. For this reason the enemy was never able to wipe out German formations. The junior commanders took advantage of every opportunity to counterattack with a view to destroying as many Russians as possible.[81]

Mellenthin actually blamed occurrences of static defense on local commanders, not Hitler, in relation to the 24th Corps' defensive position near Brussilov which 'broke to pieces in a very short time. Such dispositions must be blamed on local commanders.'[82]

Balck in *Order in Chaos* refused to endorse the myth of Hitler's inflexible orders, giving a more balanced view:

> Hitler never interfered in the operations of my corps. I always had complete

freedom of action. I was allowed to attack, defend, or withdraw as I thought appropriate. In the usual fashion, army and army group allocated the tasks and objectives without ever getting involved in details.[83]

Balck acknowledged inflexible orders given to other *Wehrmacht* commanders but stressed their impact had been exaggerated: 'But not everything that has been said since the war about Hitler's interference is quite true. All too often the personal shortcomings of military leaders at all levels were blamed on Hitler, "the Ignoramus".'[84]

Despite sweeping claims about Hitler's so-called refusal to allow withdrawals and forcing the *Wehrmacht* to fight a static defense, German defensive operations on the Eastern Front were more mobile and less subject to 'interference' than is commonly believed. The complaints of German veterans that they had been forced to fight a purely 'static war' are misleading as Eastern Front combat naturally transitioned between mobile and static operations due to geography, as historian Richard Harrison explained:

> . . . the conflict in the East was in many ways a war of position, in which intense bursts of maneuver warfare alternated with extended periods of inactivity along the front. This was particularly true along such secondary strategic directions as the northern and northwestern, where in many areas the front remained unchanged for more than two years.[85]

Hitler had a preference for fixed defense as a general principle but did not always force his commanders to fight a static war as he allowed withdrawals and tolerated commanders who retreated without permission. Furthermore, the postwar German apologists never acknowledged that in some circumstances fixed defense was wiser than mobile defense given the geographical realities of the Eastern Front, as John Mosier argued:

> In western Europe, when your forces retreated over the hill, they could take up new positions in another ancient and equally durable town and begin the defense all over again. In Russia. . . it was easy to retreat, hard to find a new defensive position, harder still to coordinate the troops into a defensive line.[86]

Fixed defense and mobile defense are both completely valid tactics and shrewd commanders will form a judgment based on context to determine which method best suits their circumstances. Nevertheless, postwar German accounts convinced the US Army of the superiority of mobile defense as a general principle.[87] A belief in the inherent superiority of mobile defense is just as foolish as Hitler's preference for static defense. Yet the maneuver warfare theorists embraced an ideological view of mobile defense based on dishonest German generals and Liddell Hart's fraudulent history, which they applied to the defense of NATO, but their plan was savagely critiqued by none other than Balck and Mellenthin.

BALCK, MELLENTHIN AND THE VEXING PROBLEM

The maneuver warfare theorists advocated mobile defense as the answer to Soviet conventional superiority, which rested on the twin myths of 'Slavic-Mongol hordes' and 'static defense'. They did not simply rely upon postwar German memoirs to justify their solution as Balck and Mellenthin participated in US Army wargames on NATO defensive tactics, and this provided them with 'evidence' to back up their claims.

Mellenthin praised mobile defense as a general principle by re-affirming what he had written two decades earlier in *Panzer Battles* in a paper submitted to the armored warfare conference. For example, he recycled the following from *Panzer Battles*:

> In numbers of divisions the ratio of strength was 8 to 1 in favor of the Russians and these operations showed once again what German troops were able to do when led by experts in accordance with accepted tactical principles, instead of being hampered by Hitler with 'holding at all costs' as the battlecry.[88]

Lind naturally viewed Mellenthin's presence in America as an opportunity to obtain ammunition for his crusade to discredit Active Defense, and during the conference asked:

We see in the defense of the Don, what we might see as an analogy to NATO forward defense, that is to say, the corps far forward trying to hold a line without much in reserve. Could you comment on what lessons you would see from those battles that might be applied to that forward defense situation in NATO today?[89]

Mellenthin's reply naturally condemned 'static defense':

You know, my consequences for the future NATO are: avoid by all means a static defense line, because a static defense line has got terrible weakness and, as a matter of fact, can be broken through everywhere. The only thing, in my opinion, is mobile defense line.[90]

Stolfi similarly asked: 'General, from your experience, which is preferable from the defenders' standpoint — a situation where you must hold the line or a situation where you can be flexible and focus more on destroying the enemy's forces?'[91] Mellenthin again channeled mythology:

Definitely, we had bad experiences with our stubborn holding of lines. Our High Command, Hitler, did not give in one step and sacrificed division after division for this purpose, which is stupid nonsense. The only answer is a flexible defense — the only answer.[92]

Of course, Mellenthin made these statements in the spirit of defending the *Wehrmacht*'s reputation, but he was only talking about 'flexible defense' at the tactical level. When the conference moved beyond general principles and began considering the defense of West Germany in detail, he rejected operational mobile defense.

West Germany, unlike the Russian steppes, contains limited depth and this geographic reality alone makes large-scale mobile defense a poor option to employ there, as Mellenthin well understood. Therefore, as the conference continued, he strongly argued against operational mobile defense in West Germany:

The frontier of the Warsaw Pact area is only approximately 100 miles away from the Rhine. In World War II, Manstein could generously withdraw his troops from the Caucasus and Stalingrad area of a few hundred miles according to plan and launch a great successful counteroffensive in the Kharkov area. NATO cannot afford to give up space on a large scale. . . Today we have a densely populated and highly industrialized area which will become the field of battle; there is no space for a generous free tank battle.[93]

Mellenthin also rejected operational-level mobile defense in West Germany for political and strategic reasons as a retreat to the Rhine might trigger a NATO nuclear strike against the Soviets.[94] Therefore, he rejected operational mobile defense in West Germany given limited depth and the need to integrate conventional strategy with nuclear deterrence — two factors which did not exist on the Russian steppes during World War II.

In May 1980, Balck and Mellenthin participated in a conference and wargame on NATO tactics at the Army War College hosted by the BDM Corporation. DePuy arranged the event 'to examine twentieth century German military experience in battle against Russian forces' in order to develop 'insights useful in aiding our understanding of the challenges NATO faces today in Europe as it prepares to confront the Soviets in any future conflict'.[95]

The activities included a wargame in which Balck and Mellenthin assumed command of the 3rd Armored Division to defend West Germany against a Warsaw Pact invasion in the Hünfeld–Lauterbach–Bad Hersfeld sector of the country, which included the Kassel–Frankfurt Autobahn. Balck and Mellenthin had to deploy the division to defend as close as possible to the East German border to keep the Red Army out of the West German heartland. They were expected to slow the Warsaw Pact advance, locate its main effort and destroy the enemy force as far forward as possible.[96]

Balck and Mellenthin's plan involved deploying three cavalry squadrons as a covering force to screen the battlefield between the border and the main battle position. Two brigades would defend the southern sector, supported by artillery, tactical airpower and attack helicopters with orders to defend the area. They left the north-western sector open to entice the Red Army to commit two tank divisions to advance along the Autobahn toward Alsfeld

William E. DePuy (left) and Friedrich von Mellenthin (right) consider the defense of NATO
(Author's Collection)

and Giessen, hoping to create an operational breakthrough. As these Soviet divisions advanced along the Autobahn, five American battalions would attack their flank just north of Lauterbach and destroy the entire force. After Warsaw Pact forces advanced beyond Alsfeld, a NATO counterattack would strike the rear of the lead enemy division and the vanguard of the next division. This plan applied tactical mobile defense, by only allowing the Red Army to advance over 40 miles into West Germany, and was forward defense at the operational level.

Lieutenant General Paul Gorman independently conducted the same wargame and his solution involved defending the northern sector and deploying a covering force to draw Warsaw Pact forces into a pocket near Fulda, where they would be destroyed in a counterattack from the south. A brigade would defend the sector east of Fulda while two brigades with artillery support would conduct an 'active defense' in the rugged Hohe Rhön region where some ground could be yielded to the Soviets without allowing a significant enemy advance. A large brigade of three tank and one mechanized battalions would form a mobile reserve south of Fulda and would either counterattack the south flank of the Soviet main advance as its vanguard reached the defensive position near Fulda or against the Soviets near Alsfeld, if their main effort approached that region.

Balck and Mellenthin praised Gorman's plan and noted that it conformed with their concept on how to fight the Red Army. DePuy also noted the convergence of American and German operational thinking:

> The similarity between the two concepts — the German and American — was remarkable. In both cases, the larger part of the sector was held by the smallest part of the force. In both cases, the enemy was 'invited in' to a selected avenue or pocket. In both cases, a large reserve was held out for a decisive counterattack. The principal (and only significant) difference lay in the fact that the German generals wished to let the Russians go on — the farther the better — while General Gorman planned to stop them cold in front of Fulda.[97]

DePuy believed that Balck and Mellenthin had helped demonstrate that a smaller well-led force could synchronize its operations and defeat a larger less-organized force consistent with Active Defense. Therefore, DePuy's vision of Active Defense deserves reassessment.

ACTIVE DEFENSE RECONSIDERED

Active Defense represented a better NATO defense plan compared with the maneuver warfare mobile defense solution as West Germany did not have the geography to facilitate retreats into great depth.[98] DePuy made this point perfectly clear:

> Manstein's counterattack around Kharkov, had it taken place in central Germany, would have carried from Frankfurt to Hannover and across the industrial area of the Ruhr. Free-wheeling, mobile defense operations require more space than the NATO center can afford.[99]

The maneuver warfare theorists also ignored the political impossibility of their plan as the West German Government would never have agreed to the sacrifices it demanded, and logically insisted upon a strategy of containing any conflict to the border region.[100] DePuy accordingly built Active Defense around the reality of West German political constraints: 'The German Army was formed to protect Germany not to destroy Germany.'[101] He had to formulate a plan which his ally would agree with, and General Rüdiger von Reichert, Vice Chief of Staff of the West German Army, endorsed Active Defense.[102] The maneuver warfare defense plan ignored reality, as historian Lawrence Freedman concluded:

> The failure to consider the geopolitical context illustrated the problem with considering operational art in isolation from a broader strategy in which holding together an alliance might be more important than developing clever moves for a hypothetical war.[103]

In contrast to Lind's critique, Active Defense never sought a war of attrition with the Warsaw Pact and always emphasized tactical maneuver, counterattacks and the importance of superior leadership, within an operational-level forward defensive posture, reflecting West Germany's lack of depth.[104] At the tactical level, DePuy advocated elastic defense in which reconnaissance would identify the axis of the Soviet advance, enabling a concentration of force to be applied at the 'critical point'.[105]

DePuy's vision of tactical elastic defense would involve each division deploying a reconnaissance screen forward to determine the main axis of the Soviet advance, followed by six to eight battalions concentrating at this critical point while three or four battalions conducted mobile operations to screen the rest of the sector.[106] He explained Active Defense was mobile defense 'compressed into the first 20 to 30 kilometers from the border. It would still be very mobile, a lot of movement but far forward.'[107] DePuy defended Active Defense against its critics by accusing them of overstating the level of attrition in the doctrine and by asserting that it was inspired by Bruce Clarke's 'elastic defense' of St. Vith during the Battle of the Bulge.[108]

Active Defense was not an isolated concept and existed within the framework of nuclear deterrence; it was designed to buy time for domestic and international pressure to end the conflict before an escalation to nuclear war.[109] Therefore, DePuy's insistence on winning the first battle, so heavily criticized by Lind, made perfect sense in the context of deterring a nuclear holocaust. Operational mobile defense, in contrast, risked a greater probability of nuclear war, as Mellenthin's advice in 1979 warned, because Red Army echelons reaching the Rhine would likely have triggered a nuclear exchange. DePuy correctly defined Active Defense in its Cold War context as 'a formula for a stalemate or for deterrence'.[110]

Although the US Army accepted maneuver warfare concepts into doctrine, given the obvious flaws in the theorists' NATO defense plan, its leadership rejected their proposal. The Army in contrast replaced Active Defense with the AirLand Battle and its architect, General Donn Starry, rejected operational mobile defense because West Germany lacked depth and also due to political reality.[111] Earlier in February 1977, when Starry commanded V Corps in West Germany, his 11th Armored Cavalry Regiment near Fulda observed 160 Soviet tanks from the 8th Guards Army suddenly appear at the border after traveling undetected 150 miles from Dresden.[112] He accordingly worried about a second Soviet echelon suddenly appearing and forcing a second battle. Starry looked for a new solution and found it in extending the battlefield to exploit Soviet depth:

> One of the hard facts that we must face in NATO today is that we do not have great depth to our battlefield. West Germany is a narrow country and much of the really good defensible terrain is close to the eastern border. Defending forward is not a slogan, it is a necessity, but we need to add depth to the battlefield.[113]

The AirLand Battle kept aspects of Active Defense by retaining DePuy's assertion that the initial Soviet assault had to be destroyed with superior firepower close to the West German border, and Starry asserted: 'The only way we will ever be able to get the Soviets' attention is to pile on and kill a lot of the bastards early.'[114] However, he looked beyond the front line into the Soviet rear:

> Simply put, those concepts tell us we must see deep to find the second echelon, move fast to concentrate forces, strike quickly to attack before he

can break into our defense, and finish the fight quickly before the second echelon closes.[115]

The AirLand Battle envisioned artillery and air strikes against the Warsaw Pact rear, targeting logistics, command and reserves to interdict and disrupt the follow-on echelons.[116] Starry believed that a deep attack targeting 'command and control' would 'disrupt the enemy timetable, complicate command and control, and frustrate his plans, thus weakening his grasp on the initiative'.[117]

The AirLand Battle's strike into Soviet depth reflected the maneuver warfare ideal of disruption over destruction as Red Army forces, such as tanks, would be difficult to locate; therefore, it would be easier to disrupt the Red Army by attacking their 'critical nodes'.[118] Starry's solution blended Active Defense and maneuver warfare by embracing both disruption and destruction:

> The defense must, therefore, begin well forward and proceed aggressively from there to destroy enemy assault echelons and at the same time slow, disrupt, break up, disperse or destroy follow-on echelons in order to quickly seize the initiative and go on the offense.[119]

The Soviet Union never invaded Western Europe and the AirLand Battle vision of extending the battlefield was never tested in Europe. However, the Gulf War would force the American military to decide how far it really embraced maneuver warfare.

CHAPTER NINE
THE GULF WAR AND THE ILLUSION OF CONFIRMATION

MANEUVER WARFARE TRIUMPHANT

Maneuver warfare concepts were first tested in combat when America invaded the tiny Caribbean island of Grenada — Operation Urgent Fury — in 1983. Lieutenant Colonel Ray Smith, a convert to the new philosophy, commanded a battalion from the 22nd Marine Amphibious Unit with highly successful results, as John Boyd's biographer Robert Coram noted:

> Elite Army rangers were pinned down at the airport, largely by Cuban construction workers, and could not move. But Smith's Marines, a much smaller group, ripped around Grenada as if they owned the island. They bypassed enemy strongholds, put strength against weakness, and moved like water flowing downhill. They created such confusion and uncertainty that hundreds of enemy soldiers surrendered to Smith because, as one of them said, 'The Marines are everywhere'.[1]

Smith concluded, 'the secret to our rapid success was the fact that we went in with the idea that speed alone would make all the difference'.[2] General Alfred Gray, the Marine Commandant who made maneuver warfare doctrine, also praised Marine performance in Grenada:

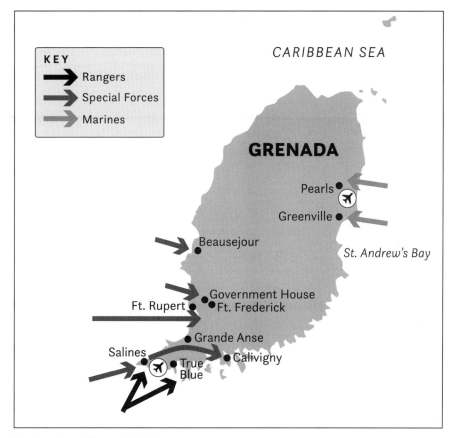

The invasion of Grenada, 1983

Maneuver warfare tactics demoralized the Cubans and the People's Revolutionary Army. One Cuban officer. . . said that he surrendered to the Marines because they kept popping up in the most unexpected places and he figured further resistance was futile. His comments speak volumes about the psychological impact of well-executed maneuver warfare operations.[3]

Smith criticized the Army's 82nd Airborne Division for spending two days preparing for a 'frontal attack on the highest piece of ground in Grenada with two brigades abreast' while the Marines 'were already there and in place'.[4]

William S. Lind similarly claimed that Grenada vindicated maneuver warfare:

> The speed with which the Marines acted and moved decisively, for example the surrender of the Grenadian platoon that surrendered rather than fight because your forces appear where they were not expected, this convinced the Grenadian high command that resistance was hopeless.[5]

Lind applauded the swift Marine operation in eastern Grenada and criticized the Army's slow advance in the west; however, in reality the Army had a harder time as communist forces had concentrated in western Grenada.[6] Smith even acknowledged that 'Marine units on Grenada never met much opposition'.[7]

The swift American invasion of Grenada involved aspects of maneuver warfare, but as the operation was conducted by a superpower fighting a tiny nation, the conflict cannot validate any concept. The Gulf War in 1991, a major regional conflict, on the other hand, did provide a laboratory to test maneuver warfare on a meaningful scale.

After the Gulf War, maneuver warfare true believers claimed vindication, crediting their theory for the victory and the surprisingly low coalition casualties. For example, General Charles Krulak, Commandant of the Marine Corps, credited Boyd with this outcome:

> . . . the Iraqi army collapsed morally and intellectually under the onslaught of American and Coalition forces. John Boyd was an architect of that victory as surely as if he'd commanded a fighter wing or a maneuver division in the desert. His thinking, his theories, his larger than life influence were there with us in Desert Storm.[8]

Lind similarly announced that in 'Desert Storm, the American ground forces, Army and Marine Corps, on the whole practiced maneuver warfare'.[9] Robert Coram concluded, 'Everything successful about the Gulf War is a direct reflection of Boyd's "Patterns of Conflict".'[10]

The theorists, in particular, praised the Marine Corps' performance during the conflict. General Norman Schwarzkopf, commander of the

John Boyd testifying at the
Hearing of the House Armed
Services Committee on the
Gulf War in 1991
(Author's Collection)

Norman Schwarzkopf during
the Gulf War
(Contributor: Trinity Mirror/Alamy
Stock Photo)

coalition forces, planned the decisive attack — the armored left hook from the US Army's VII and XVIII Corps — as a wide flanking move through southern Iraq. In order to achieve surprise, he devised a deception plan to be conducted by the Marines. A naval task force with embarked Marines rehearsed an amphibious invasion of Kuwait which never eventuated but this threat tied down six Iraqi divisions along the coast.

On 24 February 1991, the I Marine Expeditionary Force, as part of the wider ground campaign, attacked Iraqi defenses in the southern sector of the Kuwaiti border at the Persian Gulf. The Marine assault was a feint to distract the Iraqis away from the decisive 'left hook' further north through southern Iraq which planned to attack the enemy from the rear.

The 1st Marine Division, commanded by General James Myatt, infiltrated reconnaissance units into Kuwait three days earlier and led the Marine assault and the next day his forces captured over 2,000 prisoners and destroyed 18 tanks and 100 other vehicles. By the third day, Myatt's soldiers had reached Kuwait City. Myatt had looked for 'gaps' to infiltrate through under the influence of Boyd as 'maneuver warfare to me is a way of life'.[11] Robert Coram praised Myatt's men:

> They bypassed strong points, forgot their flanks, and penetrated so deeply and caused such confusion that the Iraqi Army rushed in reinforcements against what they anticipated would be the main thrust of the American invasion. Then they began surrendering by the thousands. Nowhere can be found a better example of Boyd's ideas on 'folding the enemy in on himself' than in the fact that some fifteen Iraqi divisions surrendered to two divisions of Marines.[12]

The Gulf War resulted in Boyd's ideas becoming widely discussed in the media and, as Robert Leonhard recalled, 'the term maneuver warfare came suddenly into everyday usage'.[13] Boyd's fame massively increased, as Grant Hammond from the Air War College explained: 'Suddenly, it seemed as if Boyd were everywhere in a variety of publications covering the war.'[14] However, the problem with the seeming triumph of maneuver warfare following the Gulf War is Schwarzkopf — the genuine architect of the victory — who did not believe in Boyd's theories.

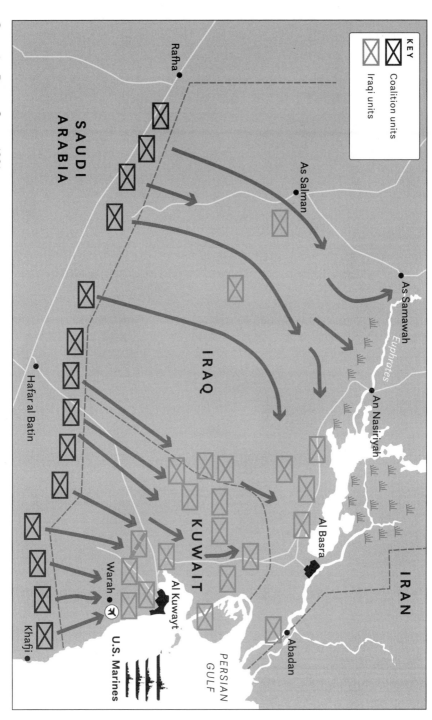

Operation Desert Storm, 1991

KEY

Coalition units

Iraqi units

SAUDI ARABIA

Rafha

As Salman

As Samawah

Euphrates

An Nasiriyah

IRAQ

Hafar al Batin

Al Basra

KUWAIT

Warah

Al Kuwayt

Khafji

U.S. Marines

IRAN

Abadan

PERSIAN GULF

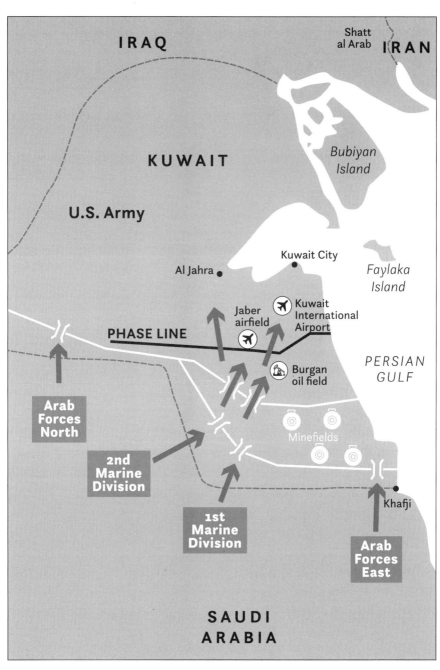

The Marine Expeditionary Force during the Gulf War, 1991

AN AMERICAN CANNAE

The United States Army had a long tradition of emulating Schlieffen's Cannae ideal, embracing his vision of fighting the 'perfect battle of annihilation'. Schlieffen's book *Cannae* first came to the attention of the Army's Command and General Staff School during a lecture by Colonel Wilson Burtt in 1916, based on the observations of a military mission which had recently visited Germany.[15] The Army War College translated *Cannae* into English, influencing a generation of American officers.[16] For example, Eisenhower, as historian Gregory Daly explained, had a 'lifelong dream. . . to emulate Hannibal's victory at Cannae'.[17]

Schwarzkopf personified the American Cannae tradition and dreamed of recreating Hannibal's 'perfect battle' and during the Gulf War he announced that the ground campaign 'was literally about to become a battle of Cannae, a battle of annihilation'.[18] As such, General Dieter Brand declared, the 'latest "Cannae" in military history was Operation Desert Storm'.[19] Although Schwarzkopf envisaged a modern Cannae to completely destroy the enemy, the Gulf War resulted in a strong impression of a maneuver warfare triumph. This confusion originated in part from the Secretary of Defense who wanted the war fought according to Boyd's concepts.

Congressman Dick Cheney sat through *Patterns of Conflict* and became impressed with Boyd's ideas: 'I was intrigued by the concepts he was working on. He was a creative and innovative thinker with respect to the military.'[20] Cheney and Boyd, according to the acolyte James Burton, 'spent hours together discussing the fundamentals of Boyd's theories and the importance of strategy'.[21] As Schwarzkopf planned the liberation of Kuwait, Cheney, now Secretary of Defense, sought Boyd's advice and both frequently met before Desert Storm.[22] Robert Coram even implied that Boyd, through his access to Cheney, secretly planned the Gulf War.[23]

Cheney rejected Schwarzkopf's first campaign plan as it failed to conform with maneuver warfare, declaring to Colin Powell, Chairman of the Joint Chiefs of Staff, 'I can't let Norm do this high diddle up the middle plan.'[24] These words are significant as Robert Coram explained: 'Not only did Cheney reject Schwarzkopf's plan but he used Boyd's language to do so.'[25] Cheney later recalled, 'I found the plan unimaginative.'[26] He confirmed that Boyd 'clearly was a factor in my thinking' and 'nobody' wanted to go 'straight up the middle into the heart of Iraqi offenses'.[27] Cheney accordingly demanded a new plan and Schwarzkopf sought assistance to shape the revision.[28]

After FM 100-5 *Operations* (1982) incorporated maneuver warfare concepts into doctrine, Lieutenant Colonel Huba Wass de Czege, who drafted the manual, founded the School of Advanced Military Studies (SAMS) at Fort Leavenworth, which gave the Army's best graduates from Staff College the option of studying for an additional year, and its curriculum initially made Boyd's ideas compulsory learning.[29]

Schwarzkopf, after Cheney rejected his first plan, augmented his Central Command planning team with four SAMS graduates tasked with improving the concept of operations. The original plan had envisaged a single corps attack seizing the high ground near the Mutla Pass in central Kuwait which aimed to cut off the highway to Iraq. The revised plan, which the SAMS graduates shaped, included the Marine feint in the south and the famous 'left hook' through southern Iraq.

The SAMS graduates called themselves the 'Jedi Knights' and they are often portrayed as an elite cohort schooled in maneuver warfare who ensured Schwarzkopf's campaign plan conformed with Boyd's theories. For example, journalist Fred Kaplan reported in an article 'The Force Was With Them' in the *Boston Globe* that the victory 'was largely the work of a small, little-known group of Army officers who call themselves the Jedi Knights'.[30] Kaplan continued:

> The adoption of their ideas by Gen. H. Norman Schwarzkopf, the commander of Operation Desert Storm, marks a radical revision in the way the US Army wages war, and represents a triumph for a way of thinking known as 'maneuver warfare.'[31]

Boyd himself made this claim after the war when testifying at Capitol Hill, declaring that the 'Jedi Knights' were 'heavily represented on Schwarzkopf's operations and plans staff'.[32] James Burton similarly claimed, 'Schwarzkopf's "Jedi Knights," the people to whom he gives credit for planning his operations, studied Boyd's theories.'[33]

Although the curriculum at SAMS included maneuver warfare, it focused on military strategy, operational art and campaign planning. De Czege, more an admirer of Clausewitz than Boyd, taught his students to seek the destruction of enemy forces as 'campaigns are decided by battles in all but the rarest cases'.[34] Although influenced by Boyd to some degree, the 'Jedi Knights' did not inject maneuver warfare into Schwarzkopf's campaign plan and their contribution improved operational-level planning, as Dwight Phillips explained:

> The SAMS school notion of 'pure' operational fires absorbed the ideas of John Boyd, but subordinated them to a ground campaign. . . Now, the SAMS school proposed using firepower to fix enemy units so that maneuver units could destroy them. Of course, the destruction of the enemy force would necessarily achieve national objectives.[35]

The 'Jedi Knights' shared Schwarzkopf's Cannae vision of annihilation, although they brought a higher appreciation of operational art to the planning process. Furthermore, as James Burton acknowledged, 'when Wass de Czege left the [SAMS] school for another assignment, the lecture invitations to Boyd stopped'.[36] Therefore, there is no evidence that the 'Jedi Knights' studied maneuver warfare in detail as Boyd's influence in the SAMS curriculum had progressively declined long before the Gulf War.

Cheney actually denied being the architect of the 'left hook' and claimed 'no direct influence' on the final plan, adding, 'It was not my job to figure out the nitty gritty. That was Schwarzkopf's mission.'[37] Therefore, Cheney did not use his authority to force Schwarzkopf to follow maneuver warfare and Boyd did not secretly plan the campaign. Schwarzkopf had no intention of allowing maneuver warfare to dominate Desert Storm and, true to Schlieffen's Cannae ideal, destruction of Iraqi forces would be his overriding goal as he declared on 14 November 1990:

> We need to destroy — not attack, not damage, not surround — I want you to *destroy* the Republican Guard. When you're done with them, I don't want them to be an effective fighting force anymore. I don't want them to exist as a military organization.[38]

Iraqi Army armored vehicles on Highway 8 which were destroyed by coalition aircraft during the Gulf War
(Contributor: US Army Photo/Alamy Stock Photo)

Schwarzkopf wanted to use his absolute air superiority to attack 'critical vulnerabilities' to disrupt and paralyze the Iraqi 'center of gravity' and, as such, embraced aspects of maneuver warfare:

> Because of Iraq's highly centralized system of command and control, Saddam was what military theorists call an enemy center of gravity — an aspect of the opposing force that, if destroyed, will cause the enemy to lose its will to fight. . . For our purposes, it was sufficient to *silence* Saddam — to destroy his ability to command the forces arrayed against ours.[39]

Nevertheless, Schwarzkopf viewed the air campaign primarily as an attritional means of inflicting mass destruction, as he articulated to the air planners, 'I'd need fifty percent of the Iraqi occupying forces destroyed before launching whatever ground offensive we might eventually plan.'[40] Schwarzkopf's ultimate aim was destruction, which he made clear:

I want to make sure you understand your mission from here on out. It is
to inflict maximum destruction, *maximum destruction*, on the Iraqi military
machine. You are to destroy all war-fighting equipment. Do not just pass it
on the battlefield. We don't want the Iraqis coming at us again five years
from now.[41]

A firmer rejection of maneuver warfare would be difficult to articulate.
Schwarzkopf perceived maneuver warfare tenets as a means of achieving
the complete destruction of the enemy, which is entirely consistent with the
AirLand Battle, as Israeli military theorist Shimon Naveh concluded: 'Desert
Storm served as the workshop in which the operational theory of Airland
Battle was examined.'[42]

Maneuver warfare did not win the Gulf War and at best played a
subordinate role. The conflict, however, successfully popularized Boyd's
ideas, but a closer look at the conflict reveals that keys aspects of maneuver
warfare were never applied despite the triumphalist rhetoric.

THE ABSENCE OF MANEUVER WARFARE

The Gulf War did not truly reflect maneuver warfare as Schwarzkopf
oversaw a centralized campaign with high degrees of 'synchronization', a
concept the theorists condemn because it contradicts 'mission tactics' by
preventing low-level initiative as subordinates must act in accordance with
carefully timed precision. For example, Lind condemned synchronization
because conflict is 'dominated by surprise, rapid change, and friction cannot
be synchronized; it is not a railway timetable'.[43]

Although the AirLand Battle accepted maneuver warfare concepts
such as 'mission tactics', the new doctrine also included synchronization
alongside initiative, agility and depth. Schwarzkopf emphasized the aspects
of the AirLand Battle which focused on 'destruction' and 'synchronization',
downplaying the maneuver warfare elements. In his memoir *It Doesn't Take a
Hero* (1992), he does not directly offer an opinion on maneuver warfare but
praised General William DePuy, the arch-enemy of Boyd and Lind:

DePuy had envisaged a battlefield that was expanding and becoming more complex. To have any hope of victory, Army units would have to be prepared to exercise greater intelligence, flexibility, and initiative than could be prepared by rote. His solution was to take an army whose grand tradition of drill stretched all the way back to General Friedrich von Steuben at Valley Forge and turn it into an army that could *think*.[44]

Schwarzkopf similarly praised the AirLand Battle:

The new doctrine abolished the traditional concept of head-on, grind-the-enemy-down warfare. . . The way to win, therefore, was to use our new technology to offset their numerical superiority; synchronize our combat power; and encourage commanders at every level to exercise initiative and flexibility, and ingenuity on the battlefield.[45]

Therefore, Schwarzkopf strongly identified with the 'synchronization' aspect of the AirLand Battle. This is no coincidence as Schlieffen's Cannae ideal requires perfect synchronization in order to effectively execute the envelopment.[46]

Schwarzkopf succeeded in 'synchronizing' a set piece battle as Robert Leonhard, who served in the Gulf War commanding an infantry battalion, confirmed:

I saw no freedom for small unit commanders to make any decisions regarding battlefield maneuver. Brigade, battalion, and company commanders were told where to go, when to move, when to shoot, and when to cease fire. Above all, they were warned to keep their flanks tied in with friendly units.[47]

Leonhard complained that 'command push' prevented 'recon pull' and Army forces made no effort to exploit 'gaps' and avoid 'surfaces': 'Like rigidly disciplined Macedonian phalanxes, divisions and brigades had to march and stay dressed to the flanks throughout the advance, crashing through both strong and weak points in the enemy's defenses.'[48]

A key objective Schwarzkopf gave the commanders of VII and XVIII Corps for their 'left hook' was the complete destruction of the Iraqi

Abrams tanks from the 3rd Armored Division during Operation Desert Storm
(Contributor: DOD Photo/Alamy Stock Photo)

Republican Guard: 'I do not want a slow, ponderous, pachyderm mentality. This is not a deliberate attack. I want to *slam* into the Republican Guard. The enemy is not worth shit.'[49] Unhappy with the slow advance on the second day of the ground campaign, Schwarzkopf ordered General Frederick Franks, commander of VII Corps, to resume the advance after he ordered his troops south to mop up bypassed enemy resistance.[50]

James Burton blamed 'synchronization' for slowing down the 'left hook' which permitted the Republican Guard to escape: 'Clearly, General Franks's failure to cut off the Republican Guard's escape can be traced to his strict adherence to the synchronization element of the Army's new doctrine.'[51] Burton concluded that Boyd 'was absolutely correct' as he 'had argued with the Army then that synchronizing was a dumb idea and that it would slow down the pace of operations. . . We now have empirical evidence to confirm that argument.'[52]

Although the escape of the Republican Guard can be attributed to the excessive synchronization of VII Corps, the correct response is not to ditch synchronization — nor is this a realistic option anyway. The real question is the degree of synchronization to adopt, which exists along a spectrum with a wide degree of choice — there is no binary choice to have synchronization or not. All military commanders apply some degree of synchronization in their plans and the precise level to apply in a given situation, as DePuy points out, must always be a judgment call: 'The question arises as to just how one decides how much synchronization is desired or required. This question carries us to the heart of the military art. Only the commander can decide (and he must decide).'[53]

Another aspect of the Gulf War which prevented genuine maneuver warfare from being applied was ever present confusion concerning its 'center of gravity' concept. Despite the rhetoric about undermining the Iraqi 'center of gravity', American campaign planners had no consistent view on what it actually was, even among the 'Jedi Knights'.[54] The Air Force considered Iraqi's national infrastructure — its electricity grid, communications and industry — to be its 'center of gravity' so its planes targeted these assets, hoping the Iraqi Government would agree to withdraw from Kuwait.[55] The Army identified the Republican Guard as the 'center of gravity', believing its destruction would remove Saddam from power.[56] The Navy viewed Iraq's oil industry as its 'center of gravity' and accordingly hoped to undermine it through maritime blockade.[57] This concept became meaningless as General Charles Horner, the air campaign commander, identified three separate 'centers of gravity' — Saddam Hussein, the Republican Guard and Iraq's weapons of mass destruction.[58] However, targeting these 'centers of gravity' failed to bring about the collapse of the Iraqi military or convince Saddam to leave Kuwait.[59]

The planners had wasted time and focus constructing 'center of gravity' concepts in the elusive hope of targeting 'critical vulnerabilities' but these failed to provide useful tools. They looked for short cuts to instantly trigger the collapse of the enemy in accordance with maneuver warfare, but applying operational art actually requires a long-term campaign plan with the successive planning of phases in which one phase establishes the conditions for the next until the end state is reached.

Despite widespread boasting that the Gulf War 'vindicated' maneuver warfare, the theorists mostly knew this was not true as they bitterly complained that their ideas had not been properly applied during the conflict. The war demonstrated that the military had somewhat adopted maneuver warfare in theory but had limited interest in putting the concepts into practice. This observation put the theorists in a dilemma regarding what to do about this contradiction.

THE UNFINISHED REVOLUTION

After the Gulf War, the maneuver warfare true believers realized that their rebellion in the American military had only partially succeeded. For example, Leonhard argued that the Army had initially made progress toward institutionalizing maneuver warfare only to regress to 'attrition':

> AirLand Battle is the closest the U.S. Army has ever come to maneuver warfare, but since 1982 the doctrine has migrated back toward the traditional attrition approach to warfare that has characterized the army since the days of the Revolution. The road back to doctrinal purity is a difficult one.[60]

The 'purists' faced a significant challenge as they wanted another wave of reform to complete their revolution during a time of jubilation. The reforming efforts of Boyd and Lind had originally gained traction in the dark days following America's defeat in Vietnam. At that time, widespread disillusionment at every level of the military encouraged new ideas but the euphoria generated by the Gulf War's victory destroyed the 'Vietnam Syndrome'.[61] The conflict vindicated the AirLand Battle status quo and the Army lost any remaining appetite for reform. In this new climate, criticism became heresy, as Roger Spiller from the Army's Combat Studies Institute explained: 'Inside the Army, any suggestion that the Army's performance was less than sterling was viewed as rank disloyalty, or at least unnecessarily troublesome.'[62]

To true believers, maneuver warfare is a closed system and its concepts cannot coexist with other ideas, effectively making the theory an all or nothing proposition. This explains why the purists are so troubled by their concepts existing in the AirLand Battle alongside destruction and synchronization. As their revolution remains an unfinished enterprise, a dangerous disconnect now exists between theory and practice, generating poisonous mistrust between the ranks.

The American military perceives itself as a maneuver warfare force and junior officers are taught its concepts such as 'mission tactics' and 'main effort'. However, junior leaders in practice are rarely given the opportunity to apply these concepts in any meaningful way, as Lind correctly argued, 'the Marine Corps formally adopted maneuver warfare as doctrine', but it does not actually practice it 'to the frustration of many junior officers'.[63] He also correctly observed:

> [The] central maneuver warfare concepts are commonly used, but mostly as buzzwords. Young officers receive classes on the concepts, but when their training moves to the field, they quickly see that what is done is mostly top-down, rigid 2GW [Second Generation Warfare].[64]

In 2016, Lind repeated this assertion after attending a Marine Corps Training and Education Command conference at Quantico which addressed the question, 'Are we doing maneuver warfare?': 'Not one person said the Marine Corps has institutionalized maneuver warfare. On the contrary, the conference concluded Marines can talk about maneuver warfare but they cannot do it.'[65]

Captain B.A. Friedman, a Marine officer, confirmed Lind's assessment:

> The most damning attack on *Warfighting* is that the Marine Corps has yet to implement it. While the document was signed, it is still an ideal that we are striving to reach. Micromanagers are cursed in *Warfighting*, but are not only tolerated in the Marine Corps, they flourish.[66]

Major Ian Brown made a similar point in 2018:

> While not universally shared, a number of Marines harbored the belief that there existed a disconnect between what the Marine Corps preached and what it practiced when it came to maneuver warfare. Curiously, this split roughly followed rank, with the senior 'preachers' evincing a rather different outlook from the lower-grade 'practitioners,' who argued that

the rank and file were denied the opportunity to use maneuver warfare in the field.[67]

The reality of preaching maneuver warfare but not practicing it generates mistrust, as Friedman concluded, because 'when NCOs read and reread that document [*Warfighting*] and then witness senior leaders ignoring it, they will lose that vital faith in the organization'.[68] However, the genuine *Wehrmacht* command system can actually solve this crisis.

As the *Wehrmacht* never preached or practiced *Auftragstaktik* as maneuver warfare theorists define the term, German soldiers expected to exercise high levels of initiative, but they also expected that at any time the forward commander, either in person or over the radio, could override their actions. Therefore, when they experienced transitions from *Auftragstaktik* to micro-management, they did not view their commanders as hypocrites because their education system never indoctrinated them with maneuver warfare dogma and, as such, they never had false expectations. Soldiers, NCOs and junior officers can be trained to transition from 'mission tactics' to 'forward command' without any perception of hypocrisy if maneuver warfare dogma is removed from doctrine. Therefore, the heart of the poisonous mistrust is not the imperfect application of doctrine but doctrine itself.

Maneuver warfare, while never fully implemented or practiced, continues to exist in doctrine and is the ideal upheld by many and continues to exert a powerful influence. Furthermore, commanders can choose to apply maneuver warfare if they happen to believe in its principles. Therefore, the maneuver warfare mindset remains and can still be applied in practice, which caused critical blunders the next time America fought Saddam Hussein.

CHAPTER TEN
THE WAR ON TERROR AND THE RETURN OF ATTRITION

THE MYTH OF PURE OPERATIONS

The German Army before and during the Nazi era participated in politics and the *Wehrmacht* willingly aligned its operations with the policy goals of the Third Reich. However, after the war, in an attempt to separate the *Wehrmacht*'s reputation from Nazi crimes, former German generals stressed the supposed apolitical nature of the army, attempting to distance their actions from Hitler. For example, Franz Halder falsely stressed the apolitical nature of the *Wehrmacht*, as historians Rolf-Dieter Muller and Hans-Erich Volkmann noted:

> [Halder's] plan was simple: to present the Army High Command as Hitler's victim, an instrument misused in the pursuit of a criminal policy . . . The High Command and its military achievements were thus separated from the political sphere, propagating the myth of the blameless *Wehrmacht* and separating it from the crimes of the SS.[1]

Erich von Manstein in *Lost Victories* similarly explained that his book 'is the personal narrative of a *soldier*, in which I have deliberately refrained from discussing political problems or matters with no direct bearing on events in the military field'.[2] Manstein's desire to avoid politics, as historians Ronald Smelser and Edward Davies concluded, 'is convenient, because it enables him to avoid entirely discussing the war in the East as one of racial enslavement and annihilation'.[3]

The postwar German accounts dishonestly present the *Wehrmacht* as an organization detached from politics.[4] Liddell Hart in *The German Generals Talk* helped spread this myth to the English-speaking world: 'The German generals had studied their profession with the greatest thoroughness, devoting themselves from youth on to the mastery of its technique, with little regard to politics and still less to the world outside.'[5]

Colonel Verner Carlson, when interviewing Friedrich von Mellenthin for *Military Review*, raised the issue of politics and he responded, 'Soldiers may not engage in political activity' as 'the officer does not become a politician; he remains a soldier'.[6] Carlson unsurprisingly accepted the myth of an apolitical *Wehrmacht*:

> Mellenthin and 150 of his colleagues were locked up for two and a half years while the Allies sought to prove them guilty of war crimes . . . The General Staff was acquitted. It was concluded that its officers were essentially technicians, brilliant in the pursuit of their profession, but politically naive. Their political deficiencies were best noted by Liddell Hart.[7]

The postwar mythology also depicted the *Wehrmacht* as liberators in the east opposed to Nazi occupation policies. Halder's manuscripts and the memoirs describe an initial benevolent *Wehrmacht* occupation of Soviet territory, until the arrival of brutal *SS* and Nazi functionaries who turn the population against Germany. For example, the manuscript *Rear Area Security in Russia* claimed: 'The German combat forces, at least during the initial period of the campaign, made every effort to restore normal conditions in the areas they occupied and to gain the confidence of the local population.'[8] Furthermore, the manuscript noted the happiness of the population after being liberated from Stalinism:

> Any arbitrary acts by German troops, such as the unwarranted slaughtering of cattle, plunder in any form, or the wanton destruction

of property, were most severely punished. This served to protect the few possessions which the Soviet regime had left in the hands of private individuals and strengthened the confidence of the people in the fairness and justice of the German forces.[9]

This happy occupation apparently ended with the arrival of Nazi authorities.[10] *Rear Area Security in Russia* even made the extraordinary claim that the Soviet partisan movement established itself by exploiting the *Wehrmacht*'s chivalrous nature:

Russian agents under the guise of helpless civilians took advantage of the kindheartedness of the German soldier by passing through the lines and infiltrating into the army group rear areas. Other agents who had been left behind during the retreat of the Red Army gradually began their work. Many of them were women who felt that they could count on protection by the German soldiers.[11]

Heinz Guderian in *Panzer Leader* also depicted happily liberated civilians until the military occupation ended:

Unfortunately this friendly attitude towards the Germans lasted only so long as the more benevolent military administration was in control. The so-called 'Reich commissars' soon managed to alienate all sympathy from the Germans and thus to prepare the ground for all the horrors of partisan warfare.[12]

The postwar German accounts stress efforts made to ensure the civil population had food. For example, *Rear Area Security in Russia* claimed in relation to Bobruysk in 1941:

In numerous meetings with the town council, arrangements were made for the resumption of work in local crafts and trades, as well as for the assurance of an adequate food supply. Soon the harvest was under way; then grist mills and distributing agencies resumed operation.[13]

Guderian similarly claimed: 'The 1941 harvest had been a rich one throughout the country and there was ample grain for bread' and 'the needs of our troops were assured as were those of the Russian civilians in the towns'.[14] However, Ronald Smelser and Edward Davies rejected Guderian's account:

> This is sublime nonsense. The 1941 harvest could hardly have been a rich one because the Ukraine, Russia's breadbasket, was the scene of ferocious battles during that period. Moreover, the German policy in Russia was precisely to channel all available resources back to Germany, assuming that the Russian population, especially in the cities, would largely starve. The General Plan for the East assumed an attrition rate of 14 million people.[15]

Despite the postwar claims of liberated populations, *Wehrmacht* brutality turned the population against the occupiers. It is true that initially German forces were often welcomed as liberators from populations weary of Stalinist rule, especially in the Baltic States, Belorussia and the Ukraine.[16] However, the alienation these people experienced resulted from *Wehrmacht* actions in addition to the brutality of Nazi organizations.

The *Wehrmacht* implemented a hunger strategy to steal food from Soviet citizens to feed the army and the home front, a policy designed to create famine which General Hans Leykauf referred to as the 'annihilation of superfluous eaters'.[17] Halder raised no objections to starving civilians in his diary: 'It is the Fuehrer's firm decision to level Moscow and Leningrad, and make them uninhabitable, so as to relieve us of the necessity of having to feed the populations through the winter.'[18] In May 1942, an Army Group Rear report confirmed the reality of the *Wehrmacht* occupation:

> . . . the population is afflicted by hunger and is therefore under pressure to wander around the countryside to barter for foodstuffs. The fact that the German *Wehrmacht* has done nothing to guarantee the nourishment of the civilian population has influenced opinion and made the population distrustful towards the victorious German forces.[19]

The 'hunger strategy' strongly contributed to the 7.5 million deaths of non-Jewish civilians in the east and demolishes the myth that *SS* and Nazi functionaries solely eroded civilian goodwill.[20]

The *Wehrmacht* never intended to liberate civilian populations in the Soviet Union, as Hermann Hoth explained to his troops: 'We are the masters of this land we have conquered. . . The fear of the population of our countermeasures is to be stronger than that of Stalinist intimidation. Compassion toward the population is completely misguided.'[21] Nevertheless, the myths of military operations free from politics and *Wehrmacht* liberation became entrenched in the American military mind.

POLITICS AND OPERATIONAL ART

The American military after Vietnam misinterpreted Clausewitz when its officers sought a scapegoat to explain their defeat. During the war, the American commander General William Westmoreland formulated an attrition based strategy to convince Hanoi to abandon its desire to forcefully unify the country: 'We'll just go on bleeding them until Hanoi wakes up to the fact that they have bled their country to the point of national disaster for generations.'[22] However, Hanoi had other ideas, which doomed Westmoreland's ambition.

The North Vietnamese leadership viewed the conflict as a total war and mobilized its population and conditioned it to suffer profound casualties. Every year in North Vietnam 120,000 men became old enough for the draft and this fact alone doomed Westmorland's strategy as Robert McNamara, the Secretary of Defense, acknowledged: 'We have no prospects of attriting the enemy force at a rate equal to or greater than his ability to infiltrate or recruit.'[23]

American strategy fatally assumed that Hanoi would act 'rationally' and think in terms of Western 'cost-benefit' analysis.[24] Westmoreland failed to formulate a winning strategy, but after the war many American officers blamed their defeat on political 'interference'. In doing so, they embraced the *Wehrmacht* myth that wars are won by a caste of military professionals free to conduct pure operations far removed from politicians who cannot understand the esoteric mysteries of war.

After Vietnam, the American military 'discovered' Clausewitz and used his famous maximum that 'war is continuation of politics by other means' to explain their defeat.[25] Clausewitz stressed that war must serve a purpose determined by state policy within the context of a proper political–military relationship.[26] Colonel Harry Summers, from the United States Army War College, wrote *On Strategy: A Critical Analysis of the Vietnam War*, which blamed the defeat on a failure to follow the civil–military interaction principles expressed by Clausewitz. This was because the military was too narrowly focused on tactical matters, which allowed the civilian leadership to shape military strategy.[27] Summers ignored the fact that Westmoreland did indeed formulate a military strategy, albeit one that failed to produce victory, and incorrectly blamed the defeat on Washington for 'interfering' in operations as politicians did not give the military the freedom it required to win the war.[28]

Summers essentially created a betrayal myth as his rhetoric about Clausewitz, according to scholar Bill Sweetman, 'was an academically respectable way of saying that Lyndon Johnson and Robert McNamara had stabbed the troops in the back'.[29] Of course, in reality the Johnson administration supported Westmoreland's strategy, which had been founded on illusions, but belief in government betrayal became entrenched and subsequent American presidents needed to reassure their people that they would allow the troops to win. For example, Reagan during an address on Memorial Day in 1988 said, 'Perhaps at this late date we can all agree that we've learned one lesson: that young Americans must never again be sent to fight and die unless we are prepared to let them win.'[30] George H.W. Bush before the Gulf War similarly announced, 'This will not be a protracted, drawn-out war. . . we will not permit our troops to have their hands tied behind their backs.'[31]

After Vietnam, American military theorists wrongly interpreted Clausewitz's famous maxim to mean that the government should set the strategic goals of the war and limit themselves to approving operational plans, developed by military experts who will implement them free from political interference. The maneuver warfare theorists accepted and expanded upon this understanding based upon their idolization of *Wehrmacht* generals.

The belief that military operations should be run by professionals free from political constraints became widespread in America after Vietnam.

Verner Carlson, in his interview with Mellenthin, accepted this myth:

> Mellenthin could never envision that Hitler would totally reverse
> Clausewitz, turning the relationship between the politicians and the
> military upside down. The politician would order war; the military would
> counsel restraint. He would order attack; they would counsel delay.[32]

Maneuver warfare theorists embraced this myth and advocated the removal
of political interference from operational art as they, according to General
Daniel Bolger, encouraged 'commanders to win wars at the operational level,
free from the intrusion of politics from above and friction from below'.[33] For
example, Russel Stolfi in *Hitler's Panzer's East* attributed the *Wehrmacht*'s early
success to the absence of political interference: 'the Balkan campaign retains
its luster, and set in the context of Barbarossa, it displays the formidable
nature of the Hitler-army synthesis in war-fighting when Hitler did not
intrude into military operations'.[34] Richard Hooker, editor of *Maneuver
Warfare: An Anthology*, also condemned the interfering politician Hitler who
prevented pure military operations:

> By any standard, the quality of the military advice offered to Hitler was
> uniformly high. . . Hitler rejected it, believing himself more capable than
> his experts. His fate and that of the German nation should remind us that
> when political leaders disregard military advice and professionalism to
> intervene in military operations, they do so at great risk.[35]

Robert Leonhard in *The Art of Maneuver* complained about political
interference during the Gulf War, which slowed down the military 'decision
cycle':

> . . . the unexpectedly successful advance through southern Kuwait had to
> stop in front of Kuwait City in order to allow the Arab allies the chance
> to formally retake the city. Further, operations within southern Iraq were
> conducted with a noticeable amount of political sensitivity and restraint,
> even at the tactical level, out of concern for the alliance. . . The problem with
> alliances is that they tend to interrupt the Boyd cycle at the decision stage.[36]

General Norman Schwarzkopf meeting with Shaikh Isa Bin Sulman Al-Khalifa and
Bahraini dignitaries
(Contributor: Everett Collection Historical/Alamy Stock Photo)

Leonhard gave no thought to the fragile nature of the Arab coalition partners
or the negative fallout that would have resulted from a failure to respect this
sensitivity. In contrast, General Norman Schwarzkopf wisely understood
the importance of political context in operational art:

> I wanted to make absolutely sure that if we took on Saddam, we would
> win not only on the battlefield but in the history books — and that
> included *Arab* history books. This was not strictly speaking a military
> concern. But we had to avoid giving the impression that western
> 'colonialists' had unilaterally imposed their will, and I was determined
> to plan smart. So Central Command organized what we called an 'Arab
> reaction seminar'. In a small briefing room a dozen experts. . . [reviewed]
> a long list of possible military actions the United States could take against
> Iraq and to figure out which — if any — would be acceptable to Arab
> governments and populations.[37]

Therefore, during the Gulf War, for the sake of achieving an unimportant tactical success, the maneuver warfare mindset could have created a strategic disaster if the Marines entered Kuwait City before Arab armies.[38]

The vision of military professionals conducting operational-level missions without political interference is at odds with the legacy of Aleksandr Svechin, the Soviet inventor of operational art. He firmly believed that political masters should play a role in shaping operations and stressed that complaints about interference are unprofessional: 'Operations on all fronts must be coordinated by politics' and strategists 'should not complain about political interference in the leadership of military operations because strategy itself is a projection of politics'.[39] Svechin concluded that politics cannot be separated from operations: 'It is natural for strategy to try to gain emancipation from bad politics, but strategy cannot exist in a vacuum without politics and is condemned to pay for all the sins of politics.'[40] He also condemned the myth of pure military operations:

Each moment of a war represents a wide range of political interests and every basic decision is made under pressure from a number of political demands. War is not waged in a vacuum. The suggestion that war is a free conflict between two armies understands nothing about the nature of warfare.[41]

Svechin argued that understanding political context is vital when planning operations, and to illustrate his point he cited the Schlieffen Plan, which was formulated in a military vacuum and not discussed in detail at the political level. In a purely military context, it rightly advocated avoiding the French border forts by advancing through Belgium but, as no political analysis had been done, the Germans disastrously failed to understand that violating Belgium's neutrality would draw Britain into the conflict.[42]

Mellenthin, despite his myth-making rhetoric about an apolitical *Wehrmacht*, did not genuinely believe in pure military operations. In *German Generals of World War II* he made a statement that could have been said by Svechin: 'The supreme military commander must in future be drawn into all political decision making, and a right of participation is his due. A prerequisite, naturally, is that he has learned to apply his mind to political matters.'[43] Mellenthin firmly rejected the idea that operations can be removed from political context as a 'soldier must always include political considerations in his military estimate of a situation'.[44]

The maneuver warfare theorists also undermined American operational art by spreading the myth of *Wehrmacht* liberation. This fantasy had earlier become widely believed in the American military. For example, Lieutenant Colonel F.O. Miksche contended in *Military Review* in 1949:

> It is no longer a secret that the German troops were greeted as liberators in the Baltic States, the Ukraine, and many other areas of the Soviet Union. The general mood changed later, but this was not the result of love for the Communist regime but a consequence of the ruthless requisition of peasants and of the senseless cruelties of the S.S. Troops.[45]

Enrique Martinez Codo made a similar statement in *Military Review* in 1960: 'General Heinz Guderian confirms in his Memoirs the favorable reception tendered the Germans by the Ukrainians and the subsequent deterioration of the good relations between the two.'[46]

John Boyd attributed the hostility in occupied lands to Hitler as the Russians 'were welcomed in, but then, Hitler came down harder than' Stalin, so 'they said, "Well, we're going to have a dictator, we're going to have our own".'[47] William S. Lind similarly separated *Wehrmacht* operations from the unpleasant world of Nazi crimes:

> Some Marine officers reject all German ideas because of Germany's defeat in both world wars. . . And some confuse German military practices with the policies of the National Socialist government, even though the former, almost without exception, were developed before or apart from the latter.[48]

Stolfi incorrectly claimed that Hitler kept the *Wehrmacht*'s leadership in the dark when planning his crimes:

> Hitler conceived the invasion of the Soviet Union. . . obsessed by the ambitious national socialist goal to colonize large areas of European

Russia. The reasons for the invasion were so radical that Hitler could not pass them to either his distinguished senior military commanders and staff or the German people.[49]

However, Hitler made his criminal policy goals perfectly clear to senior *Wehrmacht* leaders in his speech at the Reich Chancellery on 30 March 1941.[50]

Boyd, Lind and Stolfi uncritically accepted the myth of *Wehrmacht* liberation which created an impression in the American military that liberating oppressed populations is a naturally occurring phenomenon, provided that liberators arrive with benevolent intentions and subsequent actions do not betray civilian expectations. The theorists, as believers in postwar German misinformation, had no interest in political context or the problems associated with occupation policy, preferring instead an exclusive focus on pure military operations just like postwar *Wehrmacht* generals. As such, their ignorance contributed to the American military's poor application of operational art in Afghanistan and Iraq.

OPERATION ENDURING FREEDOM

The United States never intended to fight a full spectrum conflict in Afghanistan involving conventional operations, counterinsurgency and nation building. Before 2001, the 'transformation' program overseen by Secretary of Defense Donald Rumsfeld did not envisage American soldiers conducting open-ended peacekeeping or nation building; this was a reaction to perceived Clinton-era quagmires in the former Yugoslavia and Somalia.[51] Rumsfeld's 'transformation' centered on the so-called 'revolution in military affairs', which placed faith in new high-technology weapons and 'network centric solutions' that would enable relatively small forces to defeat much larger adversaries.[52] As such, the American military oriented towards a force designed for rapid deployment to short duration conflicts, which would avoid the quagmire of politics. However, the American military would soon fight the longest war in its history, deep in the quagmire, after 9/11 resulted in the invasion of Afghanistan.

General Tommy Franks, commander of Central Command (CENTCOM), had responsibility for Afghanistan in 2001. Franks, a long-

Tommy Franks in 2001
(Contributor: ZUMA Press, Inc/Alamy Stock Photo)

time convert to maneuver warfare, recalled his enthusiasm for the new ideas when stationed in Germany during the Cold War: 'I was eager to learn more about maneuver warfare.'[53] He added, 'I was working at my desk on new tactical *maneuver* concepts, listening to classical music on the radio as I struggled to transform theory into practical training procedures.'[54]

After 9/11, Franks had no contingency plan for an invasion of Afghanistan as 'CENTCOM had not developed a plan for conventional ground operations in Afghanistan.'[55] He explained the difficulty of formulating a plan from scratch: 'There were so many problems inherent in waging war in remote, landlocked, mountainous Afghanistan that any workable plan would have to transcend conventional thinking.'[56] Franks was correct, but it would not be his command which came up with the plan.

George Tenet, Director of the CIA, proposed a plan to President George W. Bush involving the insertion of CIA teams with large sums of cash into northern Afghanistan to assist Northern Alliance commanders in their fight against the Taliban, in advance of American Special Forces teams who would arrive later to direct high-tech air attacks against Taliban and al-

Qaeda targets.[57] Tenet's plan could be quickly implemented and promised to avoid large-scale troop deployments and, given the absence of a plan from CENTCOM, President Bush approved it on 17 September 2001.[58] Nine days later the first CIA team, code-named 'Jawbreaker', inserted into the Panjshir Valley in north-east Afghanistan and, armed with three million US dollars, entered the world of tribal-warlord politics in the Tajik, Uzbek and Hazara dominated Northern Alliance.[59] The emptiness of maneuver warfare at the operational level and Franks' inability to respond to an unconventional scenario resulted in a civilian agency taking the lead in applying operational art — a truly incredible development.

In October 2001, coalition airpower initiated Operation Enduring Freedom by bombing static Taliban and al-Qaeda targets, but CIA teams could not direct aircraft, as only the military had the required equipment, so frontline enemy positions could not be bombed as the Northern Alliance requested. However, the arrival of Special Forces teams enabled the direct targeting of the enemy front line and the air campaign concentrated on direct support missions to assist the Northern Alliance.[60] Taliban defenders were either destroyed or withdrew and the Northern Alliance captured Mazar on 10 November. The importance of political context became even more important as the decline of Taliban control necessitated a search for an anti-Taliban Pashtun leader to represent the largest ethnic group, as the minority dominated Northern Alliance could never be acceptable to the entire country. Hamid Karzai, from an influential Pashtun tribe, emerged from the political vacuum and, with the support of the CIA team 'Echo' and Special Forces troops, rallied Pashtuns to fight the Taliban, initiating an offensive toward Kandahar.[61] The CIA had once again taken the lead in applying operational art as Franks acknowledged: 'The CIA station in Islamabad — virtually our Afghanistan embassy in exile — supported Karzai as a future national leader who could unite the disparate ethnic factions. And I too was impressed.'[62]

During the campaign, Franks never came to grips with operational art, as historian Thomas Ricks noted:

> The inside word in the U.S. military long had been that Franks didn't think strategically. For example, when the general held an off-the-record session

with officers studying at the Naval War College. . . . one student posed
the classic Clausewitzian question: What is the nature of the war you are
fighting in Afghanistan? 'That's a great question for historians', Franks
sidestepped, recalled another officer who was there. 'Let me tell you what
we are doing'. Franks proceeded to discuss how U.S. troops cleared cave
complexes in Afghanistan. It was the most tactical answer possible.[63]

Franks, with his maneuver warfare mindset, failed as an operational leader
in Afghanistan, which allowed the CIA to step up to the challenge. An
Army War College report on the first phase of Enduring Freedom noted:
'The lack of a war plan or theater campaign plan has hindered operations
and led to a tactical focus that ignores long-term objectives.'[64] Franks
would again fail during another invasion, but this time maneuver warfare
would take center stage.

OPERATION IRAQI FREEDOM

The United States planned to invade Iraq in 2003 with an understanding
between political and military leaders that Washington would not intrude
into the operational level. President Bush made this clear before Operation
Iraqi Freedom as 'politics ought to stay out of fighting a war. There was too
much politics during the Vietnam War.'[65] Franks accordingly conceived his
operational plan in splendid isolation free from political context as advocated
by the maneuver warfare theorists. Even after Afghanistan, Franks still
viewed the operational level as removed from politics:

On March 17 [2003], two days before D-Day, I had faxed a 'letter of
concern' to Rumsfeld's deputy, Paul Wolfowitz. Although I couched the
message in polite terms, its intent was blunt: Keep Washington focused
on policy and strategy. *Leave me the hell alone to run the war.* . . . My
point was simple: While we at CENTCOM were executing the war plan,
Washington should focus on 'policy-level issues'.[66]

Operation Iraqi Freedom would be fought according to maneuver warfare
principles and Franks sincerely believed in 'mission tactics':

I trusted my subordinates. I would observe their actions, but not try to control their individual engagements, even though I had the ability to do so from CENTCOM's high-technology headquarters. I'd witnessed politicians and generals choosing targets in Vietnam; it hadn't worked then, and it wouldn't work now.[67]

Franks believed that capturing Baghdad — the enemy 'center of gravity' — would win the war:

The capital was the center of gravity of the Baathist regime; as long as his troops still controlled the city, Saddam Hussein would never relinquish power. Therefore, Coalition forces had to advance on Baghdad so rapidly — bypassing and fixing enemy formations in place — that the capital would be cut off before Iraqi divisions could fall back and turn the sprawling city into a 'fortress', as many feared it might become.[68]

General David McKiernan, the ground component commander, accordingly planned a two-pronged drive to Baghdad — the Army's V Corps would advance west of the Euphrates while the I Marine Expeditionary Force would approach between the Tigris and the Euphrates.[69] To assist this offensive, Franks explained the importance of John Boyd's O–O–D–A loop to his staff:

You all know my thoughts on battle tempo. . . Remember — speed and momentum. . . By striking hard and fast, our units would disrupt the Iraqis' ability to react effectively. . . We are going to win this fight — and we'll do it by getting inside the enemy's decision cycle.[70]

General James Mattis, commander of the 1st Marine Division, similarly told his subordinates, 'Our overriding principle will be speed, speed, speed.'[71] Mattis, a convert to maneuver warfare, deeply admired Boyd's ideas:

Success in war requires seizing and maintaining the initiative — and the Marines had adopted Boyd's OODA loop as the intellectual framework

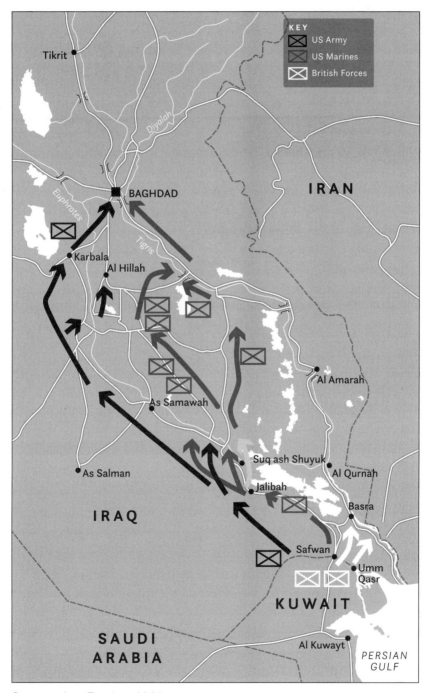

Operation Iraqi Freedom, 2003

for maneuver warfare. Used with decentralized decision-making, accelerating our OODA loops results in a cascading series of disasters confronting the enemy.[72]

Unlike the Gulf War, which involved an air campaign prior to the ground offensive, Operation Iraqi Freedom would involve the air and ground campaigns commencing simultaneously in order to completely overwhelm the Iraqis. The operational plan, as scholar Adam Elkus explained, 'was heavily inspired by Boydian theory. US forces isolated, paralyzed, and destroyed Saddam Hussein's government in record-breaking speed'.[73] Colonel Howard Belote similarly noted that as coalition forces 'bypassed Iraqi strongholds' and advanced quickly to Baghdad 'the campaign plan appeared to be a textbook application of Liddell Hart's indirect-approach theory'.[74]

Evan Wright, a *Rolling Stone* journalist, was embedded with the Marine 1st Reconnaissance Battalion and his experiences became the basis of his book *Generation Kill* (2004). Wright witnessed how the Marines were eager to prove maneuver warfare: 'The Iraq campaign would showcase the Corps' embrace of maneuver warfare.'[75] Wright continued:

The point of Mattis's plan to send First Recon ahead of his main battle forces is that this battalion will be among the fastest on the battlefield . . . According to the doctrine of maneuver warfare, their relative speed, not their meager firepower, is their primary weapon. True to his radio call sign, 'Chaos,' Mattis will use First Recon as his main agent for causing disorder on the battlefield by sending the Recon Marines into places where no one is expecting them.[76]

During the invasion, the rapid Marine advance toward Baghdad caught the Iraqis by surprise. On 5 April, Mattis ordered his famed 'Thunder Run' into Baghdad — a lightning surprise 'recon pull' in which the Marines advanced deep into Baghdad. Anthony Piscitelli in *The Marine Corps Way of War* argued that this constituted maneuver warfare:

After the first 'Thunder Run,' the Marines realized the Iraqis were unable to deal with an attack from a direction they were not expecting. The

Marines thus focused on 'Thunder Runs' aimed at the Iraqi rear. These ultimately led to the capturing of Baghdad earlier than expected and with minimum casualties. . . These 'Thunder Runs' were a successful and effective application of maneuver warfare.[77]

Bing West, a former Marine who served in Vietnam and later became Assistant Secretary of Defense for International Security Affairs under Reagan, and Ray Smith, a retired Marine General, were embedded within the 1st Marine Division. They declared Operation Iraqi Freedom 'the first major war fought according to that doctrine [maneuver warfare]'.[78] 'Maneuver Warfare,' they noted, 'moved from being a theoretical doctrine to a real battlefield, where it proved itself.'[79]

West and Smith cited an example of maneuver warfare working in practice. During the Battle of Baghdad, Fedayeen paramilitary fighters dug in at Al Karrada, a suburb containing Saddam's palaces and embassies on the Tigris River. Major John McDonough, a Marine operations officer, devised a plan to take the suburb, dubbed the Snoozle. West and Smith described McDonough as a 'charter member of the Maneuver Warfare movement'.[80] 'McDonough had the chance to show that Maneuver Warfare was real,' they continued, 'not just a theory and not only the province of generals.'[81] McDonough's plan involved a swift armored operation to seize the embassies and other key assets, using surprise and shock, while bypassing points of resistance. West and Smith noted that the conflict was a 'Colonels' War' as battalion commanders were trusted to fight in accordance with 'mission tactics'.

Despite rhetoric about a 'Colonels' War', Mattis unjustifiably destroyed the career of a colonel who made the mistake of applying 'mission tactics'. Colonel Joe Dowdy commanded the 1st Regiment from the 1st Marine Division during the advance to Baghdad, which became stopped for twenty-four hours outside the city Nasiriyah, south-east of Baghdad. General John Kelly, the assistant division commander, concerned about the pause, asked Dowdy over the radio, 'Are you attacking?' Dowdy explained that his troops were engaging the enemy and Kelly asked, 'Why don't you drive through al-Kut?', which Dowdy earlier had been directed to bypass as it was a strong point.[82] Dowdy questioned the wisdom of such a move and stressed that he intended to avoid Kut. True to 'mission tactics', Dowdy insisted that as the commander on the spot, he was best placed to make the decision. However, Kelly later asked, 'What's wrong with you?' Dowdy replied, 'There's nothing wrong' before adding 'I'm the commander on the ground'. Kelly accused the regiment of 'sitting on its ass' and threated to recommend that Mattis relieve Dowdy of command: 'Maybe General Mattis won't do it. Maybe he'll decide he can get along with a regiment that isn't worth a shit. But that's what I'm going to recommend.'[83]

Dowdy resisted Kelly's 'command push' and bypassed Kut in complete conformity with maneuver warfare and in the morning his soldiers seized the bridges beyond the city. Despite capturing a key objective, he received orders to report to Mattis, who relieved him of command. Mattis accused Dowdy of being excessively concerned about enemy resistance and lacking combat experience, to which he replied, 'I've been fighting my way up this motherfucking road for the past two weeks.'[84] Mattis stated that he 'needed to go away' and Dowdy was flown out of Iraq and left the Marines the next year.[85]

Mattis' decision received criticism in the press as Christopher Cooper reported in the *Wall Street Journal*: 'One of the cardinal rules of maneuver warfare stipulates that generals should allow commanders in the field, such as Col. Dowdy, to make tactical decisions.'[86] Dowdy made the fatal mistake of trusting his commander and believing in the doctrinal principles without understanding that his superiors considered maneuver warfare doctrine optional.

Although Operation Iraqi Freedom witnessed aspects of maneuver warfare at the tactical level, at the operational level the invasion focused on destruction, as Howard Belote stated:

> The regime was not paralyzed; it lacked the capability to act. The war was rapidly concluded in Baghdad in part due to the effect of joint and coalition airpower on Republican Guard divisions. In conjunction with landpower, the air component crushed Saddam's major source of power in decisive battle — and once again validated the enduring insights of Carl von Clausewitz.[87]

General T. Michael Moseley, the air commander, focused on supporting the ground invasion by destroying Iraqi units: 'I find it interesting when folks say we're softening them up. We're not softening them up. We're killing them.'[88] By 4 April, the air campaign had directed 85 percent of missions to destroying Iraqi troops and equipment, especially the three Republican Guard divisions, and, as Murray Williamson and Robert Scales observed, this 'rapid rate of attrition left the Iraqis with virtually no means to defend their capital'.[89] By 8 April, the Republican Guard divisions only had 19 of their original 850 tanks left and only 40 of their 550 artillery pieces.[90] Therefore, the 'Thunder Run' into Baghdad had been made possible by attrition and this had actually been going on for years before the invasion.

After the Gulf War, coalition air forces patrolled no-fly zones in southern and northern Iraq. When Saddam attempted to shoot down American and British planes, the coalition retaliated with strikes against the Iraqi air defense system, completely destroying it before the invasion.[91] The lightning advance to Baghdad during the ground campaign had been enabled by attrition as Williamson and Scales explained: 'The conflict with Iraq engaged an enemy who had virtually no military capabilities left after an air war of attrition lasting over twelve years.'[92] As successful as Operation Iraqi Freedom may have been in terms of destroying Saddam's regime, it also sowed the seeds of a strategic nightmare.

STRATEGIC FAILURE AND THE NEW WAR

Operation Iraqi Freedom was a superficial operational plan which created a strategic disaster in large part due to Franks' attachment to maneuver warfare. As he failed to contemplate political context, he never properly defined the strategic purpose of the operation and his campaign plan stressed: 'The purpose of this operation is to force the collapse of the Iraqi regime and deny it the use of WMD to threaten its neighbors and U.S. interests in regions. . . The endstate for this operation is regime change.'[93] Therefore, the plan exclusively focused on eliminating Saddam rather than shaping postwar Iraq.[94]

The key aspect of Franks' shallow understanding of operational art was his belief in the maneuver warfare ideal of undermining the enemy 'center of gravity'. As such, he believed capturing Baghdad would translate into victory and his operational plan, as Thomas Ricks contended, 'resembled a banana republic coup d'état more than a full-scale war plan'.[95] This mindset betrayed limited operational thinking as it equated capturing a capital with winning a war, the antithesis of genuine operational art. Boyd and Lind's idea of securing victory by rapid strikes against a 'critical vulnerability' to paralyze and collapse the enemy was an illusion, and Thomas Ricks observed, 'Most generals, at worst, get the opportunity to lose one war. Franks bungled two in just three years.'[96]

Franks and Mattis' obsession with speed was counter-productive and an Army War College analysis of Operation Iraqi Freedom concluded that little evidence existed that speed contributed to success and a slower pace would have made it easier to secure urban areas and establish order following major combat operations.[97] Evan Wright witnessed this firsthand:

> Not only would the Marines in First Recon spearhead the invasion on the ground, they would be at the forefront of a grand American experiment in maneuver warfare. Abstract theories of transforming U.S. military doctrine would come down on their shoulders in the form of sleepless nights and driving into bullets and bombs day after day, often with no idea what their objective was. This experiment would succeed in producing an astonishingly fast invasion. It would also result, in the view of some Marines who witnessed the descent of liberated Baghdad into chaos, in a Pyrrhic victory for a conquering force ill-trained and unequipped to impose order on the country it occupied.[98]

Furthermore, Franks and Mattis misinterpreted Boyd who never advocated speed for its own sake but instead stressed relative speed compared with the enemy. Mattis viewed his 'Thunder Run' as the epitome of maneuver warfare; however, Boyd warned, 'Maneuver warfare is not just a bunch of guys going down the highway at a high speed.'[99]

The swift capture of Baghdad destroyed Saddam's regime but failed to secure a stable new government as little planning had been done on how Iraq would be occupied.[100] The coalition ground force consisted of 145,000 troops, a sufficient number to defeat Saddam but not enough to secure the country and protect the civilian population. This resulted in part from a belief that liberation is easy, as the scholar Cora Sol Goldstein stated:

> The Pentagon and the State Department had mistaken expectations concerning Iraq. They believed that Iraqis would greet the coalition troops as liberators and that Iraqis would want to emulate the American model of society.[101]

A Pentagon review led by former Defense Secretaries James Schlesinger and Harold Brown confirmed this conclusion: 'The October 2002 Centcom war plan presupposed that relatively benign stability and security operations would precede a handover to Iraq's authorities.'[102]

America invaded Iraq without understanding the country's political landscape and, as such, the military leadership did not appreciate the complexity of Iraqi society and history; it failed to anticipate the various factions prepared to wage insurgencies. The Coalition Provisional Authority accordingly made key mistakes such as excessive de-Baathification and the dismantling of the Iraqi Army, which fueled Sunni resentment. The authority did not anticipate a Sunni backlash and utterly failed to predict the Shiite rebellion of Muqtada al-Sadr.

Before the Iraq War, the maneuver warfare theorists rarely expressed any interest in counterinsurgency operations or the politics of being an occupying power. This is unsurprising given their faith in *Wehrmacht* veterans who spoke of pure military operations and conveniently avoided discussing the reality of their brutal occupation and the barbarism of anti-partisan warfare. Their accounts presented a rosy picture of the mythical short-lived military occupation of Soviet populations until the brutal Nazis took over. Therefore, it is unsurprising that Franks and other maneuver warfare zealots expected occupation work to occur by default, provided they arrived as liberators as they incorrectly imagined the *Wehrmacht* behaved in Russia.

Maneuver warfare concepts provided no help to the occupation army fighting insurgencies, which represented a new war of attrition, as General Bernard Trainor noted:

> Iraqi Freedom I (OIF), started out as Maneuver Warfare at its best,

but came a cropper early when the enemy did not turn out to be the
Republican Guard, but the Fedayeen on our flanks. The following eight
years of Iraqi Freedom II saw no Maneuver Warfare option and became a
war of attrition, so detested by Bill Lind.[103]

However, this attrition did not turn out to be the demonic force of the
maneuver warfare imagination as Lieutenant Colonel Ralph Peters explained:
'Operation Iraqi Freedom, for all its dashing maneuvers, provided a new
example of a postmodern war of attrition — one in which the casualties are
overwhelmingly on one side [the enemy].'[104]

As maneuver warfare rejects the application of attrition in all
circumstances, it offered no real insight into fighting this kind of war. 'There
is no magic maneuver waiting to be plotted on a map,' Peters warned.
'While sharp tactical movements that bring firepower to bear will bring
us important successes along the way, this war is going to be a long, hard
slog.'[105] Major Ian Brown confirmed the decline of maneuver warfare being
practiced on operations by Marines:

> In surveying the timeline of the diverging perspectives on Enduring
> Freedom and Iraqi Freedom, the split becomes clearer. Those Marines
> who were adamant that they employed maneuver warfare generally took
> part in the initial invasions, while many of the critics who argued that
> the Corps had fallen away from it were those who deployed and wrote
> during the later counterinsurgency phases. There were a handful of
> exceptions to this.[106]

Brown added:

> The maneuver warfare of highways and deserts did not seem applicable
> in close-quarters urban combat with faceless insurgents. And so, along
> with their Army brethren, many Marines who were engaged in occupation
> duties struggled during a long and dangerous period of adapting to what
> seemed a different warfighting style.[107]

Rather than getting inside 'decision cycles' to create paralysis and collapse, fighting insurgents requires patience and, as Captain Zachary Martin, an Iraq War veteran, explained, 'insurgencies are defeated not by lightning, focused actions but instead by persistent, comprehensive actions'.[108] He stressed the necessity of understanding the political context as 'we continue to treat the insurgency as an enemy to be defeated by force of arms, instead of a Hydra that is generated by the political and structural conditions in Iraq'.[109]

After jettisoning maneuver warfare dogma, the American military learned from its mistakes and turned the situation around by allowing political context to enter operational-level planning. In June 2003, the Americans began developing a suitable campaign plan with five lines of operations: security, essential services, governance, economy and strategic communications. In 2006, the Army published FM 3-24 *Counterinsurgency* which reversed the neglect of doctrine required for the new war.

General David Petraeus took command of coalition forces in 2007 and coordinated these responses into a comprehensive counterinsurgency plan. The Americans also began to understand that political accommodation within Iraqi society was required. Sunnis had been alienated by de-Baathification and the disbanding of the Iraqi Army, causing many Sunni insurgents to join forces with international Jihadists. However, by 2006 many Sunnis began seeing the Jihadists as their primary enemy due to their atrocities and attempts to spark a full-scale sectarian civil war. At the same time, perceptions about Americans began to change as many Sunnis noted American regret over past mistakes. The resulting 'Anbar Awakening' saw Sunnis turning against Jihadists and, as the Americans now understood the political nature of the conflict, they were well placed to take advantage of the changed circumstances by allying with Sunni groups. This significantly improved security during President Bush's 'surge' of an additional 20,000 troops to Iraq in 2007.

During the 'surge', Petraeus ordered troops to spread out from large bases into small outposts to enable them to live among the population while initiating negotiations with insurgent groups. Colonel Peter Mansoor, Petraeus's executive officer, noted, 'By the beginning of the surge in early 2007, the military had undergone a renaissance in its ability to connect with the Iraqi people, an adaptation that greatly assisted its ability to conduct counterinsurgency

David Petraeus in Baghdad in 2008
(Contributor: PJF Military Collection/Alamy Stock Photo)

operations.'[110] Thomas Ricks noted how this approach succeeded:

> By June 2007 the new approach had begun to show results. As
> summer began, Sunni insurgents began coming over to the American
> side — not surrendering, but keeping their weapons and going on
> the American payroll in return for agreeing to cease their attacks on
> Americans. Eventually, more than 100,000 insurgents would turn. As
> they did, the sanctuaries of their more hard-core former comrades
> began evaporating.[111]

Petraeus explained the importance of understanding political context as
'counterinsurgency operations depend on a keen understanding of the
political, historical, cultural, economic, and military situation in each area'.[112]
He also warned about a return to dogma because 'clearly, we can't go back

American soldiers in Iraq in 2009
(Contributor: Everett Collection Historical/Alamy Stock Photo)

to the days of training that we used to do at the National Training Center where there were no civilians on the battlefield, no urban sites, it was just tank on tank and maneuver warfare'.[113] Furthermore, Petraeus warned that success requires careful coordination between civil and military authorities:

> At the core there are the insurgents that have certain needs to sustain the insurgency (money, ammunition, explosives, leadership, communications, popular support, ideology, command and control, sanctuaries). To deal with that you need a comprehensive civil-military effort that aims to squeeze the life out of the insurgency like an Anaconda snake.[114]

As the Americans began making positive steps toward a broad civil–military strategy, Lind criticized this development for generating bureaucracy and instead advocated co-coordinating the fight against insurgents through slim headquarters modeled on panzer divisions:

> Here, it is helpful to return to the source, namely the German Army.
> Not only did World War II German companies have no staff, neither did
> German battalions. At more senior levels, staffs were very small; a Panzer
> division staff had about twelve officers.[115]

Professor Jim Lacey from the Marine Corps War College criticized Lind's
disconnect from reality:

> During the invasion of Iraq the 3rd Infantry Division went from Kuwait to
> Baghdad in 21 days, destroying half a dozen Iraqi divisions along the way.
> During that time, the division was maneuvered by Brigadier General Lloyd
> Austin from the back of a couple of vehicles, and he was supported by a staff
> of less than a dozen officers. Moreover, when I visited the 101st Airborne
> Division headquarters during the invasion, it was working out of two tents.[116]

Lacey continued:

> Only during the occupation did headquarters begin to grow. This was
> not a result of needing more officers to coordinate the combat side
> of the equation. Rather, division headquarters were given diplomatic
> responsibilities, told to establish local economies, and help establish
> civic government (the list is almost endless). The reason military officers
> handled these positions is that, for the most part, the government's civilian
> agencies failed to show up in anything near the numbers required to do
> the job.[117]

Lacey concluded that Lind 'diagnosed the wrong ailment and offered the wrong
cure' and has 'lost contact with the realities of our current military'.[118] However,
Lind in more recent years rejected the universal truth of maneuver warfare
by demoting the concept to a specific period of history — Third Generation
Warfare — which is only of limited utility today as conflicts are now apparently
taking place according to the rules of Fourth Generation Warfare.

CHAPTER ELEVEN
FOURTH GENERATION WARFARE AND EDUCATING THE ENEMY

FOURTH GENERATION WARFARE

William S. Lind significantly modified maneuver warfare theory by articulating fourth generation warfare.[1] In 1989, he co-authored an article with Keith Nightengale, John Schmitt, Joseph Sutton and Gary Wilson, 'The Changing Face of War: Into the Fourth Generation' published in the *Marine Corps Gazette*, which introduced the concept. According to this theory, first generation warfare began after the Treaty of Westphalia in 1648 as the state began to monopolize warfare and ended with the conclusion of the Napoleonic Wars in 1815. Conflict during this period was characterized by infantry armed with muskets using line and column tactics.[2] Second generation warfare lasted until 1918, and witnessed mass infantry supported by the rise of industrialized firepower reaching its zenith in the trenches of World War I.[3] Third generation warfare, or maneuver warfare, commenced with German stormtrooper 'infiltration tactics' and evolved into the mechanized *Blitzkrieg*, which bypassed enemy strengths and achieved collapse through paralysis or disruption, as explained by Liddell Hart and John Boyd.[4]

Fourth generation warfare developed after World War II, as the emergence of unconventional forces using guerrilla tactics and terrorism largely replaced conventional state-versus-state conflict. The fourth generation is characterized by non-state actors, unable to directly challenge state power, instead using unconventional means to undermine government will. 'All over the world,' Lind explained, 'state militaries find themselves fighting nonstate opponents such as al-Qaeda, Hamas, Hezbollah, and the Revolutionary Armed Forces of Colombia. Almost everywhere, the state is losing.'[5] Lind, Schmitt and Gray further explained the decline of state power:

> A creation of the West, the nation-state never became the primary loyalty in much of Africa, Asia, and the Middle East. . . Most of their citizens continued to see themselves as members of a clan or tribe or religious grouping, not a nation. As Western power recedes, the old loyalties are reasserting themselves. West Africa, as one example, is rapidly returning to its precolonial status, with a coastal rim of trading stations fronting a tribal hinterland.[6]

The critics of fourth generation warfare acknowledge that it makes useful insights on contemporary conflicts and the difficulties faced by conventional militaries in dealing with them, but object to dividing the history of warfare into contrived stages. For example, Antulio Echevarria from the United States Army War College contended that 'insurgency as a way of waging war actually dates back to classical antiquity, and thus predates the so-called second and third generations'.[7] As such, fourth generation warfare theorists have little interest in pre-1945 unconventional leaders as if Spartacus, Pancho Villa, Michael Collins and the Boer *Kommandos* never existed.

Boyd, however, described guerrilla and revolutionary warfare in *Patterns of Conflict* without the dogma of confining it to the so-called fourth generation. He spoke of Lawrence of Arabia gaining the support and trust of the Arab population and using hit and run tactics to get inside the Turkish mind.[8] Boyd also mentioned the Soviet revolutionary strategy of Lenin which focused on disintegrating the existing 'regime's ability to govern' through agitation and propaganda.[9] Furthermore, Boyd declared that 'Mao Tse-Tung synthesized Sun Tzu's ideas, classic guerrilla strategy and tactics, and Napoleonic style mobile operations under an umbrella of Soviet revolutionary ideas to create a powerful way for waging modern (guerrilla) war.'[10] As these ideas originated before 1945, Lind's fourth generation framework is truly his own creation and it did not originate from Boyd.

Lind and the other founders of fourth generation theory initially believed the American military was making good progress toward transitioning into a third generation force.[11] However, Lind no longer believes this is the case as the American military refused to model itself exclusively on his concepts; therefore, he now dismisses the superpower as a second generation force:

> . . . the U.S. Army and USMC learned second Generation war from the French during and after World War I, and it remains the American way of war, as we are seeing in Afghanistan and Iraq. To Americans, war means 'putting steel on target'. Aviation has replaced artillery as the source of most firepower, but otherwise. . . the U.S. military today is as French as white wine and cheese.[12]

Lind argued that the American military is a second generation force losing fourth generation wars because it applies the tactics of firepower and attrition to politically complex insurgencies. He accordingly urged the American military to become a fourth generation force to successfully fight the new enemies. However, before this can occur, it must first transition into the third generation:

> . . . we need to move our doctrine from the Second to the Third Generation: from dumping firepower on opponents in a contest of attrition to maneuver warfare. . . once we have institutionalized the culture of maneuver warfare, with its outward focus on combat results, we must tackle the difficult intellectual challenge posed by 4GW.[13]

According to this logic, the American military cannot simply adapt to the challenges posed by contemporary conflict as it must first fully embrace maneuver warfare as the Germans supposedly did between 1918 and 1945. Following this logic, Lind urged the Marine Corps to embrace stormtrooper 'infiltration tactics' because this would constitute a move into the third generation.[14] In other words, the American military must emulate the *Wehrmacht* before it can properly fight unconventional wars and this explains Lind's advice to soldiers fighting insurgents in Iraq to model their headquarters on panzer divisions. The option of transitioning from the second generation directly to the fourth is never considered in Lind's Hegelian-Marxist mindset in which historical processes must follow precise stages.

The most significant flaw in Lind's proposal is that third generation warfare is entirely mythical as stormtroopers never applied 'infiltration tactics' and the *Wehrmacht* never practiced maneuver warfare. Therefore the entire structure of fourth generation warfare has absolutely no basis in reality. Maneuver warfare concepts cannot be effectively applied to counterinsurgency operations anyway as Boyd's vision of conflict as a time-competitive series of 'decision cycles' has limited usefulness when fighting insurgents.

POLARITY AND THE O-O-D-A LOOP

Clausewitz understood war to be a polarized contest between two adversaries locked in a struggle resembling a 'giant duel'.[15] One side will be attacking when the other is defending; one will be victorious and the other will be defeated. Furthermore, the progress of war could be measured using polarity as one side would be winning relative to how much the other is losing, or as Captain Emile Simpson, a British officer, explained: 'according to the principle of polarity, war provided a single, mutually-recognised scale which determined the relative superiority that set military conditions for a political outcome'.[16] However, polarity has little meaning when applied to wars involving non-state actors and the British blundered in Afghanistan because they tried in vain to understand the conflict by applying polarity to a stateless enemy.

The British Task Force which deployed into Helmand Province in 2006 failed to understand the complex networks of local tribes and militias because they viewed the war in terms of polarity. The British understood themselves to be on the 'side' of the Afghan Government while opposing the other side, the 'Taliban'. They failed to consider local complexity in which loyalty to a 'side' was not clearly defined. For example, Sher Mohammed

Akhundzada was the Governor of Helmand from 2001 to 2005 until being removed from power for being a narcotics trafficker. Akhundzada and his followers subsequently fought the British who viewed this as a defection to the 'Taliban', but in reality he was a militia commander fighting for his own interests. Simpson blamed polarity for creating this false impression:

> Akhundzada's actions following his dismissal are only to be considered a change of 'sides' if one erroneously imposes a polarised model of war on the conflict. Akhundzada and his men did not 'change sides'; they remained on their own side.[17]

Simpson explained that the majority of insurgents in Helmand were members of militias who in reality were only notional members of the 'Taliban'.[18] The British also failed to understand their own 'side' by not realizing that many of the supposedly pro-Government militias were beyond the control of Kabul and were constantly fighting each other.[19]

Like the British Army in Afghanistan, Liddell Hart understood war in terms of polarity by perceiving it as a contest between two opposing minds as historian Correlli Barnett concluded:

> Liddell Hart as a thinker took a very old-fashioned view of war — far more old-fashioned than that of Sir Douglas Haig, indeed more old-fashioned than Clausewitz. He saw it as a game of skill, a battle of wits, a psychological contest, almost bloodless: and himself as the commentator awarding points for clever footwork and stroke-play.[20]

The same is true of maneuver warfare as Boyd's ideas are entirely based on polarity with two sides locked in a contest trying to get inside each other's 'decision cycle'. General John Kiszely correctly concluded that maneuver warfare 'involves one opponent seeking to *mentally* outmanoeuvre the other, as in a game of chess'.[21] Boyd, a fighter pilot, superimposed the notion of a time-competitive dogfight onto all conflict, but this does not reflect the reality of land warfare and, as Major Craig Tucker noted, there 'is considerable difference between maneuvering a fighter and maneuvering an army'.[22] Maneuver warfare does not reflect the reality of conflicts like

Afghanistan, as Major Gary Anderson explained in relation to the earlier Soviet–Afghan War:

> Some enemies simply don't have OODA loops that are complicated and efficient enough to disrupt. For instance, the Soviets have launched numerous combined arms campaigns designed to paralyze the command, control, and communications of the Afghan resistance, but the Afghans simply don't have a system that is susceptible to conventional-type attack.[23]

The American military in Afghanistan also learned that insurgent groups avoid time-competitive contests and instead patiently wait for the superpower to exhaust itself, as historian Patrick Porter explained:

> In their propaganda, the Taliban play on the simple view that time is on their side. In their 'night letters' of handwritten messages, face-to-face warning and radio broadcasts, they remind Afghan communities that their enemies will run out of 'political time', and that the Taliban will be there long after demoralised foreigners leave.[24]

In a typical example of this logic, a Taliban prisoner told his American captor, 'You may have the watches, but we have the time.'[25]

The whole point of guerrilla warfare is to outlast an opponent, as scholar James Hasik concluded: 'Consider Boyd's emphasis on speed: it is not, contrary to the tenor of his work, always of the essence. It certainly wasn't for Mao, that great insurgent; he preferred going slowly, and did so to great effect.'[26] Even Lind questions the utility of 'decision cycles' in contemporary conflict: 'Exactly how the OODA Loop works in 4th Generation conflicts remains an open question; it is possible that 4th Generation forces can out-cycle state armed forces not by being faster, but by moving so slowly that they are unobservable.'[27] However, the most problematic aspect of fourth generation warfare is its continuation of the maneuver warfare myth that victory comes through undermining a 'center of gravity' by striking at 'critical vulnerabilities'.

THE 'CRITICAL VULNERABILITY' OF CIVIL SOCIETY

Fourth generation warfare depicts terrorists as an almost invisible threat living inside societies, seeking to destroy them by attacking 'critical' targets.[28] For example, Lind and the other founders argued:

> Terrorism must seek to collapse the enemy from within as it has little capability (at least at present) to inflict widespread destruction. . . Terrorism takes this a major step further. It attempts to bypass the enemy's military entirely and strike directly at his homeland, at civilian targets.[29]

In this context, the goal of terrorism is the destruction of society, as Antulio Echevarria articulated:

> The kind of terrorists that 4GW theorists described, for instance, behaved more like German storm troopers of 1918, or Robert Heinlein's starship troopers of the distant future. . . these future terrorists would first seek to infiltrate a society and then attempt to collapse it from within by means of an ill-defined psychocultural 'judo throw' of sorts.[30]

Fourth generation warfare views the civilian populations of Western democracies as sources of weakness because their perspectives can easily be shaped by terrorists who manipulate the media with shock effects to undermine their will. Therefore, fourth generation warfare is the latest reincarnation of Liddell Hart's mythical Achilles heel. Instead of strategic bombers striking the 'critical node' of civilian morale, unconventional enemies will generate the same effect through terrorism. However, the same flawed logic remains as civilian populations are more resilient and adaptable than the theorists assume, as historian Lawrence Freedman concluded:

> The idea that societies, and their associated military systems might be comprehended as complex systems encouraged the view, reflected in the perplexing searches for enemy centers of gravity, that hitting an enemy system in exactly the right place would cause it to crumble quickly, as the impact would reverberate and affect all the interconnected parts. The

frustration of the search was a result of the fact that effects would not
simply radiate out from some vital center. Societies could adapt to shocks.[31]

For example, 9/11 strengthened American civilian will and the resilience
displayed by Londoners in the aftermath of the 2005 terrorist attacks
immediately echoed the 'The Blitz'. Nevertheless, the notion of weak civilian
populations ready to fold at the first sight of blood is firmly entrenched in
the minds of America's political and military leadership by virtue of a self-
fulfilling prophecy.

The media is commonly blamed for America's defeat in Vietnam as it
supposedly undermined the will of the civilian population through incorrect
reporting which labeled the Tet Offensive in 1968 a defeat; however, in
reality, the media after Tet truthfully reported that American strategy was
not working.[32] Nevertheless, a widespread myth developed in which North
Vietnam supposedly identified the weakness of the American people and
'manipulated' the media to undermine their will, as Jeffrey Record, who
worked for the State Department in Vietnam, concluded: 'Hanoi seemed
to understand better than Washington that the center of gravity of the
American war effort was domestic public opinion, not Westmoreland's
legions traipsing around the Central Highlands.'[33]

The belief in the power of the media to undermine public opinion is
widespread. For example, Lieutenant Colonel Margaret Belknap stated:
'Inaccurate depictions of operations can have a devastating effect on what is
often the US strategic center of gravity, the will of the American people.'[34]
However, the Soviet experience in Afghanistan contradicts this legend
because the totalitarian state fought its 'Vietnam' without the handicap of
an independent media and, therefore, should have won.[35] The Soviets strictly
controlled their media in Afghanistan, but this did not alter the outcome
of the conflict.[36] The role played by the media in winning or losing wars
has been completely overstated, but obsession with media control remains
widespread and to believers in this fantasy, controlling the press is more
important than focusing on the enemy.[37]

Lind views the American people as weak, making them a 'critical
vulnerability'. For example, he declared in relation to Vietnam:

> Our ability to win battles was ultimately meaningless. Unfortunately,
> our opponent did understand the operational art. The Tet Offensive,
> although it resulted in a tactical defeat, was a major operational victory.
> It struck a decisive blow at our center of gravity, the home front's
> support for the war.[38]

Fourth generation warfare depicts civilians as being highly susceptible to media manipulation, as Lind and the other founders expressed:

> Fourth generation adversaries will be adept at manipulating the media
> to alter domestic and world opinion to the point where skillful use of
> psychological operations will sometimes preclude the commitment of
> combat forces. A major target will be the enemy population's support of
> its government and the war. Television news may become a more powerful
> operational weapon than armed divisions.[39]

However, negative media reporting did not erode American public support for the Vietnam War and, contrary to mythology, public support for the war actually increased after Tet.[40] During the Korean and Vietnam wars, public opinion tended to support presidential war policies despite negative media reporting.[41] Colonel William Darley accordingly concluded that public opinion is more influenced by 'strength and resolve of leadership in defining war policy as reflected in successful military operations' than 'the critical tone or editorial bias of press reports'.[42] Therefore, the eventual decline in public support during Vietnam was not attributable to media bias but rather President Johnson's failed leadership.[43] Bernard Schwarz, in a RAND Corporation study, similarly noted, 'Much anti-war sentiment, in fact, reflected disillusionment with the war and the concomitant desire not to withdraw troops but instead to escalate the war to get it over on terms favorable to the United States.'[44] Nevertheless, fear of the media created a self-fulfilling prophecy.

American operations in Bosnia, Kosovo and initially in Afghanistan aimed to minimize the presence of ground troops due to a perceived fear of casualties eroding domestic support.[45] This fear, however, did not reflect the actual nature of the public, which is willing to accept casualties when sound strategy exists.[46] The general population, in fact, tends to be more hawkish than the civil-military establishment and, as Jeffery Record concluded, 'political and military elites have convinced themselves that the American public's intolerance is significantly higher and more intractable than is actually the case'.[47] Lieutenant Colonel Ralph Peters similarly noted, 'In the bitter years after Vietnam, when our national leaders succumbed to the myth that the American people would not tolerate casualties, elements within our military. . . grew morally and practically timid.'[48] The civilian population is not a source of weakness, but fourth generation warfare zealots created an artificial 'critical vulnerability' which only exists in their imagination. Unfortunately, in the real world this myth encourages belligerents to attack civilians.

THE PAPER TIGER

Saddam Hussein and Osama bin Laden challenged American power under the assumption that its weak civilian population would not tolerate casualties. They saw the American superpower as a 'paper tiger' and both lost their lives after fatally underestimating their enemy.

Before the Gulf War, Saddam had no respect for the United States following humiliating withdrawals from Vietnam in 1975 and Lebanon in 1983.[49] This belief gave him the confidence to invade Kuwait as he falsely believed America would not intervene.[50] Saddam repeated this mistake before the American invasion of Iraq in 2003, again believing that fear of casualties would prevent America from forcing a regime change and he accordingly worried more about internal threats.[51] Saddam's overconfidence also resulted from America's humiliating retreat from Somalia after nineteen soldiers died during the 'Black Hawk Down' incident in 1993.[52]

Bin Laden had a similar perception of American weakness during his campaign to overthrow the pro-American 'apostate' governments in the Middle East.[53] He believed defeating America would be an easier task than fighting the Soviet Union:

> . . . our battle against America is much simpler than the war against
> the Soviet Union, because some of our mujahedeen who fought here

in Afghanistan also participated in operations against the Americans in Somalia — and they were surprised at the collapse of American morale. This convinced us that the Americans are a paper tiger.[54]

Bin Laden similarly boasted:

We have seen in the last decade the decline of the American government and the weakness of the American soldier, who is ready to wage cold wars and unprepared to fight long wars. This was proven in Beirut when the Marines fled after two explosions. It also proves that they can run in less than twenty-four hours, and this was also repeated in Somalia.[55]

Weak American responses, limited to cruise missile strikes, following the East Africa embassy bombings in 1998 and the attack on the USS *Cole* in 2000 reinforced this prejudice.[56] However, Bin Laden fatally misjudged the American psyche when he attacked their homeland in the belief that it would provoke an American invasion of Afghanistan, resulting in another humiliating withdrawal.[57] However, the 9/11 sneak attack on American soil mirrored the Japanese attack on Pearl Harbor, generating widespread public anger and desire for retaliation.[58] The public response to 9/11 demonstrated that previous American timidity had been a self-fulfilling delusion among the military and foreign policy establishments.[59]

Bin Laden, in forming his distorted perception of American weakness, had been influenced by fourth generation warfare. For example, Abu Ubayd al-Qurashi, an aide to Bin Laden, argued in the jihadist magazine *Majallat al-Ansar*:

In 1989, some American military experts predicted a fundamental change in the future form of warfare. . . They predicted that the wars of the 21st century would be dominated by a kind of warfare they called 'the fourth generation of wars.' . . . The time has come for the Islamic movements facing a general crusader offensive to internalize the rules of fourth-generation warfare.[60]

Abu Ubayd al-Qurashi added that fourth generation warfare 'presents significant difficulties for the Western war machine'.[61]

Lind noted that al-Qaeda read his foundational article from the *Marine Corps Gazette*: 'Our troops reportedly found copies of the article in the caves at Tora Bora, the al-Qaeda hideout in Afghanistan.'[62] He also said that the article 'was cited in 2002 by al-Qaeda, who declared, "This is our doctrine"'.[63] Furthermore, Lind reflected, 'The eternal nightmare of the military theorist is that only the enemy will pay attention to his work.'[64]

Lind, when commenting on fourth generation warfare, preached a pessimistic view of his fellow countrymen: 'Americans, driven by sensation-seeking media, will panic. . . Osama himself has said that al-Qaeda's main target is the American economy, since that is what Americans seem to care most about.'[65] Following the invasion of Iraq in 2003, Lind constantly predicted the defeat of Western forces, who no longer listened to his advice, while praising the cunning of fourth generation forces who are his new students.

According to Lind, American operations in Afghanistan and Iraq were doomed from day one because the military, stuck in second generation warfare, could never prevail over foes who personified the fourth generation:

> As the U.S. sends thousands more American soldiers to Afghanistan, it risks speeding its own defeat in that graveyard of empires. Why? Because the 2nd Generation practice of the U.S. military reduces tactics to little more than bumping into the enemy and calling for fire.[66]

Lind has been a consistent critic of American intervention in Iraq, citing the blunders of de-Baathification and the dismantling of the Iraqi Army: 'Washington is now making noises about reversing both of those early decisions, but it is simply too late.'[67] Even when American forces recovered from their initial mistakes and turned the situation around during the 'surge' and 'Anbar Awakening', Lind again predicted defeat:

> The war in Iraq is irredeemably lost. . . The passions of ethnic and religious hatred unleashed by the disintegration of the Iraqi state will not cool because a few more American patrols pass through the streets. Iraqis are quite capable of fighting us and each other at the same time.[68]

Maneuver warfare and its fourth generation update encourage attacks on civilian targets because the theorists spread a 'paper tiger' myth by falsely depicting civilian populations as 'critical vulnerabilities', which emboldened Bin Laden to attack the American homeland. Fourth generation warfare incorrectly views terrorist attacks on civilian targets as logical methods of undermining the 'center of gravity' of the governments they oppose, encouraging such groups to launch attacks in the false hope that they will achieve their aims. However, such actions are extremely unlikely to translate into victory because they are based on myths which contradict the well-researched resilience of civilian populations. Nevertheless, so-called fourth generation terrorists will create much human suffering before eventually disappearing into obscurity.

Despite Lind's prophecies of doom, American combat forces withdrew from Iraq in 2011 and left behind an imperfect but functioning state. Although the rise of the Islamic State three years later sparked a new war after the failed Arab Spring and civil war in Syria spilled over into Sunni areas of Iraq, Lind's prophecies of unstoppable fourth generation forces never materialized and the Islamic State eventually declined.

EPILOGUE

John Boyd initially made intriguing observations concerning air combat over Korea but made the fatal mistake of assuming he had uncovered a universal truth and, as the scholar James Hasik concluded, 'to generalize at the grand strategic level of all warfare from the tactical requirements of aerial dogfighting is a considerable leap'.[1] When searching for confirmation of his theory, he encountered the misinformation of *Wehrmacht* veterans and Liddell Hart and, unable to distinguish historical truth from fantasy, seemingly found his Holy Grail. The result of his quest, maneuver warfare, was founded upon mythology, but this became apparent only after professional historians exposed the historical fraud concocted by German generals and Liddell Hart.

Franz Halder's manuscripts contain much deliberate deception as his priority was the rehabilitation of the *Wehrmacht*'s reputation by fraudulently championing its supposed unparalleled military excellence and clean hands. This disinformation grew with popular accounts such as Heinz Guderian's *Panzer Leader*, Erich von Manstein's *Lost Victories* and Friedrich von Mellenthin's *Panzer Battles*. The postwar German accounts received legitimate historical status in part through Liddell Hart's endorsement, but he created further distortions by fabricating his self-serving definition of *Blitzkrieg*, motivated by a desire to restore his lost reputation. Liddell Hart's mythology seemingly made *Blitzkrieg* his intellectual property and this illusion became widely accepted in the English-speaking world.

As maneuver warfare began to gain traction in the Pentagon in the late 1970s, Mellenthin and Hermann Balck visited America and they rejected the theory's key concepts while insisting that the *Wehrmacht* never fought

Colonel John Boyd
(Author's Collection)

according to its tenets. Boyd and William S. Lind refused to use Mellenthin and Balck's testimony as an opportunity to revise maneuver warfare and instead inaccurately depicted the *Wehrmacht* as masters of maneuver warfare. As such, maneuver warfare remained a theory based on the disinformation and fraudulent concepts it inherited from others. As Boyd never applied the discipline of an historian to his research, he was a blind strategist trapped in the darkness of the fraudulent history of Liddell Hart and German generals, guided by the confirmation bias inherent within the logic of his grail quest.

Boyd and Lind oversaw the revolution in the American military which elevated maneuver warfare into doctrine. However, the acceptance of these concepts in the military actually reflected the trauma unleashed by defeat in Vietnam, not the truth of their ideas.[2] In much the same way, the acceptance of J.F.C. Fuller and Liddell Hart's theories reflected the post-World War I desire to avoid another Somme.

Maneuver warfare continues to be military orthodoxy in most Western countries and is upheld in doctrine as an ideal, although it is not always practiced. From the beginning its concepts have been critiqued by officers who see through its dogma. For example, General Daniel Bolger declared:

Maneuver warfare is bunk. No competent soldier, let alone the entire U.S. military establishment, should embrace it. Subjected to serious scrutiny, maneuver warfare's theoretical assumptions turn out to be laughably flimsy. Not surprisingly, so are the battlefield prescriptions that flow from such flawed premises.[3]

However, this does not mean that its concepts have no value and, on the contrary, the theorists had something to offer, as Bolger acknowledged:

Maneuver warfare stresses that wars are won by men, not machines. Its proponents prefer history (albeit versions distorted by social science smash-and-grab techniques) to technology and, consequently, people to things. Their emphasis upon leadership is right on target and, in an age of computerized 'command and control', maneuverists stand tall for the central importance of leader initiative.[4]

Even though the theorists unfairly destroyed the legacy of General William DePuy, who created Active Defense, he graciously noted their positive accomplishments:

Maneuver doctrine is active as opposed to reactive and thus fits, more comfortably, the American temperament. . . [and] seeks to keep the opposing force forever off balance, forever reacting to U.S. initiatives but always one futile step behind. . . Maneuver doctrine as expressed in FM 100-5 [1982] is a sound, logical step forward on the long road of tactical evolution.[5]

The scholar Eliot Cohen similarly stated: 'Lind and Hart's innuendos not withstanding, nobody disputes the abstract merits of cleverness over stupidity, of outflanking maneuver over frontal assault, or surprise over predictability.'[6]

The problem with maneuver warfare is not that its concepts are individually bad ideas; the problem is its claim to be an historically proven formula for success in all situations, which appeals to people on grail quests, as strategist Colin Gray warned: 'War is so serious, complex, and uncertain an undertaking that its practitioners and interpreters are always on the alert for some "key" to victory, some philosopher's stone for military art.'[7] Boyd and Lind presented their ideas as an all or nothing package which ignores complexity, narrows options and discourages creativity through a self-imposed straitjacket, restricting pragmatism and common sense. As such, General Bernard Trainor stated that maneuver warfare is 'a prescriptive formula' which 'calls for subordinate freedom of action within a framework of dogma'.[8] Major Kenneth McKenzie similarly concluded:

> The hard-line 'maneuverists'. . . choose to craft their criticism in an 'either-or' framework that accentuates extreme positions. Their criticisms are very useful, and many of them should give us pause, but we do not need to make the choice they demand. . . Their thinking certainly answers part of the puzzle, but standing alone it is not the key.[9]

There are times when attrition, synchronization, command push and centralized control are the best available options, but maneuver warfare maintains that these are always bad ideas. Therefore, the theory encourages soldiers to go to war with a half-empty toolbox and, as DePuy observed, it provides a 'one-dimensional answer to multidimensional problems on the battlefield'.[10] Major Andrew Walker similarly noted: 'Although maneuver warfare is valid under certain circumstances, the nature of war and the realities of the modern battlefield call for a much more flexible doctrine of warfare.'[11] Trainor similarly stressed that maneuver warfare cannot work in all situations:

> I fought in Korea as a rifle platoon leader and upon reflection can state with confidence that Maneuver Warfare would have had no place during the Outpost War phase of the Korean War short of another Inchon-style landing. The enemy had too much defense-in-depth. I commanded two battalions on Vietnam tours, and Maneuver Warfare would not have worked there either.[12]

Western militaries can overcome addiction to maneuver warfare by rediscovering pragmatism. The positive aspects of maneuver warfare such as re-emphasizing the human factor can be better applied by exploiting enemy mistakes, as Major Gary Anderson argued:

> Marines were able to use the Japanese banzai charge against the Japanese by inviting such forays over ground chosen by Marine commanders. These charges were generally considered to be the backbreaking climax of the battle because they drained the Japanese of their manpower. These defensive Marine Corps tactics didn't celebrate firepower attrition any more than they rejected maneuver. By exploiting the Japanese tendency to play into the hands of our superior firepower, Marine planners validated the tactics of mistake.[13]

Rommel also praised the tactics of mistakes:

> Victory in battle — save where it is brought about by sheer weight of numbers, and omitting all question of the courage of the troops engaged — never comes solely as the result of the victor's planning. It is not only the merits of the victor that decide the issue, but also mistakes on the part of the vanquished.[14]

Many officers in Western militaries have written countless articles critiquing maneuver warfare but have thus far failed to reverse the revolution as the theory remains in doctrine. They incorrectly assumed that rational debate would decide the issue, but criticism limited to the conceptual level of a theory is unlikely to change anything, as historian John Mearsheimer explained:

> It is impossible to argue against maneuver as an abstract concept, just as it is very difficult to be against a strategy which calls for inflicting a decisive defeat on an opponent without having to engage in bloody battles. Before such an argument can be taken seriously, it must be taken out of the realm of the abstract.[15]

A successful critique of maneuver warfare consequently must target its 'critical vulnerability', its foundational base built upon the deception of

Wehrmacht generals and Liddell Hart as well as Boyd and Lind's evasion of Balck and Mellenthin's inconvenient testimony which rejected the fundamentals of the theory. This places the true believers in the 'horns of a dilemma' as they must either reconsider their views or defend the existence of the misinformation and fraud in military thinking concocted by German generals and Liddell Hart — an indefensible position.

BIBLIOGRAPHY

Primary Sources

Armored Warfare in World War II: Conference Featuring F.W. Von Mellenthin, Battelle Columbus Laboratories, Columbus, 1979

Balck, Hermann, *Translation of Taped Conversation with General Hermann Balck, 12 January 1979*, Battelle Columbus Laboratories, Columbus, 1979

Balck, Hermann, *Translation of Taped Conversation with General Hermann Balck, 13 April 1979*, Battelle Columbus Laboratories, Columbus, 1979

Boyd, John R., *A Discourse on Winning and Losing (Abstract)*, 1987

Boyd, John R., *Aerial Attack Study*, 11 August 1964

Boyd, John R., *Conceptual Spiral*, July/August 1992

Boyd, John R., *Organic Design for Command and Control*, May 1987

Boyd, John R., *Patterns of Conflict*, December 1986

Boyd, John R., 'Patterns of Conflict (Delivered on 26 May 1978)', in *Proceedings of Seminar on Air Antitank Warfare*, Battelle Columbus Laboratories, Columbus, 1978

Boyd, John R., *The Strategic Game of ? and ?*, June 1987

Generals Balck and Von Mellenthin on Tactics: Implications for NATO Military Doctrine, BDM Corporation, McLean, 1980

The Private War Journal of Generaloberst Franz Halder: 14 August 1939 to 24 September 1942

United States Army Historical Division

Halder, Franz, *Analysis of US Field Service Regulations*, Historical Division, 1953

Halder, Franz, *The German Campaign in Russia: Planning and Operations (1940–1942)*, Pamphlet Number 20–261a, Department of the Army, Washington, 1955

Military Improvisations During the Russian Campaign, Pamphlet 20–201, Department of the Army, Washington, 1951

Night Combat, Pamphlet 20–236, Department of the Army, Washington, 1953

Operations of Encircled Forces: German Experiences in Russia, Pamphlet 20–234, Department of the Army, Washington, 1952

Rear Area Security in Russia: The Soviet Second Front Behind the German Lines, Pamphlet 20–240, Department of the Army, Washington, 1951

Russian Combat Methods in World War II, Pamphlet 20–230, Department of the Army, Washington, 1950

Military Manuals

Air Force Doctrine Document 1 *Air Force Basic Doctrine*, United States Air Force, 1997

Army Doctrine Publication *Operations*, Ministry of Defence, Swindon, 2010

Field Manual 100–5 *Operations*, Headquarters Department of the Army, Washington, 1982

Field Manual 100–5 *Operations*, Headquarters Department of the Army, Washington, 1986

Field Manual 100–5 *Operations*, Headquarters Department of the Army, Washington, 1993

Field Manual 3–0 *Operations*, Headquarters Department of the Army, Washington, 2008

Fleet Marine Force Manual 1 *Warfighting*, Department of the Navy, Washington, 1989

Marine Corps Doctrinal Publication 1 *Warfighting*, Department of the Navy, Washington, 1997

Naval Doctrine Publication 1 *Naval Warfare*, Department of the Navy, Washington, 1994

On the German Art of War: Truppenführung, Stackpole Books, Mechanicsburg, 2001

Monographs and Papers

Baumann, Robert F., 'Soviet Media Performance during the Afghan War: STRATCOM Utopia or Dystopia?', Kendall Gott, ed., in *The US Army and the Media in Wartime: Historical Perspectives*, The Proceedings of the Combat Studies Institute 2009 Military History Symposium, 2010

Boyd, John R., *A Discourse on Winning and Losing*, Grant T. Hammond, ed. Air University Press, 2018

Boyd, John R., *Destruction and Creation*, 3 September 1976

Boyd, John R., *Discourse on Winning and Losing* (Quantico, VA: Marine Corps University, 1989)

Boyd, John R., *Patterns of Conflict (Slides)*, Chet Richards and Chuck Spinney, eds, Defense and the National Interest, 2007

Damian, Fideleon, *The Road to FMFM 1: The United States Marine Corps and Maneuver Warfare Doctrine, 1979–1989*, Kansas State University, Manhattan, Kansas, 2008

Due, Jonathan Lee, *Seizing the Initiative: The Intellectual Renaissance that Changed U.S. Army Doctrine, 1970–1982*, University of North Carolina, 2007

Evans, Michael, *The Continental School of Strategy: The Past, Present and Future of Land Power*, Land Warfare Studies Centre, 2004

Ghiz, Christopher J., *Specialized Assault Units of the World War I Western Front: A Comparative Study of the German Stormtrooper Battalions, and Canadian Trench Raiders*, U.S. Army Command and General Staff College, Fort Leavenworth, Kansas, 2010

Hammond, Grant T., 'On the Making of History: John Boyd and American Security', in *The Harmon Memorial Lecture*, United States Air Force Academy, 2012

Lauer, G.S., *Maneuver Warfare Theory: Creating a Tactically Unbalanced Fleet Marine*

Force?, U.S. Army Command and General Staff College, Fort Leavenworth, 1991

Liddell-Hart, B.H., 'The "Man-in-the-Dark" Theory of Infantry Tactics and the "Expanding Torrent" System of Attack', Lecture Presented on 3 November 1920, in *Journal of the Royal United Service Institution*, February, 1921

Lupfer, Timothy T., *The Dynamics of Doctrine: The Changes in German Tactical Doctrine During the First World War*, Combat Studies Institute, Fort Leavenworth, 1981

Michel, Marshall L., *The Revolt of the Majors: How the Air Force Changed After Vietnam*, Auburn University, 2006

Park, Francis Joon Hong, *The Unfulfilled Promise: The Development of Operational Art in the U.S. Military, 1973–1997*, University of Kansas, 2012

Phillips Jr., Dwight E., *Reengineering Institutional Culture and the American Way of War in the Post-Vietnam U.S. Army, 1968–1989*, University of Chicago, 2014

Stackpole, Patrick T., *German Tactics in the Michael Offensive March 1918*, United States Military Academy, West Point, New York, 1981

Trauschweizer, Ingo Wolfgang, *Creating Deterrence for Limited War: The U.S. Army and the Defense of West Germany, 1953–1982*, University of Maryland, 2016

Tucker, Craig A., *False Prophets: The Myth of Maneuver Warfare and the Inadequacies of FMFM–1 Warfighting*, U.S. Army Command and General Staff College, Fort Leavenworth, 1995

Welch, Steven R., *'The Annihilation of Superfluous Eaters': Nazi Plans for and Uses of Famine in Eastern Europe*, Yale University, New Haven, 2001

Newspapers and Magazines

Cohen, Eliot A., 'Uncertain Trumpets', in *The New Republic*, Volume 195, Number 9 (Sep 1986)

Cooper, Christopher, 'Speed Trap: How a Marine Lost His Command in Race to Baghdad', in *Wall Street Journal*, 5 Apr 2004

Correll, John T., 'The Reformers,' in *Air Force Magazine* (Feb 2008)

Evans, David, 'Schwarzkopf's "Jedi Knights" Praised for Winning Strategy', in *Chicago Tribune*, 1 May 1991

Fallows, James, 'Councils of War', in *The Atlantic Monthly*, Boston, Volume 289, Issue 2 (Feb 2002)

Fallows, James, 'Muscle-Bound Superpower: The State of America's Defense', in *The Atlantic Monthly*, Oct 1979

Kaplan, Fred, 'Marine Who Fought Tradition is Out', in *Boston Globe*, 1 May 1991

Kaplan, Fred, 'Military Dissenter Endured Adversity But Won Brass Ring', in *Sun Sentinel*, 30 Nov 1986

Kaplan, Fred, 'The Force Was With Them: Army's Jedi Knights Forged Gulf War Strategy', in *Boston Globe*, 17 Mar 1991

Kondracke, Morton, 'Defense Without Mirrors', in *The New Republic*, 24 Jan 1981

Journal Articles and Book Reviews

Anderson, Gary W., 'Maneuver, Attrition, or the Tactics of Mistake?', in *Marine Corps Gazette*, Volume 69, Number 9 (Sep 1985)

Andrade, Dale, 'Westmoreland Was Right: Learning the Wrong Lessons From the Vietnam War', in *Small Wars and Insurgencies*, Volume 19, Number 2 (2008)

Anonymous, 'Maneuver Warfare Board at Lejeune', in *Marine Corps Gazette*, Volume 65, Number 10 (Oct 1981)

Anonymous, 'Professional Reading', in *Marine Corps Gazette*, Volume 71, Number 11 (Nov 1987)

Anonymous, 'Saddam's Eye View: JFCOM Releases Unclassified Report', in *Defense Daily*, Volume 229, Number 58 (27 Mar 2006)

Barnett, Correlli, 'Basil faulty?', in *RUSI Journal*, Volume 144, Number 2 (Apr/May 1999)

Bayerlein, Fritz, 'With the Panzers in Russia 1941 & 43', in *Marine Corps Gazette*, Volume 38, Number 12 (Dec 1954)

Beaumont, Roger A., 'On the Wehrmacht Mystique', in *Military Review*, Volume 66, Number 7 (July 1986)

Belknap, Margaret H., 'The CNN Effect: Strategic Enabler or Operational Risk?', in *Parameters*, Volume 32, Number 3 (Autumn 2002)

Belote, Howard D., 'Paralyzed or Pulverized? The Fall of the Republican Guard', in *Joint Force Quarterly*, Volume 37 (Second Quarter 2005)

Belote, Howard D., 'Warden and the Air Corps Tactical School', in *Airpower Journal*, Volume 13, Number 3 (Fall 1999)

Benson, J.R., 'The Apostles of Mobility: The Theory and Practice of Armored Warfare', in *Marine Corps Gazette*, Volume 64, Number 12 (Dec 1980)

Betts, Richard K., 'Thesis, Antithesis, Synthesis?: Reply to Luttwak', in *International Security*, Volume 8, Number 2 (1983)

Brand, Dieter, 'The Origins of Freie Operationen', in *Military Review*, Volume 80, Number 4 (Jul/Aug 2000)

Brown, G.M., 'The Significance of Stalingrad in World War II', in *Australian Army Journal*, Number 250 (Mar 1970)

Brown, Ian T., 'Opportunity Lost,' in *Journal of Advanced Military Studies*, Volume 12, Number 2 (Fall 2021)

Brown, R.J., 'Maneuver Warfare at Tinian — 1944', in *Marine Corps Gazette*, Volume 68, Number 7 (Jul 1984)

Cancian, Mark, 'Centers of Gravity are a Myth', in *United States Naval Institute Proceedings,* Volume 124, Number 9 (Sep 1998)

Carlson, Verner R., 'Portrait of a German General Staff Officer', in *Military Review*, Volume 70, Number 4 (April 1990)

Castel, Albert, 'Liddell Hart's Sherman: Propaganda as History', in *The Journal of Military History*, Volume 67, Number 2 (Apr 2003)

Citino, Robert, 'The War Hitler Won: The Battle for Europe, 1939–1941', in *Journal of Military and Strategic Studies*, Volume 14, Issue 1 (Fall 2011)

Clover, Kevin R., 'Maneuver Warfare: Where Are We Now?', *Marine Corps Gazette*, Volume 72, Number 2 (Feb 1988)

Codo, Enrique Martinez, 'Guerrilla Warfare in the Ukraine', in *Military Review*, Volume 40, Number 8 (Nov 1960)

Cook, Samuel, 'The German Breakthrough at Sedan', *Armor*, Volume 113, Number 5 (Sept–Oct 2004)

Corum, James S., 'How to Prepare for a Battle', in *MHQ: The Quarterly Journal of Military History*, Volume 27, Number 1 (Autumn 2014)

Corum, James S., 'The Spanish Civil War: Lessons Learned and Not Learned by the Great Powers', in *The Journal of Military History*, Volume 62, Number 2 (Apr 1998)

Cowan, Jeffrey L., 'Warfighting Brought To You By...', in *United States Naval Institute Proceedings*, Volume 127, Number 11 (Nov 2001)

Crawley, Vince, 'While U.S. is Winning "On Paper" Balance Could Shift', in *Air Force Times* (1 Dec 2003)

Creveld, Martin van, 'On Learning From the Wehrmacht and Other Things', in *Military Review*, Volume 67, Number 1 (Jan 1988)

Czege, Huba Wass de, 'Lessons from the Past: Getting the Army's Doctrine "Right Enough" Today', in *Australian Army Journal*, Volume 3, Number 3 (Summer 2006)

Czege, Huba Wass de and Holder, L.D., 'The New FM 100–5', in *Military Review*, Volume 82, Number 7 (Jul 1982)

Danchev, Alex, 'Liddell Hart and the Indirect Approach', in *The Journal of Military History*, Volume 63, Number 2 (Apr 1999)

Danchev, Alex, 'Liddell Hart and Manoeuvre', in *RUSI Journal*, Volume 143, Number 6 (Dec 1998)

Darley, William M., 'War Policy, Public Support, and the Media', in *Parameters*, Volume 35, Number 2 (Summer 2005)

Doran, Michael, 'The Pragmatic Fanaticism of al Qaeda: An Anatomy of Extremism in Middle Eastern Politics', in *Political Science Quarterly*, Volume 117, Number 2 (Summer 2002)

Downing, Wayne A., 'Training to Fight', in *Military Review*, Volume 66, Number 5 (May 1986)

Echevarria, Antulio J., 'Clausewitz's Center of Gravity: It's Not What We Thought', in *Naval War College Review*, Volume 56, Number 1 (Winter 2003)

Echevarria, Antulio J., 'Reining in the Center of Gravity Concept', in *Air & Space Power Journal*, Volume 17, Number 2 (Summer 2003)

Evans, Michael, 'Captains of the Soul: Stoic Philosophy and the Western Profession of Arms in the Twenty-first Century', in *Naval War College Review*, Volume 64, Number 1 (Winter 2011)

Fanning, William J., Jr., 'The Origin of the Term "Blitzkrieg": Another View', in *The Journal of Military History*, Volume 61, Number 2 (Apr 1997)

Forster, Jurgen, 'Barbarossa Revisited: Strategy and Ideology in the East', in *Jewish Social Studies*, Volume 50, Number 1/2 (Winter 1988–Spring 1992)

Forster, Jurgen and Mawdsley, Evan, 'Hitler and Stalin in Perspective: Secret Speeches on the Eve of Barbarossa', in *War in History*, Volume 11, Number 1 (Jan 2004)

Friedman, B.A., 'Maneuver Warfare: A Defense', in *Marine Corps Gazette*, Volume 98, Number 12 (Dec 2014)

Frothingham, J.L., 'Panzer Leader', in *Marine Corps Gazette*, Volume 37, Number 3 (Mar 1953)

Gat, Azar, 'British Influence and the Evolution of the Panzer Arm: Myth or Reality? Part I', in *War in History*, Volume 4, Number 2 (Apr 1997)

Gat, Azar, 'British Influence and the Evolution of the Panzer Arm: Myth or Reality? Part II', in *War in History*, Volume 4, Number 3 (Jul 1997)

Glantz, David M., 'Soviet Operational Formation for Battle: A Perspective', in *Military Review*, Volume 63, Number 2 (Feb 1983)

Glantz, David M., 'The Red Army at War, 1941–1945: Sources and Interpretations', in *The Journal of Military History*, Volume 62, Number 3 (Jul 1998)

Goldstein, Cora Sol, '2003 Iraq, 1945 Germany, and 1940 France: Success and Failure in Military Occupations', in *Military Review*, Volume 90, Number 4 (Jul/Aug 2010)

Gole, Henry G., 'The Relevance of Gen. William E. DePuy', in *Army*, Volume 58, Number 3 (Mar 2008)

Gray, Colin S., 'Understanding Airpower: Bonfire of the Fallacies', in *Strategic Studies Quarterly*, Volume 2, Number 4 (Winter 2008)

Guderian, Heinz, 'The Experiences of the War in Russia', in *Military Review*, Volume 37, Number 4 (Jul 1957)

Gudmundsson, Bruce, 'Field Stripping the Schwerpunkt', in *Marine Corps Gazette*, Volume 73, Number 12 (Dec 1989)

Hamilton, Mark R., 'Maneuver Warfare and All That', in *Military Review*, Volume 67, Number 1 (Jan 1987)

Hankins, Michael W., 'The Blind Strategist: John Boyd and the American Art of War (Review)', in *Journal of Military History*, Volume 85 Issue 4 (Oct 2021)

Herwig, Holger H., 'Military History Reconsidered', in *Joint Force Quarterly*, Volume 30 (Spring 2002)

Hofmann, George F., 'The Tactical and Strategic Use of Attaché Intelligence: The Spanish Civil War and the U.S. Army's Misguided Quest for a Modern Tank Doctrine', in *The Journal of Military History*, Volume 62, Number 1 (Jan 1998)

Hoffman, Jon T., 'The Limits of Light Infantry Doctrine', in *Marine Corps Gazette*, Volume 74, Number 9 (Sep 1990)

Holmes, Terence M., 'Classical Blitzkrieg: The Untimely Modernity of Schlieffen's Cannae Programme', in *The Journal of Military History*, Volume 67, Number 3 (Jul 2003)

Hooker, Richard D., Jr., 'Redefining Maneuver Warfare', in *Military Review*, Volume 92, Number 2 (February 1992)

Hooker, R.D., 'The World Will Hold its Breath: Reinterpreting Operation Barbarossa', in *Parameters*, Volume 29, Number 1 (Spring 1999)

Hughes, Daniel J., 'Abuses of German Military History', in *Military Review*, Volume 86, Number 12 (Dec 1986)

Jordan, Jonathan W., 'The Wehrmacht's Worst Defeat', in *World War II*, Volume 21, Number 4 (Jul/Aug 2006)

Joyce, Adam, 'The Micropolitics of "the Army You Have": Explaining the Development of U.S. Military Doctrine After Vietnam', in *Studies in American Political Development*, Volume 26, Number 2 (Oct 2012)

Kinase, Michael G., 'Classical Strategists and the Indirect Approach', in *Australian Defence Force Journal*, Issue 119 (Jul/Aug 1996)

Kiszely, John, 'The Meaning of Manoeuvre', in *RUSI Journal*, Volume 143, Number 6 (Dec 1998)

Kiszely, John, 'Thinking About the Operational Level', in *RUSI Journal*, Volume 150, Number 6 (Dec 2005)

Liddell Hart, B.H., 'New Warfare — New Tactics', in *Marine Corps Gazette*, Volume 39, Number 10 (Oct 1955)

Liddell Hart, B.H., 'The Great Illusions of 1939', in *Military Review*, Volume 36, Number 10 (Jan 1957)

Liddell Hart, B.H., 'Was the 1940 Collapse Avoidable?', in *Military Review*, Volume 30, Number 3 (Jun 1950)

Lind, William S., 'Defining Maneuver Warfare for the Marine Corps', in *Marine Corps Gazette*, Volume 64, Number 3 (Mar 1980)

Lind, William S., 'Fourth Generation Warfare's First Blow: A Quick Look', in *Marine Corps Gazette*, Volume 85, Number 11 (Nov 2001)

Lind, William S., 'Light Infantry Tactics', in *Marine Corps Gazette*, Volume 74, Number 6 (Jun 1990)

Lind, William S., 'Misconceptions of Maneuver Warfare', in *Marine Corps Gazette*, Volume 72, Number 1 (Jan 1988)

Lind, William S., 'Rationalizing Army and Marine Corps Roles and Missions Through Operational Art', in *Marine Corps Gazette*, Volume 78, Number 7 (Jul 1994)

Lind, William S., 'Some Doctrinal Questions for the United States Army', in *Military Review*, Volume 77, Number 1 (Jan/Feb 1997)

Lind, William S., 'Tactics in Maneuver Warfare', in *Marine Corps Gazette*, Volume 65, Number 9 (Sep 1981)

Lind, William S., 'The Operational Art', in *Marine Corps Gazette*, Volume 72, Number 4 (Apr 1988)

Lind, William S., 'Understanding Fourth Generation War', in *Military Review*, Volume 84, Number 5 (Sep/Oct 2004)

Lind, William S., 'Why the German Example?', in *Marine Corps Gazette*, Volume 66, Number 6 (Jun 1982)

Lind, William S., Nightengale, Keith, Schmitt, John F., Sutton, Joseph W., and Wilson, Gary I., 'The Changing Face of War: Into the Fourth Generation', in *Marine Corps Gazette*, Volume 85, Number 11 (Nov 2001)

Lind, William S., Schmitt, John F., and Wilson, Gary I., 'Fourth Generation Warfare: Another Look', in *Marine Corps Gazette*, Volume 85, Number 11 (Nov 2001)

Lock-Pullan, Richard, '"An Inward Looking Time": The United States Army, 1973–1976', in *The Journal of Military History*, Volume 67, Number 2 (Apr 2003)

Lord, David, 'Liddell Hart and the Napoleonic Fallacy', in *RUSI Journal*, Volume 142, Number 2 (Apr 1997)

Malkasian, Carter, 'Toward a Better Understanding of Attrition: The Korean and Vietnam Wars', in *The Journal of Military History*, Volume 68, Number 3 (Jul 2004)

Marshall, S.L.A., 'Lost Victories', in *Marine Corps Gazette*, Volume 42, Number 12 (Dec 1958)

Martin, Zachary D., 'By Other Means', in *Marine Corps Gazette*, Volume 89, Number 9 (Sep 2005)

May, Ernest R., 'Conscience and Command', in *MHQ: The Quarterly Journal of Military History*, Volume 12, Number 4 (Summer 2000)

McIntosh, Scott E., 'The Wingman-Philosopher of MiG Alley: John Boyd and the OODA Loop', in *Air Power History*, Volume 58, Number (Winter 2011)

McKenzie, Jr., Kenneth F., 'They Shoot Synchronizers, Don't They?', in *Marine Corps Gazette*, Volume 78, Number 8 (Aug 1994)

Mearsheimer, John J., 'Maneuver, Mobile Defense, and the NATO Central Front', in *International Security*, Volume 6, Number 3 (Winter 1981/1982)

Meilinger, Phillip S., 'The Historiography of Airpower: Theory and Doctrine', in *The Journal of Military History*, Volume 64, Number 2 (Apr 2000)

Mets, David R., 'Boydmania', in *Air & Space Power Journal*, Volume 18, Issue 3 (Fall 2004)

Miksche, F.O., 'The Strategic Importance of Western Europe', in *Military Review*, Volume 29, Number 4 (Jul 1949)

Morelock Jerry D., 'The Legacy of Liddell Hart', in *Military Review*, Volume 67, Number 5 (May 1986)

Morgan, J.H., 'The German Officers' Corps: Attempts to Efface the Stains of Defeat', in *Australian Army Journal*, Number 6 (April–May 1949)

Newland, Samuel J., 'Blitzkrieg in Retrospect', in *Military Review*, Volume 84, Number 4 (Jul/Aug 2004)

Nihart, Brooke, 'Strategy — The Indirect Approach', in *Marine Corps Gazette*, Volume 38, Number 9 (Sep 1954)

O'Brien Browne, 'The Kaiser's Last Battle', in *MHQ: The Quarterly Journal of Military History*, Volume 13, Number 3 (Spring 2001)

O'Neill, Robert, 'Sir Basil Liddell Hart: An Appreciation', in *Australian Army Journal*, Number 251 (Apr 1970)

Olsen, John Andreas, 'Boyd Revisited: A Great Mind with a Touch of Madness', in *Air Power History*, Volume 63, Issue 4 (Winter 2016)

Ottestad, P.N., 'Why Germany Lost the War', in *Military Review*, Volume 30, Number 5 (Aug 1950)

Peters, Ralph, 'Bloodless Theories, Bloody Wars: Easy-Win Concepts Crumble in Combat', in *Armed Forces Journal* (1 Apr 2006)

Peters, Ralph, 'In Praise of Attrition', in *Parameters*, Volume 41, Number 4 (Winter 2011/2012)

Priest, Andrew, 'The Rhetoric of Revisionism: Presidential Rhetoric about the Vietnam War since 9/11', in *Presidential Studies Quarterly*, Volume 43, Number 3 (Sep 2013)

Record, Jeffrey, 'Collapsed Countries, Casualty Dread, and the New American Way of War', in *Parameters*, Volume 32, Number 2 (Summer 2002)

Record, Jeffrey, 'Vietnam in Retrospect: Could We Have Won?', in *Parameters*, Volume 26, Number 4 (Winter 1996–1997)

Reid, Brian Holden, '"Young Turks, or Not So Young?": The Frustrated Quest of Major General J.F.C. Fuller and Captain B.H. Liddell Hart', in *The Journal of Military History*, Volume 73, Number 1 (Jan 2009)

Rippe, Stephen T., 'Leadership, Firepower and Maneuver: The British and Germans', in *Military Review*, Volume 65, Number 10 (Oct 1985)

Robinson, James R., 'The Rommel Myth', in *Military Review*, Volume 77, Number 5 (Sep/Oct 1997)

Rubin, Barry, 'The Real Roots of Arab Anti-Americanism', in *Foreign Affairs*, Volume 81, Number 6 (Nov/Dec 2002)

Sanford, Jr., F.G., 'Maneuver Warfare Handbook', in *Marine Corps Gazette*, Volume 70, Number 1 (Jan 1986)

Sanibel, Michael and Smith, Dick, 'Quest To Build A Better Fighter', in *Aviation History*, Volume 21, Issue 3 (Jan 2011)

Soutor, Kevin, 'To Stem the Red Tide: The German Report Series and its Effect on

American Defense Doctrine, 1948–1954', in *The Journal of Military History*, Volume 57, Number 4 (1993)

Spiller, Roger J., 'In the Shadow of the Dragon: Doctrine and the US Army After Vietnam', in *RUSI Journal*, Volume 142, Number 6 (Dec 1997)

Spinney, Franklin C., 'Genghis John', in *United States Naval Institute Proceedings*, Volume 123, Number 7 (Jul 1997)

Starry, Donn A., 'To Change an Army', in *Military Review*, Volume 63, Number 3 (Mar 1983)

Starry, Donn A., 'With Patience and Careful Teaching of Sound Doctrine: The U.S. Army on the Brink of Change', in *Armor*, Volume 115, Number 5 (Sep/Oct 2006)

Stolfi, Russel H.S., 'Barbarossa: Hitler's Invasion of Russia, 1941', in *The Journal of Military History*, Volume 66, Number 3 (Jul 2002)

Strachan, Hew, 'John Buchan and the First World War: Fact into Fiction', in *War in History*, Volume 6, Number 3 (Jul 2009)

Strong, R.A., 'In the Graveyard of Empires: America's War in Afghanistan', in *Choice*, Volume 47 (Jan 2010)

Sweetman, Bill, 'Clausewitzless', in *Aviation Week & Space Technology*, Volume 176, Number 30 (Sep 2014)

Tompkins, R. McC., 'War of Movement', in *Marine Corps Gazette*, Volume 40, Number 7 (Jul 1956)

Trauschweizer, Ingo Wolfgang, 'Learning with an Ally: The U.S. Army and the Bundeswehr in the Cold War', in *The Journal of Military History*, Volume 72, Number 2 (Apr 2008)

Trevor-Roper, Hugh, 'The Germans Reappraise the War', in *Foreign Affairs*, Volume 31, Number 2 (Jan 1953)

Ullman, Harlan, 'Slogan or Strategy? Shock and Awe Reassessed', in *The National Interest*, Volume 84 (Summer 2006)

Vego, Milan, 'Clausewitz' Schwerpunkt: Mistranslated from German — Misunderstood in English', *Military Review*, Volume 87, Number 1 (Jan/Feb 2007)

Vernon, Graham D., 'Soviet Combat Operations in World War II: Part I', in *Military Review*, Volume 60, Number 2 (Mar 1980)

Vernon, Graham D., 'Soviet Combat Operations in World War II: Part II', in *Military Review*, Volume 60, Number 2 (Apr 1980)

Walden, John W., 'Liddell Hart', in *Military Review*, Volume 34, Number 6 (Sep 1954)

Walker, Andrew D., 'An Alternative to Maneuver Warfare', in *Marine Corps Gazette*, Volume 75, Number 11 (Nov 1991)

Walter, Eric M., 'Synchronization: The U.S. Inheritance of Soviet Military Doctrine?', in *Marine Corps Gazette*, Volume 78, Number 8 (Aug 1994)

Walters, Robert E., 'Interview with Capt B.H. Liddell Hart', in *Marine Corps Gazette*, Volume 45, Number 11 (Nov 1961)

West, F.J. 'Bing' and Smith, Ray L., 'Implications from Operation Iraqi Freedom for the Marine Corps', in *Marine Corps Gazette*, Volume 87, Number 11 (Nov 2003)

Wheeler, Scott L., 'Terrorist Tactics for War with the West', in *Insight on the News*, Volume 19, Number 1 (24 Dec 2002–6 Jan 2003)

Wood, James A., 'Captive Historians, Captivated Audience: The German Military

History Program, 1945–1961', in *The Journal of Military History*, Volume 69, Number 1 (Jan 2005)

Woodmansee John W., Jr., 'Blitzkrieg and the AirLand Battle', in *Military Review*, Volume 64, Number 8 (Aug 1984)

Wyly, Michael D., 'Attack or Defend?', in *Marine Corps Gazette*, Volume 67, Number 6 (Jun 1983)

Wyly, Michael D., 'Doctrinal Change: The Move to Maneuver Theory', in *Marine Corps Gazette*, Volume 77, Number 10 (Oct 1993)

Wyly, Michael D., 'Ideas for Changing Doctrine', in *Marine Corps Gazette*, Volume 72, Number 8 (Aug 1988)

Wyly, Michael D., 'Lost Victories', in *Marine Corps Gazette*, Volume 66, Number 6 (Jun 1982)

Wyly, Michael D., 'NATO Under Attack', in *Marine Corps Gazette*, Volume 68, Number 9 (Sep 1984)

Zambernardi, Lorenzo, 'The Impotence of Power: Morgenthau's Critique of American Intervention in Vietnam', *Review of International Studies*, Volume 37, Number 3 (Jul 2011)

Books

Balck, Hermann, *Order in Chaos: The Memoirs of General of Panzer Troops Hermann Balck*, The University Press of Kentucky, Lexington, 2015

Balck, Wilhelm, *Development of Tactics — World War*, The General Service School Press, Fort Leavenworth, 1922

Barnett, Correlli, ed., *Hitler's Generals*, Grove Weidenfeld, New York, 1989

Bird, Tim and Marshall, Alex, *Afghanistan: How the West Lost Its Way*, Yale University Press, New Haven, 2011

Bond, Brian, *Liddell Hart: A Study of his Military Thought*, Cassell, London, 1977

Brown, Ian T., *A New Conception of War: John Boyd, The U.S. Marines, and Maneuver Warfare*, Marine Corps University Press, Quantico, 2018

Bull, Stephen, *German Assault Troops of the First World War: Stosstrupptaktik — The First Stormtroopers*, The History Press (Kindle Edition), Gloucestershire, 2014

Burton, James G., *Pentagon Wars: Reformers Challenge the Old Guard*, Naval Institute Press, Annapolis, Maryland, 1993

Citino, Robert M., *The Path to Blitzkrieg: Doctrine and Training in the German Army, 1920–1939*, Lynne Rienner Publishers, London, 1999

Clark, Alan, *Barbarossa: The Russian German Conflict 1941–1945*, Cassell, London, 1995

Clausewitz, Carl von, *On War*, Princeton University Press, Princeton, 1976 (original 1832)

Coram, Robert, *Boyd: The Fighter Pilot Who Changed the Art of War*, Hachette Book Group (Kindle Edition), 2010

Creveld, Martin van, *A History of Strategy: From Sun Tzu to William S. Lind*, Castalia House (Kindle Edition), Kouvola, 2000

Creveld, Martin van, *Air Power and Maneuver Warfare*, Air University Press, Maxwell Air Force Base, Alabama, 1994

Creveld, Martin van, *Fighting Power: German and U.S. Army Performance, 1939–*

1945, Arms and Armour Press, London, 1982

Crown Prince William of Germany, *My War Experiences*, Hurst and Blackett, London, 1922

Daly, Gregory, *Cannae: The Experience of Battle in the Second Punic War*, Routledge (Kindle Edition), London, 2002

Danchev, Alex, *Alchemist of War: The Life of Basil Liddell Hart*, Weidenfeld & Nicolson, London, 1998

Davis, Robert T., *The Challenge of Adaptation: The US Army in the Aftermath of Conflict, 1953–2000*, Combat Studies Institute Press, Fort Leavenworth, 2008

Dennis, Peter and Grey, Jeffrey, eds., *Victory or Defeat: Armies in the Aftermath of Conflict*, Big Sky Publishing, Warriewood, 2010

DePuy, William E., Compiled by Richard M. Swain, *Selected Papers of General William E. DePuy*, Combat Studies Institute, Fort Leavenworth, 1995

Doughty, Robert A., *The Breaking Point: Sedan and the Fall of France, 1940*, Stackpole Books (Kindle Edition), Mechanicsburg, 1990

Doughty, Robert Allan, *The Seeds of Disaster: The Development of French Army Doctrine, 1919–39*, Archon Books, Hamden, 1985

Dupuy, Trevor N., *A Genius for War: The German Army and General Staff, 1807–1945*, Nova Publications, Falls Church, 1977

Fick, Nathaniel, *One Bullet Away: The Making of a US Marine Officer*, Orion, London, 2005

Ford, Daniel, *A Vision So Noble: John Boyd, the OODA Loop, and America's War on Terror*, Warbird Books (Kindle Edition), 2013

Franks, Tommy R., *American Soldier*, HarperCollins (Kindle Edition), New York, 2004

Freedman, Lawrence, *Strategy: A History*, Oxford University Press, New York, 2013

Frieser, Karl-Heinz, *The Blitzkrieg Legend: The 1940 Campaign in the West*, Naval Institute Press (Kindle Edition), Annapolis, 2005

Fuller, J.F.C., *The Conduct of War 1789–1961: A Study of the Impact of the French, Industrial and Russian Revolutions on War and Its Conduct*, Greenwood Press, Westport, 1961

Fuller, J.F.C., *The Foundation of the Science of War*, Hutchinson & Co., London, 1926

Glantz, David M., *August Storm: The Soviet 1945 Strategic Offensive in Manchuria*, Combat Studies Institute, Fort Leavenworth, 1983

Glantz, David M., *Operation Barbarossa: Hitler's Invasion of Russia 1941*, The History Press (Kindle Edition), Stroud, 2001

Gole, Henry G., *General William E. DePuy*, The University Press of Kentucky, Lexington, 2008

Guderian, Heinz, *Achtung Panzer!: The Development of Tank Warfare*, Cassell (Kindle Edition), London, 1937

Guderian, Heinz, *Panzer Leader*, Penguin Books, London, 1952

Gudmundsson, Bruce I., *On Armor*, Praeger, Westport, 2004

Gudmundsson, Bruce I., *Stormtroop Tactics: Innovation in the German Army, 1914–1918*, Praeger, Westport, 1989

Halder, Franz, *Hitler as Warlord*, Putnam, London, 1949

Hammes, Thomas X., *The Sling and the Stone: On War in the 21st Century*, Zenith

Press (Kindle Edition), Minneapolis, 2004

Hammond, Grant, *The Mind of War: John Boyd and American Security*, Smithsonian (Kindle Edition), Washington DC, 2012

Harris, J.P., *Douglas Haig and the First World War*, Cambridge University Press, Cambridge, 2008

Harrison, Richard W., *Architect of Soviet Victory in World War II: The Life and Theories of G.S. Isserson*, McFarland & Company (Kindle Edition), Jefferson, 2010

Hart, Gary, *The Shield and the Cloak*, Oxford University Press, New York, 2006

Hart, Russell, *Guderian: Panzer Pioneer or Myth Maker?*, Potomac Books, Dulles, 2006

Hoffenaar, Jan, Krüger, Dieter and Zabecki, David T., eds., *Blueprints for Battle: Planning War in Central Europe, 1948–1968*, The University Press of Kentucky, Lexington, 2012

Hooker, Richard D., ed., *Maneuver Warfare: An Anthology*, Presidio Press, Novato, 1993

Hoth, Hermann, *Panzer Operations: Germany's Panzer Group 3 During the Invasion of Russia, 1941*, Casemate (Kindle Edition), Havertown, 2015

Kesselring, Albert, *The Memoirs of Field Marshal Kesselring*, Presidio, Novato, 1989

Kuhn, Thomas S., *The Structure of Scientific Revolutions*, The University of Chicago Press, London, 1962

Leonhard, Robert, *The Art of Maneuver: Maneuver Warfare Theory and AirLand Battle*, Ballantine Books (Kindle Edition), New York, 1991

Liddell Hart, B.H., *Europe in Arms*, Faber and Faber, London, 1937

Liddell Hart, B.H., *Foch: The Man of Orleans*, Greenwood Press, Westport, 1931

Liddell Hart, B.H., *Great Captains Unveiled*, William Blackwood & Sons, London, 1927

Liddell Hart, B.H., *Paris: Or the Future of War*, Garland Publishing, New York, 1925

Liddell Hart, B.H., *Strategy of Indirect Approach*, Faber and Faber, London, 1941

Liddell Hart, B.H., *Strategy: Second Revised Edition*, Meridian, New York, 1991

Liddell Hart, B.H., *The Defence of Britain*, Faber and Faber, London, 1939

Liddell Hart, B.H., *The Future of Infantry*, Faber and Faber, London, 1933

Liddell Hart, B.H., *The German Generals Talk*, Quill (Kindle Edition), New York, 1948

Liddell Hart, B.H., *The Liddell Hart Memoirs Vol I*, Cassell & Company (Kindle Edition), London, 1965

Liddell Hart, B.H., *The Liddell Hart Memoirs Vol II*, Cassell & Company (Kindle Edition), London, 1965

Liddell Hart, B.H., *When Britain Goes to War*, Faber and Faber, London, 1935

Lind, William S., *Maneuver Warfare Handbook*, Westview Press, Boulder, 1985

Lind, William S., *On War: The Collected Columns of William S. Lind, 2003–2009*, Castalia House (Kindle Edition), Kouvola, 2014

Lind, William S., and Thiele, Gregory, *4th Generation Warfare Handbook*, Castalia House (Kindle Edition), Kouvola, 2015

Macksey, Kenneth, *Why the Germans Lose at War*, Greenhill Books, London, 1996

Manstein, Erich von, *Lost Victories*, Greenhill Books, London, 1958

Malkasian, Carter, *A History of Modern Wars of Attrition*, Praeger Publishers, Westport, 2002

Mattis, Jim, and West, Bing, *Call Sign Chaos: Learning to Lead*, Random House

Publishing Group, New York, 2019

Mearsheimer, John J., *Liddell Hart and the Weight of History*, Brassey's Defence Publishers, New York, 1988

Megargee, Geoffrey, *Barbarossa 1941: Hitler's War of Annihilation*, Tempus, Stroud, 2006

Mellenthin, F.W. von, *German Generals of World War II*, University of Oklahoma Press, Norman, 1977

Mellenthin, F.W. von, *Panzer Battles*, Spellmount, Gloucestershire, 1956

Mellenthin, F.W., Stolfi, R.H.S., and Sobik, E., *NATO Under Attack: Why the Western Alliance Can Fight Outnumbered and Win in Central Europe Without Nuclear Weapons*, Duke University Press, Durham, 1984

Mitcham, Samuel W., Jr., *The Rise of the Wehrmacht*, Westport, Praeger, 2008

Mosier, John, *Cross of Iron: The Rise and Fall of the German War Machine, 1918–1945*, Henry Holt and Co., New York, 2006

Mosier, John, *Deathride: Hitler vs. Stalin — The Eastern Front, 1941–1945*, Simon & Schuster, New York, 2010

Mosier, John, *The Blitzkrieg Myth: How Hitler and the Allies Misread the Strategic Realities of World War II*, HarperCollins, New York, 2003

Murray, Williamson, and Scales, Robert H., *The Iraq War*, Harvard University Press, Massachusetts, 2003

Naveh, Shimon, *In Pursuit of Military Excellence: The Evolution of Operational Theory*, Frank Cass, London, 1997

Newland, Samuel J., *Victories Are Not Enough: Limitations of the German Way of War*, Strategic Studies Institute, Carlisle, 2005

Osinga, Frans P.B., *Science, Strategy and War: The Strategic Theory of John Boyd*, Taylor and Francis, Abingdon, 2007

Oslen, John Andreas, ed., *Airpower Reborn: The Strategic Concepts of John Warden and John Boyd*, Naval Institute Press, Annapolis, 2015

Passingham, Ian, *The German Offensives of 1918: The Last Desperate Gamble*, Pen & Sword Military (Kindle Edition), South Yorkshire, 2008

Piscitelli, Anthony, *The Marine Corps Way of War*, Savas Beattie, California, 2017

Porter, Patrick, *Military Orientalism*, Oxford University Press, New York, 2013

Richards, Chester, *Certain to Win: The Strategy of John Boyd, Applied to Business*, Xlibris, Bloomington, 2004

Ricks, Thomas E., *Fiasco: The American Military Adventure in Iraq*, Penguin Books, London, 2006

Ricks, Thomas E., *The Generals: American Military Command from World War II to Today*, Penguin (Kindle Edition), New York, 2013

Rommel, Erwin, *The Rommel Papers*, Collins, London, 1953

Santamaria, Jason A., Martino, Vincent, and Clemons, Erik K., *The Marine Corps Way: Using Maneuver Warfare to Lead a Winning Organization*, McGraw-Hill, New York, 2003

Schlieffen, Alfred von, *Cannae*, The Command and General Staff School Press, Fort Leavenworth, 1931 (original 1909)

Schwarzkopf, Norman H., *It Doesn't Take a Hero*, Bantam Books, New York, 1993

Simpkin, Richard E., *Race to the Swift: Thoughts on Twenty-First Century Warfare*, Brassey's Defence Publishers, Exeter, 1985

Simpson, Emile, *War from the Ground Up: Twenty-First Century Combat as Politics*, Columbia University Press, New York, 2012

Showalter, Dennis, *Hitler's Panzers: The Lightning Attacks that Revolutionized Warfare*, Penguin (Kindle Edition), New York, 2009

Smelser, Ronald, and Davies, Edward J., *The Myth of the Eastern Front: The Nazi–Soviet War in American Popular Culture*, Cambridge University Press, Cambridge, 2008

Sorley, Lewis, ed., *Press On! Selected Works of General Donn A. Starry: Volume I*, Combat Studies Institute Press, Fort Leavenworth, 2009

Sorley, Lewis, ed., *Press On! Selected Works of General Donn A. Starry: Volume II*, Combat Studies Institute Press, Fort Leavenworth, 2009

Smith, Hugh, ed., *The Strategists*, Australian Defence Studies Centre, Canberra, 2001

Stalk, George, *Competing Against Time: How Time-Based Competition is Reshaping Global Markets*, The Free Press, New York, 1990

Stolfi, R.H.S., *German Panzers on the Offensive*, Schiffer Military History, Atglen, 2003

Stolfi, Russel, *Hitler's Panzers East: World War II Reinterpreted*, University of Oklahoma Press, Norman, 1992

Svechin, Aleksandr, *Strategy*, East View Press (Kindle Edition), Minneapolis, 1992

Wallach, Jehuda L., *The Dogma of the Battle of Annihilation*, Greenwood Press, Westport, 1986

West, Bing, and Smith, Ray L., *The March Up: Taking Baghdad with the 1st Marine Division*, Random House, London, 2004

Wette, Wolfram, *The Wehrmacht: History, Myth, Reality*, Harvard University Press, London, 2006

Wright, Evan, *Generation Kill*, Transworld, 2004

Zabecki, David T., *The German 1918 Offensives: A Case Study in The Operational Level of War*, Routledge (Kindle Edition), New York, 2006

Websites

Echevarria, Antulio J., *Fourth-Generation War and Other Myths*, Strategic Studies Institute, 2005, http://www.strategicstudiesinstitute.army.mil/pdffiles/pub632

Elkus, Adam, 'Applying Boyd: Iraq and Strategy', in Safranski, Mark, ed., *The John Boyd Roundtable: Debating Science, Strategy, and War*, https://www.academia.edu/12575835/Applying_Boyd_Iraq_and_Strategy

Elkus, Adam, 'The Rise and Decline of Strategic Paralysis', in *Small Wars Journal*, 2011, smallwarsjournal.com/printpdf/11489

Gates, Roberts, 'Remarks to Air War College', in *As Delivered by Secretary of Defense Robert M. Gates, Maxwell-Gunter Air Force Base*, 21 April 2008, https://archive.defense.gov/Speeches/Speech.aspx?SpeechID=1231

Glantz, David M., *American Perspectives on Eastern Front Operations in World War II*, Foreign Military Studies Office, Fort Leavenworth, 1987, http://fmso.leavenworth.army.mil/documents/e-front.htm

Gray, Colin S., *Defining and Achieving Decisive Victory*, Strategic Studies Institute, 2002, 23, http://www.strategicstudiesinstitute.army.mil/pdffiles/pub272.pdf

Gingrich, Newt, *Memo: The Challenge Confronting the Republican Party*, 21 December 2012, https://www.gingrich360.com/2012/12/memo-the-challenge-confronting-the-republican-party/

Hankins, Michael, 'A Discourse on John Boyd: A Brief Summary of the US Air Force's Most Controversial Pilot and Thinker', in *Air Power History* (August 2018), https://balloonstodrones.com/2018/08/22/a-discourse-on-john-boyd-a-brief-summary-of-the-us-air-forces-most-controversial-pilot-and-thinker/

Hasik, James, *Beyond Hagiography: Theoretical and Practical Problems in the Works and Legacy of John Boyd*, LBJ School of Public Affairs, The University of Texas at Austin, May 2012, http://www.jameshasik.com/files/20120515_problems_of_boyd.pdf

Interview with Ronald Smelser and Edward Davies, 29 June 2013, http://orientalreview.org/2013/06/29/myth-of-the-eastern-front-in-american-popular-culture/

Lacey, Jim, 'The Continuing Irrelevance of William Lind', in *Small Wars Journal*, 2014, http://smallwarsjournal.com/jrnl/art/the-continuing-irrelevance-of-william-lind

Lind, William S., *The View From Olympus: Is the Marine Corps Waking Up?*, 5 January 2017, https://www.traditionalright.com/the-view-from-olympus-is-the-marine-corps-waking-up/

Lind, William S., *The View From Olympus: What it Takes to Win*, 9 March 2017, https://www.traditionalright.com/the-view-from-olympus-what-it-takes-to-win/

Manea, Octavian, 'Reflections on the "Counterinsurgency Decade": Small Wars Journal Interview with General David H. Petraeus', *Small Wars Journal*, 2013, http://smallwarsjournal.com/jrnl/art/reflections-on-the-counterinsurgency-decade-small-wars-journal-interview-with-general-david

Owen, F., 'The Manoeuvre Warfare Fraud', in *Small Wars Journal*, 2008, http://smallwarsjournal.com/jrnl/art/the-manoeuvre-warfare-fraud

NOTES

Introduction

1   Coram, *Boyd*, 114/7717
2   Paul Van Riper, 'Foreword', in Brown, *A New Conception of War*, xi
3   Ford, *A Vision So Noble*, 10/1161
4   Lind, *On War*, 225/10539
5   Boyd enlisted in the Army Air Corps on 30 October 1944 and reported for duty on 16 April 1945. He arrived in Japan on 3 January 1946 and later was discharged on 7 January 1947.
6   Hankins, 'The Blind Strategist (Review)', 1154
7   Hammond, *The Mind of War*, 1096/5008
8   Hankins, 'A Discourse on John Boyd'
9   Hammond, 'On the Making of History', 5
10 Osinga, Science, *Strategy and War*, 23
11 Osinga, Science, *Strategy and War*, 24
12 Hammond, 'Introduction', in Boyd, *A Discourse on Winning and Losing*, 5
13 Burton, *Pentagon Wars*, 434/7426
14 Burton, *Pentagon Wars*, 639/7426
15 Hammond, *The Mind of War*, 218/5008
16 Hammond noted, 'As a part of the contract for the ammunition developed for the GAU-8 gun, several former Nazi officers were brought clandestinely from Germany in the early 1970s to CIA safe houses on Maryland's eastern shore.' Hammond, *The Mind of War*, 2655/5008
17 Burton, *The Pentagon Wars*, 206/7426
18 Correll, 'The Reformers', 40
19 Kaplan, 'Military Dissenter Endured Adversity But Won Brass Ring'
20 Kaplan, 'The Force Was With Them'
21 Burton, *Pentagon Wars*, 5527/7426
22 Hart, *The Shield and the Cloak*, 25
23 Boyd declared that the 'OODA loop came from work and anomalies associated with evolution and flight tests of YF-16/17'.
    Brown, *A New Conception of War*, 283

24 Brown, *A New Conception of War*, 88
25 Spinney, 'Genghis John', 46–7
26 Spinney, 'Genghis John', 47
27 Boyd declared: 'Pretty soon you realize that when we talk about fast transient we are talking about operating at a faster tempo or a faster rhythm than our adversary.' Boyd also declared: 'Let us go to the F-86 versus Mig-15 as they were used in Korea. Now let us look at those airplanes and examine the observation-decision-action loop.' Furthermore, Boyd's slides stated: 'Disrupt adversary's connections, centers, and activities that provide cohesion and permit coherent observation — orientation — decision — action.' Boyd, *Patterns of Conflict* (Delivered on 26 May 1978), 6, 7, 94
28 Hammond, 'On the Making of History', 13
29 Burton, *Pentagon Wars*, 952/7426
30 Coram, *Boyd*, 5133–6/7717
31 Fallows, 'Muscle-Bound Superpower'
32 Hammond, 'On The Making of History', 17
33 Osinga, *Science, Strategy and War*, 5
34 Gates, 'Remarks to Air War College'
35 Osinga, *Science, Strategy and War*, 4
36 Burton, *Pentagon Wars*, 941/7426
37 Stalk, *Competing Against Time*, 180
38 Richards, *Certain to Win*, 322/3927
39 Gingrich, *Memo: The Challenge Confronting the Republican Party*
40 Hammond, 'On the Making of History', 18
41 Osinga, 'The Enemy as a Complex Adaptive System: John Boyd and Airpower in the Postmodern Era', in *Airpower Reborn*, 50
42 Hammond, *The Mind of War*, 209/5008
43 Coram, *Boyd*, 7260/7717
44 Hammond, 'On the Making of History', 7
45 Evans, 'Captains Of The Soul', 48

46 Michel, *The Revolt of the Majors*, 123–4
47 Coram, *Boyd*, 5035/7717
48 Michel, *The Revolt of the Majors*, 103
49 Hankins, 'A Discourse on John Boyd'
50 Correll, 'The Reformers', 43
51 Correll, 'The Reformers', 44
52 Sanibel and Smith, 'Quest To Build A Better Fighter', 48–53
53 Mets, 'Boydmania', 101–3
54 Ricks, *Fiasco*, 115
55 Brown, *A New Conception of War*, 95

Chapter One: Emergence of Maneuver Warfare
1 Spiller, 'In the Shadow of the Dragon', 43
2 Starry, 'With Patience and Careful Teaching of Sound Doctrine', 7
3 Spiller, 'In the Shadow of the Dragon', 43
4 Spiller, 'In the Shadow of the Dragon', 44
5 Ricks, *The Generals*, 3309/10224
6 Park, *The Unfulfilled Promise*, 116
7 Ricks, *The Generals*, 3309/10224
8 Lock-Pullan, '"An Inward Looking Time"', 495
9 Due, *Seizing the Initiative*, 20
10 Trauschweizer, *Creating Deterrence for Limited War*, 19
11 Phillips, *Reengineering Institutional Culture,* 56
12 Phillips, *Reengineering Institutional Culture,* 59
13 Spiller, 'In the Shadow of the Dragon', 46
14 Spiller, 'In the Shadow of the Dragon', 46
15 Phillips, *Reengineering Institutional Culture,* 58
16 Spiller, 'In the Shadow of the Dragon', 47
17 Due, *Seizing the Initiative*, 39–40
18 Spiller, 'In the Shadow of the Dragon', 47
19 Gole, *General William E. DePuy*, 3345/4758
20 Due, *Seizing the Initiative*, 35
21 Spiller, 'In the Shadow of the Dragon', 48
22 Joyce, 'The Micropolitics of "the Army You Have"', 197
23 Trauschweizer, 'Learning with an Ally', 500
24 Phillips, *Reengineering Institutional Culture,* 63
25 Joyce, 'The Micropolitics of "the Army You Have"', 186
26 Lock-Pullan, '"An Inward Looking Time"', 488
27 Spiller, 'In the Shadow of the Dragon', 51
28 Park, *The Unfulfilled Promise*, 130
29 Due, *Seizing the Initiative*, 66–7
30 Due, *Seizing the Initiative*, 58
31 Lind, 'Some Doctrinal Questions for the United States Army', 137
32 Lind, 'Some Doctrinal Questions for the United States Army', 136–7
33 Spiller, 'In the Shadow of the Dragon', 51
34 Naveh, *In Pursuit of Military Excellence*, 263
35 Lock-Pullan, '"An Inward Looking Time"', 506
36 De Czege, 'Lessons from the Past', 50–1
37 Ricks, *The Generals*, 4673/10224
38 Hammond, 'On the Making of History', 9
39 Van Creveld, *Air Power and Maneuver Warfare*, 3
40 Boyd, *A Discourse on Winning and Losing*, 199
41 Brown, 'Opportunity Lost', 203
42 Fuller, *The Conduct of War 1789–1961*, 243
43 Fuller, *The Foundations of the Science of War*, 292
44 Fuller, *The Foundations of the Science of War*, 290
45 Van Creveld, *A History of Strategy*, 1291/1800
46 Liddell Hart, *The Liddell Hart Memoirs Vol I*, 426/7648
47 Liddell Hart, *The Liddell Hart Memoirs Vol I*, 631/7648
48 Dennis, 'J.F.C. Fuller and B.H. Liddell Hart', in Smith, *The Strategists*, 59
49 Liddell-Hart, 'The "Man-in-the-Dark" Theory of Infantry Tactics and the "Expanding Torrent" System of Attack'
50 Liddell-Hart, 'The "Man-in-the-Dark" Theory of Infantry Tactics and the "Expanding Torrent" System of Attack'
51 Liddell-Hart, 'The "Man-in-the-Dark" Theory of Infantry Tactics and the "Expanding Torrent" System of Attack'
52 Liddell-Hart, 'The "Man-in-the-Dark" Theory of Infantry Tactics and the "Expanding Torrent" System of Attack'
53 Van Creveld, *A History of Strategy*,

1318/1800
54 Liddell Hart, *Paris*, 77
55 'Absolute war' is an abstract Platonic-like concept which is never practiced in reality due to political and social constraints but is often misunderstood to mean 'total war'. Smith, 'Clausewitz: Apostle of Modern War', in Smith, *The Strategists*, 34
56 Liddell Hart, *Paris*, 10
57 Lord, 'Liddell Hart and the Napoleonic Fallacy', 58
58 Liddell Hart, *Paris*, 19–20
59 Liddell Hart, *Paris*, 21
60 Liddell Hart, *Paris*, 36
61 Liddell Hart, *Paris*, 73
62 Liddell Hart, *Paris*, 37
63 Liddell Hart, *Paris*, 40
64 Liddell Hart, *Paris*, 82
65 Liddell Hart, *Paris*, 82–3
66 Lord, 'Liddell Hart and the Napoleonic Fallacy', 59
67 Liddell Hart, *Strategy of Indirect Approach*, 4
68 Liddell Hart, *Strategy of Indirect Approach*, 5
69 Danchev, 'Liddell Hart and Manoeuvre', 34
70 Liddell Hart, *Strategy of Indirect Approach*, 278
71 Danchev, 'Liddell Hart and the Indirect Approach', 317
72 Fuller, *The Conduct of War 1789–1961*, 244
73 Fuller, *The Conduct of War 1789–1961*, 255–6
74 Liddell Hart, *The Liddell Hart Memoirs Vol I*, 920/7648
75 Hammond, *The Mind of War*, 2715/5008
76 Boyd, *Patterns of Conflict (Slides)*, 13
77 Brown, *A New Conception of War*, 215
78 Kinase, 'Classical Strategists and the Indirect Approach', 17
79 Liddell Hart, *The Liddell Hart Memoirs Vol I*, 834/7648
80 Boyd, 'Patterns of Conflict (Delivered on 26 May 1978)', 12
81 Boyd, *A Discourse on Winning and Losing*, 36 and 41
82 Boyd, *Patterns of Conflict (Slides)*, 25 and 27
83 Boyd, *Patterns of Conflict (Slides)*, 25
84 Boyd, *A Discourse on Winning and Losing*, 45
85 Boyd, 'Patterns of Conflict (Delivered on 26 May 1978)', 15
86 Hammond, *The Mind of War*, 2777/5008
87 Boyd, 'Patterns of Conflict (Delivered on 26 May 1978)', 17
88 Boyd, 'Patterns of Conflict (Delivered on 26 May 1978)', 18–9
89 Boyd, *Patterns of Conflict (Slides)*, 42
90 McIntosh, 'The Wingman-Philosopher of MiG Alley', 31
91 Boyd, *A Discourse on Winning and Losing*, 66
92 Boyd, *Patterns of Conflict (Slides)*, 57
93 Boyd, *Patterns of Conflict (Slides)*, 57
94 Boyd, *Patterns of Conflict (Slides)*, 66
95 Boyd, *A Discourse on Winning and Losing*, 87
96 Boyd, *Patterns of Conflict (Slides)*, 76
97 Boyd, *Patterns of Conflict (Slides)*, 78
98 Boyd, *A Discourse on Winning and Losing*, 97
99 Boyd, 'Patterns of Conflict (Delivered on 26 May 1978)', 7
100 Boyd, *Patterns of Conflict (Slides)*, 111
101 Boyd, *Patterns of Conflict (Slides)*, 112
102 Brown, *A New Conception of War*, 214–5
103 Boyd, *A Discourse on Winning and Losing*, 135–6
104 Boyd, 'Patterns of Conflict (Delivered on 26 May 1978)', 35
105 Boyd, *A Discourse on Winning and Losing*, 141
106 Brown, *A New Conception of War*, 248–9
107 Hammond, *The Mind of War*, 3383/5008
108 Hammond, 'On the Making of History', 15
109 Coram, *Boyd*, 5433/7717
110 Lind, *Maneuver Warfare Handbook*, 2
111 Lind, *Maneuver Warfare Handbook*, 13
112 Lind, *Maneuver Warfare Handbook*, 17–8
113 Lind, 'The Theory and Practice of Maneuver Warfare' in Hooker, *Maneuver Warfare: An Anthology*, 10
114 Lind, *Maneuver Warfare Handbook*, 18
115 Simpkin, *Race to the Swift*, 20
116 Simpkin, *Race to the Swift*, 22
117 Leonhard, *The Art of Maneuver*, 1140/5341
118 Leonhard, *The Art of Maneuver*, 397/5341
119 Hooker, 'Redefining Maneuver Warfare', 51
120 Park, *The Unfulfilled Promise*, 200

Chapter Two: The Maneuver Warfare Revolution

1 Kaplan, 'The Force Was With Them'
2 Coram, *Boyd*, 5995/7717
3 Burton, *Pentagon Wars*, 1156/7426
4 De Czege, 'Lessons from the Past', 51
5 Joyce, 'The Micropolitics of "the Army You Have"', 195
6 Joyce, 'The Micropolitics of "the Army You Have"', 196
7 FM 100-5 *Operations* (1982), 2–2
8 Due, *Seizing the Initiative*, 35
9 Burton, *Pentagon Wars*, 109/7426
10 FM 100-5 *Operations* (1982), 2–1
11 FM 100-5 *Operations* (1982), 2–1
12 De Czega and Holder explained that the AirLand Battle 'stresses the importance of the initiative, stating that, in all operations, commanders will attempt to throw the enemy off balance with a powerful blow from an unexpected direction and continue vigorous operations until the enemy is destroyed.' De Czega and Holder, 'The New FM 100–5', 55
13 Coram, *Boyd*, 6007–6016/7717
14 Burton, *The Pentagon Wars*, 1187/7426
15 Coram, *Boyd*, 6142/7717
16 Burton, *Pentagon Wars*, 1176/7426
17 Leonhard, *The Art of Maneuver*, 4458/5341
18 Coram, *Boyd*, 6080/7717
19 Kaplan, 'Marine Who Fought Tradition is Out'
20 Cowan, 'Warfighting Brought To You By...', 61–4
21 Brown, *A New Conception of War*, 157–8
22 Coram, *Boyd*, 6173/7717
23 Wyly, 'Teaching Maneuver Warfare', in Hooker, *Maneuver Warfare: An Anthology*, 265
24 Damian, *The Road To FMFM 1*, 34
25 Damian, *The Road To FMFM 1*, 35
26 Damian, *The Road To FMFM 1*, 72
27 Wyly, 'Doctrinal Change', 44
28 Damian, *The Road To FMFM 1*, 31–2
29 Clover, 'Maneuver Warfare: Where Are We Now?', 59
30 Damian, *The Road To FMFM 1*, 35
31 Coram, *Boyd*, 6207/7717
32 Anonymous, 'Maneuver Warfare Board at Lejeune', 6
33 Damian, *The Road To FMFM 1*, 90 and 93
34 Piscitelli, *The Marine Corps Way of War*, 4882/5506
35 Damian, *The Road To FMFM 1*, 103–4
36 Wyly, 'Ideas for Changing Doctrine', 43
37 Damian, *The Road To FMFM 1*, 105
38 Coram, *Boyd*, 6349/7717
39 Damian, *The Road To FMFM 1*, 104
40 *Warfighting*, 60
41 Lind, *On War*, 215/10539
42 Piscitelli, *The Marine Corps Way of War*, 4722/5506
43 Fick, *One Bullet Away*, 37
44 Sorley, *Press On! Selected Works of General Donn A. Starry: Volume II*, 1268
45 Sorley, *Press On! Selected Works of General Donn A. Starry: Volume II*, 1290
46 Joyce, 'The Micropolitics of "the Army You Have"', 197
47 Lind, 'Defining Maneuver Warfare for the Marine Corps', 55
48 Betts, 'Thesis, Antithesis, Synthesis?', 180
49 Malkasian, *A History of Modern Wars of Attrition*, 2 and 6
50 Harris, *Douglas Haig and the First World War*, 222
51 Malkasian, 'Toward a Better Understanding of Attrition', 939–40
52 Owen, 'The Manoeuvre Warfare Fraud'
53 Lind, 'Defining Maneuver Warfare for the Marine Corps', 56
54 Piscitelli, *The Marine Corps Way of War*, 363/5506
55 Lind, *Maneuver Warfare Handbook*, 6
56 Sanford, 'Maneuver Warfare Handbook', 82–3
57 Lind, 'Tactics in Maneuver Warfare', 38
58 Lind, *Maneuver Warfare Handbook*, 4
59 Hooker, 'Redefining Maneuver Warfare', 51
60 Lind, 'Misconceptions of Maneuver Warfare', 16
61 Lind, *Maneuver Warfare Handbook*, 4
62 Boyd, *Patterns of Conflict (Slides)*, 19
63 Lind, *Maneuver Warfare Handbook*, 6
64 Daly, *Cannae*, 166/7889
65 Boyd, 'Patterns of Conflict (Delivered on 26 May 1978)', 15
66 Daly, *Cannae*, 3826/7889
67 Daly, *Cannae*, 3678/7889
68 Hamilton explained, 'In the Battle of Cannae 216 B.C., Hannibal used the double envelopment to virtually annihilate the opposing Roman army. We do ourselves a disservice to box this battle neatly into solely a victory for maneuver warfare.' Hamilton, 'Maneuver Warfare and All That', 4

69 Bolger noted, 'While Epaminondas did execute an unconventional movement that unhinged the Spartans' flank, he has left no record that this was anything more than a battlefield trick. Firepower was not an issue. Undaunted by the facts, Lind makes similar maneuverist claims for Hannibal at Cannae, and then blithely remarks that "this is what happened in many of history's most decisive battles and wars". So there.' Bolger, 'Maneuver Warfare Reconsidered', in Hooker, *Maneuver Warfare: An Anthology*, 27

Chapter Three: History Written by the Vanquished
1 Soutor, 'To Stem the Red Tide', 659
2 Soutor, 'To Stem the Red Tide', 653
3 Wood, 'Captive Historians, Captivated Audience', 126
4 Wood, 'Captive Historians, Captivated Audience', 143–4
5 Smelser and Davies, *The Myth of the Eastern Front*, 56
6 Smelser and Davies, *The Myth of the Eastern Front*, 57
7 Smelser and Davies, *The Myth of the Eastern Front*, 57
8 Trevor-Roper, 'The Germans Reappraise the War', 230–1
9 Wood, 'Captive Historians, Captivated Audience', 127
10 Trevor-Roper, 'The Germans Reappraise the War', 329
11 Smelser and Davies, *The Myth of the Eastern Front*, 66
12 Wette, *The Wehrmacht*, 230
13 Wood, 'Captive Historians, Captivated Audience', 145–7
14 Wette, *The Wehrmacht*, 232
15 Smelser and Davies, *The Myth of the Eastern Front*, 66
16 Smelser and Davies, *The Myth of the Eastern Front*, 67
17 Smelser and Davies, *The Myth of the Eastern Front*, 66
18 Guderian, *Panzer Leader*, 449
19 Manstein, *Lost Victories*, 274
20 Manstein, *Lost Victories*, 284
21 Wolfram Wette concluded that Guderian, Manstein and Mellenthin tended 'to depict Hitler as a little corporal who interfered with the professional military's handling of the war'. Wette, *The Wehrmacht*, 234
22 Megargee, *Barbarossa 1941*, 11

23 David T. Zabecki and Dieter Biedekarken, 'Preface', in Balck, *Order in Chaos*, x
24 Beaumont, 'On the Wehrmacht Mystique', 53
25 Ottestad, 'Why Germany Lost the War', 103
26 May, 'Conscience and Command', 72
27 Ottestad, 'Why Germany Lost the War', 104
28 Guderian, *Panzer Leader*, 90
29 Halder, *Hitler as Warlord*, 28
30 Ziemke, 'Rundstedt', in Barnett, *Hitler's Generals*, 191
31 Halder, *Hitler as Warlord*, 13
32 Guderian, *Panzer Leader*, 119
33 Macksey, 'Guderian', in Barnett, *Hitler's Generals*, 450
34 Macksey, *Why the Germans Lose at War*, 89
35 Hart, *Guderian*, 63
36 Smelser and Davies, *The Myth of the Eastern Front*, 62–3
37 Halder, *Hitler as Warlord*, 19
38 Wette, *The Wehrmacht*, 14
39 Forster and Mawdsley, 'Hitler and Stalin in Perspective', 69
40 *The Private War Journal of Generaloberst Franz Halder: Volume 6*, 196
41 *The Private War Journal of Generaloberst Franz Halder: Volume 7*, 36
42 Mitcham, *The Rise of the Wehrmacht*, 459–96
43 Guderian, 'The Experiences of the War in Russia', 91
44 Hart, *Guderian*, 77
45 Glantz, *Operation Barbarossa*, 2619/6987
46 Halder, *Hitler as Warlord*, 42
47 Glantz, *Operation Barbarossa*, 2603/6987
48 Halder, *Hitler as Warlord*, 51
49 Guderian, *Panzer Leader*, 259
50 Balck, *Order in Chaos*, 227
51 Balck, *Order in Chaos*, 230
52 Bayerlein, 'With the Panzers in Russia 1941 & 43', 57
53 Halder, *The German Campaign in Russia*, 124
54 Mellenthin, *Panzer Battles*, 112
55 Brown, 'The Significance of Stalingrad in World War II', 35
56 Halder, *The German Campaign in Russia*, 167
57 Halder, *Hitler as Warlord*, 59
58 Manstein, *Lost Victories*, 290
59 Manstein, *Lost Victories*, 279

60   Brown, 'The Significance of Stalingrad in World War II', 39 and 41
61   Manstein, *Lost Victories*, 313
62   Manstein, *Lost Victories*, 307–8
63   Mellenthin, *German Generals of World War II*, 122
64   Mellenthin, *German Generals of World War II*, 121–2
65   Balck, *Order in Chaos*, 283
66   Wette, *The Wehrmacht*, 207
67   *Russian Combat Methods in World War II*, 10
68   Smelser and Davies, *The Myth of the Eastern Front*, 58
69   Wette, *The Wehrmacht*, 23–4
70   Smelser and Davies, *The Myth of the Eastern Front*, 58
71   Megargee, *Barbarossa 1941*, 34
72   *The Private War Journal of Generaloberst Franz Halder: Volume 2*, 32
73   Mosier, *Cross of Iron*, 232
74   Mosier, *Cross of Iron*, 230
75   Megargee, *Barbarossa 1941*, 37–8
76   Wette, *The Wehrmacht*, 91
77   Forster and Mawdsley, 'Hitler and Stalin in Perspective', 63–4
78   Smelser and Davies, *The Myth of the Eastern Front*, 57
79   *The Private War Journal of Generaloberst Franz Halder: Volume 6*, 29
80   Hoth, *Panzer Operations*, 2723/3062
81   Smelser and Davies, *The Myth of the Eastern Front*, 60
82   Megargee, *Barbarossa 1941*, 63
83   Wette, *The Wehrmacht*, 94
84   Smelser and Davies, *The Myth of the Eastern Front*, 44
85   Guderian, *Panzer Leader*, 152
86   Forster, 'Barbarossa Revisited', 31
87   Hart, *Guderian*, 69
88   Guderian, *Panzer Leader*, 448
89   Hart, *Guderian*, 72
90   Wette, *The Wehrmacht*, 198
91   Smelser and Davies, *The Myth of the Eastern Front*, 44–5
92   Smelser and Davies, *The Myth of the Eastern Front*, 106
93   Manstein, *Lost Victories*, 180
94   Smelser and Davies, *The Myth of the Eastern Front*, 97
95   Smelser and Davies, *The Myth of the Eastern Front*, 97–98
96   Smelser and Davies, *The Myth of the Eastern Front*, 98
97   Smelser and Davies, *The Myth of the Eastern Front*, 98–9
98   Welch, '*The Annihilation of Superfluous Eaters*', 8
99   Welch, '*The Annihilation of Superfluous Eaters*', 8
100 Trauschweizer, 'Learning with an Ally', 478
101 Smelser and Davies, *The Myth of the Eastern Front*, 52
102 Smelser and Davies, *The Myth of the Eastern Front*, 74
103 *Interview with Ronald Smelser and Edward Davies*
104 Hart, *Guderian*, 114
105 Hart, *Guderian*, 114
106 Mellenthin, *German Generals of World War II*, 38
107 Morgan, 'The German Officers' Corps', 25
108 Morgan, 'The German Officers' Corps', 26
109 Wood, 'Captive Historians, Captivated Audience', 127
110 Wette, *The Wehrmacht*, 232
111 Wood, 'Captive Historians, Captivated Audience', 144–7
112 Wette, *The Wehrmacht*, 251–7
113 Wood, 'Captive Historians, Captivated Audience', 124
114 Smelser and Davies concluded, 'As our research reveals, a more specific American subculture composed of military officers, historians employed by the military, and popular historians has really succeeded in shaping the broad popular view of the German military. This view makes the German army appear as if it had operated independently of the genocidal policies and practices of the Nazi regime in the East and only played the traditional role of a military force fighting honorably for its country.' Smelser and Davies, *The Myth of the Eastern Front*, 3
115 Frothingham, 'Panzer Leader', 63
116 Marshall, 'Lost Victories', 56
117 Marshall, 'Lost Victories', 56
118 Tompkins, 'War of Movement', 60–1
119 Smelser and Davies, *The Myth of the Eastern Front*, 119
120 Gudmundsson, *Stormtroop Tactics*, xiv
121 Dupuy, *A Genius For War*, 5
122 Dupuy, *A Genius For War*, 22
123 Dupuy, *A Genius For War*, 272–3
124 Dupuy, *A Genius For War*, 344
125 Van Creveld, *Fighting Power*, 3
126 Van Creveld, *Fighting Power*, 5

127 DePuy, *Selected Papers of General William E. DePuy*, 307

128 Starry, 'To Change an Army', 26

129 Historian James Wood concluded that the 'manuscripts can add immeasurably to our understanding of the Second World War, provided that one is willing to consider the motivations, beliefs, and attitudes of their authors'. Wood, 'Captive Historians, Captivated Audience', 127

130 Coram, *Boyd*, 5351/7717

131 Burton, *Pentagon Wars*, 5547/7426

132 Boyd, 'Patterns of Conflict (Delivered on 26 May 1978)', 11

133 Lind, *Maneuver Warfare Handbook*, 61

134 Lind, *Maneuver Warfare Handbook*, 61

135 Lind, *Maneuver Warfare Handbook*, 63

136 Lind, *Maneuver Warfare Handbook*, 64

137 Wyly, 'Attack or Defend?', 60

138 Wyly, 'Attack or Defend?', 60–1

139 Wyly, 'Lost Victories', 70

140 Wyly, 'Teaching Maneuver Warfare', in Hooker, *Maneuver Warfare: An Anthology*, 267

141 Anonymous, 'Professional Reading', 81

142 Boyd, 'Patterns of Conflict (Delivered on 26 May 1978)', 36

143 Lind, 'Some Doctrinal Questions for the United States Army', 140

144 Wyly, 'Lost Victories', 70–1

Chapter Four: The Father of *Blitzkrieg*

1 Castel, 'Liddell Hart's Sherman', 418

2 Castel, 'Liddell Hart's Sherman', 418–19

3 Castel, 'Liddell Hart's Sherman', 424

4 Castel, 'Liddell Hart's Sherman', 424

5 Liddell Hart, *Great Captains Unveiled*, 7

6 Liddell Hart, *Great Captains Unveiled*, 14

7 Liddell Hart, *Great Captains Unveiled*, 31

8 Liddell Hart, *Great Captains Unveiled*, 32–3

9 Porter, *Military Orientalism*, 113

10 Porter, *Military Orientalism*, 129

11 Porter, *Military Orientalism*, 140

12 Owen, 'The Manoeuvre Warfare Fraud'

13 Danchev, 'Liddell Hart and the Indirect Approach', 331

14 Castel, 'Liddell Hart's Sherman', 425

15 Walden, 'Liddell Hart', 44

16 Danchev, 'Liddell Hart and the Indirect Approach', 326

17 Reid, '"Young Turks, or Not So Young?"',163

18 Lord, 'Liddell Hart and the Napoleonic Fallacy', 57

19 Danchev, 'Liddell Hart and the Indirect Approach', 326–7

20 Danchev, 'Liddell Hart and the Indirect Approach', 326

21 Bond, *Liddell Hart*, 97

22 Van Creveld, *A History of Strategy*, 1363/1800

23 Liddell Hart, *When Britain Goes to War*, 70

24 Bond, *Liddell Hart*, 97

25 Showalter concluded, 'Even the apostle of mobility, B. H. Liddell Hart, concluded that the lessons of Spain were that the defense was presently dominant, and that few successes had been gained by maneuver alone.' Showalter, *Hitler's Panzers*, 71

26 Hofmann, 'The Tactical and Strategic Use of Attaché Intelligence', 113

27 Peter Davies noted, 'With the ear of the Minister appointed to carry out Chamberlain's plans to restrict the Army's role in any future European war to one of "limited liability", Liddell Hart was able to give full rein to his reformist ideas.' Dennis, 'J.F.C. Fuller and B.H. Liddell Hart', in Smith, *The Strategists*, 61

28 Reid, '"Young Turks, or Not So Young?"', 170

29 Danchev, *Alchemist of War*, 191

30 Reid, '"Young Turks, or Not So Young?"', 172

31 Bond, *Liddell Hart*, 123

32 Mearsheimer, *Liddell Hart and the Weight of History*, 105–6

33 Bond, *Liddell Hart*, 130

34 Mearsheimer, *Liddell Hart and the Weight of History*, 126

35 Walden, 'Liddell Hart', 42

36 Barnett, 'Basil faulty?', 62–3

37 Mearsheimer, *Liddell Hart and the Weight of History*, 126

38 Liddell Hart, *The Defence of Britain*, 188

39 Van Creveld, *A History of Strategy*, 1237/1800

40 Mosier, *The Blitzkrieg Myth*, 200

41 Peters concluded, 'As for bombing the industrial infrastructure, at the end of the war more than 90 percent of Germany's production capabilities remained intact (contrary to popular belief). . . Those expensive attacks on "vital" nodes helped the war effort but could not have won the war alone had they lasted for a generation.' Peters, 'Bloodless Theories, Bloody Wars', 34

42 Bond, *Liddell Hart*, 137

43 Barnett explained, 'Take the Indirect Approach on the largest strategic scale, the allied campaign in the Middle East and Mediterranean in 1940–45. From first to last it was cost-ineffective, demanding forces far larger than the enemy, demanding colossal investment in shipping and logistics, and ending up in a cul-de-sac in Northern Italy.' Barnett, 'Basil faulty?', 62

44 Mosier concluded, 'The decision made in the fall of 1943 to fight up the Italian Peninsula would have a dire effect on operations in the fall of 1944, when the Allies desperately needed more infantry in Northern Europe. . . Italy sucked in more than three Allied soldiers for every German one.' Mosier, *The Blitzkrieg Myth*, 176

45 Mearsheimer concluded, 'Pursuing sideshows only worked to increase Germany's chances of winning the war. The reason is simple: a policy of horizontal escalation held no promise of inflicting a decisive defeat on Germany, yet it worked to weaken the Allies' overall position by diverting substantial numbers of British and French forces and very few German forces away from the critical Western Front.' Mearsheimer, *Liddell Hart and the Weight of History*, 69

46 Gat, 'British Influence and the Evolution of the Panzer Arm: Myth or Reality? Part II', 328

47 Liddell Hart, *Europe in Arms*, 89

48 Sheffield concluded, 'Two formations epitomise the British Desert Army's "indirect approach": the Jock Column and the Brigade Group. The former was a tiny, all-arms unit, effective enough in a raiding and screening role. . . The decision by XXX (British) Corps, after surprising Rommel during Operation CRUSADER in November 1941, to dispatch the three armoured brigades of 7th Armoured Division to divergent objectives contrasts strongly with Soviet and German practice of concentrating armour. The Gazala battles of 1942 showed again the danger of splitting the forces of Eighth Army into small units lacking in fire power and "punch".' Sheffield, 'Doctrine and Command in the British Army: An Historical Overview', in Army Doctrine Publication *Operations*, E-15

49 Mellenthin, *Panzer Battles*, 81

50 Mearsheimer, *Liddell Hart and the Weight of History*, 152–3

51 Liddell Hart, *The German Generals Talk*, 1973/4501

52 Liddell Hart, *The German Generals Talk*, 2542/4501

53 Kesselring, *The Memoirs of Field Marshal Kesselring*, 314

54 Historian Holger Herwig concluded that Halder 'used ties to Basil Liddell Hart to head off critical assessments of either the *Wehrmacht* or Third Reich'. Herwig, 'Military History Reconsidered', 114

55 Liddell Hart, *The German Generals Talk*, 55/4501

56 Liddell Hart, *The German Generals Talk*, 4432/4501

57 Bond, *Liddell Hart*, 184

58 Bond, *Liddell Hart*, 185

59 Smelser and Davies, *The Myth of the Eastern Front*, 101

60 Danchev, *Alchemist of War*, 228

61 O'Neill, 'Sir Basil Liddell Hart', 38–9

62 Bond, *Liddell Hart*, 188

63 Gat, 'British Influence and the Evolution of the Panzer Arm: Myth or Reality? Part I', 150

64 Liddell Hart, *The German Generals Talk*, 1353/4501

65 Liddell Hart, 'The Great Illusions of 1939', 10

66 Peter Dennis concluded in relation to Liddell Hart and former German generals that 'it seems that on occasions they told him what he wanted to hear and exaggerated the extent to which his ideas had influenced the development of their own'. Dennis, 'J.F.C. Fuller and B.H. Liddell Hart', in Smith, *The Strategists*, 63

67 Bond, *Liddell Hart*, 234

68 Mearsheimer, *Liddell Hart and the Weight of History*, 187–8

69 Gat, 'British Influence and the Evolution of the Panzer Arm: Myth or Reality? Part I', 151–2

70 Liddell Hart, 'Foreword', in Guderian, *Panzer Leader*, 15

71 Guderian, *Panzer Leader*, 20

72 Gat, 'British Influence and the Evolution of the Panzer Arm: Myth or Reality? Part I', 152

73 Guderian, *Panzer Leader*, 20

74 Mearsheimer, *Liddell Hart and the Weight of History*, 190–1

75   Naveh noted, 'An exchange of letters between Liddell Hart and Guderian from the summer of 1949, intended to provide a comprehensive interpretation of the *Blitzkrieg* essentials, is particularly enlightening since it discloses the fact that Liddell Hart imposed his own fabricated version of *Blitzkrieg* on the latter and compelled him to proclaim it as the original formula.' Naveh, *In Pursuit of Military Excellence*, 109

76   Guderian, *Panzer Leader*, 32

77   Condell and Zabecki, 'Introduction', *On the German Art of War*, 7

78   Hart, *Guderian*, 33

79   Citino, *The Path to Blitzkrieg*, 202

80   Hart, *Guderian*, 23

81   Showalter, *Hitler's Panzers*, 29 and 43

82   Hart, *Guderian*, 27

83   Liddell Hart, 'Foreword', Guderian, *Panzer Leader*, 13

84   Shimon Naveh concluded that 'the Liddell Hart historical manipulation encouraged further distortions and legitimized additional fabrications. One of these convolutions centred on Guderian's autobiographical account, depicting the creation of the German armoured troops and the invention of their employment conception as his individual venture and private achievement. Guderian, with significant support from Liddell Hart, created this impression.' Naveh, *In Pursuit of Military Excellence*, 109

85   Frieser, *The Blitzkrieg Legend*, 3414/14003

86   Gat, 'British Influence and the Evolution of the Panzer Arm: Myth or Reality? Part I', 151

87   Bond, *Liddell Hart*, 232

88   Mearsheimer, *Liddell Hart and the Weight of History*, 198–9

89   Liddell Hart, 'Introduction', Rommel, *The Rommel Papers*, xv

90   Liddell Hart, *The Rommel Papers*, 84

91   Liddell Hart, *The Rommel Papers*, 401

92   Liddell Hart, *Strategy: Second Revised Edition*, Dust Jacket

93   Castel, 'Liddell Hart's Sherman', 408

94   Rommel, *The Rommel Papers*, 184

95   Mellenthin, *Panzer Battles*, 69

96   Liddell Hart, 'Foreword', in Manstein, *Lost Victories*, 13

97   Liddell Hart, 'Foreword' in Manstein, *Lost Victories*, 13

98   Bond, *Liddell Hart*, 232

99   Gat, 'British Influence and the Evolution of the Panzer Arm: Myth or Reality? Part I', 150–1

100 Liddell Hart, *The Liddell Hart Memoirs Vol II*, 4254/5932

101 Bond, *Liddell Hart*, 233

102 Mearsheimer, *Liddell Hart and the Weight of History*, ix–x

103 Danchev, *Alchemist of War*, 234

104 Mearsheimer, *Liddell Hart and the Weight of History*, 188

105 Danchev, *Alchemist of War*, 189–90

106 Liddell Hart, *Strategy: Second Revised Edition*, 218

107 Liddell Hart, *The Liddell Hart Memoirs Vol I*, 3142/7648

108 Naveh, *In Pursuit of Military Excellence*, 105

109 Citino, 'The War Hitler Won', 5–9

110 Frieser, *The Blitzkrieg Legend*, 302/14003

111 Fanning, 'The Origin of the Term "Blitzkrieg"'

112 Gat, 'British Influence and the Evolution of the Panzer Arm: Myth or Reality? Part II', 329

113 Frieser, *The Blitzkrieg Legend*, 306/14003

114 Fanning, 'The Origin of the Term "Blitzkrieg"'

115 Frieser, *The Blitzkrieg Legend*, 956/14003

116 Cook, 'The German Breakthrough at Sedan', 8

117 Frieser, *The Blitzkrieg Legend*, 294/14003

118 John Mearsheimer concluded that Liddell Hart's 'mass of writings from the late 1930s and early 1940s make him look like the proverbial general caught preparing for the last war'. Mearsheimer, *Liddell Hart and the Weight of History*, 126

119 Bond, *Liddell Hart*, 4

120 Mearsheimer, *Liddell Hart and the Weight of History*, ix–x

121 Danchev, 'Liddell Hart and the Indirect Approach', 313

122 Shimon Naveh concluded that Liddell Hart damaged 'modern historical and military research' and 'created a theoretical imbroglio that has taken more than 40 years to unravel'. Naveh, *In Pursuit of Military Excellence*, 108–9

123 Liddell Hart, 'New Warfare — New Tactics', 12

124 Nihart, 'Strategy — The Indirect Approach', 58

125 Nihart, 'Strategy — The Indirect Approach', 58

126 Nihart, 'Strategy — The Indirect Approach', 58

127 Mearsheimer, *Liddell Hart and the Weight of History*, 162

128 Walden, 'Liddell Hart', 32

129 Walden, 'Liddell Hart', 39

130 Walters, 'Interview with Capt B.H. Liddell Hart', 27

131 Walters, 'Interview with Capt B.H. Liddell Hart', 27–8

132 Woodmansee, 'Blitzkrieg and the AirLand Battle', 22

133 Morelock, 'The Legacy of Liddell Hart', 66

134 Brown, 'Maneuver Warfare at Tinian — 1944', 54

135 Benson, 'The Apostles of Mobility', 65

136 Liddell Hart, *Strategy: Second Revised Edition*, 326–7

137 Liddell Hart, 'Was the 1940 Collapse Avoidable?', 8–9

138 In a 1986 *Patterns of Conflict* briefing, Boyd declared: '… another notion here, primarily attributable to … Liddell Hart. Operate in a line, or operate in a direction that threatens alternative objectives … I'll also point out, Liddell Hart didn't even understand his own idea. I'll bring that out later on.' In this statement, Boyd disagreed with Liddell Hart's emphasis on operating on a line or a direction because these are expressions of physical dislocation. Boyd added: 'For you people who have read Liddell-Hart, I can give you a much better book. Liddell-Hart's book, I think it's a lot of garbage … how many people have read Liddell-Hart's *Strategy and the Indirect Approach*? Remember, we talked about the indirect approach being dislocation, and dislocation being the indirect approach. My God, he's got circular reasoning — he's going to dislocate a guy's mind. You don't dislocate a mind — you disorient it! He talks about dislocation … he's [sic] chiropractor of war!', Brown, 'Opportunity Lost', 207

139 In a 1989 *Patterns of Conflict* briefing Boyd declared: 'In fact, how many people have read Liddell Hart's book, Strategy? I don't necessarily recommend

it too highly.' Boyd, Discourse on Winning and Losing, 25

140 Hammond, 'On the Making of History', 10

141 Boyd, *Patterns of Conflict (Slides)*, 70–1

142 Boyd, *Patterns of Conflict (Slides)*, 70

143 Boyd, *Patterns of Conflict (Slides)*, 57

144 Lind, *Maneuver Warfare Handbook*, 62

145 Lind, 'Some Doctrinal Questions for the United States Army', 139

146 Leonhard, *The Art of Maneuver*, 866/5341

147 Simpkin, *Race to the Swift*, 133

148 Danchev noted, 'Challenged to find any alternative to that gesture, a challenge he would face again, Liddell Hart could find none. Given the circumstances of 1914, he too would have sent an expeditionary force across the Channel, either to France or to Belgium. He would have done something else later — in the antique dichotomy of "Westerners" and "Easterners" in the Great War, Liddell Hart was a slightly evasive Easterner — but this was a crucial admission for any future Way. Yet it was never publicly acknowledged. "Is it too unkind to suggest that to do so would have ruined a memorable metaphor?" Perhaps it is. Liddell Hart was already committed, to an idea and to a text.' Danchev, 'Liddell Hart and the Indirect Approach', 334

Chapter Five: *Wehrmacht* Operations: Myth and Reality

1 Boyd, *Patterns of Conflict (Slides)*, 79

2 Lind, 'Why the German Example?', 60

3 Leonhard, *The Art of Maneuver*, 934/5341

4 Hughes concluded, 'Hindered by superficial knowledge and dependent upon unreliable sources, too many writers have created false pictures of the German army's doctrine and methods. Far too often, German military history has become a storehouse to be looted in search of examples to justify current doctrinal concepts.' Hughes, 'Abuses of German Military History', 67

5 Hughes, 'Abuses of German Military History', 69

6 Bolger, 'Maneuver Warfare Reconsidered', in Hooker, *Maneuver

Warfare: An Anthology, 28

7   Citino, 'The War Hitler Won', 5–9

8   Frieser, *The Blitzkrieg Legend*, 7413/14003

9   Van Creveld, *A History of Strategy*, 1009/1800

10 Holmes, 'Classical Blitzkrieg', 745

11 Holmes, 'Classical Blitzkrieg', 745

12 Holmes, 'Classical Blitzkrieg', 746–7

13 Schlieffen, *Cannae*, 4

14 Wallach, *The Dogma of the Battle of Annihilation*, 42

15 Holmes, 'Classical Blitzkrieg', 747

16 Holmes, 'Classical Blitzkrieg', 761

17 Wallach, *The Dogma of the Battle of Annihilation*, 97

18 Holmes, 'Classical Blitzkrieg', 769

19 Holmes, 'Classical Blitzkrieg', 753

20 Holmes, 'Classical Blitzkrieg', 759

21 Frieser, *The Blitzkrieg Legend*, 1894/14003

22 Brand, 'The Origins of Freie Operationen', 99

23 Megargee, 'The German Army after the Great War', in Dennis and Grey, *Victory or Defeat*, 106

24 Frieser, *The Blitzkrieg Legend*, 7457/14003

25 Showalter, *Hitler's Panzers*, 26

26 Holmes, 'Classical Blitzkrieg', 770–1

27 Hughes, 'Abuses of German Military History', 69

28 Hughes noted, 'The *Wehrmacht* used its famous encircling maneuvers to create favorable conditions for conducting traditional battles of annihilation. Despite several recent statements to the contrary, the Germans did not embrace the theories of J.F.C. Fuller or B.H. Liddell Hart on paralyzing the enemy. Physical destruction of the opposing force remained the goal of mobile warfare.' Hughes, 'Abuses of German Military History', 70

29 Hoth, *Panzer Operations*, 2103/3062

30 Balck, *Order in Chaos*, 445–6

31 Mellenthin, *Panzer Battles*, 16

32 Frieser noted, 'Reconnaissance findings impressively confirmed Manstein's estimate of the enemy situation. Accordingly, a new Cannae was within the realm of possibility if his encirclement idea could be carried out consistently.' Frieser, *The Blitzkrieg Legend*, 1947/14003

33 *The Private War Journal of Generaloberst Franz Halder: Volume 4*, 67

34 Frieser, *The Blitzkrieg Legend*, 7346/14003

35 Frieser concluded, 'The army high command planned a "super Cannae" to smash the Soviet armies that were deployed along the border in a series of encirclement battles — and they figured that this alone would mean that the campaign had been won.' Frieser, *The Blitzkrieg Legend*, 7885/14003

36 Hughes, 'Abuses of German Military History', 70

37 Hoth, *Panzer Operations*, 446/3062

38 Wallach, *The Dogma of the Battle of Annihilation*, 273

39 Rommel, *The Rommel Papers*, 116

40 Gat, 'British Influence and the Evolution of the Panzer Arm: Myth or Reality? Part I', 153

41 Gat, 'British Influence and the Evolution of the Panzer Arm: Myth or Reality? Part I', 153

42 Gat, 'British Influence and the Evolution of the Panzer Arm: Myth or Reality? Part I', 159

43 Gat, 'British Influence and the Evolution of the Panzer Arm: Myth or Reality? Part I', 171

44 Gat, 'British Influence and the Evolution of the Panzer Arm: Myth or Reality? Part II', 328

45 Liddell Hart, *When Britain Goes to War*, 71

46 Sheffield, 'Doctrine and Command in the British Army: An Historical Overview', in Army Doctrine Publication *Operations*, E-15

47 Guderian, *Achtung Panzer!*, 3752/5003

48 Liddell Hart, *Paris*, 27

49 Guderian, *Panzer Leader*, 97

50 Hughes remarked, 'The German army's mobile forces had as their primary objectives the destruction or forced dislocation of enemy artillery, not of his command and control systems. . . The task of Guderian's 2nd Panzer Group was to destroy the enemy units in the Bialystok area and then to move eastward toward Smolensk. Guderian's order, which repeatedly stressed the need to clear the roads for rapid exploitation to the east, mentioned neither enemy headquarters nor

communications.' Hughes, 'Abuses of
German Military History', 70

51   Guderian, *Panzer Leader*, 274
52   Megargee, 'The German Army after the
Great War: A Case Study in Selective
Self-Deception', in Dennis and Grey,
Victory or Defeat, 110
53   Newland, 'Blitzkrieg in Retrospect', 87
54   Balck, *Translation of Taped Conversation
with General Hermann Balck, 13 April
1979*, 13
55   Mellenthin, *Panzer Battles*, 17
56   Mellenthin, *German Generals of World
War II*, 196
57   Mellenthin, *Panzer Battles*, 17
58   Mearsheimer, *Liddell Hart and the
Weight of History*, 206
59   Liddell Hart, *The Liddell Hart Memoirs
Vol I*, 662/7648
60   Liddell Hart, *Paris*, 82
61   Liddell Hart, *The Liddell Hart Memoirs
Vol I*, 1735/7648
62   Mearsheimer concluded, 'Contrary
to what Liddell Hart implied *after*
World War II, *before* that conflict he
occasionally came close to advocating
an all-tank army, whereas Fuller
often emphasized that infantry and
artillery would not disappear from the
battlefield.' Mearsheimer, *Liddell Hart
and the Weight of History*, 207
63   Brian Bond noted that 'it would be
straining the evidence too far to
suggest that the first three Panzer
divisions created in 1935 closely
resembled Liddell Hart's "New Model"
division of a decade earlier. . . whereas
Liddell Hart pictured a small number of
infantrymen being attached to a *tank*
force, the Germans joined together
large units of infantry, artillery and
tanks to make a new type of formation
which was not followed elsewhere.'
Bond, *Liddell Hart*, 223–4
64   Gat, 'British Influence and the Evolution
of the Panzer Arm: Myth or Reality? Part
II', 335
65   Gary Sheffield concluded: 'armoured
commanders, influenced by radical
thinkers such as Liddell Hart, improvised
new tactics, which had the fatal flaw
of neglecting the coordination of all
arms. Armoured units in particular
were prone to try to fight independent
battles. This was especially unfortunate

given the propensity of some units for
the frontal "Balaclava" charge and the
German tactic of using panzers to lure
British tanks onto their anti-tank guns.'
Sheffield, 'Doctrine and Command in the
British Army', E-15
66   Rippe, 'Leadership, Firepower and
Maneuver', 30
67   Mellenthin, *Panzer Battles*, 11
68   Mellenthin, *Panzer Battles*, 60
69   Hart, *Guderian*, 68
70   Gudmundsson, *On Armor*, 132
71   Showalter, *Hitler's Panzers*, 134–5
72   Gat, 'British Influence and the Evolution
of the Panzer Arm: Myth or Reality? Part
II', 336–7
73   Liddell Hart, *The German Generals Talk*,
1438/4501
74   Gat, 'British Influence and the Evolution
of the Panzer Arm: Myth or Reality? Part
II', 336
75   Hart, *Guderian*, 34
76   Hart, *Guderian*, 39
77   Hart, *Guderian*, 39
78   Hart, *Guderian*, 94
79   Mosier, *Cross of Iron*, 189
80   Boyd, *Patterns of Conflict (Slides)*, 118
81   Simpkin, *Race to the Swift*, 53
82   Mellenthin, *Panzer Battles*, 27
83   *On the German Art of War*, 17
84   Lind, *Maneuver Warfare Handbook*, 22
85   Guderian, *Panzer Leader*, 70
86   Balck, *Order in Chaos*, 179
87   Balck, *Translation of Taped Conversation
with General Hermann Balck, 13 April
1979*, 20
88   *Generals Balck and Von Mellenthin on
Tactics*, 16–17
89   Rommel, *The Rommel Papers*, 226
90   Hart, *Guderian*, 29
91   Frieser, *The Blitzkrieg Legend*,
7657/14003
92   Balck, *Order in Chaos*, 193
93   Balck, *Translation of Taped Conversations
with General Hermann Balck, 12 January
1979*, 20
94   Balck, *Translation of Taped Conversation
with General Hermann Balck, 12 January
1979*, 20
95   Lind, *Maneuver Warfare Handbook*, 14
96   Hart, *Guderian*, 74
97   Naveh, *In Pursuit of Military Excellence*,
144
98   Naveh, *In Pursuit of Military Excellence*,
143

99   Hart, *Guderian*, 79
100 Balck, *Order in Chaos*, 229
101 Wyly, 'Appendix: Fundamentals of
     Tactics', in Lind, *Maneuver Warfare
     Handbook*, 96
102 Balck, *Order in Chaos*, 230
103 Rommel, *The Rommel Papers*, 517
104 *The Private War Journal of Generaloberst
     Franz Halder: Volume 6*, 206
105 Lind 'Defining Maneuver Warfare for the
     Marine Corps', 57
106 Lind, 'Some Doctrinal Questions for the
     United States Army', 139
107 Citino, *The Path to Blitzkrieg*, 250
108 Frieser, *The Blitzkrieg Legend*,
     2070/14003
109 Showalter, *Hitler's Panzers*, 106
110 Hart, *Guderian*, 64
111 Frieser, *The Blitzkrieg Legend*,
     1979/14003
112 Frieser, *The Blitzkrieg Legend*,
     1964/14003
113 Doughty, *The Breaking Point*, 1961/7793
114 Frieser, *The Blitzkrieg Legend*,
     4774/14003
115 Frieser, *The Blitzkrieg Legend*,
     5751/14003
116 Frieser, *The Blitzkrieg Legend*,
     5758/14003
117 Frieser, *The Blitzkrieg Legend*,
     4300/14003
118 Frieser, *The Blitzkrieg Legend*,
     7087/14003
119 Mellenthin, *Panzer Battles*, 24
120 Doughty, *The Seeds of Disaster*, 71
121 Mosier, *Deathride*, 27
122 Frieser, *The Blitzkrieg Legend*,
     3439/14003
123 Kesselring, *The Memoirs of Field Marshal
     Kesselring*, 30
124 Corum, 'The Spanish Civil War', 326
125 Mosier, *Cross of Iron*, 113
126 Mellenthin, *Panzer Battles*, 17

Chapter Six: Riddle of the Stormtroopers
1   Liddell Hart, *The Future of Infantry*, 27
2   Liddell Hart, *The Liddell Hart Memoirs
     Vol I*, 4304/7648
3   Boyd, 'Patterns of Conflict (Delivered on
     26 May 1978)', 23
4   Boyd, 'Patterns of Conflict (Delivered on
     26 May 1978)', 22
5   Boyd, 'Patterns of Conflict (Delivered on
     26 May 1978)', 24
6   Boyd, 'Patterns of Conflict (Delivered on

26 May 1978)', 27
7   Fallows, 'Muscle-Bound Superpower'
8   Lind and Thiele, *4th Generation Warfare
     Handbook*, 1450/1578
9   Lind, 'Light Infantry Tactics', 44
10   Leonhard, *The Art of Maneuver*,
     927/5341
11   Wyly, 'Fundamentals of Tactics', in Lind,
     Maneuver Warfare Handbook, 73
12   Liddell Hart, *Strategy: Second Revised
     Edition*, 218
13   Fuller, *The Conduct of War 1789–1961*,
     256–7
14   Boyd, 'Patterns of Conflict (Delivered on
     26 May 1978)', 29
15   Boyd, *Patterns of Conflict (Slides)*, 113
16   Lind, 'Some Doctrinal Questions for the
     United States Army', 138
17   Lind, 'Some Doctrinal Questions for the
     United States Army', 140
18   Leonhard, 'Maneuver Warfare and
     the United States Army', in *Maneuver
     Warfare: An Anthology*, 52
19   Simpkin, *Race to the Swift*, 33
20   Doughty, *The Breaking Point*, 6009/7793
21   Doughty, *The Breaking Point*, 6006/7793
22   Tucker, *False Prophets*, 17
23   Roger Beaumont concluded: 'very few
     West German works criticizing the
     German–Nazi military tradition were
     published in Great Britain or the United
     States'. Beaumont, 'On the Wehrmacht
     Mystique', 46
24   *Armored Warfare in World War II*, 8
25   *Armored Warfare in World War II*, 11
26   *Armored Warfare in World War II*, 11
27   *Armored Warfare in World War II*, 28
28   *Armored Warfare in World War II*, 28
29   *Armored Warfare in World War II*, 28
30   *Armored Warfare in World War II*, 28
31   *Armored Warfare in World War II*, 29
32   *Armored Warfare in World War II*, 31
33   *Armored Warfare in World War II*, 31
34   Mellenthin, *Panzer Battles*, 167
35   Lauer, *Maneuver Warfare Theory*, 40
36   Lauer, *Maneuver Warfare Theory*, 41
37   Balck, *Translation of Taped Conversation
     with General Hermann Balck, 12 January
     1979*, 18
38   *Generals Balck and Von Mellenthin on
     Tactics*, 53
39   *Generals Balck and Von Mellenthin on
     Tactics*, 53
40   *Generals Balck and Von Mellenthin on
     Tactics*, 53

41   *Generals Balck and Von Mellenthin on Tactics*, 53

42   *Generals Balck and Von Mellenthin on Tactics*, 53

43   *Generals Balck and Von Mellenthin on Tactics*, 53

44   *Generals Balck and Von Mellenthin on Tactics*, 52

45   *Generals Balck and Von Mellenthin on Tactics*, 53

46   Stackpole noted, 'Often, the first Germans the British defenders saw were already behind their positions.' Stackpole, *German Tactics in the Michael Offensive March 1918*, 88

47   Bull remarked, 'Although the merits and demerits of Gough's generalship may continue to be debated, there can be little doubt that he himself helped to encourage the idea of von Hutier as a maverick tactical genius and bogeyman.' Bull, *German Assault Troops of the First World War*, 2498/3406

48   Bull, *German Assault Troops of the First World War*, 2511/3406

49   Gudmundsson, *Stormtroop Tactics*, 193–4

50   Gudmundsson, *Stormtroop Tactics*, 194–5

51   Gudmundsson, *Stormtroop Tactics*, 195

52   Gudmundsson, *Stormtroop Tactics*, 193

53   Bull, *German Assault Troops of the First World War*, 799/3406

54   Bull, *German Assault Troops of the First World War*, 793/3406

55   Liddell Hart, *Foch*, 400

56   Strachan, 'John Buchan and the First World War', 313

57   Strachan, 'John Buchan and the First World War', 313

58   Strachan, 'John Buchan and the First World War', 313

59   Strachan noted, 'The 'military philosophy' deployed in *The Courts of the Morning*, published in 1929, was a much more sophisticated blending of Liddell Hart's themes, a cross of 'infiltration tactics' with what was to become the 'strategy of the indirect approach', and Buchan declared himself 'proud indeed' that Liddell Hart 'approved of it'. Strachan, 'John Buchan and the First World War', 314–5

60   Lupfer, *The Dynamics of Doctrine*, 27–8

61   O'Brien Browne, 'The Kaiser's Last Battle', 86

62   Gudmundsson, *Stormtroop Tactics*, 85

63   Lupfer, *The Dynamics of Doctrine*, 28

64   Gudmundsson, *Stormtroop Tactics*, 49

65   Gudmundsson, *Stormtroop Tactics*, 51–2

66   Gudmundsson, *Stormtroop Tactics*, 67

67   Gudmundsson, *Stormtroop Tactics*, 72

68   Lind and Thiele, *4th Generation Warfare Handbook*, 879/1578

69   Lind, 'Light Infantry Tactics', 44

70   Stackpole noted, 'The Germans emphasized firepower to make their penetration. Stormtroopers sought gaps in the line, but expected to fight through enemy positions.' Stackpole, *German Tactics in the Michael Offensive March 1918*, 104

71   Gudmundsson, *Stormtroop Tactics*, 78

72   Ghiz, *Specialized Assault Units of the World War I Western Front*, 18

73   Gudmundsson, *Stormtroop Tactics*, 78

74   Bull, *German Assault Troops of the First World War*, 627/3406

75   Stackpole, *German Tactics in the Michael Offensive March 1918*, 104

76   Hoffman, 'The Limits of Light Infantry Doctrine', 20

77   Corum, 'How to Prepare for a Battle', 58–9

78   Corum, 'How to Prepare for a Battle', 60–1

79   Corum, 'How to Prepare for a Battle', 60–1

80   Stackpole, *German Tactics in the Michael Offensive March 1918*, 4

81   Gudmundsson, *Stormtroop Tactics*, 149

82   Crown Prince William of Germany, *My War Experiences*, 295

83   Lupfer, *The Dynamics of Doctrine*, 46–7

84   Stackpole, *German Tactics in the Michael Offensive March 1918*, 23–4

85   Ghiz, *Specialized Assault Units of the World War I Western Front*, 30–1

86   Gudmundsson, 'Field Stripping the Schwerpunkt', 32

87   Gudmundsson, *Stormtroop Tactics*, 164

88   Stackpole, *German Tactics in the Michael Offensive March 1918*, 88–9

89   Bull, *German Assault Troops of the First World War*, 24/3406

90   Stackpole, *German Tactics in the Michael Offensive March 1918*, 89

91   Gudmundsson, *Stormtroop Tactics*, 167

92   Stackpole, *German Tactics in the Michael Offensive March 1918*, 99

93   Bull, *German Assault Troops of the First World War*, 96/3406

94   Gudmundsson, *Stormtroop Tactics*, 168

95   O'Brien Browne, 'The Kaiser's Last Battle', 86

96   Balck, *Development of Tactics*, 277

97   Wilhelm Balck explained that 'special assault battalions were formed which, armed with the auxiliary weapons (machine guns, flame throwers and infantry guns), were attached by groups or platoons to the infantry. . . The shock squads (1 non-commissioned officer and 6 to 8 men) "lead the infantry at difficult points to open the points of entry into the hostile position, roll up hostile trenches, capture hostile machine guns and pill boxes and support the infantry in consolidating the captured position" (Field Training Regulations, I, 389)' Balck, *Development of Tactics*, 85

98   Balck, *Development of Tactics*, 86

99   Balck, *Order in Chaos*, 81

100   Balck, *Order in Chaos*, 83

101   Balck, *Order in Chaos*, 83

102   Balck, *Order in Chaos*, 84

103   Balck, *Order in Chaos*, 175

104   Boyd, *Destruction and Creation*, 3

105   Boyd, *Destruction and Creation*, 3

106   Boyd, *Destruction and Creation*, 5

107   Boyd, *Destruction and Creation*, 7

108   Boyd, *Destruction and Creation*, 7

109   Boyd, *Destruction and Creation*, 7

110   Kuhn, *The Structure of Scientific Revolutions*, 75

111   Spinney, 'Genghis John', 42

112   Spinney, 'Genghis John', 43

113   Osinga, *Science, Strategy and War*, 42

114   Hammond, *The Mind of War*, 2639/5008

115   Coram, *Boyd*, 901/7717

116   In the final version of Boyd's *Patterns of Conflict* slides, the notion that the Wehrmacht avoided destruction is contained in slides 111–17 in which he compares maneuver to attrition. Boyd, *Patterns of Conflict (Slides)*, 111-17. In a 1989 Patterns of Conflict verbal transcript Boyd added: 'Remember, in blitzkrieg you're trying to avoid the battle.' This is another example of Boyd insisting that the Wehrmacht avoided destruction. Boyd, *Discourse on Winning and Losing*, 125

117   Boyd, *Patterns of Conflict (Slides)*, 194

118   In the final version of Boyd's *Patterns of Conflict* slides, the historically inaccurate concept of infiltration tactics dominates slides 58–65. In slide 66, Boyd defined *blitzkrieg* as follows: 'Infiltration tactics of 1918 were mated with: Tank, Motorized Artillery, Tactical Aircraft, Motor Transport [and] Better Communications.' Boyd, *Patterns of Conflict (Slides)*, 58–66. In a 1989 Patterns of Conflict verbal transcript, Boyd stated: 'The Germans captured some of those pamphlets, and then they augmented it even more. And eventually, of course, it was used against the West in 1918, so-called German infiltration techniques. Today they're known — some people call them Hutier Tactics. That's why I put a question mark after him, because he was not an architect. He just happened to be commander on the German side that used them, and either a French or English correspondent used that name. And ever since then, it's been called the Hutier Tactics. But he wasn't an architect.' Boyd's use of the words 'so-called' concerns the question of whether the concept should be called 'infiltration tactics' or 'Hutier Tactics'. He is not doubting the existence of the tactics but what its proper name should be. Boyd added: 'So my point then, is until the rise of the infiltration tactics, and of course the use of tanks by the allies, neither the 19th century nor the early 20th century commanders were able to evolve tactical penetration maneuvers to offset the increase in weapons' lethality until these things start showing up.' Boyd added: 'But out in the field, the infiltration tactics, a la Ludendorff, are very similar to the guerrilla tactics as seen through Lawrence's eyes, very similar.' Boyd also added: 'And so he [Guderian] was familiar and privy to the German infiltration techniques. He read the British pamphlets. Plus, he understood the importance of communications. He put all that together, and therefore he became the innovator of the blitzkrieg.' Boyd, *Discourse on Winning and Losing*, 74, 79, 84, 85

119   Burton, *The Pentagon Wars*, 1051/7426

120   Burton, *The Pentagon Wars*, 5552/7426

121   Lind, *Maneuver Warfare Handbook*, 63

122   Lind, *Maneuver Warfare Handbook*, 58–9

123   Lind, *Maneuver Warfare Handbook: An*

Anthology, 7

124 Lind, 'The Theory and Practice of Maneuver Warfare', in Hooker, *Maneuver Warfare" An Anthology*, 5–7

125 Lind stated, 'When asked if the bulk of German thinking on maneuver warfare had been developed 1914–1918 or 1918–1939, he [Balck] replied that it had all been developed 1914–1918.' It is clear from the context of this discussion that Balck understood 'maneuver warfare' to mean 'mobile warfare' in opposition to 'static warfare' and not John Boyd's philosophy which would have been completely alien to him. Lind, 'The Theory and Practice of Maneuver Warfare', in Hooker, *Maneuver Warfare: An Anthology*, 17

126 Sanford, 'Maneuver Warfare Handbook', 82

127 Michel, *The Revolt of the Majors*, 91

128 General Wayne Downing explained that 'Battelle's series of interviews with the German generals (Hermann Balck, Gaedcke and von Mellenthin) are difficult to locate but contain excellent treatment of German application of the doctrine.' Downing, 'Training to Fight', 20

Chapter Seven: Maneuver Warfare and Operational Art

1 Freedman, *Strategy*, 84

2 Kipp, 'General-Major A. A. Svechin and Modern Warfare', in Svechin, *Strategy*, 858/9533

3 Glantz, 'Soviet Operational Formation for Battle', 3–4

4 Evans, *The Continental School of Strategy*, 49–50

5 Kiszely, 'Thinking About the Operational Level', 38

6 Svechin, *Strategy*, 1753/9533

7 Harrison, *Architect of Soviet Victory in World War II*, 1131/8272

8 Harrison, *Architect of Soviet Victory in World War II*, 1397/8272

9 Harrison, *Architect of Soviet Victory in World War II*, 2484/8272

10 Glantz, 'Soviet Operational Formation for Battle', 4–5

11 Naveh, *In Pursuit of Military Excellence*, 10–11

12 Leonhard, *The Art of Maneuver*, 970/5341

13 Leonhard, *The Art of Maneuver*, 978/5341

14 Leonhard, *The Art of Maneuver*, 1018/5341

15 Simpkin, *Race to the Swift*, 49

16 Zabecki, *The German 1918 Offensives*, 674/10246

17 Zabecki, *The German 1918 Offensives*, 671/10246

18 Glantz, 'Soviet Operational Formation for Battle', 4

19 Evans, *The Continental School of Strategy*, 57

20 Ricks, *The Generals*, 3390/10224

21 Lind, 'Why the German Example?', 63

22 Lind, 'The Operational Art', 47

23 Van Creveld, 'On Learning From the Wehrmacht and Other Things', 66

24 Halder, *Hitler as Warlord*, 23

25 Manstein, *Lost Victories*, 547

26 Mellenthin, *German Generals of World War II*, 286

27 Balck, *Order in Chaos*, 432

28 Balck, *Order in Chaos*, 435

29 Glantz, *Operation Barbarossa*, 202/6987

30 Naveh, *In Pursuit of Military Excellence*, 126

31 Forster and Mawdsley, 'Hitler and Stalin in Perspective', 63

32 Manstein, *Lost Victories*, 177–8

33 Guderian, *Panzer Leader*, 142

34 Halder, *The German Campaign in Russia*, 30–1

35 Megargee, *Barbarossa 1941*, 50

36 Glantz, *Operation Barbarossa*, 978/6987

37 Megargee, *Barbarossa 1941*, 49

38 Megargee, *Barbarossa 1941*, 52

39 Megargee, *Barbarossa 1941*, 119

40 Halder, *The German Campaign in Russia*, 89

41 Robinson, 'The Rommel Myth', 83

42 Naveh, *In Pursuit of Military Excellence*, 134

43 Robinson, 'The Rommel Myth', 89

44 Rommel, *The Rommel Papers*, 116

45 Macksey, *Why the Germans Lose at War*, 125

46 Robinson, 'The Rommel Myth', 84

47 Newland, *Victories Are Not Enough*, 74

48 Daly, *Cannae*, 1397/7889

49 Frieser, *The Blitzkrieg Legend*, 7867/14003

50 Richard Swain, 'Preface', in Schlieffen, *Cannae*, ii

51 Balck, *Order in Chaos*, 373–4

52   Condell and Zabecki, 'Introduction', *On the German Art of War*, 3

53   Naveh concluded, 'The greater their tactical successes and the deeper their penetration into the adversary's territory, the flimsier their operational position became. The German inclination to grab the largest possible number of enemy troops into the cauldrons created by the deep penetrating armoured blows overstretched their resources, split the mechanized formations from the infantry, and severed the succession of operations, thus bringing complete exhaustion upon themselves.' Naveh, *In Pursuit of Military Excellence*, 125

54   Naveh, *In Pursuit of Military Excellence*, 127

55   Hofmann, 'The Tactical and Strategic Use of Attaché Intelligence', 105

56   Hofmann, 'The Tactical and Strategic Use of Attaché Intelligence', 120

57   Naveh, *In Pursuit of Military Excellence*, 165

58   Showalter, *Hitler's Panzers*, 162

59   Mosier, *Deathride*, 63

60   Clark, *Barbarossa*, 34

61   Glantz, *Operation Barbarossa*, 361/6987

62   Glantz, *Operation Barbarossa*, 916/6987

63   Glantz, *August Storm*, 58

64   Jordan, 'The Wehrmacht's Worst Defeat', 39

65   Naveh, *In Pursuit of Military Excellence*, 237

66   Glantz, *August Storm*, xiii–xiv

67   *Russian Combat Methods in World War II*, 8

68   *Russian Combat Methods in World War II*, 11

69   Manstein, *Lost Victories*, 438–9

70   Liddell Hart, *The German Generals Talk*, 3292/4501

71   Balck, *Order in Chaos*, 291–2

72   Balck, *Order in Chaos*, 292

73   Balck, *Order in Chaos*, 263

74   Brown, *A New Conception of War*, 257

75   Brown, *A New Conception of War*, 110

76   Clausewitz, *On War*, 642

77   Clausewitz, *On War*, 518

78   Boyd, *Patterns of Conflict (Slides)*, 41

79   Lind, 'The Operational Art', 45

80   Leonhard, *The Art of Maneuver*, 439/5341

81   Leonhard, 'Maneuver Warfare and the United States Army', *Maneuver Warfare: An Anthology*, 52

82   FM 100-5 *Operations* (1986), 30

83   De Czege, 'Lessons from the Past', 59

84   *Warfighting*, 47

85   Elkus, 'The Rise and Decline of Strategic Paralysis'

86   Cancian, 'Centers of Gravity are a Myth', 30–4

87   Cancian, 'Centers of Gravity are a Myth', 30–4

88   Brown, *A New Conception of War*, 220–1

89   Brown, *A New Conception of War*, 233

90   Cancian, 'Centers of Gravity are a Myth', 30–4

91   Cohen, 'Uncertain Trumpets', 37

92   Tucker, *False Prophets*, 36

93   Cancian, 'Centers of Gravity are a Myth', 30–4

94   Freedman, *Strategy*, 208

95   Cancian, 'Centers of Gravity are a Myth', 30–4

96   Echevarria, 'Clausewitz's Center of Gravity', 110

97   Echevarria, 'Clausewitz's Center of Gravity', 111

98   Echevarria, 'Clausewitz's Center of Gravity', 115

99   Vego, 'Clausewitz' Schwerpunkt', 101

100   Vego, 'Clausewitz' Schwerpunkt', 102

101   Vego, 'Clausewitz' Schwerpunkt', 102

102   Frieser, *The Blitzkrieg Legend*, 7485/14003

103   Vego, 'Clausewitz' Schwerpunkt', 103

104   Brown, *A New Conception of War*, 231–2

105   Brown, *A New Conception of War*, 230

106   Hamilton, 'Maneuver Warfare and All That', 12

107   Megargee, *Barbarossa 1941*, 55

108   Halder, *The German Campaign in Russia*, 89

109   Guderian, *Panzer Leader*, 199

110   Manstein, *Lost Victories*, 177

111   Clark, *Barbarossa*, 92

112   Glantz, *Operation Barbarossa*, 2186/6987

113   Stolfi, *Hitler's Panzers East*, 108

114   Stolfi, *Hitler's Panzers East*, 110

115   Stolfi, *Hitler's Panzers East*, 111

116   Stolfi, *Hitler's Panzers East*, 127

117   Stolfi, 'Barbarossa', 889

118   Stolfi, *Hitler's Panzers East*, x

119   Stolfi, *Hitler's Panzers East*, ix

120   Stolfi, *Hitler's Panzers East*, 89

121   Stolfi, *German Panzers on the Offensive*, 13

122   Stolfi, *Hitler's Panzers East*, 28

123   Stolfi, *Hitler's Panzers East*, 18

124 Stolfi, *Hitler's Panzers East*, xii
125 Smelser and Davies concluded, 'Stolfi recycles many of the myths that he inherited from former German generals as to the possibilities of German victory in the summer of 1941.' Smelser and Davies, *The Myth of the Eastern Front*, 244
126 Hooker, 'The World Will Hold its Breath', 150
127 Hooker, 'The World Will Hold its Breath', 152
128 Hooker, 'The World Will Hold its Breath', 155
129 Hooker, 'The World Will Hold its Breath', 162
130 Hooker, 'The World Will Hold its Breath', 157
131 Hooker, 'The World Will Hold its Breath', 156
132 Mosier, *Cross of Iron*, 202
133 Halder, *The German Campaign in Russia*, 79
134 Showalter, *Hitler's Panzers*, 193
135 Guderian, 'The Experiences of the War in Russia', 96
136 Balck, *Translation of Taped Conversation with General Hermann Balck, 12 January 1979*, 23
137 Halder, *The German Campaign in Russia*, 63
138 Manstein, *Lost Victories*, 177
139 Hoth, *Panzer Operations*, 1881/3062
140 Mosier concluded, 'Hitler demanded a vast expansion. For him, the war was not about symbols, it was about resources. He saw, correctly, that although the Moscow–Leningrad axis was arguably the brain and the heart of the USSR, those organs were dependent on the resources at the other end of European Russia, in Ukraine, the Caucasus, and the fertile lands lying along the lower reaches of the Don and Volga Rivers, historically known as "Black Earth" Russia.' Mosier, *Deathride*, 93

Chapter Eight: Maneuver Warfare and the Defense of NATO
1 Carter, 'War Games in Europe', in Hoffenaar, Krüger and Zabecki, *Blueprints for Battle*, 3411/5843
2 Smelser and Davies, *The Myth of the Eastern Front*, 70
3 Smelser and Davies, *The Myth of the*

Eastern Front, 70
4 Carter, 'War Games in Europe', 3411/5843
5 Soutor, 'To Stem the Red Tide', 669
6 Wood, 'Captive Historians, Captivated Audience', 140–1
7 Soutor, 'To Stem the Red Tide', 678–9
8 Wood, 'Captive Historians, Captivated Audience', 146
9 Soutor, 'To Stem the Red Tide', 682–3
10 Davis, *The Challenge of Adaptation*, 45
11 Sorley, *Press On! Selected Works of General Donn A. Starry: Volume I*, 126–7
12 Lind, 'Some Doctrinal Questions for the United States Army', 143
13 Lind, 'Some Doctrinal Questions for the United States Army', 142
14 Leonhard, *The Art of Maneuver*, 2218/5341
15 Lind, 'Some Doctrinal Questions for the United States Army', 139–40
16 Wood, 'Captive Historians, Captivated Audience', 138–9
17 Smelser and Davies, *The Myth of the Eastern Front*, 2
18 Wood, 'Captive Historians, Captivated Audience', 138–9
19 *Night Combat*, 19 and 21
20 *Russian Combat Methods in World War II*, 3
21 *Russian Combat Methods in World War II*, 7
22 *Russian Combat Methods in World War II*, 24
23 Smelser and Davies, *The Myth of the Eastern Front*, 69
24 *Night Combat*, 20
25 Glantz, *American Perspectives on Eastern Front Operations in World War II*
26 Manstein, *Lost Victories*, 255
27 Mellenthin, *Panzer Battles*, 180
28 Mellenthin, *Panzer Battles*, 181
29 Mellenthin, *Panzer Battles*, 189
30 Glantz, 'The Red Army at War', 602
31 Glantz, *American Perspectives on Eastern Front Operations in World War II*
32 Lind, *Maneuver Warfare Handbook*, 64–6
33 Vernon, 'Soviet Combat Operations in World War II: Part I', 32
34 Vernon, 'Soviet Combat Operations in World War II: Part II', 48
35 *Armored Warfare in World War II*, 157
36 *Generals Balck and Von Mellenthin on Tactics*, 10

37 Generals Balck and Von Mellenthin on
    Tactics, 10
38 Generals Balck and Von Mellenthin on
    Tactics, 10
39 Generals Balck and Von Mellenthin on
    Tactics, 1
40 Mellenthin, Stolfi and Sobik, NATO
    Under Attack, 70
41 Mellenthin, Stolfi and Sobik, NATO
    Under Attack, 55 (the same statement
    can be found in Mellenthin, Panzer
    Battles, 138)
42 Mellenthin, Stolfi and Sobik, NATO
    Under Attack, 87
43 Mellenthin, Stolfi and Sobik, NATO
    Under Attack, 51
44 Glantz, American Perspectives on
    Eastern Front Operations in World War II
45 Glantz, American Perspectives on
    Eastern Front Operations in World War II
46 Wyly, 'NATO Under Attack', 70
47 Wyly, 'NATO Under Attack', 70
48 Simpkin, Race to the Swift, 50
49 Mosier, Deathride, 275
50 Jordan, 'The Wehrmacht's Worst Defeat',
    40
51 Glantz, August Storm, 41
52 Glantz, August Storm, 153
53 Glantz, August Storm, 156–7
54 Glantz, August Storm, 157
55 Walters, 'Synchronization', 24
56 Selected Papers of General William E.
    DePuy, 321
57 Soutor concluded, 'With scanty
    information available from other sources,
    the Army became convinced by the
    German generals' belief that they would
    have achieved victory without Adolf
    Hitler's misguided command efforts and
    eagerly pointed to the series [the Halder
    manuscripts] as proof that the mobile
    defense doctrine would succeed against
    a Soviet attack in Western Europe.'
    Soutor, 'To Stem the Red Tide', 6748–9
58 Halder, Hitler as Warlord, 62
59 Military Improvisations During the
    Russian Campaign, 27–8
60 Operations of Encircled Forces: German
    Experiences in Russia, 13
61 Military Improvisations During the
    Russian Campaign, 36
62 Manstein, Lost Victories, 279
63 Manstein, Lost Victories, 179–80
64 Guderian, Panzer Leader, 266
65 Mellenthin, Panzer Battles, 171
66 Liddell Hart, The German Generals Talk,
    3114/5932
67 Liddell Hart, The Liddell Hart Memoirs
    Vol II, 5749/5932
68 Liddell Hart, The Liddell Hart Memoirs
    Vol II, 4964/5932
69 Liddell Hart, The Liddell Hart Memoirs
    Vol II, 4984/5932
70 Walters, 'Interview with Capt B.H. Liddell
    Hart', 27
71 Hart, Europe in Arms, 296
72 Liddell Hart, The Defence of Britain, 216
73 Liddell Hart, The Defence of Britain, 56
74 Liddell Hart, The Liddell Hart Memoirs
    Vol II, 4965/5932
75 Manstein, Lost Victories, 362
76 Manstein, Lost Victories, 456
77 Manstein, Lost Victories, 513 and 517
78 Manstein, Lost Victories, 530
79 Guderian, Panzer Leader, 367
80 Mellenthin, Panzer Battles, 154
81 Mellenthin, Panzer Battles, 170
82 Mellenthin, Panzer Battles, 170
83 Balck, Order in Chaos, 327
84 Balck, Order in Chaos, 433
85 Harrison, Architect of Soviet Victory in
    World War II, 5890/8272
86 Mosier, Cross of Iron, 186
87 Smelser and Davies concluded,
    'Manstein's memoir, Lost Victories,
    has influenced Americans, particularly
    the military for decades. Aware of the
    possibility of a Soviet attack on Western
    Europe during the Cold War with an
    accompanying U.S. retreat, the Americans
    viewed with awe Manstein's description
    of the series of fluid, tactical retreats of
    the Wehrmacht in Russia.' Smelser and
    Davies, The Myth of the Eastern Front, 90
88 Armored Warfare in World War II, 93
89 Armored Warfare in World War II, 30
90 Armored Warfare in World War II, 30
91 Armored Warfare in World War II, 41
92 Armored Warfare in World War II, 41
93 Armored Warfare in World War II, 36
94 Armored Warfare in World War II, 36
95 Generals Balck and Von Mellenthin on
    Tactics, 1
96 Generals Balck and Von Mellenthin on
    Tactics, 23–4
97 Generals Balck and Von Mellenthin on
    Tactics, 37
98 Mearsheimer explained, 'West Germany
    is a long and narrow country and, as
    such, has little strategic depth. The

defender, should he attempt to trade space for time as called for with a mobile defense, would quickly find himself backed up against the Rhine and the West German border.' Mearsheimer, 'Maneuver, Mobile Defense, and the NATO Central Front', 114–16

99   Selected Papers of General William E. DePuy, 289
100   Spiller, 'In the Shadow of the Dragon', 50
101   Gole, General William E. DePuy, 3438/4758
102   Gole, General William E. DePuy, 3439/4758
103   Freedman, Strategy, 211
104   Gole, 'The Relevance Of Gen. William E. DePuy', 70
105   Trauschweizer, 'Learning with an Ally', 500
106   Trauschweizer, Creating Deterrence for Limited War, 366–7
107   Gole, General William E. DePuy, 3439/4758
108   Trauschweizer, Creating Deterrence for Limited War, 378–9
109   Joyce, 'The Micropolitics of "the Army You Have"', 186
110   Spiller, 'In the Shadow of the Dragon', 50
111   Sorley, Press On! Selected Works of General Donn A. Starry: Volume I, 406
112   Park, The Unfulfilled Promise, 156
113   Sorley, Press On! Selected Works of General Donn A. Starry: Volume I, 190
114   Joyce, 'The Micropolitics of "the Army You Have"', 199
115   Park, The Unfulfilled Promise, 156
116   Joyce, 'The Micropolitics of "the Army You Have"', 201
117   Sorley, Press On! Selected Works of General Donn A. Starry: Volume I, 201
118   Joyce, 'The Micropolitics of "the Army You Have"', 202
119   Sorley, Press On! Selected Works of General Donn A. Starry: Volume I, 203

Chapter Nine: The Gulf War and the Illusion of Confirmation

1   Coram, Boyd, 6284/7717
2   Piscitelli, The Marine Corps Way of War, 1355/5506
3   Damian, The Road To FMFM 1, 93
4   Piscitelli, The Marine Corps Way of War, 1360/5506
5   Piscitelli, The Marine Corps Way of War, 1400/5506
6   Cohen, 'Uncertain Trumpets', 37
7   Lind, Maneuver Warfare Handbook, 1
8   Hammond, The Mind of War, 204/5008
9   Lind, 'The Theory and Practice of Maneuver Warfare', in Hooker, Maneuver Warfare: An Anthology, 15
10   Coram, Boyd, 6912/7717
11   Piscitelli, The Marine Corps Way of War, 1581/5506
12   Coram, Boyd, 6904/7717
13   Leonhard, The Art of Maneuver, 4595/5341
14   Hammond, The Mind of War, 4096/5008
15   Stuart Heintzelman, 'Foreword', in Schlieffen, Cannae, v
16   Richard Swain, 'Preface', in Schlieffen, Cannae, ii
17   Daly, Cannae, 177/7889
18   Evans, The Continental School of Strategy, 54
19   Brand, 'The Origins of Freie Operationen', 100
20   Coram, Boyd, 5761/7717
21   Burton, Pentagon Wars, 1035/7426
22   Hammond, 'On the Making of History', 17
23   Coram, Boyd, 6867/7717
24   Coram, Boyd, 6891/7717
25   Coram, Boyd, 6892/7717
26   Ricks, The Generals, 4997/10224
27   Coram, Boyd, 6896/7717
28   Coram, Boyd, 6896/7717
29   Burton, Pentagon Wars, 1193/7426
30   Kaplan, 'The Force Was With Them'
31   Kaplan, 'The Force Was With Them'
32   Evans, 'Schwarzkopf's "Jedi Knights" Praised for Winning Strategy'
33   Burton, The Pentagon Wars, 122/7426
34   Phillips, Reengineering Institutional Culture, 279
35   Phillips, Reengineering Institutional Culture, 280
36   Burton, The Pentagon Wars, 1195/7426
37   Coram, Boyd, 6898/7717
38   Schwarzkopf, It Doesn't Take a Hero, 381
39   Schwarzkopf, It Doesn't Take a Hero, 319
40   Schwarzkopf, It Doesn't Take a Hero, 319
41   Schwarzkopf, It Doesn't Take a Hero, 462
42   Naveh, In Pursuit of Military Excellence,

252

43 Lind, 'The Theory and Practice of Maneuver Warfare', in Hooker, *Maneuver Warfare: An Anthology*, 8

44 Schwarzkopf, *It Doesn't Take a Hero*, 200

45 Schwarzkopf, *It Doesn't Take a Hero*, 225

46 Holmes, 'Classical Blitzkrieg', 749

47 Leonhard, 'Maneuver Warfare and the United States Army', *Maneuver Warfare: An Anthology*, 47

48 Leonhard, *The Art of Maneuver*, 4642/5341

49 Burton, *The Pentagon Wars*, 5348/7426

50 Burton, *The Pentagon Wars*, 5341/7426

51 Burton, *The Pentagon Wars*, 5390/7426

52 Burton, *The Pentagon Wars*, 5390/7426

53 *Selected Papers of General William E. DePuy*, 318

54 Echevarria, 'Clausewitz's Center of Gravity', 116

55 Cancian, 'Centers of Gravity are a Myth', 30–4

56 Cancian, 'Centers of Gravity are a Myth', 30–4

57 Cancian, 'Centers of Gravity are a Myth', 30–4

58 Echevarria, 'Reining in the Center of Gravity Concept', 88

59 Cancian, 'Centers of Gravity are a Myth', 30–4

60 Leonhard, *The Art of Maneuver*, 4022/5341

61 Priest, 'The Rhetoric of Revisionism', 546

62 Spiller, 'In the Shadow of the Dragon', 42

63 Lind, *On War*, 1690/10539

64 Lind, *On War*, 6810/10539

65 Lind, *The View From Olympus: Is the Marine Corps Waking Up?*

66 Friedman, 'Maneuver Warfare', 28

67 Brown, *A New Conception of War*, 184

68 Friedman, 'Maneuver Warfare', 28

Chapter Ten: The War on Terror and the Return of Attrition

1 Wood, 'Captive Historians, Captivated Audience', 126

2 Manstein, *Lost Victories*, 17

3 Smelser and Davies, *The Myth of the Eastern Front*, 94–5

4 Smelser and Davies, *The Myth of the Eastern Front*, 135

5 Liddell Hart, *The German Generals Talk*, 2471/4501

6 Carlson, 'Portrait of a German General Staff Officer', 80

7 Carlson, 'Portrait of a German General Staff Officer', 80–1

8 *Rear Area Security in Russia*, 15

9 *Rear Area Security in Russia*, 17

10 *Rear Area Security in Russia*, 19

11 *Rear Area Security in Russia*, 19

12 Guderian, *Panzer Leader*, 194

13 *Rear Area Security in Russia*, 18

14 Guderian, *Panzer Leader*, 249

15 Smelser and Davies, *The Myth of the Eastern Front*, 105

16 Megargee, *Barbarossa 1941*, 91

17 Welch, 'The Annihilation of Superfluous Eaters', 7

18 *The Private War Journal of Generaloberst Franz Halder: Volume 6*, 212

19 Welch, 'The Annihilation of Superfluous Eaters', 7–8

20 Welch, 'The Annihilation of Superfluous Eaters', 11

21 Hoth, *Panzer Operations*, 2742/3062

22 Andrade, 'Westmoreland Was Right', 163

23 Andrade, 'Westmoreland Was Right', 163

24 Zambernardi, 'The Impotence of Power', 1335–1356

25 Clausewitz, *On War*, 94

26 Smith, 'Clausewitz', in Smith, *The Strategists*, 32

27 Davis, *The Challenge of Adaptation*, 61

28 Davis, *The Challenge of Adaptation*, 61, and Priest, 'The Rhetoric of Revisionism', 544–5

29 Sweetman, 'Clausewitzless', 14

30 Priest, 'The Rhetoric of Revisionism', 543

31 Priest, 'The Rhetoric of Revisionism', 545

32 Carlson, 'Portrait of a German General Staff Officer', 80

33 Bolger, 'Maneuver Warfare Reconsidered', in Hooker, *Maneuver Warfare: An Anthology*, 22

34 Stolfi, *Hitler's Panzers East*, 34

35 Hooker, 'The World Will Hold its Breath', 162

36 Leonhard, *The Art of Maneuver*, 4776 and 4785/5341

37 Schwarzkopf, *It Doesn't Take a Hero*, 355

38 Park noted, 'Taken in isolation, maneuver warfare could be counterproductive to the exercise of operational art, as Schwarzkopf found during Desert Storm when Marine forces were in danger of entering Kuwait

City first during the war, which made perfect sense from a tactical sense but would have been a strategic blunder.' Park, *The Unfulfilled Promise*, 411

39 Svechin, *Strategy*, 2016 and 2116/9533
40 Svechin, *Strategy*, 2126/9533
41 Svechin, *Strategy*, 3731/9533
42 Svechin, *Strategy*, 3771/9533
43 Mellenthin, *German Generals of World War II*, 282
44 *Armored Warfare in World War II*, 4
45 Miksche, 'The Strategic Importance of Western Europe', 40
46 Codo, 'Guerrilla Warfare in the Ukraine', 4
47 Brown, *A New Conception of War*, 246
48 Lind, 'Why the German Example?', 59
49 Stolfi, *Hitler's Panzers East*, 14
50 Wette, *The Wehrmacht*, 91
51 Bird and Marshall, *Afghanistan*, 49–50
52 Bird and Marshall, *Afghanistan*, 49
53 Franks, *American Soldier*, 2099/10402
54 Franks, *American Soldier*, 2483/10402
55 Franks, *American Soldier*, 4201/10402
56 Franks, *American Soldier*, 4209/10402
57 Bird and Marshall, *Afghanistan*, 66
58 Bird and Marshall, *Afghanistan*, 66
59 Bird and Marshall, *Afghanistan*, 73
60 Bird and Marshall, *Afghanistan*, 79
61 Bird and Marshall, *Afghanistan*, 85
62 Franks, *American Soldier*, 5237/10402
63 Ricks, *Fiasco*, 127
64 Ricks, *The Generals*, 5356/10224
65 Priest, 'The Rhetoric of Revisionism', 549
66 Franks, *American Soldier*, 7375 and 7386/10402
67 Franks, *American Soldier*, 5271/10402
68 Franks, *American Soldier*, 7971/10402
69 Murray and Scales, *The Iraq War*, 59–60
70 Franks, *American Soldier*, 7804 and 7814/10402
71 West and Smith, *The March Up*, 5
72 Mattis and West, *Call Sign Chaos*, 90
73 Elkus, 'Applying Boyd'
74 Belote, 'Paralyzed or Pulverized?', 40–1
75 Wright, *Generation Kill*, 11
76 Wright, *Generation Kill*, 49
77 Piscitelli, *The Marine Corps Way of War*, 4136 and 4141/5506
78 West and Smith, 'Implications from Operation Iraqi Freedom for the Marine Corps', 43
79 West and Smith, 'Implications from Operation Iraqi Freedom for the Marine Corps', 46

80 . West and Smith, *The March Up*, 219
81 West and Smith, *The March Up*, 222
82 Ricks, *The Generals*, 5430/10224
83 Ricks, *The Generals*, 5438/10224
84 Cooper, 'Speed Trap'
85 Ricks, *The Generals*, 5458/10224
86 Cooper, 'Speed Trap'
87 Belote, 'Paralyzed or Pulverized?', 45
88 Belote, 'Paralyzed or Pulverized?', 41
89 Murray and Scales, *The Iraq War*, 174
90 Murray and Scales, *The Iraq War*, 176
91 Murray and Scales, *The Iraq War*, 163
92 Murray and Scales, *The Iraq War*, 183
93 Ricks, *Fiasco*, 116
94 Thomas Ricks explains that in the plan for Operation Iraqi Freedom 'there was a disconnect between the stated strategic goal of transforming the politics of Iraq and the Mideast and the plan's focus on the far more limited aim of simply removing Saddam Hussein's regime'. Ricks, *Fiasco*, 116
95 Ricks, *Fiasco*, 128
96 Ricks, *The Generals*, 5317/10224
97 Cooper, 'Speed Trap'
98 Wright, *Generation Kill*, 12
99 Brown, *A New Conception of War*, 143
100 Ricks, *Fiasco*, 112
101 Goldstein, '2003 Iraq, 1945 Germany, and 1940 France', 48
102 Ricks, *The Generals*, 5401/10224
103 Piscitelli, *The Marine Corps Way of War*, 4906/5506
104 Peters, 'In Praise of Attrition', 3
105 Peters, 'In Praise of Attrition', 8
106 Brown, *A New Conception of War*, 191
107 Brown, *A New Conception of War*, 192
108 Martin, 'By Other Means', 68
109 Martin, 'By Other Means', 69
110 Ricks, *The Generals*, 5812/10224
111 Ricks, *The Generals*, 5834/10224
112 Manea, 'Reflections on the "Counterinsurgency Decade"'
113 Manea, 'Reflections on the "Counterinsurgency Decade"'
114 Manea, 'Reflections on the "Counterinsurgency Decade"'
115 Lind, *On War*, 6815/10539
116 Lacey, 'The Continuing Irrelevance of William Lind'
117 Lacey, 'The Continuing Irrelevance of William Lind'
118 Lacey, 'The Continuing Irrelevance of William Lind'

Chapter Eleven: Fourth Generation Warfare and Educating the Enemy

1 Van Creveld, *A History of Strategy*, 1651/1800
2 Lind, Nightengale, Schmitt, Sutton and Wilson, 'The Changing Face of War: Into the Fourth Generation', 65
3 Lind, Nightengale, Schmitt, Sutton and Wilson, 'The Changing Face of War', 65–6
4 Lind, Nightengale, Schmitt, Sutton and Wilson, 'The Changing Face of War', 66
5 Lind, 'Understanding Fourth Generation War', 13
6 Lind, Schmitt and Wilson, 'Fourth Generation Warfare: Another Look', 70
7 Echevarria, *Fourth-Generation War and Other Myths*, 10
8 Boyd, *Patterns of Conflict (Slides)*, 64
9 Boyd, *Patterns of Conflict (Slides)*, 67–8
10 Boyd, *Patterns of Conflict (Slides)*, 66
11 Lind, Nightengale, Schmitt, Sutton and Wilson, 'The Changing Face of War', 68
12 Lind, 'Understanding Fourth Generation War', 12–13
13 Lind, *The View From Olympus: What it Takes to Win*
14 Lind, 'Rationalizing Army and Marine Corps Roles and Missions Through Operational Art', 35
15 Simpson, *War from the Ground Up*, 54
16 Simpson, *War from the Ground Up*, 55
17 Simpson, *War from the Ground Up*, 45
18 Simpson, *War from the Ground Up*, 45
19 Simpson, *War from the Ground Up*, 46
20 Barnett, 'Basil faulty?', 62
21 Kiszely, 'The Meaning of Manoeuvre', 36
22 Tucker, *False Prophets*, 25
23 Anderson, 'Maneuver, Attrition, or the Tactics of Mistake?', 74
24 Porter, *Military Orientalism*, 148
25 Strong, 'In the Graveyard of Empires', 977
26 Hasik, *Beyond Hagiography*
27 Lind, *On War*, 4198/10539
28 Lind, Nightengale, Schmitt, Sutton and Wilson, 'The Changing Face of War', 66
29 Lind, Nightengale, Schmitt, Sutton and Wilson, 'The Changing Face of War', 67
30 Echevarria, *Fourth-Generation War and Other Myths*, 2–3
31 Freedman, *Strategy*, 239
32 Hammes, *The Sling and the Stone*, 72
33 Record, 'Vietnam in Retrospect', 53
34 Belknap, 'The CNN Effect', 111
35 Baumann, 'Soviet News Media Performance During the Afghan War', 175
36 Baumann, 'Soviet News Media Performance During the Afghan War', 177
37 Belknap, 'The CNN Effect', 102
38 Lind, 'The Operational Art', 46
39 Lind, Nightengale, Schmitt, Sutton and Wilson, 'The Changing Face of War', 67
40 Darley, 'War Policy, Public Support, and the Media', 128
41 Darley, 'War Policy, Public Support, and the Media', 122–3
42 Darley, 'War Policy, Public Support, and the Media', 127
43 Darley, 'War Policy, Public Support, and the Media', 129
44 Darley, 'War Policy, Public Support, and the Media', 130
45 Record, 'Collapsed Countries, Casualty Dread, and the New American Way of War', 4
46 Record, 'Collapsed Countries, Casualty Dread, and the New American Way of War', 11
47 Record, 'Collapsed Countries, Casualty Dread, and the New American Way of War', 11–12
48 Peters, 'In Praise of Attrition', 4
49 Rubin, 'The Real Roots of Arab Anti-Americanism', 73–85
50 Record, 'Collapsed Countries, Casualty Dread, and the New American Way of War', 13
51 A declassified American Government report concluded: 'Saddam Hussein's number one priority as the U.S.-led coalition prepared to invade in 2003 was to preserve himself and his regime from an attempted internal coup and his worldview led him to believe the United States was casualty-averse, thus the regime would survive.' 'Saddam's Eye View: JFCOM Releases Unclassified Report', 1
52 Crawley, 'While U.S. is Winning "On Paper" Balance Could Shift', 22
53 Hammes, *The Sling and the Stone*, 143
54 Record, 'Collapsed Countries, Casualty Dread, and the New American Way of War', 13–14
55 Record, 'Collapsed Countries, Casualty Dread, and the New American Way of War', 14

56 Doran, 'The Pragmatic Fanaticism of al Qaeda', 183
57 Doran, 'The Pragmatic Fanaticism of al Qaeda', 183
58 Priest 'The Rhetoric of Revisionism', 546
59 Record, 'Collapsed Countries, Casualty Dread, and the New American Way of War', 11
60 Hart, *The Shield and the Cloak*, 69–70
61 Wheeler, 'Terrorist Tactics for War with the West', 24–5
62 Lind, 'Understanding Fourth Generation War', 12
63 Lind, *On War*, 220/10539
64 Hart, *The Shield and the Cloak*, 70
65 Lind, *On War*, 9624/10539
66 Lind, *On War*, 9541/10539
67 Lind, *On War*, 818/10539
68 Lind, *On War*, 5798/10539

Epilogue
1   Hasik, *Beyond Hagiography*
2   Damian, *The Road To FMFM 1*, 16
3   Bolger, 'Maneuver Warfare Reconsidered', in Hooker, *Maneuver Warfare: An Anthology*, 21
4   Bolger, 'Maneuver Warfare Reconsidered', in Hooker, *Maneuver Warfare: An Anthology*, 37
5   *Selected Papers of General William E. DePuy*, 315
6   Cohen, 'Uncertain Trumpets', 37
7   Gray, *Defining and Achieving Decisive Victory*, 23
8   Piscitelli, *The Marine Corps Way of War*, 4901/5506
9   McKenzie, 'They Shoot Synchronizers, Don't They?', 30
10 *Selected Papers of General William E. DePuy*, 315
11 Walker, 'An Alternative to Maneuver Warfare', 51
12 Piscitelli, *The Marine Corps Way of War*, 4906/5506
13 Anderson, 'Maneuver, Attrition, or the Tactics of Mistake?', 77
14 Rommel, *The Rommel Papers*, 519
15 Mearsheimer, 'Maneuver, Mobile Defense, and the NATO Central Front', 108

INDEX